Gender in Transition
A New Frontier

Gender in Transition
A New Frontier

EDITED BY
Joan Offerman-Zuckerberg, Ph.D.

PLENUM MEDICAL BOOK COMPANY
NEW YORK AND LONDON

Library of Congress Cataloging in Publication Data

Gender in transition: a new frontier / edited by Joan Offerman-Zuckerberg.
  p.   cm.
  Includes bibliographies and index.
  ISBN 0-306-43132-7
  1. Human reproduction technology—Psychological aspects. 2. Human reproduction technology—Social aspects. 3. Sex role—Psychological aspects. I. Offerman-Zuckerberg, Joan.
  [DNLM: 1. Identification (Psychology) 2. Mothers—psychology. 3. Reproduction Technics—psychology. BF 692.2 G3255]
  RG133.5.G46 1989
  306.7—dc20
  DNLM/DLC   89-8737
  for Library of Congress   CIP

© 1989 Plenum Publishing Corporation
233 Spring Street, New York, N.Y. 10013

Plenum Medical Book Company is an imprint of Plenum Publishing Corporation

All rights reserved

No part of this book may be reproduced, stored in a retrieval system, or transmitted in any form or by any means, electronic, mechanical, photocopying, microfilming, recording, or otherwise, without written permission from the Publisher

Printed in the United States of America

To Joshua and Benjamin—

" . . . make the world a better place, if you can."

Contributors

Betsy P. Aigen, Psy.D. • Surrogate Mother Program of New York, New York, New York 10024

Bonnie R. Aronowitz, M.A. • Ph.D. Clinical Psychology Candidate, Ferkauf Graduate School, Yeshiva University–Einstein College of Medicine, Bronx, New York 10461; Neurological Institute and Anxiety Disorders Clinic, Psychiatric Institute, Columbia Presbyterian Medical Center, New York, New York 10302

Donna Bassin, Ph.D. • Institute of Psychoanalytic Training and Research, New York, New York 10028

Susan Bram, Ph.D. • New York State Psychiatric Institute, Columbia Presbyterian Medical Center, New York, New York 10032

Aphrodite Clamar, Ph.D. • Private practice, 162 East 80th Street, New York, New York 10021

Mary Beth M. Cresci, Ph.D. • The Psychoanalytic Institute, Postgraduate Center for Mental Health, New York, New York 10016; Brooklyn Institute for Psychotherapy, Brooklyn, New York 11215; National Institute for the Psychotherapies, New York, New York 10019

Leanne Domash, Ph.D. • Beth Israel Medical Center, New York, New York 10003; Mount Sinai School of Medicine, New York, New York 10029

Joan E. Donner, Ph.D. • Private practice, 1100 Glendon Avenue, Los Angeles, California 90024

Alice Eichholz, Ph.D. • Vermont College of Norwich University, Montpelier, Vermont 05602

Joan Einwohner, Ph.D. • The Infertility Center of New York, New York, New York 10022

Joseph Feldschuh, M.D. • Cornell Medical College, New York, New York 10021; Montefiore Hospital, Bronx, New York 10467; IDANT Laboratories, New York, New York 10022

Linda S. Fidell, Ph.D. • Department of Psychology, California State University, Northridge, California 91330

Gwendolyn L. Gerber, Ph.D. • Department of Psychology, John Jay College of Criminal Justice, The City University of New York, New York, New York 10019

Stephen B. Goldman, Ph.D. • Psychology Externship Program, New Hope Guild Centers, Brooklyn, New York

Chris Jenkins-Burk, M.A. • Richard G. Jones, Ph.D., and Associates, and Adjunct Faculty, Psychology Department, Houston Community College System, Houston, Texas 77054

Harriette Kaley, Ph.D. • City University of New York–Brooklyn College, Brooklyn, New York 11210

Janie Koenigsberg, M.A. • Educational Therapy Programs, 10877 Rose Avenue, Los Angeles, California 90034

Susan S. Lichtendorf • Medical Science Journalist, New York, New York 10128; Member, National Association of Science Writers, Author's Guild

Kathy Magnussen • Department of Psychology, California State University, Northridge, California 91330

Jaroslav Marik, M.D. • The Tyler Medical Clinic, Inc., Los Angeles, California 90024

April Martin, Ph.D. • Private practice, 429 West 24th Street, New York, New York 10011

Dorothea S. McArthur, Ph.D. • Private practice, 2362 Cove Avenue, Los Angeles, California 90039

Randy Milden, Ph.D. • Dean's Office and Departments of Psychology and General Programs, Haverford College, Haverford, Pennsylvania 19041

Cynthia Morgan, Ph.D. • Institute for Psychological Development, Thousand Oaks, California 91360

Joan Offerman-Zuckerberg, Ph.D. • Psychoanalytic Society of the Postdoctoral Program for Study and Research in Psychology, New York, New York; Brooklyn Institute for Psychotherapy, Brooklyn, New York 11215; National Institute for the Psychotherapies, New York, New York 10019; Yeshiva University, New York, New York 10033

Sophia Richman, Ph.D. • Institute for Contemporary Psychotherapy, New York, New York 10024; Postdoctoral Program, New York University, New York, New York 10003

Barbara Katz Rothman, Ph.D. • Department of Sociology, Baruch College, New York, New York 10010

Isadore Schmukler, Ph.D. • Surrogate Mother Program of New York, New York, New York 10024

Nadine Taub, L.L.D. • Women's Rights Litigation Clinic, Rutgers University School of Law, Newark, New Jersey 07102-3192

Jodie B. Ullman, M.A. • Department of Psychology, California State University, Northridge, California 91330

Richard M. Zuckerberg, Ph.D. • Brooklyn Institute for Psychotherapy, Brooklyn, New York 11215; Kingsbrook Jewish Medical Center, Brooklyn, New York 11203

Preface

The wish for a child runs deep, as does the desire for parenthood. It is a wish that is essential to the continuance of the human species. It derives its motive power from many interrelated sources: psychobiological, sociological, historical. Yet it is a power that is changing hands. A short decade ago, Louise Brown was born. Prior to this event, human beings had begun biological life deep inside a female body. Louise Brown's birth signaled the beginning of a new era: The door to a new biotechnological world was opened, a world of artificial insemination, *in vitro* fertilization, surrogacy, embryo transplants, amniocentesis, gender preselection—procedures imagined but never before realized, leading perhaps to the injection of new genetic material into frozen embryos. Indeed, what had been, since Eve, an exclusively female power and prerogative has now been invaded by 20th-century biotechnology. The womb has been replaced, and sperm and egg can now be joined without love and romance.

Change brings with it new questions: A complex inquiry has been generated by issues that are psychological, ethical, moral, biological, sociological, and legal. Simultaneously, and not incidentally or accidentally, gender psychology is in transition. As we enter an androgynous zone, cultural heroes shift, new couples emerge. Gender roles are redefined, and renegotiated, not without struggle and apprehension. We are approaching a new frontier—hopeful, self-conscious, and anxious. The possibilities are endless, as are the problems. The ultimate determinant of how benevolently we will use our new freedoms, technologically based and otherwise, will fundamentally reside in our humanity.

JOAN OFFERMAN-ZUCKERBERG

Contents

Introduction	•	Gender in Transition: A Brave New World? .... JOAN OFFERMAN-ZUCKERBERG	1
Part I	•	Gender in Transition: The Androgynous Zone	7
Chapter 1	•	That Old Black Magic of Femininity: Then and Now .... LEANNE DOMASH	9
Chapter 2	•	From John Wayne to Tootsie: The Masculine Struggle with Psychological Integration .... RICHARD M. ZUCKERBERG	17
Chapter 3	•	Preparation for Fatherhood: Dreams of Transition .... MARY BETH M. CRESCI	35
Chapter 4	•	Gender Stereotypes: A New Egalitarian Couple Emerges .... GWENDOLYN L. GERBER	47
Chapter 5	•	New Parents in a Changing World: Existential and Interpersonal Dilemmas .... SOPHIA RICHMAN	67
Part II	•	New Reproductive Technologies: From Test Tubes to Surrogates	79
Chapter 6	•	A Psychoanalytic Case Study: Infertility, in Vitro Fertilization, and Countertransference .... HARRIETTE KALEY	81
Chapter 7	•	Paternity by Proxy: Artificial Insemination with Donor Sperm ..... LINDA S. FIDELL AND JAROSLAV MARIK (WITH JOAN E. DONNER, CHRIS JENKINS-BURK, JANIE KOENIGSBERG, KATHY MAGNUSSEN, CYNTHIA MORGAN, JODIE B. ULLMAN)	93

Chapter 8	•	Psychological Implications of the Anonymous Pregnancy .... 111 APHRODITE CLAMAR
Chapter 9	•	Who Becomes a Surrogate: Personality Characteristics .... 123 JOAN EINWOHNER
Chapter 10	•	Contemporary Adoption: A Cooperative Enterprise .... 133 DOROTHEA S. MCARTHUR
Chapter 11	•	Artificial Insemination by Donor: Yours, Mine, or Theirs? .... 151 BONNIE R. ARONOWITZ AND JOSEPH FELDSCHUH
Chapter 12	•	Infertility and the New Reproductive Technologies: Speculations from a Psychodynamic Perspective .... 163 RANDY MILDEN
Chapter 13	•	Amniocentesis: The Experience of Invasion and the Ambivalence of Foreknowledge .... 173 ALICE EICHHOLZ
Chapter 14	•	Gender Selection and Society .... 179 JODIE B. ULLMAN AND LINDA S. FIDELL
Chapter 15	•	Woman's Shifting Sense of Self: The Impact of Reproductive Technology .... 189 DONNA BASSIN
Part III	•	The 21st Century: Futuristic Patterns, Concerns, and Issues 203
Chapter 16	•	Divided Loyalties: Ongoing Reactions to Baby M .... 205 SUSAN S. LICHTENDORF
Chapter 17	•	Feminist Tensions: Concepts of Motherhood and Reproductive Choice .... 217 NADINE TAUB
Chapter 18	•	On Surrogacy: Constructing Social Policy .... 227 BARBARA KATZ ROTHMAN
Chapter 19	•	The Terror of Surrogate Motherhood: Fantasies, Realities, and Viable Legislation .... 235 ISADORE SCHMUKLER AND BETSY P. AIGEN
Chapter 20	•	Lesbian Parenting: A Personal Odyssey .... 249 APRIL MARTIN
Chapter 21	•	Bearing the Unbearable: The Psychological Impact of AIDS .... 263 STEPHEN B. GOLDMAN

Chapter 22 •	*Toward a Sense of Immortality: Case Studies of Voluntarily Childless Couples* .... 275 SUSAN BRAM	
Chapter 23 •	*21st Century: Changing Concepts of Masculinity and Femininity* ... 285 ALICE EICHHOLZ	
Overview •	*Reflections* .... 297 JOAN OFFERMAN-ZUCKERBERG	
Index	 299	

Introduction
Gender in Transition
A Brave New World?

JOAN OFFERMAN-ZUCKERBERG

Sue Anne, an attractive middle-aged woman, comes into my office for the first time. She had been referred by a friend, a former patient of mine who had just given birth to her first child—a son. She looked familiar. As it turned out, some 10 years ago, she had been my travel agent briefly. She began speaking slowly and to the point. The scenario seemed familiar. I want a child—he doesn't. I'm 42 years old and I'm running out of time. Everyone around me is having babies. My life is empty; it has no meaning. My marriage feels repetitive, boring; please help me. A week later, Tom enters. An attractive middle-aged man, he seemed familiar as well, for different reasons. He just never felt the urge to have children, and until this baby boom, things with her were going OK. I don't know what it is, I just like things the way they are. *She's my baby—* maybe it's my freedom, and losing it; maybe it's because I fear the unknown: I'm not doing such a great job providing for us anyway. It's breaking us up. She's so depressed, it's unbearable.

As a psychoanalyst one can look (and has to) to the individual psychodynamic histories and arrive at some tentative hypotheses regarding the possible psychogenic origins of these presenting problems. One considers Sue Anne's depression as possibly derived from multiple sources, that her delay in childbearing was "overdetermined"; perhaps there were "unconscious" conflicts regarding the assumption of a maternal role; perhaps unresolved negative identification issues with the mother were involved. There may be developmental arrest and/or fixation due to the presence of early oral symbiotic needs that were unmet. Perhaps her anger at a rejecting husband is a displacement, belonging to a shadowy and negligent father. In like manner, Tom's refusal may indicate unresolved Oedipal issues with his father, an inability to move beyond "boyhood" into fatherhood because of some unconscious fears of Oedipal

---

JOAN OFFERMAN-ZUCKERBERG • Psychoanalytic Society of the Postdoctoral Program for Study and Research in Psychology, New York, New York; Brooklyn Institute for Psychotherapy, Brooklyn, New York 11215; National Institute for the Psychotherapies, New York, New York 10019; Yeshiva University, New York, New York 10033.

competition and/or retaliation. Perhaps his refusal and rigidity reveals an underlying hatred toward women (mother), who historically may have made excessive demands on his autonomy or authority.

Though all these hypotheses may, upon psychoanalytic investigation, bear fruit (as it were), the more general contemporary themes that strike one are powerful as well. Gender and gender-related psychodynamics are critical to understanding all human beings. Gender is a biologically assigned aspect of identity. It is an inherited given. Until this century, it was an irrevocable stamp. It served to define, prescribe, limit, and guide. Gender dynamics and related roles are culturally embedded molds that are undergoing, in this age and into the future, dramatic revisions. Sue Anne and Tom are knowable entities to us. We respond to the ache and anger of a woman of 40-plus who "feels empty" and driven to bear now, under the pressure of a time bomb. We understand the childless man of 42, who embraces his freedom as passionately as his wife embraces her childless grief. We have become aware of the time warp, realizing that the "woman's" liberation movement's focus on female self-actualization in a "man's world" (i.e., defined as work outside the home, salaried, and status-defined) has changed course, that women now 40 are taking a look inside and rediscovering old urges, suppressed but not repressed, and that many of their men are now coming along for the ride.

We are also familiar with the pain of infertility: A patient recently reminded me of his feelings of being less than a man. His low sperm count—meaning soft man, weak, inadequate, insecure, damaged, never to bear a biological offspring, never to father the sons he yearned for, never to be the father he never had—seemed an unbearable injustice. And the guilt—not to be able to give to his wife a child, to feel depriving once again. We are familiar, too, with the professional woman who, after two daughters, chooses to abort the third, fearing the stress on the marriage, fearing the loss of attention to the other children, guilty about the murderous act. Herself a pediatrician and a child of the Holocaust, she truly values life but is starting to feel a healthy commitment to herself and to the quality of life. Terribly torn by the decision to keep or abort, she attempts to choose, as a mature adult woman, an option that has been available to human beings for only a couple of decades. It is an agonizing choice for many. We can understand the relief and we can understand her words—Please forgive me. We turn to her husband, who's not sure he has a choice. After all, how can I impose my desire for a third child, perhaps this time a son, when it's her body, her fatigue, her breasts nursing all hours of the day and night? Do I have a right? Now, two weeks later, after the choice to abort is made, there is an unspoken grief between them, his anger rekindled, other losses returning. Silent hopes are shattered and she is startled by the mourning recharged, not necessarily for the pea-sized fetus, but for the loss of a fantasy, already elaborate, somehow almost constructed instantly on an unconscious level.

And we are becoming more familiar with the lovely, ambitious woman who talks of her close marriage, her moneyed position in the computer-banking world, and her dream of starting an art school in France. There she is: competent, gracious, feminine, and wondering how she will ever fit it all in—family, children. What will she have to give up? What will be the psychological and physical costs of more delay? These are questions coming from choice, a new freedom, a new existential burden.

In the course of the day, I listen and respond to feelings emerging from an "empty nest" syndrome to overflowing nest—different variations on a common theme in women and men of all generations. The question, ultimately, of "Who am I?" In the course of a day, I listen to the pregnant father talk of fears of sharing his wife with another baby besides himself; I hear the grief of a mother saying *au revoir* to her son, now 18, going off to college; minutes later, a mother's protests that her baby prefers the bottle to her breast. This evening, it will be a father's joy and regret at becoming a grandfather, a moment for him mixed with pride and sadness, forlorn that what he sees as marital love between his daughter and her husband was never his, in that way.

In the course of a clinical day, one is sometimes struck by how very much the same things remain, despite contemporary trends. In front of me is a 29-year-old graduate student with a B.A. from Harvard and an M.A. from Columbia. She is a concert flutist, a painter, a champion swimmer, and is now embarking on a Ph.D. in history. Over 40 myself, I look to this new breed of woman with respect and awe—only to catch myself knowing full well that self-esteem regulation in this woman is related almost exclusively to being loved by a man. She proclaims that unless she meets someone by 45 and has a child, she would consider suicide a viable solution. This is a woman of tremendous inner resources, highly educated, very attractive, with a personality that is magnetic, feeling intrapsychically cheated of what remains most important to her—as she says: children, a home, a man who loves her.

A couple enters treatment on the verge of separation. He's leaving; he's had it. She has rejected me one too many times. I can't satisfy her. I am not ambitious enough for her. I like being with the children after my day's over. I like my life. She doesn't and she's furious. She moans, he's a horrible provider; he can't face reality. He doesn't plan. I'm furious. I have to worry about the finances. As a woman, it's OK to make money; I like to work, but "I don't like the feeling as if I *have* to." Now it's all on my shoulders. It is 1988, the modern couple has spoken. Shared parenting, joint salaries. He complains: She doesn't make me feel like a man, I can't please her. She complains: He doesn't take care of me.

A patient bemoans her marriage. I love him and I don't want to hurt him—but I just know that every time I assert myself, when I win an argument, he will be impotent sexually; he won't be able to have intercourse with me. He can have oral sex though! When I concede or act submissive, there's no problem. I feel I'm being punished for being strong. I feel I'm hurting him, damaging his manhood. Is he getting even with me? Do I have to act like someone I'm not anymore?

What has changed? Genuine integrated growth originates deep within, in the darkest recesses of our unconscious. For real growth to occur, our "wishes" must change. If we as men and women truly wish for a benevolent form of androgyny, i.e., a rich integration of masculinity and femininity, then we will, through struggle, gradually achieve it. But obstacles must be removed first; conflicts over male–female autonomy, territorial attachments, sexual fidelity, ambivalence in men regarding the female as competitor, ambivalence in women regarding the male as nurturer must be worked through and resolved. These ambivalences have to be faced first within, intrapsychically, and without, interpersonally.

Why has infertility risen dramatically? Is it related to the lack of deep conflict resolution? We can cite many of the commonly reported reasons: sexual promiscuity, exposure to viral agents, efforts at conception after 35, to name a few. But perhaps some cases of infertility are psychosomatic in origin, a *bodily* expression and barometer of the depth of some pervasive psychological conflicts, stressful conflicts between men and women that are attended by powerful emotions. And these feelings can register in the body in very real ways, lowering sperm count, contracting the uterus under stress, interfering with sexual life.

On a societal level, we reach out to the biotechnological god to make possible what is improbable, but we are not acknowledging and/or resolving many psychological issues within. It seems that only in the therapist's office can you hear the underlying feelings, the joys and pains, the fears and apprehensions, the conflicts and struggles of attachment and separation, of closeness and distance, of letting go, of loss and necessary mourning.

Now in 1988, after 18 years of practice as a psychotherapist, the scenarios are changing. I feel like a pioneer on a new frontier. Now that I have become somewhat comfortable with certain ways of understanding, suddenly the music has changed; and not only is the melody unrecognizable, but I never heard of the composer. What remains familiar are the notes. The language of emotion, of human conflict, remains the same. What is different is the composition.

A man of 45 speaks of leaving semen sperm deposits in a cold clinic bathroom, resenting the paradoxical reversal of an archaic parental prohibition. Now it is, do masturbate! He speaks of feeling mutilated, embarrassed, humiliated, and denigrated. A single woman, a teacher of 40, is planning to have a child through a surrogate she chose, whose pregnancy she is following month by month and supporting financially. A lesbian woman, after years of accepting her childlessness, is considering adoption. The options are expanding; the terrors are as well. A woman, a former patient, calls me after several years of a particularly good adjustment. She is distraught. Her husband, once a heroin user, is tested (+) for AIDS; she feels she's living with death. AIDS—the 20th-century plague, a horror that casts a dark shadow affecting us on all levels, including sexual habits, and, paradoxically, a force shaping a renewed affirmation of monogamy and commitment.

The year 1984 has passed and Orwell's reality is upon us. For the first time, we can separate male and female, producing sperm by machine (cloning). Babies are coming from test tubes, and insemination is not necessarily an act of love. Motherhood, typically once residing ultimately in one's own body, is undergoing revision. The body as a container of gender and gender-related privileges is being surpassed by other more capable and willing bodies or by biotechnology.

All of this is occurring in a society already undergoing dramatic transitions in roles and identity. Our heroes have changed from John Wayne to Tootsie, from Ginger Rogers to Yentl. Shared parenting and increasing options for men and women are exposing our children to a new interpretation of masculinity and femininity leading to the possibility of a new intrapsychic integration. All of this movement on one level—yet as psychoanalysts, we know that the pace of the unconscious is painstakingly slow, that childhood prototypes bear powerful imprints, that change is undertaken by humans with great reluctance. It is a change that carries with it the gift of increasing choice and freedom and the burden of decision making and the frightening unknown.

All of this biotechnological "progress" is happening, it seems to us, and fundamental questions of rather weighty ethical and moral dimensions are being asked. How do we draw the line between organ transplantation to save a life and embryo transplantation to create life? How do we differentiate morally between blood donations and anonymous sperm donation? We are coming to a historical point in time in which we can both control our evolution and destroy it. Are we wise enough to make human decisions, given this awesome power?

In the year 1918, Freud's reference to civilization and its many discontents is terribly applicable:

> Long ago he [man] formed an ideal conception of the omnipotence and omniscience which he embodies in his gods. To these gods he attributed everything that seemed unattainable to his wishes, or that was forbidden to him. One may say, therefore, that these gods were cultural ideals.
>
> Today, he has come very close to the attainment of this ideal, he has almost become a god himself. Only, it is true, in the fashion in which ideals are usually attained according to the general judgment of humanity. Not completely, in some respects not at all, in others only half way. Man has, as it were, become a kind of *prosthetic god*.
>
> Future ages will bring with them new and probably unimaginably great advances in this field of civilization and will increase man's likeness to God still more. But in the interests of our investigations, we will not forget that present day man does not feel happy in his Godlike character. (Freud, 1918)

We feel troubled and ofttimes unhappy about all this control, for reasons not always easy to articulate. Rather, sophisticated couples will opt to undergo the invasive procedure of amniocentesis but will choose "not to know" the gender, preferring the magic of the unknown, the belief that nature will give me what I will have, that God's will will be done, and that what will be will be. One can't help but think that the problems in success encountered with *in vitro* fertilization are similar to those in organ transplant rejection: that beyond the biochemistry of biocompatibility, the unconscious has a stake in keeping things natural, conservative, and familiar. The unconscious is a rather careful and staid host.

And when we think of Baby M (as if she didn't have a name), do we not feel for Shelley's monster? How far away is this fictionalized specimen of perfection, lamenting the awesomeness of his own creation: "Remember [Frankenstein] that I am thy creature; I ought to be thy Adam, but I am rather the Fallen Angel, whom thou drivest from joy for the misdeed." For this creature becomes, in Frankenstein's eyes, an "abhorred monster! Fiend thou art! The tortures of hell are too mild a vengeance for thy crime. Wretched devil! You reproach me with your creation; come on then, that I may extinguish the spark which I so negligently bestowed" (Shelley, 1818/1984).

Given the incredible media naïveté, coloring the way we receive news, we assume that the Baby Ms, the adopted children of this world, the children of anonymous donors and wombs, are the innocent players in this biological game, the passionately wanted members of the human species; forgetting that they are also the salaried by-products of our unconscious, symbols of the "unknown" monsters from the deep, projections of pieces of ourselves. In this darkened and divided arena, there are new fears: Did they confuse the tubes of sperm? Who is this anonymous donor? There are fantasies about the inseminating stranger, doctor, a white-uniformed lover with metallic hands. Lacking good follow-up data as yet, as psychoanalysts we cannot help but speculate that the conditions surrounding one's conception, birth, and early mothering will have an effect, and that the innocent can readily and unwittingly become monstrous projections, given the right amount of agonizing conflict and pain. If, on the other hand, all goes well, and society can find a way of tolerating this new arrangement, the Baby Ms may have many people who love them, and children of technology will feel *truly chosen*. We shall see.

What is difficult to predict is whether this new frontier is more of a mirage than real, that—as in the 1960s—we're experimenting politically, psychologically, and sociologically. The loud protest marches of the 1960s have quieted substantially. Only 25 years later, we seem to be reimmersed in highly conservative waters. Civil rights, women's rights, and political ideals are causes that seem to belong to a bygone era. Are we involved in a cycle that will return to its point of origin? The forces of tradition, sameness, predictability, and familiarity are powerful. We are alarmed by the new hype, such as "baby brokers," "institutionalized slavery" (referring to surrogate motherhood), the "industrialization of reproduction." We enter an age in which it may soon be possible that a woman's embryo can be manipulated in the laboratory to produce numerous genetically identical babies, carried to term in the wombs of surrogate mothers.

We read of the Vatican's 40-page document entitled "Instruction on Respect for Human Life in the Origin and Dignity of Procreation: Replies to Certain Questions of the Day." And we hear Pope John Paul II's absolute objection to human beings' being treated as objects available for scientific manipulation, an objection understandable as well, his having lived for years under Nazi rule.

What I hear now in my practice are the wishes of older mothers to stay home with their young children, the decision of some couples to adopt rather than suffer the long-term humiliation and hardship, both psychological and financial, of biotechnological intervention.

The divorce rate is slowing down somewhat. Is this the product of role redefinition and sharing, or a return to simpler modes of being? Simultaneously, legislation reacts to all of this almost phobically, in spurts, somehow, always lagging behind in its attunement to the complexity of the issues.

Clearly, we progress, amoebalike—jutting forward, retreating back. Clearly, scientific grandiosity is the flip side of human temerity. Clearly, we revel in power and control and live with the anxiety of hubris. In this collection of writings, we will explore and expose this new frontier; what human being settles here, and how many, is something to ponder.

REFERENCES

Freud, S. (1918). *Civilization and its discontents*. In *Collected works of Sigmund Freud*. (Reprinted in *Harper's* magazine, September 1987).
Shelley, M. W. (1984). *Frankenstein*. New York: Random House. (Original work published 1818).

Part I
Gender in Transition
The Androgynous Zone

In Part I of this book, we explore the psychological substratum of society's new gender arrangements. We gradually enter the 21st century, slowly debunking deeply cherished and familiar myths. As wombs become replaced and displaced, as sperm becomes detached from identity and person, we challenge law, religion, and tradition. We provoke the unconscious (by nature and definition, a highly conservative reservoir of memory and feeling) and invoke the courage to change. New couples emerge, stronger, more fulfilled (Gerber); cultural heroes shift from John Wayne to Tootsie. The struggle for integration of masculinity, femininity, and wholeness is examined, from an intrapsychic viewpoint (i.e., the blend *within* the person him/herself) (Zuckerberg) and from the interpersonal (*between* man and woman) (Domash). The developmental stage upon which we see much of this struggle enacted is in the transition to parenthood. This is explored by looking into our dreams (Cresci) and by reflecting on our changing existential and interpersonal problems (Richman).

Chapter 1

That Old Black Magic of Femininity
Then and Now

LEANNE DOMASH

The unconscious source of tension between the sexes has long been a subject of fascination and concern. This essay will explore the lure of femininity, the "black magic" power of it, to help explain what can still be called the battle between the sexes. We can think of it as an envy war. Each sex symbolizes a force the other craves. In this essay, we will focus on the male's conflict based on a wish for, and fear of, merger. However, there are reciprocal feelings in the female toward the male concerning power. These will also be discussed later in the essay. Early mother–son interactions that contribute to the adult male's ambivalence will be detailed. Our hope is that by making these, at times, nearly invisible conflicts visible, we can lessen the schism that still exists. Also, while there have been many recent societal advances in greater equality between the sexes, it is felt that attention to these unconscious factors may facilitate greater, more permanent change.

Why was the allure of the Sirens so great that Ulysses had to be tied to his boat to resist their charms? What is the fear behind the biblical myth of Delilah's robbing Samson of his strength by cutting his hair? What is behind the horror and rage of the witch burnings at Salem? Is this ancient and mysterious allure that the female has held for the male in the process of change? This attraction, related to the universal wish for reunion and fusion, may be more or less fraught with anxiety, in part depending on how secure the man's sense of maleness is, including boundaries and gender identity. We are focusing on these salient aspects while acknowledging that man's conflict in this regard can have many sources simultaneously.

Resolving fears about this wish is crucial for the male since this universal wish can be a very positive force in a mature love relationship. It fosters the relative openness between lovers that creates opportunities for personal reorganization and growth. If not afraid of this openness, lovers offer each other a healing process and rich possibilities for greater wholeness. For example, I have explored elsewhere the many levels of experience in the act of intercourse (Domash, 1988). In addition to sexual excitement and satisfaction, there is an analogy to Winnicott's discussion of the path

---

LEANNE DOMASH • Beth Israel Medical Center, New York, New York 10003; Mount Sinai School of Medicine, New York, New York 10029.

the infant traverses from initial union with the mother to a final sense of separateness (Winnicott, 1969). Initially, mother and child are merged. As part of this process, the infant enters the transitional area of illusion. In this there is a sense of freedom linked to a limitless feeling of wholeness with the mother. To then attempt to make the mother real and separate, the infant tries to destroy her, and she must survive his attack. The mother becomes the object of the infant's instinctual desires. The destructiveness creates the externality, and the mother is finally a separate presence who is appreciated as coming through the potential destruction.

This process involves a simultaneity of love, destruction, and survival. The infant feels grateful that he can destroy and love the object, and that the object survives. The feeling is that integrity is possible without destroying self or other. Love is strong enough to use destructiveness creatively.

The analogy may be that in each act of intercourse, one level of meaning is the following: The original physical and emotional merger is replicated and each person goes through a dual feeling of complete union (and with it an exultation, a limitless feeling of wholeness, a sense of freedom) and a need to destroy (a cataclysmic feeling of violent excitement sometimes coupled with destructive or hostile fantasies of harm or revenge) and yet finally a need to make the other real and still survive the instinctual attack (the gratitude and affection expressed in afterplay). All of these feelings contribute to the sexual excitement and are condensed in the pleasurable act of orgasm and afterplay. Part of the motivation for the afterplay is the renewed appreciation of the otherness of the partner and the gratitude that the partner has both helped one participate in the healing area of merger and illusion as well as survived the instinctual attack. I am postulating these feelings as present in normal mature loving and that they bring with them a deep sense of renewal in each act of sexual love.

The Universal Wish for Reunion

Silverman, Lachman, and Milich (1982) describe this wish for reunion in adults as wishes and fantasies, usually unconscious, that are directed toward a state of oneness with another person; in psychoanalytic terms it is a state in which, in varying degrees, representations of self and object are merged. It is akin to the experience of the oceanic feeling described by Werman (1986), which is characterized by an unbounded sensation of eternity and limitlessness. Ghent (1983) discusses this as the universal wish to surrender, as distinguished from submission. This includes a surrender of the false self and the longing for the rebirth of the true self. He writes that while in the West our concern is with information, in the East surrender leads to transcendence and ultimately to the central concern: transformation. Eigen (1981) locates an area of faith that is similar to surrender. Faith is a way of experiencing, with one's whole being, a core sense of creativeness. It is a giving of body and soul to an act, a kind of blanking out of ordinary consciousness where the sense of self is submerged in an oceanic feeling. This leap of faith, this immersion fosters the breakdown of inner rigidities of organization and therefore facilitates growth.

As these writers remark, this need can serve many functions, including positive and adaptive or defensive and regressive. That is, this need can be used for purposes of creative self-healing or for defensive retreat from unpleasant feelings, including disturbing erotic and aggressive impulses.

An example of a defensive use of this experience is described by Ghent, who explores masochism as a perversion of the wish to surrender. In the masochistic stance, surrender becomes submission. There becomes a continual need for impingement (sadism), yet there is a yearning to be reached in a deeper way. There may also be the need for punishment in the expression of sexuality. Another example is a man who becomes involved in oceanic feelings to dampen his aggressive and assertive feelings, which would allow him to become more successful in the world. He thus assumes a defensively regressive posture to retreat from competing.

Examples of adaptive uses of these fantasies are described by Silverman *et al.* (1982). They report numerous instances in which unconscious oneness fantasies can enhance adaptation if, at the same time, a sense of self is preserved. They describe experiments using a research technique in which the subject is exposed to subliminal messages, including "Mommy and I are one." Using these methods, they report improvement in severely disturbed schizophrenic patients as well as in nonpsychotic people, such as for weight loss, anxiety, depression, alcoholism, and other addictions.

MAN'S AMBIVALENCE ABOUT THIS WISH

The love relationship holds the promise of the fulfillment of this wish for the man. As Freud remarked, "At the height of being in love, the boundaries between ego and object threaten to melt away" (Freud, 1930, p. 66). Yet if a man's sense of himself as a male is tenuous, he may also dread this union, this surrender. The possibility of realization of this wish can be deeply threatening both to the societal expectations of him as a male and to inner processes such as gender identity, sense of boundaries, and feelings of envy. In these instances, part of the woman's mysterious allure is that she will provide fulfillment of this wish that man needs to hide from himself. This is part of the ineluctable and slightly dangerous attraction the female has for some men.

We have a piece of our answer to the question at the beginning of this chapter, of the lure of the Sirens for Ulysses, of the Lorelei for the boatmen of the Rhine; of the fear in the story of Samson's being robbed of his strength as Delilah cut his hair. Women hold the promise of total satisfaction, but because of their lure they also have the power to stop the man from going back out into the world, thereby symbolically castrating him and, on a deeper level, to threaten his sense of male identity by threatening his boundaries. An example of this problem is Mr. S., a 36-year-old man in psychoanalytic treatment who cannot achieve the wished-for intimacy in his marriage. He frequently feels alienated from his wife and, many times, experiences a sense of dread in anticipating sexual relations with her. He cannot "surrender to her" and does not feel "in love" with her; yet he wanted to marry her and feels as if he "loves" her.

This is related to an overly close early mother–son relationship. This mother had him sleep with her, and she also performed many bodily functions for him long beyond the appropriate time. The father–son relationship was weak. Consequently, closeness again with a woman is fraught with anxiety since his mother was sexually overstimulating, in part to block his growing separateness. To some extent, his sense of self and masculinity are threatened by his closeness to his wife. It also arouses intense anxiety about incestuous wishes.

In addition to psychic fears, men have repressed this wish for oneness because of biological and social imperatives. Karen Horney (1932) got right to the point when she emphasized the difference between being and doing, based in part on biology. Woman, she argues, performs her part—that is, being female—merely by *being*. Man, because of the biological differences between the sexes, has to *do*. He is actually obliged to go on proving his manhood to the woman. There is no analogous necessity for woman; even if she is frigid, she can engage in sexual intercourse and have a child. That she performs her part by merely being, without any doing, has always filled men with admiration and resentment. The man has to *do* something in order to fulfill himself, not only biologically (that is, to be potent) but also in terms of our society (to go out and act on the world). As Block (1973) has reported, men in our society are socialized for agency—that is, to be independent and autonomous. Because this wish for reunion and merger is so denied, it becomes more insistent, and the attraction for the female becomes fraught with ambivalence.

Development of a Sense of Maleness

Regarding the male's sense of gender identity, in our culture, the young boy needs to disidentify from the mother to develop a core sense of maleness. The need to disidentify with the mother is a special vicissitude in the normal psychological development of the boy in the first few years of life. As discussed by Greenson (1968), to achieve a healthy sense of maleness, the boy must replace the primary object of his identification, the mother, and identify instead with his father. This is what is meant by the term *to disidentify*.

The difficulties inherent in this additional step of development are responsible for certain special problems in the man's gender identity: his sense of belonging to the male sex. Because of this additional step, it may be said that men have a greater insecurity about their maleness than women do about their femaleness. Women's certainty about their gender identity and men's uncertainty are rooted in their early identifications with the mother. The young boy has to shift his identification while the girl does not. To *disidentify* with his mother is a struggle for the boy; he must free himself from the early closeness with the mother and separate from her, in some instances, prematurely. The little girl does not have to make this early separation and can form a solid early identification that does not have to shift. The male child's ability to disidentify will determine the success or failure of his later identification with his father. The outcome of this attempt will be determined in part by the mother's willingness to allow the boy to identify with the father. She can facilitate this by enjoying and admiring the boy's boyish features and skills and looking forward to his further development in this regard. However, if the mother devalues her own femininity and/or has strong envy of the male, she may block the young boy's attempt to disidentify and make this step difficult for him.

When the male's later identification with the father is weak, and consequently his sense of maleness shaky in the extreme, this can lead to transsexualism or homosexuality. An addictive involvement with pornography is another possible outcome. Still another, much less extreme, more likely outcome is a "macho" quality, including the male's need to be on guard about being influenced by, or being too close to, female elements. Especially when the sense of masculinity has not been strongly established, primarily because of a longer than usual symbiotic period with the mother and an unavailable father, there is a feeling of unconscious bondage to the female that must be denied. This is experienced as a sense of dread and gets rearoused as the male becomes intimate with a woman. Therefore, in these kinds of instances, when the attraction to the female is aroused, there will be a dread of intimacy, in fear of a dissolution of ego boundaries and a loss of a sense of maleness, yet there is also the wish for closeness and the strong erotic attraction. So the male feels both the pull and the dread.

Primordial Masculinity in a Primitive Culture

For the purposes of illustration, let me refer to a primitive stone-age culture in New Guinea, the Sambia, who, almost in grotesque relief, uncannily illustrate these dynamics in their childrearing practices, as reported by Lidz and Lidz (1977) and Stoller and Herdt (1982). The purpose of this culture is to create fierce men: warriors and hunters—that is, a primordial masculinity. To achieve this, their childrearing customs are as follows. There are prolonged and warm mother–son relationships and simultaneously weak father–son relationships. For the most part, the son remains with his mother and siblings for the first 7 to 10 years of life. At the same time, the marital couple's relationship has little warmth or affection. Then the young boy is abruptly separated from his mother and stays with the men as he undergoes a series of traumatic rituals. Men in this culture feel that attaining adult reproductive competence is far less certain for males than for females. This psychological fact (due to childrearing practices) is translated into a concrete belief that they can acquire maleness only by acquiring semen. Only this can produce male biology and masculine behavioral capacities (prowess). They believe that the boys may have been polluted by the mother's body (menstrual blood) and also that they innately lack semen. Maleness is not natural but is a power men and boys seize only through the initiations of their ritual cult. Men regard constant insemination as the only means for boys to grow and mature to men. This includes frightening initiation rites, which terrorize and forcibly harm the boys and also compel them to engage in fellatio with (take semen from) the bachelors. At the same time a female avoidance taboo is instituted. Women are seen as polluting, depleting inferiors that a man distrusts his entire life. Then, at 18, these young men must become heterosexual, although terrified, and this perverse state is channeled into becoming a successful warrior. The society has shrewdly created a fiercely angry man who will become a successful warrior. They have overstimulated him, then forcibly separated him from his mother, traumatized him, shaped a perversion, and then told him he must return to the dreaded woman. He longs to return yet is in a state of intense anxiety and fear.

This very dramatic series of enactments captures the flavor of the dread: a longing to return to a blissful state coupled with adult eroticism and a terrible fear of loss of maleness if one is close to the female. This is not meant to say our culture is comparable to that of the Sambia, but to emphasize that an overstimulating mother–son relationship, a weak father–son relationship, and a shaky sense of maleness can lead to a compensatory "macho" quality that contains a dread of the woman combined with a longing to reunite with her. In another context, I did present similarities between the Sambia culture and Marine Corps training, which takes vulnerable males, those who may be uncertain about their masculinity, and systematically separates them from women, humiliates and degrades them, and finally enrages them sufficiently for them to want to kill (Domash, 1986).

The Receptive Nature of Femininity

Women are not as anxious about dissolution of boundaries and gender identification. The latter is more secure and the former more permeable and, therefore, flexible. This flexibility grows out of a natural close association and identification with the mother. There is a longer closeness with the mother, with no need, in normal development, to prematurely turn away. This may allow a natural and lifelong greater accessibility to unconscious processes, including the wish to fuse. This may be related to man's dread of the sinister powers of the witch. As suggested, possibly the generally greater permeability of boundaries between women and others allows them greater access to unconscious processes. These intuitive powers may seem magical and, if hostile intent is attributed, then witchlike.

Chassequet-Smirgel (1984) writes in a moving way about how, in normal development, women are at ease with the receptive aspects of being: how women have the wisdom to wait, again related to procreation. Women know the meaning of waiting to arrive at puberty, of the need for time to gestate a child, of the long, at times chaotic nature of development. She hypothesizes that women can sustain the waiting more easily than men because they have the fantasy of gestation. They know they have the ability to carry life within, which is the closest any of us can get to the universal wish to return to a state of total satisfaction. This fantasy sustains women in the wait.

For example, in undertaking psychoanalysis with a patient, it is this feminine capacity, whether in a male or a female analyst, that allows us to stay with and accept the slow, seemingly imperceptible changes that finally make for palpable change in treatment. As analysts containing the patient in the long stretch of the analysis, we are close to a symbolic reenactment of the gestation fantasy—containing, digesting, eliminating, and finally giving birth to a more fully creative and loving person.

Distortions of Femininity

However, Chassequet-Smirgel's is a description of normal, perhaps ideal, female development. Women have not always appreciated this receptive capacity and have felt powerless with what they perceived as this relatively more passive stance. This receptive aspect of the essence of femininity has always been elusive, in part because of its subtlety, in part because of man's envy and consequent societal devaluation.

In addition, socialization in this culture has been to reinforce biological givens: women for communion, or to promote the smooth functioning of the group; men for agency, to be autonomous and have power. In a sense, each sex is cheated, in that each has longings for both. Women are also often oversocialized for communion. Then receptivity becomes passivity and an inadequate sense of self.

Women have, at times, partly in response to these various factors, perverted their femininity in various ways, largely because of their envy of the autonomous, powerful aspect of male functioning. One of the many possibilities of this perversion is masochism, which is a victimized way to seize power, as well as a chance to get vicarious pleasure from identification with the sadist with whom the masochist is in concert. Another is the "phallic," overly aggressive female who mimics a male model of power. Still another is the woman who attaches herself to a powerful man and, in what can be a very adaptive manner, feels fulfilled vicariously.

INDIA AND AMERICA CONTRASTED

To add a cross-cultural perspective, Roland (1980) contrasts intimacy relationships in America and India. He describes the atmosphere of relating in India as a symbiotic mode of relating, or symbiotic reciprocity, where there is tremendous mutual giving and asking, caring for and depending on, in an emotional atmosphere of affection and warmth. Emotional connectedness is always central, and everything is done so as not to disturb or interrupt it. There is a heightened asking, wanting, and depending on in a mutual or reciprocal way. He views the American childrearing system as fostering a highly individualized, autonomous self with a high level of ego skills. Self-actualization has become the profound goal of American psychological development. He adds that women in American society tend to have more and closer intimacy relationships than men, even while seeking realization of the individual self. He does acknowledge some shift in social climate from a preoccupation with a competitive ethos to one more concerned with intimacy relationships.

As Roland comments regarding American society, you can't have your cake and eat it too. One cannot have the degree of individual autonomy and self-creation present in American society and have intimacy relationships to the degree that is present in India and many other non-Western countries. As previously discussed, this emphasis on autonomy and achievement leads to a denial of the wish for symbiotic reciprocity, especially in men. This makes the wish itself even more intense, heightening men's anxiety in relation to women. Consequently, women who can acknowledge these wishes more easily feel frustrated by men who are afraid. At the same time, there may be envy of the male's power because achievement is so valued in our culture, culminating in considerable alienation between the sexes.

CONCLUSION

In many ways our culture has been caught in a state of mutual envy between the sexes. This chapter has addressed some of the unconscious roots of this to deepen our understanding and then integrate it with biological and social factors. To review, the woman, although inherently more able to be receptive, has frequently either not appreciated or distorted this quality. This is, in part, due to societal devaluation of the receptive capacity, labeling it "passivity" and Western adulation of power and materialism. In women, a few of the many possible results of this envy has been either a "masculinized" approach to the world or the development of a masochistic stance.

In childrearing this problem has, in some instances, led women to bond the male child to her—that is, not let him "disidentify." This latter fosters a particularly vicious cycle since it creates a male who is uncertain about his sense of maleness and may then need to be even more "macho" to prove himself. He is frightened of intimacy with a woman, creating a still greater schism between the sexes for the next generation. The lure of the woman becomes equal to the dread of the woman.

Despite woman's conflicts about power, she still has relatively greater ability to enter a relationship and a relatively greater ease with surrender. Consequently, we have a society where many women are "looking for a relationship" and many men are "unable to commit." Ideally, a greater understanding of these unconscious forces will help lessen the schism. For many, relationships seem like little more than temporary shelters. Our hope is to make a contribution toward men and women forming the kind of unlimited partnership that facilitates creativity and renewal.

References

Block, J. H. (1973). Conceptions of sex-role: Some cross-cultural and longitudinal perspectives. *American Psychologist, 28,* 512–526.

Chassequet-Smirgel (1984). The femininity of the analyst in professional practice. *International Journal of Psychoanalysis, 65,* 169–178.

Domash, L. (1986, June). Panel on women and war. The International Psychohistorical Meetings.

Domash, L. (1988). Perversion: the terror of tenderness. In J. Lasky & H. Silverman (Eds.), *Love: Psychoanalytic Perspectives.* New York: New York University Press.

Eigen, M. (1981). The area of faith in Winnicott, Lacan and Bion. *International Journal of Psychoanalysis, 62,* 413–433.

Freud, S. (1930). *Civilization and its discontents. Standard Edition, 21,* 66.

Ghent, E. (1983, December 2). Masochism, submission, surrender. Colloquium. New York University Postdoctoral Program in Psychoanalysis.

Greenson, R. (1968). Disidentifying from mother: Its special importance for the boy. In *Explorations in psychoanalysis* (pp. 305–312). New York: International Universities Press.

Horney, K. (1932). The dread of woman: Observations on a specific difference in the dread felt by men and by women respectively for the opposite sex. *International Journal of Psychoanalysis, 13,* 348–360.

Lidz, R. W., & Lidz, T. (1977). Male menstruation: A ritual alternate to the oedipal transition. *International Journal of Psychoanalysis, 58,* 17–31.

Roland, A. (1980). Intimacy as viewed from a cross-cultural perspective: Aspects of the self in India and America. *Modern Psychoanalysis, 5,* 177–185.

Silverman, L. H., Lachman, F. M., & Milich, R. H. (1982). *The search for oneness.* New York: International Universities Press.

Stoller, R. J., & Herdt, G. H. (1982). The development of masculinity: A cross-cultural contribution. *Journal of the American Psychoanalytic Association, 30,* 29–59.

Werman, D. S. (1986). On the nature of the oceanic experience. *Journal of the American Psychoanalytic Association, 34,* 123–139.

Winnicott, D. W. (1980). The use of an object and relating through identifications. In *Playing and reality* (pp. 101–111). New York: Penguin Books.

Chapter 2

From John Wayne to Tootsie
The Masculine Struggle with Psychological Integration

RICHARD M. ZUCKERBERG

The ideas and evidence presented here are both timeless and timely. In fact, much of what is to be said here has the ring of familiarity in spite of years of change. Whenever it was that man first began to explore his outer world, and his inner nature, one of his first discoveries clearly must have been that his own kind was divided into two sexes, that there was man and woman. What we are seeing in contemporary society is the continuing evaluation of man and woman, reflecting our ongoing search and fascination with the image of who we are, and how we are related to each other, as man and woman. Perpetually, the fact that emerges to catch our attention is how we, as man and woman, are both similar and different. We acknowledge our similarity on the basis of our shared biological fate as *Homo sapiens*, but also we see ourselves as divided into two groups on the basis of our sex. At a psychological level, we too share a common fate as human beings, and yet, as man and woman, our fates seem to possess the character of both convergence and divergence. This fact of our oneness and separateness was articulated early in the history of the recording of our ideas. In the work of the ancient Greeks, most notably Plato's "Symposium," we are informed that the "original nature of man was not like the present, but different. The sexes were not two as they are now, but originally three in number; there was man, woman, and the union of the two, having a name corresponding to that double nature, which once had a real existence, but is now lost . . . androgynous" (1952, p. 157). Plato goes on to tell us that "man was then split into two by the Gods to teach them a lesson of humility in their divided state. And, because of the original unity of man's nature, the humbled state of living only a part of his existence as a piece of this whole, there is a primordial hunger in each of us, a constant yearning to re-unite this divided self" (p. 158). The process by which this reunification is accomplished is part of what motivates man's actions in life, for the desire to heal this state of separateness is what the search for a loving other is all about. It is said that the union of man and woman, between them, is what heals this divided self within. For Plato, this is what man and woman want of each other, why they seek each other out, for in

---

RICHARD M. ZUCKERBERG • Brooklyn Institute for Psychotherapy, Brooklyn, New York 11215, and Kingsbrook Jewish Medical Center, Brooklyn, New York 11203.

the yearning to be united there will be a healing of the split within. It is interesting to note that Plato clearly had in mind the idea of a split within man and woman of the feminine and masculine principles, and that love *between* the sexes was the way to reunite the split of the feminine and masculine within each sex. Thus, the search for interpersonal union is, in part, the means to self-unification. In this work, Plato provides the conceptual model for our continuing concerns about the nature of who we are, that in the beginning we were once each male-female, that through our development we became split into two sexes, that in this process of splitting we lost some part of our original nature, and that which motivates us in life is the pursuit to heal the split within, through a process of merging in love with another of the opposite sex.

Much of the history of psychological thought and investigation in the area of sex and gender has been devoted to an exploration of these ideas, which appear to us as self-evident and lasting truths, and yet as continuing questions and mysteries well worth pondering. Centuries after Plato, Freud addressed the same problem of the similarities and differences between the sexes. In Freud, too, there is the notion of an original bisexuality in human nature, and that this is, in part, expressed in the child's erotic ties to both parents. Similarly, Freud speaks of the developmental task for both boys and girls to first attach to, and then relinquish, the erotic tie to the opposite-sex parent in order to be free, later in life, to establish healthy heterosexual object choices beyond the parents. For men, this means that while one must have loved mother in order to love, one must exchange that love to love a woman. What gradually happens at an intrapsychic level also, then, is that for each sex there is an incremental gain and loss in one's sense of being masculine or feminine. For Freud, it is crucial to understand that development of the individual, in part, proceeds according to the needs of the species—i.e., that man and woman need to fill out an individual psychology, isomorphic with their biology, a mutuality of roles, which assures the procreation of the species at its most basic level. And so, in this normal developmental process a man becomes more like men, a woman more like women, and the split of man's inner bisexual nature ensures the survival of the species. And yet there are still vestiges and traces of our original bisexual, unitary nature. As Freud (1937/1961) notes, "In mental life we only find reflections of this great antithesis (male and female) . . . and no individual is limited to the modes of reaction of a single sex but always finds some room for those of the opposite one . . ." (p. 188). Still, it is within the work of Freud that we find the first great psychological theory, which purports that the uniqueness and difference of male and female psychology is traceable to a biological root, that one's psychological makeup is predetermined and designed by one's anatomy. For Freud, psychological birth of one's sense of being masculine or feminine begins at the recognition of one's own and others' sexual anatomy. With this recognition, one's psychological development takes off on a certain prescribed and predictable course, and this course will be different if the child discovers the presence or absence of a penis. Hence, boys fall under the influence of castration anxiety and girls under the influence of penis envy, the wish to have what boys have. (It is clear to developmental psychologists and naïve observers of children alike that recognitions and reactions of this kind do take place in boys and girls. I have a memory, in fact, of overhearing a conversation between my then 3-year-old son and a female friend while they were in the bath together. The topic was his penis. Whether this was the first time of recognition of this noteworthy difference between himself and girls I cannot know, but in an apparent response to something she said, he remarked in a tone mixed with certainty and sympathy, "Don't worry, you'll get one when you grow up." This unprompted and unrehearsed remark no doubt came from some deep place within, and testifies to this feeling of comparison, that he had something she did not. What her reaction was I do not know. Whether this discovery is as momentous and characterized by such far-reaching consequences for the inner psychological life of both boys and girls, and later as adult men and women, is an issue of continuing debate among psychological theoreticians.) For Freud, what the girl does with this knowledge and consequent sense of her inferiority and envy will help or obstruct her movement toward femininity and feminine identification, and the character traits associated with being feminine. If she does not give up on the wish to have what men have, if the envy is too strong, identification can proceed too much in the direction of being like a man. On the other hand, if she gives up on this wish to possess a penis, the wish persists as a character trait of jealousy. In addition, the classic formulation for Freud is that the female begins to replace the wish for the penis with the wish for a child as a substitute. For boys, the castration complex serves to explain how the boy abandons sexual love for his mother (under the threat of castration from the father) and begins to accept all the other dictates of the father that are associated with conscience and morality. Within the Freudian scheme of things, these formulations are an attempt to provide a powerful and unitary conceptual model to explain and account for a variety of clinical observations and developmental facts. Among others, these include the apparent differences in psychological traits associated with being male and female, how we come to identify with being male and female, how we come to feel we are like our mothers and fathers and yet also give up our erotic ties to our parents, and how in adulthood we find or rediscover the erotic connections to the opposite sex. This model also is an attempt to explain the importance of the complementarity of a developmental process for men and women as each moves to assume a place, and play a respective part, in the grand biosocial scheme of love, procreation, and generation of the species.

And so, for Freud, too, it is clear that in order for the normal course of development to proceed in its divine design, part of oneself must be relinquished and another part accentuated, and even exaggerated. Within the Freudian plan, the outcome of this process will be different for men and women. For women, it will mean the development of a more passive, subdued, self-sacrificing sense of self and orientation with others, and for men it will mean the development of an active, aggressive, competitive position in the world. What one sex has, the other will not.

Freud has been criticized for the starkness of his portrayals of the psychic inner life of men and women, and for the extent to which he relies on psychological fates being sealed by anatomy. While it can be argued that anatomy is certainly a determiner of who we are and what we become, there is a reluctance to assign to it Freud's fatalistic power. And yet we continue to be struck by the truth of his perceptions, and we remain impressed with the enduring similarities and differences in psychology among men and women.

Gender Similarities and Differences: A Brief Review

Research and theory continue to be spun out to further uncover both the fact and the source of differences between men and women. The result is a long history, spanning decades and based on a variety of techniques, including interviews, experimental laboratory data, naturalistic observation, and self-reports—all of which confirm that men and women are different psychologically and different in definable ways. A second order of interest has involved the construction of explanations to account for these differences—i.e., what conditions, intrapsychic and sociocultural, sustain and maintain these differences, and what is the extent of rigidity or plasticity of this apparent essential character of man and woman.

Within this context, experimental attempts at classifying male and female traits in terms of behaviors and structures have usually come up with similar results. Here's one for an example. A study by Bem (1975) asked male and female college students to rate personality characteristics that they thought belong to men and women in American society. A personality characteristic qualified as feminine if it was independently judged by both males and females to be significantly more desirable for a woman than for a man. We are not surprised by the results of this study or countless others that document the very same patterns. Women, in general, are described by traits such as tender, sympathetic, yielding, sensitive to the needs of others, and compassionate, to name just a few. On the other hand, men are described by such traits as aggressive, analytical, competitive, dominant, and self-reliant, among others. The author notes that these traits were felt to represent enduring definitions and standards of feminine and masculine behavior in our culture in spite of the atmosphere of change inspired by feminist doctrines.

Some of the other myths that we hold regarding male–female differences have also held up on closer scrutiny. For example, a recent study by Shields (1987) found evidence to support the myth that women are more emotional than men, and more prone to displays from the emotional spectrum of sadness-depression, while men display more anger-hostility. Other studies have addressed the many myths regarding gender differences with respect to communication and communication patterns. Aries (1987) constructed a study to explore the reality of this stereotype. The author concluded: "There are clearly gender differences in the patterning of both verbal and nonverbal communication and in the topics of discourse. The interactions of men can be characterized as more task-oriented, dominant, directive, hierarchical; and women's as more social-emotional, expressive, supportive, facilitative, cooperative, and egalitarian" (p. 170). A study by O'Barr and Atkins (1980) referred to this difference in communication patterns in terms of interpersonal language use, finding that men's language patterns were characterized by frequent intrusions and interruptions, and attempts at control in terms of both topics and direction of conversations.

When theoreticians have been confronted with a history of this kind of data, the focus has been on an emerging characterization of what might be referred to as the basic essence of the inner structure of man and woman, and the quality of the interaction with those around them. Thus, we see the essence of woman as being more tender and warm, and her interactions as being yielding, self-sacrificing, compassionate and soothing, sympathetic and understanding. Men, on the other hand, are experienced as hard, bounded, self-reliant, separate, and their interactions as forceful, competitive, and dominating. These salient differences have even been used to account for differences in essential structural organizing principles between men and women as well. It is said, therefore, that we can even classify the "feminine principle" as associated with cognitive and emotional orientations that emphasize concern with intimacy, relationships to others, interest in community, harmony, preservation of relationship, listening to others, empathy, and nurturance. In fact, we tend to conceptualize male and female psychopathology in terms of deviations from these essential forms so characteristic of the sexes; i.e., we evaluate individual men and women as possessing either too much or not enough of the traits considered to be characteristic of their sex. Thus, women seem to be more vulnerable to intrapsychic and interpersonal dilemmas of "losing themselves" within others, living their lives too much for others, overly sacrificing of their needs for the sake of others, too soft, and too dependent. On the other extreme, there is the problem of "not enough feminine gender," expressed in being too selfish, self-centered, hard and unbending, overly dominant and controlling in forceful ways— i.e. being too much like men. Just the opposite is the case for men. The typical or normal male is seen in terms that emphasize individuality, valuing independence, being more concerned with self-interests than the interests of others. To be a man, in the common and enduring mythology of the culture, involves self-reliance and autonomous inner structures, and relationships that are characterized by domination, control, aggressiveness, taking charge, and taking over. It has been an assumption of this perspective that *human traits can be seen in bipolar opposite terms, that we see people as existing on a continuum of these bipolar dimensions, such as weak–strong, dependent–independent, soft–hard, selfless–selfish, giving–taking,* and that the distribution of these traits and ways of being in the world are gender-linked. It is a further corollary of this kind of thinking that possession of one of these traits necessarily influences the possession of others because they are organized as a pattern, and not just randomly distributed. Secondarily, in an either/or fashion, it is assumed that possession of one set of these attributes of being man or woman would necessarily diminish the accumulation and expression of the opposite. Thus, it is assumed that if one is a man he ought to be tough, and also self-reliant, and furthermore, that he has much less of a chance of being tender or empathic. In all of this there is again the feeling of general truth and legitimacy, but at the same time an exaggeration and simplification of reality. But that is part of what the construction of pure psychological types is all about: They are both the by-products of our observations and our intellectual need to categorize reality, sometimes beyond observation. *Most* men do fall close to these expectations, as do most women. And yet, while generalizations seem to apply, we also respect individual differences and variability within men and women, as well.

The second of these questions brings us to a consideration of the relative contribution of nature and nurture to the development of psychological sex differences. This is, of course, a complex subject, and a thorough examination of this is beyond the scope of this chapter. Nevertheless, it is clear that any explanation of differences between the sexes must consider an equation that includes apparent genetic differences as determinants—i.e., differences in biological programming at a neurological and biochemical level affecting inborn dispositions and temperaments. Also, on the side of the nature argument is the fact of behavioral differences in the lower animal species, and the implication that things should not be that much different with *Homo sapiens*. Furthermore, this programming, it is said, has biologically functional and adaptive properties, in that the asymmetry of functions in the two sexes promotes survival, adaptation, and propagation of the species. From a psychological perspective it is further assumed that these biological forces emerge and express themselves in inner temperament, influence interaction patterns, and change form as the individual grows and develops. In fact, they soon become the source of information about who we are, the very material that leads to a sense of identity of what it is to be a man or a woman. It is further assumed that society and social structures have emerged in the image of these differences, so that male–female differences are sustained and maintained by institutional structures. In persons born with, and then brought up with, this sense of the average expectable way to be and feel like a boy/girl, man/woman, these differences are carried through from generation to generation, from parents to children in a continuing cycle.

So when we ask where these differences come from, how they come into being, and what sustains them, we look first to this intimate link between our biology and psychology. But when we explore these supposedly male and female traits and patterns of interaction, we are struck again both by the truth and by the oversimplification of our conclusions. Since we know, too, that traits that seem to "belong" to men or women are not the exclusive domain of one or the other sex, they just seem to be, in most cases, unevenly or disproportionately distributed between the sexes. Thus, we know that with all of the influences of biology and gender-linked identifications, individual men and women possess traits that seem more dominant in the other sex.

More recent psychological perspectives have emerged to revise and extend earlier notions of biology and anatomy as destiny in understanding the process of becoming masculine and feminine. Again, these are attempts that both acknowledge observable male–female differences and try to explain them on the basis of some inner psychological definition that we each assign to being male and female in the process of development. Thus, it is assumed that our unique biology and physical structure as man and woman provide us with a powerful source of information and meaning about ourselves. Female psychology, for example, is said to be based on, and to spring from, an early and ongoing sense of the unique capacity to bear children, to nurture and sustain life, a sense of gender-based identification with mother, and all this becomes part of the heritage of identifications with what it means to be a female.

Thus, from the beginning, our biologies begin to inform us about who we are, and we begin to associate ourselves, at a psychological level, with a subclass of human, by sex, and begin to define and identify ourselves along social lines that continue to inform the meaning of being male and female. But, of course, the first transmitters of the culture at large are the parents. And it is within this framework that the real emotional stuff, and specific pictures of what it is to be boy/girl, man/woman, begin to take shape for each of us in highly individualized ways. Ultimately, who we are and how we come to define ourselves is intimately tied up with a complicated process of identification with our parents, which serves as a first powerful link to the sense of masculinity-femininity. But this, of course, does not mean we are merely copies of our parents, for parents serve only as models, and through complicated and shadowy ways, not always understandable and certainly unpredictable, we choose to become like them in whole or in part. Consciously and unconsciously we become what they wish us to be, or rebel against them and become what they are not. Within this process, we integrate parts of who they are into a new and novel admixture of a unique identity. Eventually we become more of ourselves, a composite that grows organically out of our natural tendencies, talents, wishes, conflicts, and yearnings.

Images of Man and Woman: Wish and Resistance to Change

The theories and evidence regarding how we become what we are is especially important nowadays because we are in the midst of social forces that are encouraging men and women to change. As such, we are being pushed into a position of exploring the degree of modifiability of the traits and modes of being in the world seemingly so characteristic of most men and women. There is a near obsession with the issue of recasting our versions of what it is to be masculine and feminine in our society, and men and women are struggling with and confronting these ideas about themselves and each other. With the increase in freedom and options for both men and women to move out of familiar roles and modes of experiencing the world, and into unfamiliar roles *within* and *between* themselves, at home and in the workplace, the boundaries of what is appropriate, valued, and even necessary are changing. Men and women are each exploring aspects of themselves, at times by necessity, at times by choice, which would have been impossible, or required much more daring, years ago. There is both a sharing and an exchanging of traditional roles of what in the past was considered the exclusive province of one or the other sex. And it should be emphasized that this applies as much to explorations and utilization of our inner "stuff" as to the performance of roles. Men are thus not only taking over more of the child care or domestic work than they used to but are doing more of the "maternal work," and this calls up the experience of different aspects of themselves. They are not just being more of what fathers used to be, or what is expected of fathers, but they are trying to be more of what mothers have been. Over the past two decades the tide has turned, and we are now in the midst of full-force currents of change. But it must be acknowledged that while for some this feels freeing and rewarding, for many others it feels as if they were swimming upstream, or even drowning.

This atmosphere of social change brings with it powerful questions as to how these forces will change our perceptions of who we are, and how are they likely to influence us now and in the future. We have more options and opportunities, but have we taken advantage of them? We have more choice, but are we choosing differently? In spite of the politics and rhetoric of change, do men and women want change, and are we ready? With all the evidence of the timelessness of male and female character, are we capable of change, and at what cost? How much of this atmosphere of change has been accepted by men and women, and to what extent have attitudes been translated into transformations of perceptions, self-experiences, and real behavioral change? Does all this represent a new beginning of some permanent alterations in the psyche of man and woman, or is it simply another swing of the proverbial pendulum?

The explorations of some recent studies address these questions of where we stand now and how we are doing. The tentative answers, as usual, reveal that we are confronted with the double-edged sword of apparent resistance and desire to change, both a preference and comfort with old established patterns and a yearning to move in different directions, which seem to be rewarding but certainly are not easy, and predictably are not without conflict or sacrifice.

Again, it may be useful to present just a brief review of some pertinent literature that covers men's and women's recent attempts at *sharing* and *exchanging* the roles of mother/father, husband/wife, which for many means shifting well-established patterns of behavior and intrapsychic structures. For men, this social movement has meant increasing paternal involvement in both the "fathering" and "mothering" aspects, and women are moving out of traditional mothering and into more breadwinning, distant roles. The results of these transformations are mixed. First, in terms of the sharing of childrearing and domestic activities, the Lamb, Pleck, and Levine (1987) review suggests that there is "little evidence that appreciable changes in paternal participation have taken place in response to increases in woman's total workload . . . and moreover . . . only a minority of women seem to desire increased participation by their husbands in child-care, and that the rates are not appreciably higher for employed than for unemployed women" (Pleck, 1983). The issue of whether women even want more involvement from their husbands in child care is debatable. Pleck's (1983) study found that women did not want their husbands to be more involved in child care, and another study by Russell (1982) found that many of the wives experienced dissatisfaction with the quality of the father's home and child care performance, and this in turn was a source of marital friction. Simply stated, increased paternal involvement in child care and domestic work, in and of itself, does not make for more satisfied individuals or happier marriages. One must look to other issues, such as whether these arrangements are by choice of the partners and not forced by circumstances, or because someone else thinks it is good for them, and whether these shifts are consistent or inconsistent with self-definitions. In addition, men continue to define what is good for them in terms of their work and career, and concern with promotion, money, and prestige. Thus, in Russell's study men reported that increased family involvement adversely affected career advancement. Bailyn, in 1974, found that "increased paternal participation is inimical with overtime and moonlighting as a means of supplementing family income" (p. 117). Therefore, as Veroff and Feld found (1970), "men are often torn between their desire to establish a close relationship with their children and their desire to establish financial security for the family" (p. 180). Nevertheless, some studies suggest that men are making the sacrifices necessary to ensure better relationships with wife and child (Sheehy, 1979). That we have to look closer at individual motivation is emphasized in a study by Owen, Chase-Lansdale, and Lamb (1982), who found that men who intrinsically valued parenthood were eager to be involved and more satisfied than those for whom the act of parenting was of less value. And yet, for men these shifts are not easy, not without conflict, or sacrifice, and for many they are attempts that are only short-lived. For example, in Russell's study, husbands and wives tended to revert back to more traditional patterns after initial rearrangements were made, and many of the men complained about issues in childrearing that women have complained of for years, focusing on the isolation from the adult world, boredom, repetition, and dull routines. For the most part, however, results suggest that men who have wanted to and who have had circumstances that have allowed them to increase their involvement with family and children (and this includes women who have wanted and been willing to share) have felt a greater sense of mastery, effectiveness, and competence as men and fathers.

Internal Conflicts: Classical and Contemporary

It is clear that we are now in the midst of internal and interpersonal struggles engendered by these shifting notions of what it means to be a man or a woman, and what it means to be a man with a woman. The heroes of the past were held up for emulation. It used to be clearer what we had to be, and we knew the familiar landmarks of how to succeed, even how to know when we were failing. In fact, the old notion of what it is to be a man appears to be a timeless one, since both men and women continue to define themselves in these terms. So it is clear that most men continue to see themselves in the ways they always have. Indeed, men are used to masculine kinds of struggles emerging out of the classical definitions and feelings of being a man, and the conflicts that grow out of the dilemma of having to deal with aggressiveness, competition, and assertion. And we are used to the kinds of implications that are organized around this experience. One is that we can become too much identified with these expectations and diminish the development of other aspects of ourselves, becoming somewhat like caricatures, approximating too closely some ideal cultural masculine type. On the other hand, men's struggles have emerged out of not feeling masculine enough in the ways that are spelled out by the conventions of the culture. This has brought a whole set of conflicts around achievement, feelings that one should be more independent, stronger, earn more money, have more prestige.

In the past, and now as well, men traditionally and paradoxically have benefited and have been burdened by the typical and classical male traits and ambitions. In the development of masculinity there has been the encouragement of many wonderfully adaptive functions, capacities, and skills. But, again, we may fall victim to a tendency that the accentuation of traits of one kind may diminish the possibility of those of another and opposite kind. And a further difficulty is expressed in being able to then make use of what we have less of, or to bring it into harmony with what is already there. This relationship between the conflict of different aspects of self that compete for dominance and expression was highlighted by a man in his early 30s exploring these aspects of himself in therapy. "I really don't cultivate friendship," he says, "I haven't gone out with anybody from work for two years." His beginning statement is a lament about difficulties in friendship and intimacy with others of a social kind, although his "professional" interactions are less problematic. He says that "when I am at a party, I put people off, I can't maintain a conversation. If I'm engaged by somebody, I don't engage back." As he continues, he reflects, "I can't take the lead in the social arena," and then, catching himself on the use of the word *arena*, he adds, "You know, sometimes that's what it feels like, like I'm in an arena, like a contest. There's something preventing me from getting more personally involved, not in touch with my feelings or emotions, and not expressing them. People get used to my not interacting, and they give up on me. I push people away, but then I get angry, I miss it when I'm in the mood for it. It's lonely when you want someone around to listen and they're not there." In this reflection, he begins to talk about a friend with whom he does feel comfortable, a relationship in which he feels "there is no wall between me and my emotions, that I have to fight through." Receiving encouragement to talk more about this relationship, reluctantly, and after a pause, "I think I feel I'm better than he is, and that's why I'm comfortable. I don't feel like a follower, I can be in charge, I don't have to be conscious of what he wants of me. In fact, I see him as a lot like me; he does what other people want, so I can do what I want. I'm not going to lose to him. I'm not even going to have to fight. I won't have to engage in some kind of battle—it's safe, I don't have to be afraid of losing—or even winning, for that matter." These experiences of the conflict in interpersonal expression—How do I express myself when it always seems competitive? Will I be the killer or the one killed? How can I be assertive and powerful and maintain a bond at the same time?—are classical dilemmas with which men have special struggles. In fact, it might be argued that it is more in the male psyche that the need for, and struggle with, self-aggression is an obstacle to closeness, while for women, the need and concern with closeness obstructs the expression of self. This is dramatically expressed by a young woman in therapy struggling with her intense masochism born of this conflict. "I'm so busy servicing other people's needs, I feel like I was born a waitress. I'll do whatever the other wants me to do, just to stay together with them, even if it means giving up on what I want for myself or who I am. I would never take the credit for anything,

I would be there only to serve others, to make them feel good, by being less than them, and then less than myself." Referring to conflicts with her mother, in this regard, she agonizes, "She just won't be able to tolerate my anger, or admit that it's her fault, so there I am again, blaming myself to save her, and to save us." Much of what she begins to acknowledge is the terrible aching need to be loved, to disprove feelings of being rejected and unwanted, and the angry assertive self that must be sacrificed as the condition necessary to achieve this.

The new images of man, what men struggle with now, seems to many men like a *giving up of of a way of being, a part of what they were and are, and trying to add something new and different to what they have not been. But this new goal, this new ideal of masculinity creates problems of a new order, a new set of conflicts as well as new possibilities*. A young man in therapy finds himself in a marriage and with a son for whom he feels he is the primary emotional parent. This arrangement has no doubt occurred by virtue of his own inner dynamics and those of his wife, and it is further supported by the social ambience, which makes the arrangement all the more plausible. Involved with prior concerns about his own authority, now he also struggles with a new set of issues related to whether he should give his son ice cream before dinner, weaning him from his bottle, or how tough to be with toilet training. Speaking of his relationship to his child and to his wife, who is no indifferent bystander in these father–son exchanges, he admits, "I've been real resistant getting him off the bottle. I'm so strongly connected with him, I've grabbed hold of his connections to me so strongly. I'm having a problem giving up some of the control and responsibility for him, of letting her do more. It was instant acceptance between him and me; it felt so good. His ties to me are incredibly strong. I really like it, but I also want a break from it, but I'm not willing to make the break." To complicate matters further, at a deeper personal level for this man, his struggle is also about his own ambivalence to act as a more powerful and authoritative father by controlling, setting limits, and disciplining his son. Along with this is a kind of identification with his son's antiauthority position, and a kind of pleasure in watching the son express his own emerging power and defy the authority that he, the father, now represents. Old conflicts and new demands merge to create unusual patterns of struggle requiring novel solutions.

By the same token, women are shifting the nice neat patterns of what it has meant to be a woman. A woman in her mid-30s struggles with these issues in her therapy as she explores the meanings of being a woman in the business world. "I'm having difficulty dealing with men at work," she says, "I can't get ahead in a man's world, and I'm having difficulty being a woman, both of which could be solved if I just had a child. I can't change it, but I can't accept if either. Having a baby feels like giving up a lot of my power, having to rely more on my husband, and I'll be more vulnerable. I want to make money, travel, have a house, retire wealthy, and it feels like I have to give that all up to have a child. How are we going to get all we want? Having a baby takes it all out of my hands, my power, self-sufficiency will be gone." She also bemoans her fate as a woman, that in some way she is more haunted by having to be loved and loving than does a man. "Men," she says, "seem to be able to put that aside and focus on something else, achieving something for themselves; they've traded off being loved for the love of ambition." It is important to recognize, of course, that the new times have not created this particular woman's struggles and inner conflicts. The concern with her inner power, vulnerability, dependency, the ability to love another with the threat of self-sacrifice rather than reward of self-enhancement have existed for a long time. But the social forces of change impinge on the psychic makeup and can bring out conflict, which then requires new and different strategies and forms for coping, adaptation, and resolution.

Psychic Reverberations of Internal Change

As men and women move into unfamiliar roles and modes of experiencing themselves and each other, both are being forced to make internal and intrapsychic adjustments. Men are now being asked to fill the vacuum created by the exodus of women in much of what has been the exclusive province of women. But it is not so easy for men to become something they are not used to, maybe less capable of, or which they associate with being part of the feminine world. Nor do they want to give up what they feel they are and know how to be. In fact, these issues of *to be and not to be* resound in all of the struggling relationships within and between the new man and woman.

There are obstacles each way, in each direction—i.e. to give up what one feels to be, maybe always felt to be, by virtue of inheritance, legacy, and culture, an integral part of our identity. Men who have attained, or continue to struggle to attain, the traditional masculine ideal, or continue to need to, may not be able to relinquish it so easily. (Men who have not been able to, out of reasons of their own dynamics, resistances, or identifications, may actually feel comforted, even spared.) But while it is difficult to relinquish, *it is equally difficult to take on and assume what one has ignored, devalued, and felt to be incompatible with oneself.*

Psychological Losing and Gaining: Unconscious Components

But what is this feeling of "losing something" of what we are and "becoming" what we are not all about, at a psychological level?

It is assumed by most psychologists, an article of faith by now, that who we are is essentially an extension of what we once were, and that gender becomes an important organizing principle in the traits we develop, the ones we don't, the ways we behave, the goals we have, the very sense of our self. From Freud's version of psychological development to the present, there is no question that gender plays a crucial part in defining who we are and how we are related to others. Observations of infants and children serve to confirm our beliefs as to gender-specific differences in the establishment of temperaments, dispositions, and relatedness with parents and siblings.

There is also evidence to suggest that there is, from early on, a different course in development that is taken for boys and girls. That this development is complicated cannot be overstated, yet generalized patterns, in gender-specific terms, do emerge. Margaret Mahler (Mahler, Pine, & Bergman, 1975), in her observation-based developmental theory, for example, observes that a "boy's active, aggressive strivings, his gender-determined motor mindedness seem to help him to maintain (with many ups and downs to be sure) the buoyancy of his body-ego feelings, his belief in his body strength, and his pleasure in functioning" (p. 213). In addition, the physical moving-away behavior from mother seems to be more prominent in boys than in girls, as boys and girls move away from mother, both physically and psychologically. Furthermore, for girls, identification with mother forms a basis for feminine gender identity, while for boys, the experienced gender difference (experienced and acknowledged both by the boy and by his mother) increases the psychological separateness from each other, and the mother in fact respects and enjoys the son's "phallicity," which pushes along this separation and individuation even more. In addition, the author notes that "identification with the father and perhaps with an older brother facilitates a later early beginning of the boy's gender identity" (p. 214). In fact, it is speculated that once this separation has taken place, the son has a more difficult and conflictual experience of reunion with the mother later on—i.e., to be able to make use of the mother in a psychological sense as he turns away from her developmentally. This is true for other reasons, connoting the boy's anxiety about loss of his newly found gender-related strength and difference from the mother. The anxiety in returning to the mother is even more so if the mother finds it difficult to relinquish her son's body and ownership of his penis to him, and if she interferes with his autonomy. The mother then is perceived not as a safe oasis, where he can recoup losses from the daily battles with the world, but as a source of danger and feared potential castration. "We cannot help but speculate," says Mahler, "that the fear of re-engulfment by the dangerous mother after separation, the fear of merging that we sometimes see as a central resistance in our adult male patients, has its inception at this very early period of life" (p. 215). Thus, in the normal course of development toward separation and individuation, the boy's gender serves the purpose of disentangling him and his mother from an early bond which once served to ensure his growth, and which now, if left unchanged, threatens to sabotage it. Thus, the mother and the boy, in a mutual recognition of their separateness cued by gender and gender difference, become partners in a cooperative process spurred on by the healthy wishes of each to be freed and free. And yet, the very same gender issue that may serve the purpose of separation may also hinder the smooth prospects for reunion, since, as we have seen for the boy, return to the mother may be loaded with dangers of loss of phallus, loss of self, fear of engulfment, loss of gender, loss of control, and loss of autonomy (and later on, the sexual implications of turning back to mother make it even more difficult). The gender-linked psychological distance ensures safety of self, but then it becomes a gulf that needs to be navigated to feel connected and related with another and to help in the process of intimacy and sharing. Thus, within the context of gender, the boy's early psychological push is away from mother, to "disidentify" with her (Greenson, 1968). The father, then, further serves as a rescuer from symbiotic yearnings in the boy for the mother (which are perhaps less strong in the boy) and serves to allay separation anxiety in his presence to receive the boy as he moves away from mother. The boy, in his identification search, then, is to find other-than-mother ego ideals with which to identify, and father becomes a likely candidate in the process of facilitating such a developmental push. Boys, then, are seen to have reengulfment anxieties with mothers and, later, castration anxieties with fathers, although boys are likely to develop both sets of anxieties with mothers who are ambivalent about the boys phallic strivings, and where inadequate objects for masculine identification opportunities exist.

The Problem for Men: Intrapsychic and Interpersonal Consequences

Thus, men, through the course of development, tend to take on and *become* more of what we expect ourselves to be at a gender-linked level. We men may push ourselves away from mothers and away from maternal identifications for the sake of our masculinity, and for the safety of our penis and ourselves. In this process we begin to *disown* internal aspects of ourselves, which have become associated with the feminine, a process that may also involve distancing ourselves from females. Thus, we see that the psychological problem for men is this development of some prescribed aspects of self that have intrapsychic and interpersonal implications for us as we move in the world, implications of both gain and loss. At an intrapsychic level we see the development of internal structures and identity organized around independence and separateness. We see the development of traits of competition, autonomy, aggression, tendencies toward domination, and control. This, of course, is what men are known for, traits that clearly represent adaptive strengths—the reliance on self, protection of others, leadership, and guidance. What happens on the other hand, of course, is the lack of development, or repression, of other aspects of self related to capacities of tenderness, caring, emotional expression, and dependence—psychological structures usually identified with and encouraged within women.

There are other implications for men in this process of leaving behind aspects of self on the way to becoming a man. For most men, this developmental process is at best incomplete, and remnants of early fears and potential dangers remain still lurking in the masculine unconscious. *Men continue to be haunted in vague and ill-defined ways* with the longings and fears, wishes and avoidances which were begun in childhood, and which reawaken in the context of adult male–female relationships. The resurfacing of old conflicts rears its multifaceted head in the male experience of self and in relationship with both other men and women. The extent to which the past enacts its power, of course, depends on the degree of satisfactory resolution of these early conflicts, and for men this is expressed in variations in one's firm sense of masculinity, the character of relations with women, with one's own children, and with ambitions. There are some good reasons why men need to maintain this polarity within themselves and in relationships. Men feel more of what they are in this process of taking on certain ways of being and giving up others. For many men, this is the way it has been, and this is the way it must always be. Many men continue to need this sense of polarity within themselves and between themselves and women for other reasons. Many men wish to save the inner polarity for sexual reasons, since it may preserve one's sense of masculine sexuality, and the difference with women maintains a vital tension of sexuality, which they fear may be lost with too much sameness, equality, and equivalence. The more that men feel strong and dominant inside themselves not only reassures a sense of masculinity but continues to make women feel like women. It should also be remembered that the early pulling away from mother may lead to a devaluing of mother and women, and a devaluing and disowning of the feminine inside oneself that has been associated with mother. Men sometimes fear that too much intimacy with women may lead to a blurring of boundaries, a resurgence of the feminine inside themselves and being swept away by these feelings, leading to loss of sexual interest, loss of domination and control. Intimacy, with its corresponding loss of separateness, may also arouse old issues of dependency, of wanting to be mothered or taken care of, which can seem very wrong. The very notion of self, at times, feels as if it is on the line. Many men, thrust into roles and expectations requiring intimacy and relatedness, may be thrown back into times of childhood dependence. Thus, it may call up the little boy who needed to ask for help when feeling helpless, the wish to be mommy's little helper, the dreaded fear that asking for help might lead to humiliation and shame. The man who engages in shared responsibilities with a woman may be faced with psychic reverberations of castration anxiety. Or, in still another version, it may call up one's relationship with the father, with the male legacy, heritage, and identification. Will I disappoint my father; will I surpass him by being more or less than he was? There is a symbolic killing that goes on here beneath the surface. And sometimes, the greatest fears bespeak the most unresolved conflicts, that those with the greatest needs to be independent, separate, and different are those most afraid of the temptations, the strong forbidden or anxiety-laden wishes that require strong boundaries and defenses against expression. For many men these wishes have not been satisfied or worked through adequately in the course of development, so that situations now may evoke intense and conflictual feelings of the past, bringing anxiety, discomfort, and intense resistance.

Therefore, we should not naively assume that we are dealing with a wealth of easily discernible, accessible, or even valued treasures. In fact, there is a bit of the idea of the Pandora's box here, forces that, acknowledged and exposed, could attack and destroy. Also, we are dealing here with inner structural traits of people, structure that orders and sustains one's sense of who we are, what we are all about. So, *simply being encouraged or placed in situations by virtue of choice or chance (of life circumstances outside of our control) does not necessarily do the psychic work for us; it only serves to remind us of what needs to be done, and our behavior, it must be remembered, is always mediated by how we feel inside of ourselves.* But this is what contemporary promptings are all about, asking men to explore and use aspects of self long ago buried, diminished, or devalued. And so, this sets many men on a collision course with old and repressed longings, a course which has many obstacles but which may lead, at best, to intrapsychic and interpersonal resurrection and restoration.

And all of this movement toward or resistance against reclamation of parts of our self takes place within the context of what we may not be so well suited to do, both by virtue of the limitations of our biological programming and as a result of what years of *being man* can do on the disuse of functions that long ago were sacrificed on the road to becoming a man. And so, for most of us, at a psychological level, the issue is of getting back on a course that has been "left behind" and undeveloped in the process of growing up. In fact, this is all we can hope for, since our programming at a biopsychological level imposes limits within which we have to work, as individuals and as members of a group. This, of course, can be offset by a host of factors of internal motivation, wishes, and encouragements, and the lifting of internal psychic barriers, as well as the slow modification of sociocultural archetypes. What is increasingly clear is that the external forces of change are prominent. How we react inside is more questionable, problematic, and uncertain.

Psychological Androgyny: Conceptualizing Individual Differences in Gender

It should be underscored at this point that individual men have gained and lost more or less in this developmental process, since individual men and women only approximate the kinds of dispositions, temperaments, and conflicts associated with their gender. so, for some men, this will not feel like such a sacrifice (either the giving up, modifying, or taking on of certain traits or patterns of interaction associated with the feminine, or early childhood). For any one man it may come as a great relief and a reward to unburden oneself of the hidden and perhaps secretive, yet yearned-for, aspects of self now allowed to be expressed. For others it will feel awkward, dangerous, or even impossible.

For many men these kinds of problems and opportunities become exposed and expressed in relationships, particularly when demands from others ask or require men to be *more* than just autonomous and independent, but sympathetic, involved, and self-sacrificing. These relationships involve men as lovers, husbands, fathers to children, and caregiving adults to aging parents. This developmental process, which leaves us in a rather bifurcated version of what it means to be human in a Platonic sense, is encountering the new cultural archetypes that are moving us to a version of masculinity that *includes* the notion of being both tough and tender, independent and dependent, self-interested and altruistic. The result is that in addition to struggling with classical masculine kinds of conflicts involving aggression and competition, men are now struggling with problems related to the psychic demands of being more than tough, of asking themselves how to be both tough and tender.

And this is where the notion of psychological androgyny provides an interesting conceptual link. Within this context, it is noteworthy to cite a study on the psychological consequences of androgyny from the vantage point of adaptation. The purpose of this research (Bem, 1975) was to find out if the androgynous person (defined as men and women who see themselves as possessing both masculine and feminine traits) is better off than the "sex-typed" person (males and females who define themselves within traditional sex-stereotyped modes of behavior either for their sex or for the opposite sex). Thus, one could be considered a masculine male, a feminine male, a masculine female, or a feminine female. The highly sex-typed person, according to Bem, "keeps his or her behavior consistent with an internalized sex role standard; that is, he becomes motivated to maintain a self-image as masculine or feminine, a goal which is presumably accomplished by suppressing any behavior that might be considered undesirable or inappropriate for that sex." Thus, even the self-concepts of the "feminine male and masculine female . . . are not less sex-typed . . . being narrow and restrictive [as it is] limited in accordance with his or her self-definition of masculine or feminine" (p. 634). Designing a series of tasks that called for independence and playfulness-tenderness, the author found that only "androgynous subjects of both sexes displayed a high level of independence *and* playfulness." Another study (Bem, Martyna, & Watson, 1976) found "only androgynous males high in both the instrumental and the expressive domains; that is, only androgynous males were found to stand firm in their opinions as well as to cuddle kittens, bounce babies, and offer a sympathetic ear to someone in distress" (p. 1022). In contrast, "the feminine males were low in independence, while the masculine male was low in nurturance (whether they were interacting with a baby, a kitten, or a lonely fellow student)" (p. 1022).

In another study, LaFrance and Carmen (1980) found evidence to confirm these same kinds of differences between androgynous men and women compared with their sex-typed counterparts. Corroborating their predictions, they found that sex-typed males and females followed traditional paths; i.e., sex-typed individuals of both sexes display correspondent sex consistency and cross-sex avoidance, meaning that they respond as though feminine and masculine behaviors are antithetical to each other. On the other hand, androgynous individuals showed neither the within-sex role homogeneity of sex-typed subjects nor the cross-gender rejection. In sum, they found that androgynous individuals "demonstrate variable blending of masculinity and femininity in each situation. They have a larger repertoire and a greater range of responsiveness than sex-typed individuals" (p. 47). Moreover, this blend for androgynous persons is not less masculine for men or less feminine for women but, rather, is the "addition of some cross-sex behavior and deletion of some sex-consonant behavior" (p. 47). In addition, the authors contend that androgyny may well represent a true blend of traits out of which emerges a new, more integrated compound, which emerges and functions in its own right, a true blend, out of which a new dimension arises, consisting of these parts, but greater and something different as well. In addition. the authors contend that androgyny may be arrived at differently for males and females. Androgynous females seem to decelerate feminine display, and their masculine counterparts show less masculine behavior in sex-consonant situations. There is, in general, the "addition of some cross-sex behavior and the deletion of sex-consonant behavior" (p. 48).

Thus, the androgynous man can be as masculine as masculine men, and as feminine as feminine women. He doesn't have to sacrifice one way of being for the other. His ability to do this comes from within, and he responds to the demands of the situation, which calls for him to be one way or the other, and not just as he is restricted to do by virtue of a limited mode of responsiveness. And, of course, this applies to both men and women, as exemplified by an insight of a woman patient of mine, who feels this very issue in her relationship with her daughter. "I'm used to doing things the same old way inside, and not being able to adjust to new demands from her. I keep responding the way *I* need to, not the way she wants me to, or the way *she* needs me to." In this sense, the androgynous person is, indeed, more adaptive, since he or she has a repertoire of responsiveness that allows for interactions in a world that requires both the tough and the tender. And the world in which men find themselves nowadays is certainly one that contains these different kinds of demands.

The Masculine Struggle with Psychological Integration

Androgyny speaks to a fundamental issue in all of us. For each of us, it brings up the idea of psychological integration, the notion of being able to explore, develop, bring together, and use all aspects of our humanness, for ourselves and for others. It should not be underemphasized that this is a difficult psychological chore, since most of us are making up for lost time, and there is a sense of being handicapped by the constraints placed on us by our gender-linked identifications. Most men are coming from the traditional place, in spite of the new androgynous male spirit in the air, and most men are trying to figure our how to bring together these apparently disparate aspects of themselves. It is not easy. We still feel ourselves in very masculine ways, and want to see women from that very masculine perspective. The cultural and biological legacy, social symbols, and cultural heroic images are seemingly endless in our mythology and continue to abound in contemporary forms. We have been raised and bred on these masculine heroes, and while hearing and seeing John Wayne movies may seem a little corny nowadays, there are lasting emotional truths expressed as we see him in a movie like *The Quiet Man*, depicting the time when men were men and women were women. At one point in this love story he wistfully yearns for "things that a man doesn't get over so easy, like the sight of girl comin' through the fields, the scent of her hair, a face like a saint, comin' into a man's home and cleanin' and cookin' for him." While this no doubt represents a set of aspects that men wish for in their women and their experience of self in relation to women, we are reminded also of the new man in Dustin Hoffman's Tootsie. Here we see an incredibly accurate and insightful depiction of man's struggle for integration within himself and in his relation to women. In the course of this unfolding inner journey it is clear that a deeper kind of love of self and women becomes possible only through a process of self-exploration and self-discovery. And this is made possible through a process of identification with, and assuming the position of, the woman, which leads to the discovery of feminine aspects within himself. In the beginning, this rather harsh, narrowly sexualized man, consumed by and struggling with issues of traditional masculine success and failure, gradually transforms himself into a more tender, nurturant, whole, and loving man. And he does this by first falling in love with this inner feminine aspect of himself, which he begins to respect and cultivate. This gradual recognition of this other part of himself through identification with women, this becoming more of what a woman is allows a connection to women that he could not establish as a one-dimensional man. But this does not come at the sacrifice of his masculine strength and power, or his erotic fascination with woman. Instead, the masculine and feminine aspects begin to blend with each other, and there emerges a new inner person possessed of the character of each. In addition, his love of self and for his woman are informed by this new emergent self. Further, this gradual development allows him to see his woman more as a person, from the inside, and, in fact, even to help his woman with aspects she has denied in herself. This then leads to the development of a true love between them, a love composed of currents springing from erotic and affectional sources. The process is complicated and torturous, but ultimately resolved, as Tootsie leaves us with the resultant moral metaphor of his metamorphosis: "I was a better man with you as a woman than I ever was with a woman as a man. I just gotta learn to do it without the dress."

There is much for men to gain in this process of discovering, reclaiming, and using aspects of self given up, sacrificed, and forfeited in the course of development. Becoming more empathic with one's self, acknowledging, respecting, and using the "other sides" of self, we bring back to life that which was once ours, and become a more whole and complete person. We are then able to use ourselves differently in relation to others, with friends and lovers alike. We also give up dependencies on others, as men have done with women by needing them to be for us in ways we can't be for ourselves. It frees us of a slavish obedience and dependence on women (which many men will of course deny) to be our mothers, praising and idolizing them when they are, angry and disparaging of them when they are not. This will lead to a higher level of personal integration, a true joining and a coming together of split-off aspects of ourselves, which will make for a stronger, more resilient structure within. In many ways we have nothing to fear but the proverbial fear itself, since understanding the irrationality and source of these fears, the risks involved in exposing then, and then the courage to act in novel ways can modify these inner fears and the defensive dispositions that arise from them. We can learn that intimacy will not lead to reengulfment, to sexual impotence or castration, that experiencing the person of the woman does not necessarily diminish our sexual or romantic love, that, in fact, it can even deepen it. Thus, confrontation with our darker aspects can disprove, rather than confirm, the power it holds over us. In so doing, we begin to learn how to nurture ourselves and others, and to love, husband, and father better, with a sense of genuineness, mastery, and ownership. In all of this, a level of personal integration may be gradually achieved by a process of reciprocal accentuation and softening of bipolar aspects of self, which have lived in separate domains, with little sharing and no chance to learn or borrow from the other. The lessons are moving and considerable to be strong and powerful without domination, self-interested without denying the needs of others, autonomous and independent without sacrificing the legitimate and genuine needs for help and dependency, and loving of self and others in all the ways and nuances of meaning available to us as full, complete, and reunified human beings.

REFERENCES

Aries, E. (1987). Gender and communication. In P. Shaver & C. Hendrick (Eds.), *Sex and gender* (pp. 167–170). CA: Sage.
Bailyn, L. (1974). Accommodation as career strategy: Implications for the realm of work. Working paper 728–724, Sloan School of Management, M.I.T.
Bem, L. (1975). Sex role adaptability: One consequence of psychological androgyny. *Journal of Personality and Social Psychology*, 31, 634–643.
Bem, S. L., Martyna, and Watson, C. (1976) Sex typing and androgeny: Further explorations of the expressive domain. *Journal of Personality and Social Psychology*, 34(5), 1016–1023.
Freud, S. (1961). An example of psychoanalysis. *Standard Edition* (Vol. 23, pp. 183–195). London: Hogarth. (Original work published 1937).
Greenson, R. (1968). Disidentifying from mother: Its special importance for the boy. In *Explorations in Psychoanalysis*. New York: International Universities Press.
LaFrance, M., & Carmen, B. (1980). The nonverbal display of psychological androgyny. *Journal of Personality and Social Psychology*, 38, 36–49.
Lamb, M. E., Pleck, J., & Levine, J. A. (1987). Effects of increased paternal involvement on fathers and mothers. In C. Lewis & M. O'Brien (Eds.), Reassessing fatherhood (pp. 109–125). CA: Sage.
Mahler, M., Pine, F., & Bergman, A. (1975). *The psychological birth of the human infant*. New York: Basic Books.
O'Barr, W., & Atkins, B. (1980). "Women's language" or "powerless language"? In S. McConnell-Ginet, R. Borker, & N. Furman (Eds.), *Women and language in literature and society* (pp. 93–110). New York: Praeger.
Owen, M. T., Chase-Lansdale, P. L., & Lamb, M. E. (1982). *Mothers' and fathers' attitudes, maternal employment, and the security of infant–parent attachment*. Unpublished manuscript.
Plato (1952). The symposium. In R. M. Hutchins (Ed.), *The great books* (pp. 149–174). Chicago: University of Chicago and the Encyclopeadia Britannica.
Pleck, J. H. (1983). Husbands' paid work and family roles: Current research issues. In H. Lopata & J. H. Pleck (Eds.), *Research in the interweave of social roles, Vol. 3, Families and jobs*. Greenwich, CT: JAI Press.
Russell, G. (1982). Shared caregiving families: An Australian study. In M. E. Lamb (Ed.), *Nontraditional families: Parenting and child development*. Hillsdale, NJ: Erlbaum.
Sheehy, G. (1979). Introducing the postponing generation. *Esquire*, 92(4), 25–33.
Shields, S. A. (1987). Women, men, and the dilemma of emotion. In P. Shaver & C. Hendrick (Eds.), *Sex and gender* (pp. 229–251). CA: Sage.
Veroff, J., & Feld, S. (1970). *Marriage and work in America*. New York: Van Nostrand Reinhold.

Chapter 3
Preparation for Fatherhood
Dreams of Transition

MARY BETH M. CRESCI

In the past decade the psychoanalytic literature has shown a remarkable proliferation of articles on the topic of fatherhood, both in terms of a father's importance in his children's lives and in terms of fatherhood as an important developmental epoch in a man's life. Most likely, the professional interest in the topic has been spurred by the social changes that have so dramatically affected family life in the past 20 years. The feminist movement, changing work patterns for women, improved methods of birth control, and the higher incidence of divorce have conspired in various ways to influence both the decision to have children and the style of parenting in our homes today. The recognition that these changes have affected men as well as women, fathers as well as mothers, has caused scientists to reexamine their previous assumption that "parenting" was in many ways synonymous with "mothering." The result has been a much closer look at how men approach fatherhood and choose a fathering style.

This chapter will focus on one aspect of fatherhood—that is, a man's preparation for fatherhood as it was displayed in the course of psychoanalytic treatment. The issues that arose in the treatment prior to the baby's arrival, far from being unusual or primarily pathological, seemed to represent an orderly transition from the role of son and of one who has been fathered to the role of being a father oneself. A number of old patterns of relationships needed to be reworked within this man's psyche in order to give him the freedom to establish new patterns of relationships as a father himself. Vital to this process were a series of dreams produced by this man during his wife's pregnancy, dreams that addressed many profound issues of fatherhood.

There is an interesting parallel between the fathering that my patient, Mr. M., received as compared with the father he wished to become and the early as opposed to recent literature on the psychodynamics of fatherhood. In both cases, the "early" experiences (i.e., Mr. M.'s experience as a child and the early psychoanalytic theories) minimize the role of father, whereas the "later" experiences (Mr. M.'s view of fatherhood and later psychoanalytic theories) give much greater recognition to the

---

MARY BETH M. CRESCI • The Psychoanalytic Institute, Postgraduate Center for Mental Health, New York, New York 10016; Brooklyn Institute for Psychotherapy, Brooklyn, New York 11215; National Institute for the Psychotherapies, New York, New York 10019.

importance of the father. Freud's theory (1908, 1909), for instance, focuses on the little boy's desire to imitate his mother and to give birth to a child as she did. Freud believed that children have a "cloacal theory" of birth, in which genital and excretory organs and functions coincide, so that the little boy assumes he can give birth through the anus. As the boy comes to realize that the mother is impregnated by the father, he then develops the wish to be impregnated by the father himself. This state of development Freud (1923) labeled the "negative Oedipus complex" because it represents the boy's identification with his mother and his fantasy of the father as a sexual partner in order to have a child. In discussing this tendency to link parental ambitions of a boy or man with maternal, womanly capacities, Ross (1982) has concluded: "Psychoanalytic theorists have allowed little place for fatherhood in the developmental scheme of things. It is almost, one senses, as if to be a parent one must be a woman."

In other words, while the father's role in impregnation is emphasized, the man's desire for children and his concept of parenting are seen as being modeled primarily on the mother's contribution of bearing children. Even Reik's (1919) focus on the adult male's reaction to becoming a father, the concept of the couvade in which the man experiences many of the bodily symptoms of pregnancy and childbirth, stresses the adult male's imitation of the female's experience.

Additionally, some authors have suggested that the early psychoanalytic writings accepted and even propagated a societal view of fatherhood that minimized the father's active involvement with caretaking of the children. Robinson and Barret (1986) discuss the "traditional" father as one who fulfills his role by being the breadwinner in the family and by being a kindly but distant authoritarian figure. They suggest that traditional psychoanalytic writings provided a theoretical underpinning for this paternal stance by stressing that the father becomes a strong rival for the little boy in the boy's quest for his mother's love during the Oedipal stage. In this role, fear of castration by the father provides the impetus for the boy to resolve the Oedipal conflict by giving up his genital desires for the mother and moving on to more mature, sublimated libidinal activities, such as friendships with other boys and academic pursuits. The father's authoritarian style and his own active professional life outside the home are seen as appropriate models in drawing the little boy away from too incestuous a relationship with his mother. These activities, however, do not place much importance on the father as an active participant in household activities and childrearing.

More recent researchers have begun to reconsider some of the assumptions regarding the father's role and his impact on his children. They have begun to observe different styles of fatherhood and to consider whether the various styles have different effects on childrearing and on the father–child and father–mother relationships. They have also begun to investigate anew the developmental issues that affect a man as he becomes a father and to consider whether identifications with his own father may not be just as important as his maternal identifications. A variety of new theoretical directions have been proposed.

While there are different viewpoints as to the degree to which a father provides a different experience for his child or the degree to which he provides the child with an experience similar to the experience with the mother, all researchers agree that the tie of the child to the father is a very important one. Lamb (1978), for instance, in reviewing a number of infant studies concludes that infants develop an attachment to their mothers and fathers at about the same time. He states that they do not show the predicted preferences for their mothers during the first year, and he finds that male infants tend to develop a preference for their fathers during the second year of life. His own studies suggest that there are qualitative differences in the relationships with the two parents that may make different contributions to the child's development. For instance, the child may develop more of a sense of gender identity from his or her interaction with the father.

Yablonsky (1982) stresses that "changing sex roles have already produced fathers who 'mother' and mothers who 'father.' In fact, we would do well to recognize clearly that such traits as the ability to love compassionately and to nurture exist equally in both men and women" (p. 26).

Yablonsky believes that the father produces a cognitive map, or a mental image of what his son should become, which precedes and strongly affects the son's views of himself and his development of his life plan. The harmony or discordance of these views and the extent of the closeness between the father and the son are both important factors in helping the son to feel a sense of success and fulfillment in his life. Yablonsky also discusses various father types, such as the compassionate-loving or doubling father, the peer-type or buddy father, the macho father, and more pathological types such as the psychopathic or egocentric father.

In this same vein, Blos (1985) has emphasized the importance of the father–son relationship and its impact on the boy's developing sense of self. He stresses that many aspects of the relationship are not resolved during the Oedipal phase but persist into adolescence and beyond.

Another group of literature focuses on the man as a prospective father. Gurwitt (1976), for instance, describes a young man's fears of fatherhood as his wife went through her pregnancy and finds that they were successfully resolved at the time of the baby's birth. Herzog (1982) studied a group of men during their wives' pregnancies. He found that the degree of emotional participation in the pregnancy was correlated with the degree to which the men were involved in an ongoing empathic relationship with their wives. Additionally, he found that the more-involved men were also more attuned to their own feelings and fantasies during the pregnancy. Many of them were particularly concerned to resolve outstanding conflicts in their relationships with their own fathers. He found that those who had not been able to resolve their internal conflicts with their own fathers had the most internal difficulties during the latter half of the wives' pregnancy. He concludes, "If you are always searching for a father, it may interfere with your ability to become one, although some men make their own reparations and compensations for their defective childhoods by endeavoring to become superior parents themselves" (p. 313).

The two issues of the ongoing relationship with his wife and, most important, his relationship and identifications with his father were of paramount importance for my patient, Mr. M., during his wife's pregnancy. Mr. M. had initially consulted me for treatment when he was 34 years old. He had been married for 6 months to a 37-year-old woman who was completing her residency as a doctor. Mr. M.'s presenting complaint was that he was unable to function in his profession as a lawyer, especially in making courtroom presentations, which were frequent events in his particular job. He had become so frightened of these appearances that he had gotten a temporary dispensation from making them. It was understood that he could not keep his job if he could not shortly return to court. In addition, Mr. M. complained of general feelings of low self-esteem. He seemed happy in his marriage, although there were some adjustments to be made about issues of intimacy and his concern about his wife's dependency on him. In general, Mr. M. used an obsessive-compulsive style in both adaptive and more defensive ways.

In the early months of treatment, Mr. M. made a number of important advances in terms of his commitment to treatment, his ability to move toward self-exploration, and his ability to make substantive changes in his life. He very quickly moved into twice-a-week treatment and began to explore his most pressing problem, his stage fright at work. An intense internal conflict regarding his choice of a career became the focus of our work.

Mr. M. is the son of a Jewish family from an industrial city in the Midwest. He has a sister 4 years older than himself. His father owns a retail store. His mother is a housewife and is also active in working at the store when needed. In the immediate neighborhood lived the grandparents plus many aunts, uncles, and cousins, particularly from the mother's side of the family.

As Mr. M. described his childhood, there was a strong sense of feeling out of step with his family. He stated that his father worked long hours every day, and his mother and sister were also actively involved in the store. He, on the other hand, had no interest in the family business and chose to stay home. His parents accepted this and developed a view of him as their intellectual, scholarly son who would someday have a successful professional career. The mother's family, in particular, had many professionals in it, including several lawyers. Comparatively speaking, Mr. M.'s father was considered to have a low-status occupation and to be a "jock" rather than a serious-minded intellectual.

In high school, the parents wanted Mr. M. to join a social group from their local synagogue, young people whose parents were friends of Mr. M.'s parents. Mr. M. found this group to be very dull, with shallow, materialistic values. Instead, he eventually associated with a loosely formed group of intellectuals at school whom he greatly admired. A very significant fact for him was the coincidence that a number of these boyhood friends died in freakish accidents during or shortly after college. This increased Mr. M.'s sense of isolation and alienation, leading to a feeling of depression and a sense of his relative ordinariness and mediocrity. In college, Mr. M. greatly enjoyed the intellectual stimulation. He developed a close relationship with several young faculty members, but he experienced a real crisis when his college career came to an end. He could not choose among a number of academic fields, all of which would have required extensive graduate training, in spite of considerable encouragement from his faculty mentors. He eventually decided on law school, which greatly pleased his parents, especially his father. However, he never really enjoyed legal work, and his lack of interest in his profession, coupled with his increasing discomfort in the courtroom, brought him to the point of being unable to perform his job.

Mr. M. also had a love of music, which his family did not share. He met his wife at a summer music camp. They both belonged to amateur orchestral groups. They dated for several years prior to their marriage.

In reviewing his decision to go into the field of law, Mr. M. came to realize that in many ways his father's "cognitive map" that he should be a successful, professional man did not really coincide with his own scholarly and intellectual goals. He had not really pursued his goals because they were too far from his parents' goals for him and because he did not have enough confidence or commitment to pursue any one academic field. Simultaneously with these realizations, Mr. M. chose to quit his job and get an administrative job at a university, which felt quite comfortable to him. Now he was much closer to the atmosphere that had felt most compatible to him growing up, even though his parents were surprised by the move and saw the new job as less prestigious.

At about the same time that Mr. M. was resolving his career change, he announced that his wife had just learned she was pregnant. Mr. M. and his wife had made the decision several months before to have a baby early in their marriage because of Mrs. M.'s age, and Mr. M. seemed genuinely pleased with the idea of becoming a father. He maintained an extremely high interest in his wife's progress during the pregnancy, and he engaged in many fantasies about the baby and his relationship with the child. On an intellectual level, he read voraciously books on every aspect of pregnancy, labor and delivery, infant development, and childrearing practices. He accompanied his wife to some of her obstetrical appointments, as well as for an amniocentesis, fetal monitoring, and coaching classes for labor and delivery. He also arranged for about 6 weeks of vacation and leave time from work, so that he could stay home with the baby for 6 weeks after his wife had taken about 2 months of maternity leave herself. He was actively involved with his wife in interviewing child care workers to care for the baby after he went back to work. In addition to being present during labor and delivery, he accompanied his wife and child on several doctors' visits for minor complications after the baby was born. Throughout the early months of the baby's life, he was actively involved in the baby's care, providing supplementary bottles for feeding, giving baths, and changing diapers.

Obviously, this father was not following the pattern of the traditional, distant father. He was very active as a father even before the child's birth and showed many of the characteristics common to Herzog's highly involved fathers-to-be. The dimension that made the preparation for fatherhood most interesting in this case was a series of dreams that Mr. M. had during his wife's pregnancy. The dreams became focal points from which much of Mr. M.'s unresolved concerns about his relationship with his own father and some of the issues of intimacy in his marriage could be explored.

The first dream reported early in the pregnancy was actually a dream that Mr. M. had had repeatedly since college days. It was as follows:

> I was standing on an upper floor of a building at college. The building was built into the ground so that most of it was below ground. It had a moat all around it. The floor on which I stood was actually at ground level, but it was separated by the moat. It had a narrow balcony all around it. I was debating whether I should try to leave the building and, if so, should I try to jump from the balcony across the moat to the ground outside.

In discussing the dream, Mr. M. said the dream always reminded him of college, a relatively happy time for him, but that it always reminded him of the anxiety he felt about leaving college and making the leap into the real world. He commented that the building was a very odd one because so much of it was built below ground and that he had never seen another one like it. The odd thing was that even though he was on an upper floor he was still basically at ground level, and yet he had to jump across the moat to get out of the building. As we discussed all these spatial arrangements, it seemed that in many ways the building represented Mr. M. While he was solid and steady, there was a "moat" or gap between himself and the rest of the world. Also, much of his feeling was buried below ground, so that only the "upper stories," or intellectual functioning, were evident. The balcony represented an extension of himself to the outside world that still left a dangerous gap to fill. Mr. M. was uncertain whether he wanted to risk leaving his secure, protected fortress for whatever lay outside.

We applied this image to several aspects of Mr. M.'s life. One was his feeling of alienation within his family, and his tendency to protect himself through his intellectual pursuits while keeping his feelings well hidden. Another was a general difficulty he was having in being responsive to his wife, a quality that was being exacerbated by her special needs for attention during her pregnancy. This difficulty was experienced by Mr. M. as his desire to have peace and quiet and settle down with an interesting book at night, whereas his wife wanted him to listen to her complaints about work and give her advice. She also wanted him to talk more about his feelings. Mr. M. felt pressure to come up with good solutions to his wife's difficulties. When she complained about work, he felt like a failure. He also became exasperated with her when she continued to worry about her problems and remained indecisive. In discussing these issues in the treatment and then with his wife, he admitted that he had trouble talking about his feelings and began to make more efforts to do so. He also tried to do more listening and less problem solving with his wife so that the discussion was more open-ended and less judgmental. An awareness of his lack of expressiveness was helpful.

Toward the middle of his wife's pregnancy, Mr. M. brought in two dreams with some common elements. The first one was the following:

> I was in a theater that seemed to be made up of two different buildings. One was canal-like with two passageways. I looked down one. It was all red and there was someone at the other end of it. The other had many passageways going off it, but I didn't go down there. The second building was the theater itself. It was very dark. I was sitting in the theatre by myself watching Laurence Olivier on stage.

The second dream occurred a few nights later:

> I am sitting in a theater. At the back of the stage there are a bunch of male lions lounging around. In front of them are a group of pop singers. Some of them are kids. They're supposed to learn to perform their songs without being afraid of the lions.

Mr. M.'s immediate reaction to the first dream was that the buildings seemed like a very unusual theater because most theaters do not have all those little passageways. He also noted that he had watched a program about Laurence Olivier's life that night. The idea of the canal reminded him of the birth canal, which might be all red with blood, and he thought he might be looking down the canal at the baby. The many passageways off the other corridor felt like a labyrinth, where you might get lost and never find your way out, possibly a reference to his fears of getting enmeshed in therapy (and relationships in general) and never finding his way to health.

He saw himself as a spectator in the second half of the dream watching an actor, Laurence Olivier. He said he was enjoying the performance. However, he expressed mixed feelings about Olivier, seeing him as pretentious and overly dramatic and grandiose. The distance between himself and the actor reminded him of the distance between himself and his father. In some ways, the actor reminded him of his father, who seemed to be constantly jolly but somehow shallow, so that Mr. M. did not know if this jolliness reflected his real feelings or was "just an act." He associated the pretentiousness with his mother, especially in terms of her expectations of him and his sister and her tendency to overdramatize every event in their lives.

The dream, then, suggested that the awareness of soon coming face to face with his own child might be stimulating Mr. M. to look at his parents, his childhood relationships, and possibly his alienation and passivity as an onlooker in his family. The fact that in the dream there were two adjoining buildings and that one building had two sets of passageways also might have anatomical references. We saw one set of passageways as a birth canal; the other might refer to other internal organs, such as intestines, and the theater itself might refer to the womb. The presence of both Mr. M. and a father figure in the womb might represent the fact that both were able to impregnate a woman and become fathers, as well as that both of them originally were born from a womb. Their similar origins and fates could be focused on, along with the new third-generation inhabitant of a womb, Mr. M.'s own offspring.

The second dream also occurred in a theater in which Mr. M. is observing something on stage, but the feeling tone was quite different. The grandeur of Olivier is replaced by the chaos of a group rehearsal. In associating to the male lions, Mr. M. said that individually in the jungle they might be the king of the beasts and quite majestic. However, as a group lounging around on stage they seemed silly and out of place. Pop music also came in for some derision, since this type of music was considered quite foreign to Mr. M., a classical music lover. The word *pop* reminded him of his father, since he sometimes referred to him by that name.

Thus, the dream seemed to be an extension of the previous dream in further emphasizing Mr. M.'s conflict with regard to his father. Should he "sing" about his "pop" as a majestic figure to be respected and even feared, or was his father just a silly stage prop that could be maneuvered with ease? Clearly, this issue was a disturbing one to Mr. M. In both dreams the figure of the actor and the lions would seem to have associations of grandeur and admiration, yet Mr. M. focused on their less serious, more silly qualities. The dreams reflected his disappointment that his father was not a more serious, thoughtful, intense person.

Mr. M. took this opportunity to describe how unaware his father seemed to be of other people and their lives. He had hardly even reacted to the news that he was soon to have a grandchild. This brought up childhood memories of important events in Mr. M.'s life that his father had been too busy or not interested enough to participate in. These traits were seen as less related specifically to the boy, Mr. M., and more as part of his father's general character. Nevertheless, they were painful to Mr. M. and caused him to think further about his relationship with his own unborn child.

At about this time, Mr. M. had learned from the results of the amniocentesis that his child was a boy. If anything, having a boy made him more anxious than he might have been if the baby were a girl, possibly because it did highlight how the relationship might get off track as it had with his own father. Knowing the sex of the baby also concretized the fact that a real live child was on the way. Mr. M. talked about how he wanted this child to share his interest in music. He reflected on a brief meeting he once had with a world-famous musician who played the same instrument as Mr. M. This had been a moment of great importance for Mr. M., who highly revered this man. We discussed how Mr. M. saw him as a spiritual father with whom he had more in common than his own father.

I brought up the fact that Mr. M. had not shared many of his own father's interests, such as sports and running a business. I asked him how he would feel if his son did not share his interests. Mr. M. professed a greater willingness than his father had shown to get involved in whatever interests his son had and to introduce his son to things that interested Mr. M. in ways that would make them exciting and pleasurable to a child. He realized that he was not experienced in these matters and had a lot to learn, but he certainly wanted to try. Mr. M. thus seemed to be displaying traits of two of the father-types suggested by Yablonsky, the compassionate-loving double and the peer father or buddy. The strong desire for closeness and involvement was very marked.

A few weeks later, Mr. M. had another dream in which he himself was on center stage, or in this case, center ring:

> I was at a circus. Anyone from the audience could come up and try swinging from the trapeze. Instead of a swing, it was just a rope—like Tarzan. I went up and did it. My extended family was there, but they didn't notice me. I decided I wasn't going back to do it again just so they could see me.

Mr. M. associated swinging from a rope as a daring, dangerous feat that required a lot of courage. Tarzan was certainly a brave, fearless man who also was a man of nature, not caught up in the typical competitive, materialistic conventions of our society. While Mr. M. was in reality more interested in intellectual prowess than physical might, he could strongly identify with Tarzan's forthright, uncomplicated, helpful qualities. Thus, the dream reflected certain capacities to be daring and develop his own style that Mr. M. already possessed but needed to solidify. Examples of his ability to be his own person included his recent decision to move into a career that was much more satisfactory to him and his lifelong ability to seek out interests and friends that might have been unusual for his family background.

The two aspects of the dream that seemed more problematic to Mr. M. were, first, his demonstration of his skills before an audience and, second, the lack of attention paid to him by his family. The ability to show off in front of an audience was striking because in reality this was something Mr. M. had trouble doing. His fear of courtroom appearances and the difficulties he had playing music before an audience were examples of the trouble he had in exposing himself to others in real life. The dream certainly reflected his wish to get attention and admiration by performing well without fear. On his new job he was having more success making speeches and dealing with groups of people.

The fact that his family did not notice his performance was indicative of Mr. M.'s belief that his family did not appreciate his capacities. This disappointment was clearly centered on Mr. M.'s father. His father's lack of enthusiasm for Mr. M.'s new job and his persistence in referring to him as a lawyer even though he no longer did legal work came to mind. Even more upsetting was his father's casual reaction to the announcement that Mr. M. was soon going to be a father himself. Mr. M. reflected that this was indeed a grand feat, for which he wished to receive much recognition within the family. In this instance, Mr. M. felt he had taken center stage, and he wanted much more notice taken of him. For the most part, this did not appear to be a competition with his wife for others' attention, although there was some realization that his mother could appreciate his wife's accomplishment more than his father could appreciate his.

An additional dream that occurred a few weeks later made direct reference to Mr. M.'s father:

> I was with my father looking at a tall modern building that my father admired a lot. He showed me a large stone wall with hieroglyphics on it that he said had been found on this site. He said the building had been built around the stone, and he seemed very pleased that the builders had taken so much care to preserve it—a sign that progress needn't destroy the old. But it seemed odd to me that the stone wall was set up on the second floor rather than on the ground level where it should have been.

The dream seemed to encapsulate some of the different values and life-styles that divided Mr. M. and his father, as well as suggesting some ways in which they might become more compatible. Mr. M.'s father happily embraces the new, progressive building in this dream and seems content that the connection with the past has been fully preserved. Mr. M. is much less sanguine. He is suspicious of the fact that the stone wall is now on the second floor. Has it actually been moved to accommodate the new building or has the building been built around it in such a way that the foundation or support system of the stone has been threatened? In either case, its integrity may have been lost. Furthermore, Mr. M. is not delighted with the size of the new building as his father is. Thus, on the surface we have the interesting paradox of a father who wants to move into new ideas and structures while the son eschews the new, prefers to hold onto the mysteries of the past, and finds the juxtaposition of the old and new troublesome.

Symbolically, the tall building might be seen as a phallic representation. If so, the father in the dream seems much more comfortable with its size and shape and power. The son seems more concerned with its potential for destruction, its lack of support for the precious things inside it, and its lack of grounding or rootedness. In other words, Mr. M. seems concerned about the solidity of his masculinity and wishes to be sure that his masculine identity is sufficiently rooted in the traditions of his father and forefathers, even though much of this past is unfathomable or undeciphered by him at this point. He feels a lack of continuity, fearing that his father has broken the chain or destroyed the traditions that made him strong.

In reality, Mr. M.'s masculinity was not demonstrated in the ways that were most comfortable to his father, such as being a successful businessman/breadwinner and being an athlete. His masculinity might be considered less showy than his father's, and it encompassed other qualities, such as close relationships with his wife and child. I wondered if his intellectual pursuits and artistic interests were common in previous generations of his family, and Mr. M. indeed pointed to several ancestors and members of his extended family who had scholarly pursuits, including an uncle who was a linguistics scholar. Becoming more aware of his compatibility with these male relatives enabled Mr. M. to feel more satisfied with his own masculine style and more comfortable with his new male role as a father.

Shortly before the baby was born, Mr. M. had a dream that focused on his relationship with his wife: "I met some students from my wife's class. They said I was a doctor, too. I said no. To prove it, I assured them that I couldn't remember anything about taking care of patients, so I must not have gone to medical school."

In contrast to previous dreams, which had emphasized Mr. M.'s relationship with his father and his desire to be successful as a father himself, this dream explored Mr. M.'s disappointment with his inability to do what his wife was doing—that is, to bear children. Throughout the pregnancy, Mr. M. had commented on his wife's physical symptoms, such as her fatigue, discomfort in eating certain foods, and growing size. He had occasionally expressed admiration for his wife's ability to be pregnant and work hard. He also discussed how generally healthy she was feeling. Now, he mentioned that she was having trouble sleeping at night and that this was disturbing his rest as well. He talked about his impatience in waiting for the baby to arrive.

Until the baby was born, his wife had the greater physical involvement with the baby, and Mr. M. was quite envious of this closeness. Would it not be wonderful if the medical students were right and he could, indeed, do everything his wife did, such as taking care of patients/babies? Mr. M. readily admitted these feelings and vowed that he would be as involved with the baby and child care as his schedule and lack of certain physical maternal capacities allowed. When the baby had arrived and needed all the attention and care that a baby requires, Mr. M. did make good on those promises.

Working with Mr. M. as he was exploring his feelings and attitudes about becoming a father caused me to reconsider a number of the commonly held early psychoanalytic precepts mentioned at the beginning of this chapter. These precepts suggested that the primary conflicts for the father-to-be would focus on his rivalry with the creative processes of his wife and rivalry with the new baby as the center of his wife's attention. Both issues in different forms refer back to the primary mother–son relationship. The rivalry with the wife's creative processes suggests a revival of the man's childhood desires to bear a child as his mother did. The rivalry with the newborn child recalls earlier experiences of being mothered and resentments about losing the mother's attention, especially to a new sibling. General fears about becoming a father, including the responsibility involved, the loss of freedom, the financial burden, and the commonly held assumption that men are less interested in having children than women are, can to a great extent be explained in terms of the man's fear of loss of the nurturance provided by the wife/mother.

In Mr. M.'s case, issues related to rivalry with a mother figure or fear of loss of her love to the new baby-rival were not the most significant. Rather, his lackluster relationship with his own father was the focus of concern for Mr. M. His desire for a close relationship with his son and his strong commitment to active involvement in child care were in marked contrast to his own father's style. They represented a further step outside the "cognitive map" that Yablonsky suggests sons learn from their fathers. Confronting this substantial discrepancy involved remembering, reexperiencing, and reevaluating his painful early relationship with his father. The dreams and the resultant discussion enabled Mr. M. to express his fear of repeating the past with his own son either through ignorance or force of habit. He was able not only to consciously resolve to be different but also to become aware of some unrealized impediments to being different. These included a rigidity of his own interests and pursuits that might interfere with his ability to appreciate his child if their interests did not coincide, and a general difficulty with expressiveness of emotions.

Thus, for Mr. M., the most important issues in approaching fatherhood were not issues with maternal figures but resolving a troubled relationship and an unacceptable identification with his own father. One might wonder whether this unanticipated focus looks at the most significant developmental issues in becoming a father. It might be argued, for instance, that Mr. M.'s focus on his father makes sense for him given his particular developmental history, but is not necessarily relevant to other men in a similar life situation. Mr. M., for instance, had much less actual anxiety about becoming a father than some men do. His envy of his wife's creative processes, while evident, was not paramount. His relationship with his own mother also was one in which he felt fairly confident of her love and of his specialness in her eyes. However, these very facts also point to the difficulty in applying any general formula or universal theoretical understanding to a particular individual's development. Every story is to some extent unique and different from the norm.

Additionally, I believe something would be missed were we to see Mr. M.'s story as a slightly unusual variation on a psychoanalytic theme whose variations are caused primarily by some particular developmental aspects of Mr. M.'s childhood. I believe the issues raised by Mr. M.'s movement into fatherhood point to difficulties that many men are facing today as they also become fathers. Mr. M. is not unique in having to seriously reconsider his role as a father compared with the role played by his own father. The scenario of having grown up in a home in which the father worked long hours while the mother stayed home and had primary responsibility for raising the children is not at all uncommon. Just as women today (many of whom work outside the home, have fewer children, and yet have great expectations for motherhood) are having to reexamine their roles compared with the roles of their own mothers, so men are having to do the same. Good fathering is no longer considered to be satisfied so long as the checkbook can be balanced at the end of the month. Yet for many men, this is the standard that was used in their own homes.

Many men have the wish and expectation that they will be active in the child care and raising of their children, yet their own model of fatherhood was quite different. They, like Mr. M., must resolve the discrepancy in a way that allows them to be the kind of father they aspire to be. Resentments and disappointment in their own father–son relationship must be resolved and unconscious identifications with their own fathers must be reconsidered if the prospective father is going to establish a different relationship with his own children. In these considerations, the father as a model for the son takes precedence over the mother–son relationship.

Erik Erikson (1964) illustrated many years ago that psychological, social, and emotional development does not end as we leave childhood. As people we continue to develop and to meet new challenges at different life stages. These challenges have both biological and sociocultural components such that the timing and significance of each developmental stage have certain universal aspects, while considerable variation among cultures and among individuals within the same culture also occurs. Fatherhood is increasingly being recognized as a significant developmental epoch for a man, much as motherhood has always been recognized for women. Even as the significance of becoming a father is being given greater acknowledgment in a man's life, the role of the father within the family is being given more importance within the society. There are seemingly both more variations in this role and greater expectations for the father's active involvement in his children's lives than ever before. Yet the opportunity for considering this important transition and choosing a style of fatherhood that is feasible and desirable to both the individual and the family is quite limited. Mr. M.'s dreams are an example of the resolution of past relationships and experiences that must occur as a new developmental challenge is approached. Since we have greater expectations of the fathers in our society and since fathers have greater expectations of themselves, it will be important to give them opportunities to make these transitions with excitement and anticipation rather than anxiety and fear.

References

Blos, P. (1985). *Son and father: Before and beyond the Oedipus complex*. New York: Free Press.
Erikson, E. H. (1964). *Childhood and society* (2nd ed.). New York: Norton.
Freud, S. (1908). On the sexual theories of children. *Standard Edition* (Vol. 9, pp. 205–226). London: Hogarth Press.
Freud, S. (1909). Analysis of a phobia in a five-year-old boy. *Standard Edition* (Vol. 10, pp. 3–152). London: Hogarth Press.
Freud, S. (1923). The ego and the id. *Standard Edition* (Vol. 14, pp. 3–68). London: Hogarth Press.
Gurwitt, A. R. (1976). Aspects of prospective fatherhood. *Psychoanalytic Study of the Child, 31*, 237–270.

Herzog, J. M. (1982). Patterns of expectant fatherhood: A study of the fathers of a group of premature infants. In S. H. Cath, A. R. Gurwitt, & J. M. Ross (Eds.), *Father and child: Developmental and clinical perspective* (pp. 301–314). Boston: Little, Brown.

Lamb, M. (1978). The father's role in the infants' social world. In J. H. Stevens, Jr., & M. Mathers (Eds.), *Mother/child, father/child relationships* (pp. 87–108). Washington, DC: National Association for the Education of Young Children.

Reik, T. (1919). *Ritual*. New York: International Universities Press.

Robinson, B. E., & Barret, A. L. (1986). *The developing father*. New York: Guilford Press.

Ross, J. M. (1982). The roots of fatherhood: Excursions into a lost literature. In S. H. Cath, A. R. Gurwitt, & J. M. Ross (Eds.), *Father and child: Developmental and clinical perspectives* (pp. 3–20). Boston: Little, Brown.

Yablonsky, L. (1982). *Fathers and sons*. New York: Simon & Schuster.

Chapter 4
Gender Stereotypes
A New Egalitarian Couple Emerges

GWENDOLYN L. GERBER

One of the fundamental beliefs about women and men is that they have different personality characteristics. This belief has persisted to the present day, despite major changes in social conditions, family structures, and occupational roles (Neufeld, Langmeyer, & Seeman, 1974; Ruble, 1983; Werner & LaRussa, 1985). When people are asked to describe the personality traits that are typical of the two sexes, women are characterized as being sympathetic, compassionate, and sensitive to the needs of others, while men are depicted as being assertive, independent, and dominant (Bem, 1974; Rosenkrantz, Vogel, Bee, Broverman, & Broverman, 1968; Spence, Helmreich, & Stapp, 1975).

These personality traits are known as the "gender stereotype traits" and refer to the two different ways of behaving that people think are characteristic of the two sexes. Women are assumed to be strong in "communion," which means that they are primarily concerned with responding to the needs of other persons; men are thought to be strong in "agency," which indicates that they are concerned with enhancing their own self and exerting their own will on others (Bakan, 1966).

The persistence of these gender stereotypes reflects people's belief that they embody the true essence of masculinity and femininity (Spence & Sawin, 1985). People think that most men would describe themselves as strong in agency and weak in communion, while most women would see themselves as strong in communion and weak in agency. However, research has shown that this is not the case. In spite of what most people assume, the two sexes do *not* see themselves as having radically dissimilar personalities. Instead, when asked to describe themselves on the gender stereotype traits, men and women often portray themselves in highly similar ways, so that they are equally strong in both communion and agency.[1]

---

[1] One of the widely used scales (Bem, 1974) for measuring the traits stereotypically associated with men and women is the Bem Sex-Role Inventory (BSRI). Research with the original scale found that it measured other dimensions in addition to communion and agency (Pedhazur & Tetenbaum, 1979). New instruments based on the BSRI were then developed, which pro-

---

GWENDOLYN L. GERBER • Department of Psychology, John Jay College of Criminal Justice, The City University of New York, New York, New York 10019.

This raises some perplexing questions. Why do people persist in the mistaken belief that women and men have extremely different personality characteristics? What maintains this assumption in the face of such apparently contradictory evidence?

This chapter is concerned with examining some of the current research that relates to these questions. This shows that there is a connection between the roles that the two sexes are expected to enact and the personality traits of communion and agency. Men and women perform different roles with one another, and so they appear to have different personalities. However, the characteristics that are displayed when the two sexes interact do not necessarily reflect the range of behaviors that they are capable of expressing in other situations. They can often behave in ways that do not conform with gender stereotypes. For example, a man may act in a very nurturing, supportive way with his young son who has just fallen and hurt himself; a woman might act in an extremely directive, assertive way when organizing a social event to raise money for a political campaign in her community.

Conventional patterns of behavior by women and men are most prevalent when they interact with one another. This is because there are powerful pressures that motivate them to do so. These pressures are particularly strong within the marriage relationship, and here the enactment of traditional roles can actually interfere with people's efforts to attain personal happiness. This is illustrated with examples of couples who are in traditional marriages. Finally, some of the changes that are necessary to evolve more satisfying relationships of equality between the sexes are described.

LEADER-FOLLOWER ROLES AND GENDER STEREOTYPES

One of the major differences in the roles that men and women are expected to perform involves power. In interactions between the sexes, the man is expected to be the leader and the woman is expected to be the follower. These social expectations apply to different types of relationships—to short-term encounters between strangers or acquaintances, and to intimate, long-term involvements between engaged or married couples (Blood & Wolfe, 1960; Denmark, 1977; Megargee, 1969; Peplau & Gordon, 1985). Since people have repeatedly observed men acting as leaders and women acting as followers, they also believe that the sexes differ in the traits associated with these roles (Eagly & Steffen, 1984).

The leader in a relationship is expected to be self-assertive and to make decisions, while the follower is expected to be responsive and to accommodate to these decisions (Bass, 1973; Stogdill, 1950). In other words, the leader is expected to be strong in agency and the follower is expected to be strong in communion.

Although the follower exerts a lesser degree of influence than the leader, he or she also engages in some acts of self-assertion. The leader would be responsive and supportive toward these assertive acts whenever they occur. This means that the

---

vided more refined, internally consistent measures of agency and communion (Bem, 1981; Costos, 1986). Men and women describe themselves as dissimilar on both scales of the original BSRI (Bem, 1974). However, these differences often disappear when the more recently developed, refined measures are used. Using conventionally accepted levels of statistical significance ($p < .05$), two studies (Bem, 1981; Costos, 1986) found sex differences in communion but not in agency; one study (White, Speisman, Jackson, Bartis, & Costos, 1986) found an absence of sex differences in both communion and agency.

follower would be weak in agency and the leader would be correspondingly weak in communion.

In opposite-sex relationships, people's assumption that the man will be the leader and the woman will be the follower explains why the two sexes are believed to have different personality traits (Gerber, 1987, 1988a). The man generally acts as the leader, and so his agency and the woman's communion are both relatively strong. The woman usually plays the role of follower, and so her agency and the man's communion are both relatively weak.

Also, the expectation about male leadership determines one additional characteristic of gender stereotyping. Because leaders are perceived as having more socially desirable traits than followers (Harvey, 1953; Lippitt, Polansky, Redl, & Rosen, 1952), the man is seen as having more culturally valued traits than the woman (Gerber, 1987, 1988c; McKee & Sherriffs, 1957).

> This connection between the leader–follower roles and the gender stereotype traits can be illustrated by a couple, Mike and Cindy, who have a very traditional marriage. Mike has a well-paying position in an accounting firm, and Cindy is a housewife. They have been married 18 years and are considered to be very happy together. People often refer to them as an ideal couple.
>
> Cindy feels that Mike is an excellent husband, and she relies on him to take the primary leadership role in their relationship. She explains her dependency by saying, "He's so clever and logical. I can never seem to see the issues as clearly as he." On one occasion, when Cindy asked for a charge account of her own, Mike said that he thought this was unwise. He told her that he did not believe in having charge accounts unless they were an absolute necessity, as they were for his business. On further thought, Cindy felt that her husband was probably right. Following this discussion, Mike gave his wife an extra $500 that month to spend as she wished.
>
> They have always had an active social life with Mike's business acquaintances, and frequently spend time with them on vacations. Although Cindy feels that their social life is satisfying, she wistfully confided to one of her friends that she sometimes wished Mike felt more comfortable socializing with people that she knew. She enjoys the sports-oriented vacations that her husband likes, involving tennis or skiing, but she is not very good at sports and sometimes thinks that it would be fun to travel. However, Mike does not seem to enjoy the idea of going to Europe, or traveling around the United States. When her friend asked if she was truly happy in her marriage, Cindy hesitated a moment and then said that she thought she must be because Mike was such a good husband and father.
>
> Mike is very involved in his work and thinks that he has a very satisfying marriage. He sometimes wishes that Cindy would take more of the initiative in their sexual relationship. However, he has accepted the fact that she is somewhat inhibited. He would be surprised to find out that his wife sometimes feels unhappy, and he would have difficulty understanding her concerns, since he feels that he has always paid a great deal of attention to her needs.
>
> Mike is very much the leader in the marriage and Cindy is the follower. As the leader, Mike is seen by both persons as having more socially desirable characteristics than Cindy. He is very self-confident and thinks that he is well able to take care of his wife and act in her best interest. Cindy idealizes her husband, looks to him for guidance, and sees him as being far more capable than she.

The leader–follower roles determine the way in which both partners see themselves on the gender stereotype traits. Mike's role as leader is maintained by his strong agency and his wife's strong communion. This means that Mike makes most of the decisions and Cindy accommodates these decisions. Cindy's role as follower is maintained by her weak agency and her husband's weak communion. In terms of their behavior toward each other, Cindy makes only occasional attempts to express her desires, and Mike is minimally responsive to her tentative efforts at self-assertion.

The marriage is a very stable one, with little interpersonal conflict. This is because the strength of each persons' agency is matched by the strength of the other persons's communion. Whenever Mike feels that Cindy is acting with too much agency (or self-assertion), as he did when she asked for a charge account of her own, he did not reciprocate by acceding to her wish, since this would have increased the strength of his communion (or responsiveness to her needs). Instead, he maintained his communion at a low level and did not agree to let her have a charge account. Cindy did not insist on the legitimacy of her request, which would have led to interpersonal conflict. Rather, she acquiesced to Mike, thereby maintaining the strength of her agency at a low level. Thus, both marital partners monitor the strength of the agency and communion that they express in order to behave in ways that are consistent with cultural expectations. By doing this, they are able to maintain a stable relationship, in which the husband's role of leader and the wife's role of follower are clearly defined.

Principles Used to Form Relationships

When women and men act in stereotyped ways with one another, they are using certain implicit guidelines in order to establish a relationship that functions smoothly and without conflict. When Mike expressed high levels of agency and little communion, and Cindy reciprocated by expressing high levels of communion and little agency, they both were using these guidelines to promote the functioning of their marriage.

The basic principles that Mike and Cindy used to establish their traditional marriage relationship are the same as those that are used to establish relationships in general. The Relationship Balance model, which I have developed, describes these principles and shows how the strength of the two partners' gender stereotype traits determine different qualities of the interaction (Gerber, 1985, 1987). Not only do these traits affect the kinds of leadership roles that are created, they affect the desirability of each partner's personality, and the degree of happiness that is experienced as well.

According to the model, people conceptualize opposite-sex interchanges in terms of three dimensions, called the "relationship balances." These dimensions consist of the "leadership balance," the "positivity balance," and the "satisfaction balance." The leadership balance reflects the relative leadership that is exercised by the woman and the man, the positivity balance reflects the relative social desirability of their personalities, and the satisfaction balance reflects the degree of satisfaction that is experienced in the relationship.[2] Since all three relationship balances are based on the

---

[2]Studies have been done in order to test whether each of the three relationship balances measures the dimension of the relationship that is predicted by the model (Gerber, 1987, 1988a). Sub-

traits of communion and agency that characterize the woman and the man, they are all interdependent.

In order to apply the model to actual couples, both the woman and the man would need to describe their own personalities by filling out a questionnaire that measures the strength of their agency and communion (Gerber, 1986a). The scores that are obtained—woman's agency, woman's communion, man's agency, and man's communion—would be added together in the various ways described by the model. The resulting "balances" would indicate how the couple experiences their relationship.

The leadership balance reflects the extent to which either the man or the woman is perceived as the leader. An individual's power is dependent on the extent to which he or she is self-assertive, and also on the extent to which the other person is willing to accommodate. The man's power is computed by adding together the two "stereotypic" traits—the man's agency and the woman's communion. The woman's power is computed by adding together the two "nonstereotypic" traits—the woman's agency plus the man's communion. When the sum of the two stereotypic traits is greater than the sum of the two nonstereotypic traits, the man is the more powerful person and is perceived as the leader of the couple. When the sum of the two nonstereotypic traits is greater than the sum of the two stereotypic traits, the woman is the more powerful person and is perceived as the leader. When the stereotypic and nonstereotypic traits are equal, the man and woman share the leadership equally.

The positivity balance reflects the relative social desirability of the woman's and the man's personalities. Agency and communion are considered to be valuable characteristics for both sexes. People think that it is desirable for a person to be capable of self-assertion and also to be capable of responding to another person's needs (Pedhazur & Tetenbaum, 1979). Thus, the social desirability of an individual's personality can be determined by adding together his or her agency and communion. When the man has more of these traits than the woman, he is evaluated as having the more positive personality. When the woman has more of these two traits than the man, she is evaluated more positively and has the more socially desirable personality.

The satisfaction balance reflects the degree of satisfaction that is perceived in the relationship. This balance is of particular importance for maintaining both persons' satisfaction with the interaction, and it is crucial for the continuation of the relationship. It is based on the balance between the traits that are concerned with accommodation to the other person and those that are concerned with self-assertion. It is computed by comparing the strength of the communal traits within the relationship as a whole (the woman's communion plus the man's communion) with the strength of the agentic traits (the woman's agency plus the man's agency). When there is more communion than agency, then the partners are very responsive and accommodating toward one another and, as a consequence, are both very happy. When there is more agency than communion, then both partners continually try to assert their own needs without showing any concern for the other person. They are very unhappy, and the partnership is in danger of breaking up.

Although opposite-sex relationships can vary along the three dimensions that

---

jects were presented with a brief description of a married couple. They were asked to rate the wife and the husband on communion and agency, as well as on other scales. As predicted, the leadership balance measured the relative power of the husband and the wife, the positivity balance measured the relative social desirability of their personalities, and the satisfaction balance measured relationship satisfaction. The model has also been tested with actual persons (Gerber, 1986a).

are reflected in the relationship balances, the most central dimension involves power. A majority of interactions follow a traditional pattern, in which the man is the leader and the woman is the follower. However, other kinds of interactions are also possible. The woman and the man can share the leadership equally, or they can totally reverse roles so that the woman is the leader and the man is the follower. These different types of relationships are each structured by the relationship balances in very distinctive ways.

Traditional and Nontraditional Leadership Roles

People have images that represent different kinds of interactions between the sexes.[3] These are shared by most people in our culture and act as inner guidelines for establishing and maintaining both traditional and nontraditional relationships. These guidelines are based on the relationship balances, and so they involve the characteristics of the interaction as a whole as well as the personal qualities that are expressed by each person. Since power is such a central dimension in male–female interactions, the ways in which the relationship balances are used to establish relationships with different kinds of leadership roles will be described.

A traditional couple, with the man as leader, is perceived as having a leadership balance in which the stereotypic traits are stronger than the nonstereotypic traits (Gerber, 1988a, 1988b). As a consequence, both the woman and the man are stereotyped in an extremely conventional way. The man is highly masculine-typed (strong in agency and weak in communion), and the woman is highly feminine-typed (strong in communion and weak in agency). The positivity balance is also an inequality. Not only does the man have more power than the woman, he is evaluated as having more valuable personality traits as well. In contrast, the woman follower's traits are devalued.

A nontraditional couple, with the woman as leader, reverses the traditional relationship between the sexes. The leadership balance is an inequality, but here the nonstereotypic traits are stronger than the stereotypic traits. The conventional gender stereotypes are also reversed, so that it is the woman who is highly masculine-typed and the man who is highly feminine-typed. The positivity balance is an inequality. This indicates that the female leader's personal qualities are seen as valuable, while the male follower's qualities are devalued.

There is a close correspondence between the leadership and positivity balances, which can be seen very clearly in the two types of couples that have just been described (Gerber, 1987, 1988a). When one person is designated the leader, that person is also perceived as having very desirable personality characteristics. In contrast, the follower's personality characteristics are seen as less socially desirable. Since women commonly play a follower role in their interactions with men, they are usually seen as possessing the less valued attributes of followers. When men are assigned the role of follower, they too are perceived as having less valuable personal characteristics.

An egalitarian couple, which shares the leadership, is very different from the other two types of couples. Both the leadership and positivity balances are equalities, which means that the sexes have the same amount of power and equally positive personalities. There is a total absence of conventional gender stereotyping. Both the woman and the man are perceived in exactly the same way—they are moderately

---

[3]These images or guidelines have also been defined as "social schemata" (Fiske & Taylor, 1984).

strong in communion and in agency. This indicates that the two sexes are equally assertive and equally responsive to each other's needs, and that neither the woman's nor the man's personal qualities are devalued.

For all three different types of leadership, the satisfaction balance is an equality.[4] This means that the level of accommodation (communion) within the dyad as a whole is approximately equal to the level of self-assertion (agency), and that the different kinds of interactions are all perceived as stable and smoothly functioning (Bales, 1967; Gerber, 1987, 1988a).

Although the satisfaction balance is in a state of equality for different kinds of leadership, the degree to which either the man or the woman contributes to this overall level of satisfaction is not always the same (Gerber, 1988a). The more power an individual holds, the more support and accommodation he or she receives from the other partner.[5] In traditional relationships with a male leader, the female follower is primarily responsible for supporting the man's power, accommodating to him, and taking care of his happiness. The male leader does very little to support the woman, and need have little concern for her satisfaction. In interactions with a female leader, the conventional roles are reversed and the male follower is expected to provide most of the support and accommodation. The only type of interchange in which both persons share the same amount of concern for each other's happiness is the egalitarian one. Here both persons are equally strong in communion and, as a consequence, are equally responsive to each other's needs.[6]

Thus, the principles involved in the relationship balances, which people use to form relationships, are designed to promote the functioning of the relationship as a whole. Once the leadership roles are clearly designated, the primary goal becomes that of creating a stable, smoothly functioning interaction, without any conflicts over power. The happiness of the individuals who are actually involved in the relationship is irrelevant to this goal, and maximizing the satisfaction of each individual participant is not of any concern.

INTERACTIONS BETWEEN WOMEN AND MEN

People interact with other persons who have different types of personalities in the course of their daily lives. They need to be able to adapt to these other persons'

---

[4]The satisfaction balance was not computed directly in the study that examined relationships with different types of leadership—male leadership, egalitarian leadership, and female leadership (Gerber, 1988a). However, when each of the gender stereotype traits was analyzed separately for the three leadership conditions, the level of each persons' agency (high, medium, or low) was matched by the level of the other person's agency was matched with the strength of the other person's communion, indicating that the satisfaction balance would be essentially equal across the different leadership conditions.
[5]This is because in each of the different types of leadership conditions (male leadership, egalitarian leadership, and female leadership), the strength of one person's agency was matched with the strength of the other person's communion (Gerber, 1988a). When one person held most of the power, he or she was strong in agency and received a great deal of support and accommodation from the less powerful partner, who was strong in communion. Since the less powerful individual was weak in agency, he or she did not receive much support from the more powerful partner, who was correspondingly weak in communion.
[6]Research with actual couples has demonstrated the importance of communion for marital happiness. The husband's happiness is directly dependent on the strength of the wife's communion, and the wife's happiness is dependent on the husband's communion (Antill, 1983).

behaviors in order to create relationships that function smoothly, without conflict (Holyoak & Gordon, 1984). To do this, they have to be capable of behaving in both nontraditional and traditional ways with members of the opposite sex. When a person wants to establish a relationship with another individual, it is possible to set aside cultural expectations for behavior and act in a nonconventional as well as a conventional way. The relationship balances are employed as guidelines in this adaption process.

The cues that are available about the other participant's personality determine how a person will choose to act in a particular situation (Darley & Fazio, 1980). This means that a person's behavior will vary according to the person that he or she is with. For example, a male businessman will behave in a very different way, depending on whether he is interacting with the female vice-president of his company or his female secretary. When he has a meeting with the vice-president to discuss his role in the company's development of new products, the vice-president acts in a highly assertive way. He responds by being highly accommodating and responsive to her wishes. On the other hand, his secretary is a very accommodating individual. When he wants her to type a report, he changes his behavior so that it is very directive and assertive. As this example shows, he uses the cues that he receives about each person's personality to alter his own actions so that the interaction proceeds smoothly.

As he modifies his behavior in these different situations, he is implicitly using the guidelines described by the relationship balances in order to establish either a traditional or a nontraditional relationship with the other person. When he interacts with the female vice-president, who is highly masculine-typed (strong in agency and weak in communion), he alters his behavior so that it complements the traits exhibited by the vice-president.[7] He responds to her by acting in a highly feminine-typed way (strong in communion and weak in agency). This leads to the creation of a nontraditional interaction in which the woman is the leader and the relationship balances are the opposite of the traditional pattern. When he interacts with his feminine-typed secretary, he complements her behaviors by behaving in a masculine-typed way. The secretary plays a follower role and he enacts his socially expected leadership role. This creates a traditional interaction with stereotypic relationship balances.

Research has confirmed that perceivers who wish to promote a relationship with someone of the opposite sex are able to modify their own behavior in either conventional or nonconventional ways (von Baeyer, Sherk, & Zanna, 1981; Zanna & Pack, 1975). In one study (von Baeyer et al., 1981), female job applicants were told that a male interviewer preferred either traditional or nontraditional women. When the female applicant was told that the male interviewer preferred traditional women, she acted in a more "feminine" and less dominant way than when she was told that the interviewer preferred nontraditional women.

In continuing interactions between the sexes, there is a mutual adjustment process that takes place (Darley & Fazio, 1980; Holyoak & Gordon, 1984). Both participants alter their behaviors to complement the behaviors manifested by their partner. Their joint behaviors then promote a stable, conflict-free relationship. This process has been

---

[7]Research has shown that other persons' communal and agentic traits are assumed to be inversely related (Foushee, Helmreich, & Spence, 1979; Major, Carnevale, & Deaux, 1981), just as they are in the images that people have for opposite-sex relationships. This means that a perceiver who receives the information that another person is extremely strong in agency would assume that the other person is also extremely weak in communion, and vice versa.

demonstrated in an experiment by Skrypnek and Snyder (1982). Participants in an interaction with another partner used the information that they received about the partner to modify their own behavior in either a masculine-typed or feminine-typed direction. For example, participants who were given the information that the partner was highly feminine-typed modified their own behavior in a complementary way so that it was more masculine-typed. As the interaction progressed, both participants continued to engage in this mutual adaptation process, and to modify their behaviors so as to structure the entire interchange in a more effective way.

As this research has shown, men and women are capable of changing their behaviors when they interact with different partners. They are able to alter their behavior so that it either corresponds with cultural expectations or goes counter to them.

Maintaining Stereotypic Relationships

Even though they are capable of modifying their behavior in nontraditional ways, men and women usually enact traditional leadership roles with one another. In part, this is caused by the external social structure. Women are generally barred from the high-status roles that would allow them to assume leadership positions in relation to men. When such external constraints are absent, however, women and men still frequently choose to enact traditional leadership roles in their interactions with one another (Megargee, 1969). This choice is made jointly, by both sexes, even when these roles conflict with their basic personality dispositions and lead to personal dissatisfaction (Nyquist & Spence, 1986).[8]

It is understandable that men would be motivated to take the role of leader. This role is associated with desirable personal characteristics, as well as other benefits (Harvey, 1953; Lippitt et al., 1952). However, it is less clear as to why women would voluntarily choose the role of follower, since it is associated with less desirable personal characteristics.

One explanation is that the two sexes enact traditional roles in order to conform with social norms and maintain a predictable social structure. Certainly, conformity with social norms is viewed more positively than deviation from these norms (Thibaut & Kelley, 1959). However, "social conformity" and "social deviance" are abstract concepts, which may or may not have relevance for individuals. In order for these concepts to influence individual behavior, they must be translated into sanctions that have personal meaning for individuals and can motivate them to conform. They must also affect men and women equally, so that they are both motivated to play traditional roles. This is because the roles of leader and follower are interdependent and require the collaboration of both persons in order for them to be performed without conflict (French & Raven, 1968).

There are penalties imposed on individuals who act in socially deviant ways and do not conform with the expected behaviors for their sex. Such individuals are stereotyped as having less desirable personal attributes (Costrich, Feinstein, Kidder, Maracek, & Pascale, 1975; Falbo, Hazen, & Linimon, 1982) and as being less physically

---

[8]Women who are highly dominant voluntarily choose to enact a subordinate role with men. However, they express more dissatisfaction with this role than women who are not dominant (Nyquist & Spence, 1986).

attractive than those who conform (Unger, Hilderbrand, & Madar, 1982). This is of particular importance for interactions between the sexes, since one of the most powerful motivations for women and men is to appear attractive to the opposite sex (Hatfield & Sprecher, 1986).

Just as there are penalties for individuals who transgress social norms, there are penalties for couples who do so as well. A recent study (Gerber, 1988d) examined the stereotypes about physical attractiveness and gender identity associated with opposite-sex couples who enacted traditional and nontraditional leadership roles. The members of the couple that enacted traditional leader–follower roles were stereotyped as having the attributes that would make them most attractive to the opposite sex—both the man and the woman were highly sex-typed in their gender identity and extremely attractive. The members of the couple that shared the leadership equally were both perceived as moderately attractive; the man was moderately masculine in his gender identity and the woman was moderately feminine. The strongest sanctions were imposed on the couple that was described as reversing the traditional roles for the two sexes. When the woman was the leader, both she and the man were viewed as least attractive; the woman had the least feminine gender identity and the man had the least masculine gender identity.

In their actual behavior, individuals can give the impression that they have an appropriate gender identity and are attractive by conforming with the conduct that is expected for their sex (Gillen, 1981; Heilman & Saruwatari, 1979; Spence, Deaux, & Helmreich, 1985). Men can create an impression that they are highly masculine and women can appear highly feminine by choosing sex-typed clothing and hairstyles, and by using sex-typed body movements and gestures (Henley, 1977; Major, 1981). Many current advertising campaigns use these stereotypic associations to sell their products. They communicate the message that their product will increase a woman's femininity or a man's masculinity, thereby enhancing sexual attractiveness.

Just as personal adornments and behaviors can be used as gender displays, the enactment of traditional leader–follower roles can be employed as well (Goffman, 1979). Members of couples can enact traditional roles, thereby appearing as if they have a sex-appropriate identity and are highly attractive. However, since these roles are interdependent, men and women must cooperate in performing them. For example, if a woman wishes to present herself as a follower, she needs to enlist the cooperation of the man by having him agree to take the complementary role of leader. That is precisely what happened in the classic study by Megargee (1969), mentioned at the beginning of this section. A woman who had a dominant personality was paired with a man who had a nondominant personality. When they were asked to decide who would be the leader in a subsequent task, the woman used her dominant personality characteristics to influence the man into taking that role.

Courtship rituals, in which the man is expected to ask for a date and the woman is expected to wait to be asked, provide an opportunity for both persons to present themselves in traditional leadership roles. Since these traditional roles are associated with stereotypes of attractiveness and sex-typed gender identity, both persons can present themselves as potentially desirable members of a "couple." By enacting these traditional roles, the man and the woman can both display the personality traits that are stereotypic for their sex. The man can present himself as strong in agency and weak in communion, while the woman can present herself as strong in communion and weak in agency.

It is not that women's and men's personalities are necessarily dissimilar, therefore, but that they create the impression that they have different personality traits by the way that they present themselves in social situations (Deaux, 1977). The stereotypes about the typical man and woman act as inner guidelines for individuals who wish to enhance their apparent masculinity or femininity and attractiveness in interactions with the opposite sex. The use of these guidelines leads to the establishment of relationships that are part of a predictable social order.

Traditional Marriage

Many people continue to view a traditional marriage, in which the man enacts the role of leader and the woman enacts the role of follower, as the ideal type of marriage (Hicks & Platt, 1970). They think that the achievement of this ideal will bring them personal happiness. However, as discussed previously, this type of marriage is designed to create a stable social structure; the happiness of the individuals involved in the marriage is irrelevant to this goal.

Research with actual couples has shown that marriages in which the husband is dominant do not lead to high marital happiness (Blood & Wolfe, 1960; Gray-Little & Burks, 1983). Some studies have even found that these marriages are less happy than any other kind of marriage (Bernard, 1972, p. 324; Michel, 1967; Pond, Ryle, & Hamilton, 1963). Similar results have been obtained when the personality characteristics of marital partners have been examined. Even though the husband has been found to experience somewhat more satisfaction than the wife, a marriage between a highly masculine-typed man and a highly feminine-typed woman is one of the least happy of the different types of marriage (Antill, 1983; Antill, cited in Ickes, 1985, p. 199).

The satisfactions that are experienced in this type of marriage are related to the ability to conform to role requirements, not to the quality of the relationship (Hicks & Platt, 1970). The ability of the husband to perform his role effectively is crucial for his own satisfaction and for the wife's. The rewards that the wife experiences are based on external factors, such as the husband's prestige or social status in the community (Blood & Wolfe, 1960).

People expect that enacting traditional roles will bring them personal happiness because of a misconception. They confuse the culturally sanctioned goal of promoting stable relationships with the personal goal of promoting individual happiness. Traditional relationships promote stability, not happiness, and these two dimensions of a marriage are not equivalent (Hicks & Platt, 1970). Conforming with cultural expectations can bring some personal satisfaction, in terms of thinking of oneself as a "good wife" or a "good husband." However, this is different from the feelings of affection, companionship, and sexual enjoyment that people frequently hope to achieve.

In the hope of gaining satisfaction, people can suppress important parts of their personalities that conflict with the highly sex-typed characteristics they are expected to enact (Gerber, 1986b). They do not realize that they are doing so in order to maintain a stable equilibrium in their marriage, and that they are using the relationship balances as guidelines for this.

In a traditional relationship (Gerber, 1987; 1988a), the leadership and positivity balances are perceived as unequal, so that the husband is the leader and has more positive personal qualities than the wife. The satisfaction balance is viewed as an equality, indicating that the relationship is stable. These interrelated balances determine the strength of the husband's and wife's gender stereotype traits. The husband is perceived as very strong in agency and weak in communion and the wife is seen as strong in communion and very weak in agency. Any change in the strength of one of the gender stereotype traits associated with either the wife or the husband would lead to changes in all three relationship balances (Gerber, 1986b). Thus, any behaviors that do not fit the stereotypes need to be discounted or ignored. Goals that would lead to behaviors that conflict with cultural stereotypes have to be undermined. As a consequence, the continued enactment of these traditional leader–follower roles in marriage can exact a considerable toll in terms of personal distress.

Part of the process of psychotherapy involves helping people to examine the basic assumptions that they make about relationships. They can gain insight into how they have distorted their perceptions and modified their behavior so as to fit the cultural stereotypes. During this process, the way in which people use the relationship balances to structure their relationships can be seen more clearly.

The following case of a woman who came to me for treatment illustrates the way in which she denied important parts of her own personality because of her fear of disrupting her relationship with her husband. She was not aware that she had suppressed parts of herself that could bring her increased self-esteem. The discussion will focus on how her need to perceive her relationships with men in traditional ways led to the conflicts that motivated her to seek help. This marriage is similar to the one discussed earlier in the chapter. However, in the former relationship, both spouses were relatively content. In the present case, the wife is more in touch with her feelings, she experiences more inner conflict, and this motivates her to seek psychotherapy.

> Patricia had met her husband, Don, in college, where both of them had majored in business administration. Don was a year ahead of her, and upon graduation, he obtained a position as a junior executive in a large business firm. They decided to get married shortly thereafter, while Patricia was still in college. When Patricia started psychotherapy, they had been married for 2 years.
>
> After she graduated, Patricia spent several months looking for a job in her field without success. Finally, with her uncle's help, she found a secretarial job at a large magazine. Her male boss was very impressed with her work and, after a year, recommended that Patricia be promoted to a staff position. She saw this as an excellent opportunity but began experiencing intense anxiety. She had many self-doubts and felt that she was incapable of assuming the responsibility that the new job would entail. She had developed a close personal relationship with her boss, and he suggested that she seek psychotherapy, which she did.
>
> Patricia had attended an all-girl high school where she had been very active in student activities and had been elected vice-president of the student body. She discounted this achievement, saying that she had run for office only because her close friend had encouraged her to do so. When she started college, she decided not to get involved in student government. She felt it was because she wanted to have more time for her social life, but the fact that the college was coeducational probably influenced her decision.
>
> Before she met her husband, she had dated a man who had not gone to college. He had been very passive and had wanted her to make most of the decisions. She reluctantly accepted the leadership role but felt that when she

took charge, she appeared unattractive and unfeminine. She had felt superior to her boyfriend but was very uncomfortable with these feelings, and the relationship eventually broke up. Part of the reason she had been attracted to her husband was that he was extremely ambitious, and she saw him as superior to her. Actually, she had done somewhat better than he in some of the courses that they took together in college. She discounted this by saying that he was actually more intelligent, but she had studied more.

Patricia saw her husband as a strong leader in their marriage, even though he only rarely asserted himself directly with her. Generally, he maintained control by agreeing to do something and then not following through, or by making plans without consulting her, to which she would then accommodate. She explained his behavior by saying that it was perfectly understandable that he did not consult her, since she was such a "nag." When she disagreed with him, she often felt that he probably was "right" and she was "wrong." She had difficulty seeing that they both might have valid concerns.

There were two major areas of disagreement between them. One of these areas concerned Don's family. He had a large extended family and liked to socialize with them frequently, whereas Patricia preferred to spend more time with him alone. He would "jokingly" refer to her as "nasty" whenever she objected to seeing his family, and she felt that she had probably been overly unpleasant. Sometimes Don would agree to attend a family gathering without telling her. When Patricia complained, he would say that it was too late to back out of the commitment. She thought that his way of dealing with her objections was "cute," because he knew that she would protest if he told her about these engagements in advance.

Another area of disagreement involved Don's chronic lateness. He would frequently call while Patricia was making dinner, and say that he would be home in half an hour. He would not appear for an hour or more and would mention that he had become involved in a conversation just as he was about to leave the office. She would express her frustration in a "kidding" way. He did not take her objections seriously, and she was not sure that she had a right to object, because she knew how involved he was with his work.

Patricia thought of her marriage as basically happy, with some minor problems. She and her husband did enjoy each other's company and had a satisfying sexual relationship. However, she discounted the frustration that she frequently felt by saying that her demands were excessive and she was a mean-spirited, critical person, whereas her husband was very "nice" and never criticized her.

Without being aware of what she was doing, Patricia used the principles involved in the relationship balances to perceive her marriage. She modified her perceptions and behavior so that her view of her marriage would correspond with the traditional expectations for these balances. She suppressed her agency (or self-assertiveness) in order to maintain a traditional leadership balance, with her husband as leader. This was at considerable cost to herself, since she was capable of highly assertive behavior and had to be constantly alert to control these impulses. The only time she was able to express her agency comfortably was in relationship to women, as she did when she held an important office in her all-girl high school. When she interacted with men, she tried to avoid taking any kind of responsibility because it made her feel unattractive and uncomfortable. It was particularly anxiety-producing for her to be put in the leadership role with her previous boyfriend, and she welcomed her husband's ability to take charge in their marriage. She had great difficulty acknowledging to herself that Don was not as self-assertive and self-confident as she usually viewed him, and that he usually exercised control by either ignoring or indirectly resisting her wishes.

Patricia perceived a close correspondence between the leadership and positivity balances, regardless of whether she or the man was in charge. She viewed the leader as having superior personal qualities and the follower as having inferior qualities. In the relationship with her previous boyfriend, Patricia was the leader and also saw herself as superior to him. With her husband, she saw him as the leader and as superior to her. She was able to maintain her more positive view of her husband even when he broke promises that he had made. She perceived the fault as hers by saying that she had probably been unreasonably demanding. She distorted her perceptions so as to view her husband as "nice" and herself as "nasty." When there were disagreements between them, he was "right" and she was "wrong."

The relationship was a very stable one, and the satisfaction balance was an equality. However, Patricia worked hard to maintain this balance. She discounted her legitimate objections to Don's behavior in order to inhibit her agency (self-assertiveness), and she accommodated to him, regardless of the circumstances, in order to appear high in communion (responsive to Don's needs rather than her own).

Patricia's conflict over accepting a promotion at work can be understood in terms of the way she structures her relationships with men. Her anxiety was related to her need to maintain a traditional leadership balance in her relationship with her male boss. She felt uncomfortable accepting a more responsible position because that would mean that she would need to be more assertive. Her increased agency would change the leadership balance so that she would exert more influence in her relationship with her boss. Since she would no longer be working under his direction, she would see herself as less feminine and attractive. She had sabotaged her own initial efforts to find a job in her field upon graduation because of the same underlying fear.

Her primary concern involved her relationship with her husband. If she became more assertive as work, she might also become more assertive at home. Since all of the relationship balances are interrelated with one another, a change in the strength of Patricia's agency would change the leadership balance with her husband and would lead to changes in the other two relationship balances as well. The leadership balance would become less traditional as she tried to exert more influence with her husband. Since agency is a socially desirable quality, she would have more positive personal attributes. This would change the positivity balance so that she would perceive herself as more positive in relation to her husband. She would be more likely to insist that he show respect for her needs, and the satisfaction balance would also change. The relationship would become less satisfying, particularly for her husband. Thus, her need to maintain the relationship balances in a state of equilibrium led to her conflicts over accepting the promotion (Gerber, 1986b). The personal cost that she paid for this was high in terms of lessened self-esteem and inner tension.

Toward Egalitarian Marriage

There is another kind of marriage that many people view as ideal, in addition to the traditional type (Burgess & Locke, 1960). This is the "egalitarian" marriage, in which both participants are equal in power. In this relationship, the autonomy of the individual and mutuality in decision making are stressed. The participants' right to be happy is taken as a basis for the relationship and is used as the criterion for evaluating its success. Greater emphasis is placed on the affective aspects of the relationship, such as feelings of intimacy, the ability to communicate, and the ability of both partners to gratify each other's needs.

Research with actual couples who are in egalitarian marriages shows that they experience more relationship satisfaction than couples in any other type of marriage (Bernard, 1972, p. 324; Blood & Wolfe, 1960; Gray-Little & Burks, 1983). Similar results have been obtained when the couples' personality traits have been studied. Marriages in which the husband and the wife are strong in both agency and communion have been found to be one of the happiest types of marriage (Antill, 1983).

When the husband and wife share the leadership role, the relationship is perceived by means of the same principles as other kinds of marriage (Gerber, 1987, 1988a). The leadership and positivity balances are equal, indicating that the wife and husband are both seen as exercising power and as having the same amount of socially desirable characteristics. The satisfaction balance is an equality, indicating that the overall relationship is stable. An examination of the gender stereotype traits that constitute the relationship balances shows that the participants are perceived as having the same amount of agency and communion. This means that they are viewed as participating in the decision-making process to the same degree, while showing mutual respect and responsiveness toward each other. Since the two persons are high in communion, they are equally happy in the marriage.

Even though they are based on the same principles, the egalitarian marriage is structured in a fundamentally different way from the other types of marriage. The traditional and wife-led marriages are based on a hierarchical structure, in which one person has more power than the other. Whenever there is one person that has power and another person that does not, the possibility of a role reversal is always present. Thus, an underlying fear in a traditional marriage may be that the power positions will be reversed, and that the wife will become the leader, rather than the husband. A role reversal would be of particular concern in female–male relationships where there is no inherent superiority (Maccoby & Jacklin, 1974), only social custom, that maintains the male in the leadership position. This concern would be absent in an egalitarian marriage, where both persons have the same amount of power.

Empirical research suggests that there are qualitative as well as structural differences in the relationships between real couples who are in traditional and egalitarian marriages. In a traditional marriage, the husband and wife are both highly sex-typed (Hicks & Platt, 1970). Such highly sex-typed persons tend to confuse members of the opposite sex with one another to a greater extent than members of the same sex (Frable & Bem, 1985). This suggests that they are less likely to perceive members of the opposite sex as unique individuals. In a study of interactions within male–female pairs (Ickes & Barnes, 1978), a feminine-typed female and a masculine-typed male were found to communicate less, enjoy the interaction less, and experience less attraction for one another than participants in any other type of relationship.

In contrast, people in egalitarian marriages have been able to integrate the seeming dichotomies of agency and communion within their own personalities. Persons with strong agentic and communal qualities have been found to have a greater appreciation of the opposite sex as unique individuals (Frable & Bem, 1985). They communicate more, enjoy interacting with one another, and are more attracted to one another than participants in traditional dyads (Ickes & Barnes, 1978).

Thus, research with actual people has confirmed that egalitarian relationships are far more satisfying to the participants than are traditional relationships. As Ickes and Barnes (1978, p. 681) conclude from their own research on this issue, "social incompatibility between males and females may be the result of their *adherence* to . . . socially endorsed sex roles, not their lack of adherence to them."

Although people have an image of what an egalitarian marriage is like and can describe the characteristics of the wife and husband with a very high degree of consistency, many people are not able to attain such a marriage for themselves. What, then, keeps people who wish to achieve the ideal of an egalitarian marriage from being able to do so?

The numerous studies about gender that have been done in recent years have made it increasingly clear that, as a culture, we have many misconceptions about these issues. People with highly sex-typed characteristics still tend to be viewed as psychologically healthier than people who do not have these sex-typed traits (Broverman, Broverman, Clarkson, Rosenkrantz, & Vogel, 1970). This is not surprising. It is only in recent years that psychologists have formulated the concept of "androgyny," which refers to a person who possesses the socially desirable traits associated with women as well as men (Bem, 1974; Block, 1973; Constantinople, 1973; Spence et al., 1975). Before this development took place, psychologists thought that it was most desirable for a woman to be feminine-typed and for a man to be masculine-typed (Constantinople, 1973). The research that has been stimulated by the new concept of androgyny has shown that the personality traits of agency and communion are both necessary for fully functioning men and women—agency is necessary for self-esteem (Whitley, 1983); communion is necessary for happiness in relationships (Antill, 1983). This is consistent with the formulations of a number of personality theorists. The ability to integrate seeming dichotomies, such as communion and agency, within one's personality is a development that comes with increased personal maturity (Bakan, 1966; Block, 1973; Hefner, Rebecca, & Oleshansky, 1975; Pleck, 1975). Since the concept of androgyny is a relatively new one within psychology, it has not yet been fully communicated to the larger culture.

Many people would like to experience the satisfactions that are associated with an egalitarian marriage, but they think that these satisfactions will be obtained by enacting the stereotypic personality traits that are associated with their sex. They see an egalitarian marriage as an ideal to be sought after. However, they also hold a conflicting ideal—that it is desirable for a woman to be highly feminine-typed and for a man to be highly masculine-typed. They do not realize that an egalitarian relationship requires that the man and women manifest the personality traits of both agency *and* communion.

Gender stereotyping is part of a larger process that helps people to make sense out of their world and organize their experience (Jones, 1982). Cultural stereotypes can represent reality but can also distort the interpretation of that reality (Brigham, 1971; Campbell, 1967). People stereotype the traditional man and woman as being highly sex-typed on agency and communion and as having a strong sense of gender identity (Gerber, 1988a, 1988d). However, research with actual people has shown that these stereotypes about gender identity are misleading (Spence & Sawin, 1985). People do not actually use the traits of communion and agency as the primary defining characteristics of their own and other people's gender identity. In a study that examined this issue, the investigators conclude that gender identity is a "basic existential conviction that one is male or female" (Spence & Sawin, 1985, p. 59). Any personal qualities that conflict with people's view of their own or others' gender identity are usually discounted. For example, a woman can be seen as very womanly, while also being seen as high in agency. Similarly, a man can be viewed as very manly and also be high in communion.

Rather than reflecting a deficiency in gender identity, women and men who are able to enact roles that do not conform to cultural stereotypes may have a strong sense of their own gender identity (Block, 1973). The expression of nonstereotypic traits can reflect a basic confidence in a man's sense of his maleness and a woman's sense of her femaleness, so that they are freed from using the stereotypic traits as gender displays.

Stereotypes about physical attractiveness appear to be similarly misleading. These stereotypes have been shown to be based on the extent to which someone enacts a culturally valued role (Unger et al., 1982). People who enact culturally accepted roles are stereotyped as attractive; people who enact deviant roles are unattractive. A highly sex-typed person in a traditional marriage is stereotyped as being more attractive than an androgynous person in an egalitarian marriage (Gerber, 1988d). However, when actual women who were either androgynous or feminine-typed were rated on physical attractiveness, no difference between them was found (Andersen & Bem, 1981). This suggests that stereotypes about physical attractiveness may have little to do with the actual attractiveness of real men and women.

Many of the beliefs about gender are deeply rooted in personality and past experience. The realization that a number of the assumptions about gender and relationships are in error is an important step toward change. Rather than communion and agency being seen as the exclusive domain of one sex or the other, these traits need to be viewed as human qualities that are necessary for both sexes. They enable women and men to interact together as mature human beings in relationships that are mutually satisfying.

ACKNOWLEDGMENTS. The author wishes to express her appreciation to Peggy Donovan, Doris Howard, Raymond F. Kennedy, Ruth Shapiro, and Barbara J. Steinberg for their thoughtful comments on an earlier version of the chapter.

REFERENCES

Andersen, S. M., & Bem, S. L. (1981). Sex typing and androgyny in dyadic interaction: Individual differences in responsiveness to physical attractiveness. *Journal of Personality and Social Psychology, 41,* 74–86.
Antill, J. K. (1983). Sex role complementarity versus similarity in married couples. *Journal of Personality and Social Psychology, 45,* 145–155.
Bakan, D. (1966). *The duality of human existence.* Chicago: Rand McNally.
Bales, R. F. (1967). The equilibrium problem in small groups. In A. P. Hare, E. F. Borgatta, & R. F. Bales (Eds.), *Small groups: Studies in social interaction* (pp. 444–476). New York: Knopf.
Bass, B. M. (1973). *Leadership, psychology, and organizational behavior.* Westport, CT: Greenwood Press.
Bem, S. L. (1974). The measurement of psychological androgyny. *Journal of Consulting and Clinical Psychology, 42,* 155–162.

Bem, S. L. (1981). *Bem Sex-Role Inventory: Professional manual*. Palo Alto, CA: Consulting Psychologists Press.

Bernard, J. (1972). *The future of marriage*. New York: World Publishing.

Block, J. (1973). Conceptions of sex role: Some cross-cultural and longitudinal perspectives. *American Psychologist, 28*, 512–526.

Blood, R. O., & Wolfe, D. M. (1960). *Husbands and wives: The dynamics of married living*. New York: Free Press.

Brigham, J. (1971). Ethnic stereotypes. *Psychological Bulletin, 76*, 15–38.

Broverman, I. K., Broverman, D. M., Clarkson, F. E., Rosenkrantz, P. S., & Vogel, S. R. (1970). Sex-role stereotypes and clinical judgments of mental health. *Journal of Consulting and Clinical Psychology, 34*, 1–7.

Burgess, E. W., & Locke, H. J. (1960). *The family: From institution to companionship* (2nd ed.). New York: American Book Company.

Campbell, D. T. (1967). Stereotypes and the perception of group differences. *American Psychologist, 22*, 817–829.

Constantinople, A. (1973). Masculinity-femininity: An exception to the famous dictum? *Psychological Bulletin, 80*, 389–407.

Costos, D. (1986). Sex role identity in young adults: Its parental antecedents and relation to ego development. *Journal of Personality and Social Psychology, 50*, 602–611.

Costrich, N., Feinstein, J., Kidder, L., Maracek, J., & Pascale, L. (1975). When stereotypes hurt: Three studies of penalties for sex-role reversals. *Journal of Experimental Social Psychology, 11*, 520–530.

Darley, J. M., & Fazio, R. H. (1980). Expectancy confirmation processes arising in the social interaction sequence. *American Psychologist, 35*, 867–881.

Deaux, K. (1977). Sex differences. In T. Blass (Ed.), *Personality variables in social behavior* (pp. 357–377). Hillsdale, NJ: Erlbaum.

Denmark, F. L. (1977). Styles of leadership. *Psychology of Women Quarterly, 2*, 99–113.

Eagly, A. H., & Steffen, V. J. (1984). Gender stereotypes stem from the distribution of women and men into social roles. *Journal of Personality and Social Psychology, 46*, 735–754.

Falbo, T., Hazen, M. D., & Linimon, D. (1982). The costs of selecting power bases or messages associated with the opposite sex. *Sex Roles, 8*, 147–157.

Fiske, S. T., & Taylor, S. E. (1984). *Social cognition*. New York: Random House.

Foushee, H. C., Helmreich, R. L., & Spence, J. T. (1979). Implicit theories of masculinity and femininity: Dualistic or bipolar? *Psychology of Women Quarterly, 3*, 259–269.

Frable, D. E. S., & Bem, S. L. (1985). If you are gender schematic, all members of the opposite sex look alike. *Journal of Personality and Social Psychology, 49*, 459–468.

French, J. R. P., Jr., & Raven, B. (1968). The bases of social power. In D. Cartwright & A. Zander (Eds.), *Group dynamics: Research and theory* (3rd ed., pp. 259–269). New York: Harper & Row.

Gerber, G. L. (1985). A relationship balance model for sex-role stereotypic traits: Attributions to married couples (Summary). *Proceedings and Abstracts of the Annual Meeting of the Eastern Psychological Association, 56*, 14.

Gerber, G. L. (1986a, April). Gender and police partners: A model for describing relationships. In R. Pecorella (Chair), *Integrating the public service: Changing roles and gender*. Panel conducted at the 40th Annual Conference of the New York State Political Science Association, Albany, NY.

Gerber, G. L. (1986b). The relationship balance model and its implications for individual and couples therapy. In D. Howard (Ed.), *The dynamics of feminist therapy* (pp. 19–27). New York: Haworth Press.

Gerber, G. L. (1987). Sex stereotypes among American college students: Implications for marital happiness, social desirability, and marital power. *Genetic, Social, and General Psychology Monographs, 113*, 413–431.

Gerber, G. L. (1988a). Leadership roles and the gender stereotype traits. *Sex Roles, 18*, 649–668.

Gerber, G. L. (1988b). *The leadership balance in traditional and nontraditional male-female dyads*. Unpublished manuscript.

Gerber, G. L. (1988c). *The more positive evaluation of men than women on the gender stereotype traits.* Manuscript submitted for publication.

Gerber, G. L. (1988d). *Social desirability of married couples and their relationships: Effect of leadership roles on physical attractiveness, gender identity, self-esteem and status.* Manuscript submitted for publication.

Gillen, B. (1981). Physical attractiveness: A determinant of two types of goodness. *Personality and Social Psychology Bulletin, 7,* 277–281.

Goffman, E. (1979). *Gender advertisements.* Cambridge, MA: Harvard University Press.

Gray-Little, B., & Burks, N. (1983). Power and satisfaction in marriage: A review and critique. *Psychological Bulletin, 93,* 513–538.

Harvey, O. J. (1953). An experimental approach to the study of status relations in informal groups. *American Sociological Review, 18,* 357–367.

Hatfield, E., & Sprecher, S. (1986). *Mirror, mirror . . . The importance of looks in everyday life.* Albany: State University of New York Press.

Hefner, R., Rebecca, M., & Oleshansky, B. (1975). The development of sex-role transcendence. *Human Development, 18,* 143–158.

Heilman, M. E., & Saruwatari, L. R. (1979). When beauty is beastly: The effects of appearance and sex on evaluations of job applicants for managerial and nonmanagerial jobs. *Organizational Behavior and Human Performance, 23,* 360–372.

Henley, N. M. (1977). *Body politics: Power, sex and nonverbal communication.* Englewood Cliffs, NJ: Prentice-Hall.

Hicks, M. W., & Platt, M. (1970). Marital happiness and stability: A review of the research in the sixties. *Journal of Marriage and the Family, 32,* 533–574.

Holyoak, K. J., & Gordon, P. C. (1984). Information processing and social cognition. In R. S. Wyer, Jr., & T. K. Skrull (Eds.), *Handbook of social cognition* (Vol. 1, pp. 39–70). Hillsdale, NJ: Erlbaum.

Ickes, W. (1985). Sex-role influences on compatibility in relationships. In W. Ickes (Ed.), *Compatible and incompatible relationships* (pp. 187–208). New York: Springer-Verlag.

Ickes, W., & Barnes, R. D. (1978). Boys and girls together—and alienated: On enacting stereotyped sex roles in mixed-sex dyads. *Journal of Personality and Social Psychology, 36,* 669–683.

Jones, R. A. (1982). Perceiving other people: Stereotyping as a process of social cognition. In A. G. Miller (Ed.), *In the eye of the beholder: Contemporary issues in stereotyping* (pp. 41–91). New York: Praeger.

Lippitt, R., Polansky, N., Redl, R., & Rosen, S. (1952). The dynamics of power. *Human Relations, 5,* 37–64.

Maccoby, E. E., & Jacklin, C. N. (1974). *The psychology of sex differences.* Stanford, CA: Stanford University Press.

Major, B. (1981). Gender patterns in touching behavior. In C. Mayo & N. Henley (Eds.), *Gender, androgyny, and nonverbal behavior* (pp. 15–37). New York: Springer-Verlag.

Major, B., Carnevale, P. J. D., & Deaux, K. (1981). A differential perspective on androgyny: Evaluations of masculine and feminine personality characteristics. *Journal of Personality and Social Psychology, 41,* 988–1001.

McKee, J. P., & Sherriffs, A. C. (1957). The differential evaluation of males and females. *Journal of Personality, 25,* 356–371.

Megargee, E. I. (1969). Influence of sex roles on the manifestation of leadership. *Journal of Applied Psychology, 53,* 377–382.

Michel, A. (1967). Comparative data concerning the interaction in French and American families. *Journal of Marriage and the Family, 42,* 277–244.

Neufeld, E., Langmeyer, D., & Seeman, W. (1974). Some sex-role stereotypes and personal preferences, 1950 and 1970. *Journal of Personality Assessment, 38,* 247–254.

Nyquist, L. V., & Spence, J. T. (1986). Effects of dispositional dominance and sex role expectations on leadership behaviors. *Journal of Personality and Social Psychology, 50,* 87–93.

Pedhazur, E. J., & Tetenbaum, T. J. (1979). Bem Sex-Role Inventory: A theoretical and methodological critique. *Journal of Personality and Social Psychology, 37,* 996–1016.

Peplau, L. A., & Gordon, S. L. (1985). Women and men in love: Gender differences in close heterosexual relationships. In V. E. O'Leary, R. K. Unger, & B. S. Wallson (Eds.), *Women, gender, and social psychology* (pp. 257–292). Hillsdale, NJ: Erlbaum.

Pleck, J. (1975). Masculinity-femininity: Current and alternative paradigms. *Sex Roles, 1,* 161–178.

Pond, D. A., Ryle, A., & Hamilton, M. (1963). Marriage and neurosis in a working-class population. *British Journal of Psychiatry, 109,* 592–598.

Rosenkrantz, P., Vogel, S., Bee, H., Broverman, I., & Broverman, D. M. (1968). Sex-role stereotypes and self-concepts in college students. *Journal of Consulting and Clinical Psychology, 32,* 283–294.

Ruble, T. L. (1983). Sex stereotypes: Issues of change in the 1970s. *Sex Roles, 9,* 397–402.

Skrypnek, B. J., & Snyder, M. (1982). On the self-perpetuating nature of stereotypes about women and men. *Journal of Experimental Social Psychology, 18,* 277–291.

Spence, J. T., Deaux, K., & Helmreich, R. L. (1985). Sex roles in contemporary American society. In G. Lindzey & E. Aronson (Eds.), *Handbook of social psychology: Vol. 2. Special fields and applications* (3rd ed., pp. 149–178). New York: Random House.

Spence, J. T., Helmreich, R. L., & Stapp, J. (1975). Ratings of self and peers on sex-role attributes and their relation to self-esteem and conceptions of masculinity and femininity. *Journal of Personality and Social Psychology, 32,* 29–39.

Spence, J. T., & Sawin, L. L. (1985). Images of masculinity and femininity: A reconceptualization. In V. E. O'Leary, R. K. Unger, & B. S. Wallston (Eds.), *Women, gender, and social psychology* (pp. 35–66). Hillsdale, NJ: Erlbaum.

Stogdill, R. M. (1950). Leadership, membership and organization. *Psychological Bulletin, 47,* 1–14.

Thibaut, J. W., & Kelley, H. H. (1959). *The social psychology of groups.* New York: Wiley.

Unger, R. K., Hilderbrand, M., & Madar, T. (1982). Physical attractiveness and assumptions about social deviance: Some sex-by-sex comparisons. *Personality and Social Psychology Bulletin, 8,* 293–301.

von Baeyer, C. L., Sherk, D. L., & Zanna, M. P. (1981). Impression management in the job interview: When the female applicant meets the male (chauvinist) interviewer. *Personality and Social Psychology Bulletin, 7,* 45–51.

Werner, P. D., & LaRussa, G. W. (1985). Persistence and change in sex-role stereotypes. *Sex Roles, 12,* 1089–1100.

White, K. M., Speisman, J. C., Jackson, D., Bartis, S., & Costos, D. (1986). Intimacy maturity and its correlates in young married couples. *Journal of Personality and Social Psychology, 50,* 152–162.

Whitley, B. E., Jr. (1983). Sex role orientation and self-esteem: A critical meta-analytic review. *Journal of Personality and Social Psychology, 44,* 765–778.

Zanna, M. P., & Pack, S. J. (1975). On the self-fulfilling nature of apparent sex differences in behavior. *Journal of Experimental Social Psychology, 11,* 583–591.

Chapter 5

New Parents in a Changing World
Existential and Interpersonal Dilemmas

SOPHIA RICHMAN

Becoming a parent is a profound psychological and existential event. It is an experience that can potentially change one's perspective from the trivial preoccupations of daily life to an attitude of greater self-awareness. Often, deciding to parent raises issues of personal identity, encourages a reevaluation of values, goals, and aspirations, and involves a reordering of priorities. Irvin Yalom, the existential psychotherapist, uses the term *boundary situation* to describe events "that propel one into a confrontation with one's existential situation in the world." For Yalom, the prototypic boundary situation is death awareness, but his description could just as readily apply to birth awareness. Giving birth, like facing death, potentially creates a massive shift in the way one lives in the world. Yalom sees decisions as boundary experiences as well. He writes: "Decision, especially an irreversible decision, is a boundary situation in the same way that awareness of 'my death' is a boundary situation. Both act as a catalyst to shift one from the everyday attitude to the ontological attitude—that is, to a mode of being in which one is mindful of being" (1980, p. 319).

The commitment to parent is one of the most significant and far-reaching decisions of a person's life. Insofar as it is truly irreversible, it exposes one to the anxiety of knowing that one has to relinquish all other possibilities.

For many, becoming a parent means finally becoming an adult. Growing up also means growing older, and taking another step toward death. Birth stirs up our death anxiety. It makes us more aware of the biological life cycle. In the psyche, birth and death are related opposites, so that when we think of one, we associate the other. Being so intimately involved with the beginnings of life often makes us more conscious of the end of life as well.

The specter of death attends the birth of every child. Years ago, death in childbirth was not an uncommon reality (Shorter, 1982). For the woman who has a great fear of childbirth, even the desired baby can turn into a monster that has taken over the body, that cannot be controlled as it grows and grows and threatens to burst forth, rupturing and damaging the body, potentially destroying it.

SOPHIA RICHMAN • Institute for Contemporary Psychotherapy, New York, New York 10024; Postdoctoral Program, New York University, New York, New York 10003.

As the newborn enters the world, we are aware of its apparent fragility and helplessness, and it reminds us of the thin line between life and death. New parents visit the nursery with great trepidation, listening for sounds of life as the baby lies still in his crib. And as they watch the child grow, they see the passage of time expressed in this undeniable visible transformation. This new human being who reminds them of their mortality is paradoxically their bridge to immortality as the future stretches endlessly with new generations to follow.

Another existential concern activated by parenthood is the issue of responsibility. Creating a new life, becoming aware of the total dependence of this fragile being, is experienced by some as an overwhelming responsibility. It is particularly frightening for people who have difficulty claiming ownership of their own lives to be responsible for another. Paradoxically, a child can rescue its parents from having to take responsibility for their own lives. The child becomes the guiding principle, sometimes the rationalization for one's actions or inactions. In the face of groundlessness the child becomes the anchor. The child is planned to save a marriage, or to be offered as a gift to the grandparents, or to give meaning to a life that has no direction. Such purposes frequently remain unconscious or at the edges of awareness.

Birth highlights another ultimate concern, namely, isolation. No matter how close each of us is to another, there remains a final unbridgeable gap. The tiny newborn makes the birth journey alone. Totally on her own in that internal cavern of the womb, she struggles valiantly to be born. She enters the world alone, hopefully into her parents' loving arms. As the parents bond with their baby, they bridge the isolation momentarily.

Existential thinking holds that each of us is ultimately alone, and that there is no preordained design for us to follow; each of us must find his own meaning in life. Patients in psychotherapy often complain of a sense of malaise, a lack of direction in their lives. A child is conceived as a solution to the problem of meaninglessness. Creation of a new life, and dedication to its development, provides a sense of purpose, a direction to follow, and as such is a powerful antidote to the problem of meaninglessness. Erik Erikson (1959) believed that parenthood, or "generativity," as he called it, is a stage of development in the life cycle. The healthy personality is interested in establishing and guiding the next generation. Individuals who develop generativity are able to transcend themselves and find ultimate meaning in their existence.

From an existential perspective, birth is an urgent experience that propels us into a confrontation with fundamental concerns of human existence, such as death, isolation, responsibility, and meaninglessness. The self is changed as a result of the encounter. The ripple effects are experienced in the interpersonal world of the new parents. Relationships with various significant others undergo transformations. Prospective parents are embarking on a journey that many others have either completed or are longing to travel. Pregnancy stirs up powerful, often unconscious feelings in other people. Sometimes the lost or unused potential is reawakened in others. Childbirth is a reminder of the passage of time, of a new generation coming to replace the existing one. Furthermore, as a symbol of motherhood, the pregnant woman is ripe for the projection of complex ambivalent feelings people hold deep inside toward their own mothers. In a society such as ours, where mothers have been the primary caretakers, the mother's power is feared and envied (Dinnerstein, 1976).

While changes in relationships occur on many different fronts, with friends, relatives, co-workers, nowhere are changes experienced as profoundly as in the couple relationship. The decision to parent is a momentous one, with major consequences for every aspect of a couple's life together. The balance of power and dependency that had been reached over time suddenly shifts with new roles and demands of parenthood.

The obvious dependency of the child is a theme resonating in the household even before the child is born. In our society, dependency needs of men and women get played out in indirect ways; as Eichenbaum and Orbach (1983) point out, women are trained to be depended upon, to provide the emotional support for others, and men to rely on that emotional support without acknowledging their emotional dependency. Both men and women are discouraged from expressing their deep-seated emotional needs and are made to feel ashamed of them. The pregnancy stage with its attendant anxiety elicits further neediness. In addition to struggling with an internal sense of fragility and heightened death anxiety, prospective parents have interpersonal concerns to deal with. They are fearful of losing their relationship with each other, of being replaced by the newcomer. They may reexperience feelings of jealousy and exclusion characteristic of earlier developmental stages when their initial dyadic bond was threatened. In our culture, where women tend to be the primary caretakers, men in particular are vulnerable to experiencing such feelings of loss.

During the pregnancy, the mother-to-be readily focuses her attention on the developing child inside her. Much of the time, she seems to be preoccupied with the dramatic changes in her body. At this point, the father-to-be is already sharing her with the yet invisible baby. If he is feeling somewhat abandoned, he usually does not feel free to express such feelings and does not expect to get much sympathy for them. His mate is the one on center stage. She gets a great deal of attention from friends and relatives. Furthermore, she seems more dependent on him and in need of his reassurance. So while the father-to-be may be equally anxious and needy at this time, his role is to put his own concerns into the background and to support his mate. In addition to having to cope with her increased emotional demands and with his own powerful feelings, he also has concerns about the increased financial responsibilities lurking ahead.

The birth of the baby does not ease the situation. The newborn becomes the central focus of the relationship, its neediness and endless demands taking precedence over other concerns. If this baby is born into a traditional "mother-nurturer, father-provider" family, the woman will take on a powerful role, for she will be the one with the power to withhold or provide emotional supplies. The transference possibilities are particularly strong for the male whose experience of his own mother's immense unilateral power may be reactivated. His reaction to free himself of it by devaluing her or withdrawing from her are expressed in his relationship with his mate. His role of provider furnishes him with the opportunity to invest his energies into work with a wonderful rationalization for his withdrawal as well as a reaffirmation of his power and control.

Some men withdraw by turning to other women at this time. This can be a way of dealing with feelings of abandonment or fears of engulfment. The husband may experience the wife's intense involvement with the pregnancy or the new baby as a love affair. Since the wife has taken a new lover, he redresses the balance by finding someone for himself. Or the infant may represent a merger and intensify his feelings of attachment and dependence. Trapped by fears of engulfment, the husband finds a new lover and creates a secret life to reaffirm his separateness (Eichenbaum & Orbach, 1983).

When the couple becomes a family, the system changes and the intimacy–distance balance also shifts. Successful relationships are those in which the partners have found a comfortable place on the continuum of distance and closeness, where they are able to enjoy a sense of being merged without losing a sense of freedom and separateness. When a new baby enters the family, the balance shifts and realignments occur. The baby can be experienced as an intruder in the couple's relationship or the woman may bond with the child in a way that excludes her mate or the child may be used by both parents to avoid intimacy with each other. Potentially, however, the baby can also bring the couple closer together as they share the common concerns of parenthood. Their relationship can become more stable and mature, and a new level of commitment can be reached.

The Changing Social Context

Over the last 30 years or so there have been significant social and economic changes that have had a profound impact on parenting. Changing economic times have made it increasingly difficult to adhere to the traditional family pattern in which a father is the sole wage earner and the mother stays at home with the children. Owing to financial pressures, women are joining the work force in unprecedented numbers. Many women choose to work outside the home for personal reasons as well. They view a career as a source of self-esteem and personal fulfillment. The climate of self-expression and self-development has meant a prolonged period of exploration and experimentation, particularly for women who have enjoyed the newfound freedom of being able to fill multidimensional roles in jobs, leisure occupations, and a range of social settings.

The 1960s and early 1970s ushered in a time of political and social activism, wherein people grappled with issues of inequality and sexism. The women's movement sensitized us to the inequities and constrictions of both sexes within the patriarchal culture and stimulated a reevaluation of the gender arrangements in our society. As a result, many couples made personal and social commitments to carry egalitarianism into their home, dividing up responsibilities, sharing the housework and the care of children. Certain segments of the feminist movement downgraded motherhood and childrearing, calling it a biological trap, a method of ensuring woman's servitude in the home (Kitzinger, 1978). The social context of childbearing became less positive. Some people maintained that it is wrong to bring children into our overpopulated world, others felt that it is criminal to expose new life to the nuclear threat we all live with. Those who are ambivalent or negative about having children have been able to enlist such arguments to support their position.

With the social and economic changes taking place, parenthood is no longer the inevitable sequel to marriage. More couples than ever before are opting to remain childless or "child-free," as they would prefer to call it. Many more couples are deciding to delay parenting until their career goals are achieved. While declining fertility becomes an issue for couples who postpone parenthood, the incredible scientific advances have made it possible to consider heretofore unimaginable possibilities for conception.

As a result of all of these social, economic, and scientific developments, the modern couple is living in a world very different from that of their parents. They are faced with many more choices and possibilities and at the same time have fewer guidelines to provide them with the help they need to make wise decisions.

There is little preparation for parenthood. The support of the extended family is usually not available in our highly mobile society where young people settle many miles away from their family of origin. Notions of what it means to be a mother or a father are inevitably influenced by one's early parental figures. This influence can exist on an unconscious level and can sometimes be in conflict with current ideals of parenthood. As the society changes, the role models of the past prove inadequate. The situation that young couples face, with more options and less guidance, means more uncertainty, insecurity, and anxiety. Many search for answers from experts. The proliferation of "how to" books for new parents or prospective parents illustrates the need for guidance and support.

As parenthood no longer inevitably follows marriage, people face questions such as whether or not to have a baby, when to have a baby, whether to have one within or outside marriage. What was once assumed now becomes an issue that may involve difficult joint decision making. In my psychoanalytic practice, I often see people at such a juncture in their lives when they feel pressured to make an important decision yet feel that they do not have the inner resources to make the necessary commitment. The situation is particularly problematic when one partner is reluctant to have a child and the other feels ready. Most often in such situations, it is the woman who is wishing to become a mother while her mate is reluctant to become a father. Typically, the woman is in her 30s and aware of her declining fertility. Even among men who welcome fatherhood, it is normally the woman's wish that initiates the family. The male generally experiences more concerns over the financial responsibilities of the household and wants to feel more professionally secure before undertaking parenthood (Williams, 1988).

When parenthood unquestionably followed marriage, people had their children and later experienced their negative feelings. Absent fathers and resentful mothers are examples of the casualties. These days, when parenthood is more of a choice, we can observe agonizing struggles around the issue. An especially poignant state of affairs exists when because of emotional or psychological reasons one partner is unwilling to have a child. Unlike other differences of opinion, where some compromise is theoretically possible, the decision to have a baby or not has no middle ground. This dilemma is resolved for some by conscious or unconscious lapses in the use of birth control, the so-called accidents. For others, it leads to a dissolution of the relationship. The more fortunate ones work through their ambivalence and feelings, understand the psychodynamics involved in their positions, and ultimately arrive at a mutual decision that they can comfortably live with. A case illustration follows.

> Linda at 35 years of age was beginning to feel the pressure of having to make a decision about whether or not to have a child. A successful executive in a large corporation, she derived a good deal of satisfaction from her work and was concerned about interrupting her career. In therapy she sorted out her motivation for parenthood, examining various practical considerations, as well as less conscious feelings about becoming a mother. Eventually, it became clearer to her that she wished to have a child. Her husband, Chuck, a 40-year-old professional with high status aspirations, showed no inclination to parent. For him, having a child was associated with numerous losses—the loss of his comfortable life-style, the loss of his freedom to indulge his expensive taste, the loss of his exclusive, intimate relationship with his wife. He was especially concerned that once a baby was born, Linda would stop working and become finan-

cially dependent on him. Deep down he felt like a child himself, and he was not prepared to step aside for a child.

As Linda's desire for motherhood crystallized, the marriage reached an impasse. She was more articulate about her feelings than he, and Chuck began to feel overwhelmed and fearful that his needs would be overridden and ignored. In couples therapy, he had an opportunity to more fully express his needs and fears. Once his concerns were verbalized and heard, he felt less resentful and ultimately accepted what was for him the inevitable, since his wife's desire to have a child was stronger than his own reluctance.

If men today feel freer to reject parenthood, they also feel freer to embrace it. Concepts of masculinity and femininity are undergoing a quiet yet profound transformation. There is less pressure for a man to be aggressive, rational, and competitive, and more for him to be sensitive, emotional, and empathic. The nurturant yet strong male is gradually replacing the tough, distant hero in current films and books. The father, traditionally provider and protector of the family, is now encouraged to play a more active role in his children's development. For the woman, femininity needs no longer be defined by her motherhood; she is encouraged to develop other creative aspects of herself, to play a more active role in the outside world.

Traditional parents each had a distinct sex-linked role to play, the father as the breadwinner responsible for the financial well-being of the family, the mother as the primary caretaker and responsible for the day-to-day care of the children. These gender arrangements are gradually changing. Male and female gender roles are defined in relation to one another; a change in one produces a complementary change in the other. As women have taken on more of the financial responsibility, men have become more involved in the caretaking aspects of parenthood. In the 1960s fathers in childbirth classes and delivery rooms were considered pioneers, today they are in the mainstream. Companies are offering paternity leaves, judges are awarding custody to fathers. Even fathers in traditional roles now spend more time at home during the early years of their children's lives. Even if they see child care as primarily the woman's responsibility, they tend to be more involved than their own fathers were (Boston Women's Health Book Collective, 1978).

Moreover, a small percentage of couples are experimenting with more radical gender arrangements, like shared parenting. Parental role sharing is defined as a partnership where both mother and father share the primary daily care of their children, and work at their careers. Through this arrangement, the provider role and the nurturer role are fulfilled by both parents simultaneously. Economic pressures as well as philosophical and personal value considerations lead these couples to this form of parenting. In the remainder of this chapter we will take a closer look at the effects that the changes in gender arrangements have had on men, women, and their children.

Psychological Impact of Shared Parenting Arrangements

Couples who embark on shared parenting, by choice rather than because of financial necessity, implicitly value equality in a relationship. They have a belief that for a child to grow up relatively free of sex biases, both parents must be involved in childrearing. According to Ehrensaft (1987), who conducted a detailed study of shared parenting families, these couples fare very well in terms of their general level of satisfaction, and in how they feel about their marriage. They share the same psychological world as they both balance career and parenthood. As a result, they tend to be more empathic to each other and more respectful of each other's career needs. The equality in their relationship is particularly evident in the decision-making process. Decisions are made by consensus, involve negotiations and problem solving, and result in mutually acceptable solutions.

Sometimes negotiations get bogged down. Without a clear demarcation of roles and responsibilities there is an occasional duplication of effort. In a traditional marriage where husband and wife both have prescribed areas of competency, the functioning is smoother and more efficient than when both parents are juggling career and childrearing. Assuming responsibility for both work and family means giving up the illusion that the partner will be the perfect parent or the perfect provider on whom one can rely. "Having it all" translates into not doing anything to its fullest. A major complaint of role-sharing parents is the lack of time in their hectic lives. The feeling of fragmentation and fatigue, the absence of personal time or exclusive time with one's mate, the tyranny of intricate schedules are all recognized as the sacrifices of the new arrangements (Ehrensaft, 1987; Williams, 1988).

For most of these parents, however, the emotional fulfillment derived from joint parenting is well worth the sacrifices. The positive effect of shared parenting on fathers is evident in the warm, loving relationships they tend to develop with their children. The opportunity to learn from the parenting experience and use it for personal growth is another positive outcome. When men are exposed to daily caretaking of children they develop new strengths, such as patience, endurance, and compassion, and they get in touch with so-called feminine aspects of themselves, such as their intuitive capacity and their tenderness.

The primary concern of these parents, however, is the effect that such arrangements will have on their children. Children growing up in a democratic climate tend to internalize values of equality and fairness. Since such new gender arrangements are still in their infancy as sociological events, it is not possible with any certainty to answer questions about the long-term effects of joint parenting on the personality of the child. It is, however, important for psychologists to deal with questions such as how coparenting affects attachment and bonding, separation–individuation, and gender identity formation. While no definitive answers exist at present, we do have some data, and with the help of our theories we can speculate with some confidence.

Attachment is the first major task facing a child and its parents. Research tells us that a child is capable of multiple attachments, and that men are psychologically able to participate in all parenting behavior with the exception of gestation and lactation. Fathers can develop a powerful bond with their newborn equal in intensity to the mother–infant bond. The sense of absorption and preoccupation of new fathers with their infants has been described by various writers (Ehrensaft, 1987; Greenberg & Morris, 1982; Williams, 1988). Expressions of these feelings are reflected in comments from fathers such as "I love looking at Evin, I think he's beautiful, so perfect. I used to think that all newborns looked more or less alike until I saw him" and "When Lina was born, I looked into her eyes and talked to her while gently caressing her with my hand; it was as if we were communicating with our eyes. I told her that I would protect her and help her grow big and strong and free." Men are often surprised by the intensity of their emotional reactions toward their newborn. A father says, "I knew that I would enjoy being a father, but I never expected to find myself so passionately in love with the baby."

In contrast, women seem to experience the closeness and bonding in a less romantic way (Ehrensaft, 1987). A new mother says, "When I look at this little person and realize he came out of my body, I am completely awed. This is probably the greatest achievement of my life!" Another says, "When I take care of the baby, I sometimes feel I'm engaged in the most important job in the world, but at other times I feel overwhelmed with the work and desperately crave some time of my own, just for me." Women seem less surprised by the intensity of their feelings and more surprised by the amount of energy involved in the day-to-day care of an infant. One new mother expressed this by saying, "I love being a mother, but I didn't realize how exhausting it would be taking care of a newborn. I really underestimated the work involved."

When parents equally share childrearing responsibilities, presumably there are numerous positive consequences. First, it is more likely that a child's needs will be met when two people are committed to meeting those needs. If one parent who has been attending to the infant is exhausted or frustrated, the other can step in and relieve him or her. The child is then provided with a responsive parent rather than a resentful, depleted one.

Another advantage is that one parent's way of viewing the world does not have to become the child's only reality. The child is exposed from birth to different parenting styles as well as to a broader perspective. The differences between parents help a baby piece the world together and clarify the meaning of differences (Kaplan, 1978). Indeed, it has been reported that children raised in shared-parenting families tend to be particularly good at reading social cues. They are able to relate to different kinds of people, and to adapt more easily to new situations (Ehrensaft, 1987).

With an intense attachment to two people instead of one, it is likely that the fear of abandonment will be attenuated to some extent. The potential loss of the mother is less devastating when there is a powerful attachment to father as well. Ehrensaft's research supports this expectation. In her sample, the children seemed to experience minimum trauma to early separation. She reasoned that because these children have experienced a transition from one caretaking person to another, they are less anxious when a parent leaves, confident that their needs will continue to be met. She concluded that these children tend to be emotionally secure and trusting in the world.

It is likely that separation and individuation, as a major developmental task, is facilitated by the newer gender arrangements. In describing the early development of the human being, Kaplan (1978) writes: "In the first years of life mother and baby play dangerously on the margin between oneness and separateness. The balance between mutual envelopment and moving apart is delicate. A father's presence in their world keeps a mother and a baby in touch with the fact of their separateness" (p. 138).

Kaplan is referring to the traditional family arrangement. A variation of this interaction is expected when the father is a coparent who is as intimately involved in the care of the infant as the mother. Presumably, he too enters into a symbiotic union and develops his own dialogue with the infant. He too must struggle with the dialectic of oneness and separateness. We speculate that in the coparenting family each parent helps the other with the delicate balance between oneness and separateness.

For example, when 4-month-old Gordon sees his father or hears his voice, he gets excited, kicks, and smiles just as he does in his mother's presence. While perfectly content and secure with each parent, he appears to be able to discriminate between them. Each parent has her or his way of talking, playing, and feeding him, and Gordon seems aware of these differences. Each parent brings out somewhat different responses from him. His mother talks to him constantly, and he in turn vocalizes more with her. His father is more physical with him, rocking him, lifting him up high over his head, and cuddling with him. When his father is taking care of him, the two of them are united in a state that has been called oneness or merging. When his mother appears, that state of oneness with his father is temporarily disrupted and recreated anew with his mother, as he merges with her. The changing of the guard, so to speak, facilitates the disengagement process, which in turn helps with separation and ultimately with the achievement of selfhood.

With regard to the question of gender identity, we expect better integration and less splitting off of certain aspects of the self with the new arrangements. In a traditional culture, male children need to renounce their tie with their mother and reject their dependent, needy feelings. When masculinity includes nurturance, and fathers play an active role in raising their sons, the image of a male that is internalized is more integrated and includes the more tender, soft, "feminine" aspect. Furthermore, the female child reared by both parents can also incorporate "masculine" aspects of assertion and activity. It is anticipated that as children are freer to develop both the masculine and feminine sides of themselves, they will enjoy more expanded options in life.

The positive effects of joint parenting notwithstanding, the possibility for increased conflict is also there. When there is no longer an exclusive territory, differences of opinion have to be hammered out. The mother can no longer count on having the last word in the nursery. The father can no longer use his work as an excuse for noninvolvement in family affairs. Women who have been programmed from childhood to derive their self-esteem from their mothering role sometimes experience sharing as giving up something of value. They are reluctant to give up the power that goes with the role. Their resistance may get expressed in subtle undermining of the father's child care. While verbalizing their wish to have his involvement, they in fact become impatient and mistrustful and jump in with their own premature solutions, thereby sabotaging the arrangement.

Even with the new attitude toward fathering, the internalized traditional values are not easily discarded. In a study based on in-depth interviews with role-sharing fathers, Williams (1988) reported that these couples gradually and unexpectedly found themselves moving toward more traditional roles, with men tending to take on more career commitments as time went on and women spending more time at home with the child. The men in her sample experienced more concern about financial matters than their mates. While feeling very positive about their decision to coparent, they also had to come to terms with the career costs involved. Williams found other gender differences as well. For example, mothers seemed to be more preoccupied with the children. Similarly, Ehrensaft (1987) observed that men and women who coparent actually care for children differently and feel differently about their childrearing roles. Women "are" mothers while men "do" mothering. Thus, the father experiences himself as more separate from the child while the mother feels more connected. Ehrensaft attributes these differences to differences in socialization. Because of the way they are raised, women are more concerned with relational issues and have more fluid ego boundaries than males. Consequently, mothers tend to see the child as an extension of themselves and are preoccupied with child care matters even when away from home, while fathers are better able to set boundaries between work and family. Some quotes from parents illustrate these differences: A mother says, "I'm the worrier in the family. When Steve goes to work, he seems to be able to tune everything out. I envy him for that. I worry about my son's relationship with his friends, what he's doing with the baby-sitter, what school we should apply to, everything!" A father says, "I find that Pam is overly concerned with how the baby looks, I think it's silly to worry about whether his outfit matches or his clothes are pressed."

The facts of biological differences may also have a bearing on the woman's greater immersion in her relationship with her child. At a certain point in prenatal development, the woman and her child are literally one, and it is difficult to say where one begins and the other ends. Breastfeeding also creates a special bond between mother and baby. The intimate, physical relationship between nursing mother and infant has an interpersonal impact. It is often cause for some jealousy and envy on the part of some fathers. It is a poignant reminder of the biological limitation to true equality.

When both parents are intimately involved with their child, there is more room for subtle competition between them for the child's affection. Without clear prescribed division of roles, attachment is based on preference. Ehrensaft (1987) reported a tendency for the young baby in the egalitarian family to prefer one parent over the other. Usually that parent turned out to be the mother. Since it was also the mother who tended to spend more time with the baby, the preference seemed to be environmentally rather than biologically based. The preference was also slight and temporary, shifting as the child went from one developmental period to the next.

While alliances breed discontent and feelings of rejection, they are inevitable concomitants of family life. The Oedipal struggles are as much a reality in sharing families as they are in traditional ones. Ehrensaft (1987) has observed a reversal of the triangle usually observed in traditional families where the bond between mother and child often excludes the father. When men form a powerful bond with their child, it is the mother who may feel left out. Men who nurture their children find that they can be intimate with them in a way that they are unable to be with their wives. Because of the female-dominated childrearing of past generations, men in our culture develop a strong ambivalence toward women. While longing for intimacy, they also put up protective shields against it. Because it is safer to open up with a child who is vulnerable and all-accepting, they can more readily meet their need for connectedness in this relationship. Wives who see their husbands as more empathic and emotionally available to their children are likely to experience jealousy and feel excluded. The interpersonal tensions of family life are more readily acknowledged by couples who share parenting. It has been reported that, as a group, they tend to be more open about their feelings in general (Russell, 1983). Because open communication is crucial to the process of shared parenting, it is assumed that these couples tend to be better at it and can therefore deal with such troublesome feelings more effectively.

Even with its difficulties, the enterprise of shared parenting is attractive to many young couples. They are excited about the possibility of truly sharing in the most significant task of all, that of raising healthy children. While these couples are still in the minority, their numbers are growing. For the new arrangements to take greater hold in our society, however, certain social conditions are necessary. The structure of the economy and the workplace can facilitate or put up barriers to the success of the new arrangements. Better social and economic supports are needed for the sharing family, such as flexible working hours, job-sharing possibilities, and the availability of child care services. As a society we have a lot to gain by these changes, but we are still a long way from egalitarian parenting. We are, however, moving in that direction as fathers become increasingly more involved in family life and mothers pursue careers in greater numbers.

Genuine social and psychological change is a slow process. Even with the remarkable shift in public consciousness about gender roles, internal scripts are not easily discarded. Ideas about who mothers and fathers are derive largely from unconscious identification with one's own parents, and it is those internalized images that have the greatest impact, particularly at times of stress and in uncharted situations such as new parenthood. The deeply entrenched mythology of motherhood is reflected in our vocabulary. When we refer to men bringing up children, we say they are doing the "mothering," as if it were intrinsic to mothers to nurture children. It is likely that it will take several generations before the changes are truly internalized. But what can we expect ultimately?

We look forward to a society where choices are based on personal desire and individual capacity rather than being gender-determined or imposed by cultural stereotypes. A society in which individuals can develop themselves more fully is one that will be less subject to alienation and resentment. Presumably when women are freer to develop identities outside of motherhood, they will be less likely to use their children to fulfill their own unresolved needs. For men, the opportunity to develop the more emotional, tender sides of themselves will be a most valuable development.

We theorize that in such a society there will be fewer gender tensions. When women are the exclusive or primary caretakers, they are unconsciously imbued with incredible power (Dinnerstein, 1976). The infant first experiences the most intense primitive feelings of love and hate with its mother. She is the person who can frustrate the child or gratify its needs. It is with her that the child learns to submit, and it is against her that the child must push in order to become a separate person. Males in particular must leave the female-dominated world of early childhood in order to individuate and develop a sense of wholeness. Because of our species' prolonged dependence and vulnerability throughout life, there remains in us a sense of dread and resentment toward the mother, and a fear of engulfment. Such feelings and fears remain unconscious, exerting their influence indirectly. When men and women equally share the care of their children, the infant, dependent on two human beings to meet its needs, will come to experience the two as equally powerful. The intensity of the emotional attachment, the rage, and the love will be divided and hence less consuming. A child will experience vulnerability, disappointment, and pain, as well as gratification, pleasure, and love, with both a man and a woman. When mothers have less unilateral power, it is expected that engulfment fears will not be as acute and people will be better able to move into intimate relationships.

Finally, we hope that these changes in gender arrangements will facilitate an attitude of greater personal responsibility. If our lives are constricted and unsatisfying, it will be more difficult to hold others responsible. Dinnerstein (1976) writes that "our gender arrangement has helped us keep unintegrated the two sides of our ambivalence about becoming adults, about embracing the freedom and responsibility and loneliness of our actual condition" (p. 249).

Social changes that minimize constriction and encourage personal freedom are essential to help us with the necessary and difficult task of assuming greater responsibility for our lives. Through parenting the next generation, we ourselves have an opportunity to contribute to the changes and enhance the choices.

References

Boston Women's Health Book Collective. (1978). *Ourselves and our children*. New York: Random House.

Dinnerstein, D. (1976). *The mermaid and the minotaur: Sexual arrangements and human malaise.* New York: Harper & Row.

Ehrensaft, D. (1987). *Parenting together: Men and women sharing the care of their children.* New York: Free Press.

Eichenbaum, L., & Orbach, S. (1983). *What do women want: Exploding the myth of dependency.* New York: Coward-McCann.

Erikson, E. (1959). Growth and crises of the healthy personality. *Psychological Issues, 1,* 50–100.

Greenberg, M., & Morris, N. (1982). Engrossment: The newborn's impact upon the father. In S. Cath, A. Gurwitt, & J. M. Ross (Eds.), *Father and child* (pp. 87–100). Boston: Little, Brown.

Kaplan, L. (1978). *Oneness and separateness: From infant to individual.* New York: Simon & Schuster.

Kitzinger, S. (1978). *Women as mothers.* New York: Vintage Books.

Russell, G. (1983). *The changing role of fathers.* St. Lucia, Queensland: University of Queensland Press.

Shorter, E. (1982). *A history of women's bodies.* New York: Basic Books.

Williams, M. (1988). *Fathers involved in parental role-sharing: An experiential study.* Unpublished doctoral dissertation, New York University.

Yalom, I. D. (1980). *Existential psychotherapy.* New York: Basic Books.

Part II
New Reproductive Technologies
From Test Tubes to Surrogates

In Part II of this book, we cautiously enter the biotechnological world of the 21st century. We explore the new reproductive technologies from a unique and balanced perspective. We gather data and generate insights from many sources: empirical research data, case studies, personal experience. Infertility, a deeply painful and spreading phenomenon in our society, is examined psychodynamically (Milden) and through intensive and extensive interviews (Aronowitz and Feldschuh). A psychoanalyst discusses pregnancies that are anonymous (Clamar), and an academician speaks of paternity by proxy (Fidell and Marik *et al.*). The psychological repercussions of conception via artificial insemination are discussed. Once the province of lovemaking, conception takes on a new technological cast. From the deeply private and personal world of sexuality and romance, we enter the sterile, moneyed office of test tubes and white gloves. From the magical realm of suspense and reliance on Mother Nature, we become capable of gender selection (Ullman and Fidell). We are entrusted with sacred knowledge—the gender of our child before birth (Eichholz).

We don't stop there. Biotechnological brilliance (and/or folly) continues. We are now able to choose the baby bearer: who is this person, depicted in the media as either saint or, more likely, villain (Einwohner)? As the numbers in the conception clan increase—biological parent(s), psychological parent(s), the child—we enter into a complex world of interpersonal relationships. Can we maintain our humanity, our sense of boundaries, our human decency and cooperativeness? Or do emotion, indecision, and ultimately, damage and hurt prevail (McArthur)? In assessing the impact of all of this, we look to the individual (Kaley) and sensitively weigh the possibilities. The ultimate effect of biotechnological intervention on an individual woman's sense of self will vary from woman to woman. A healthy and strong body ego can accept change readily and creatively (Bassin).

Chapter 6

A Psychoanalytic Case Study
Infertility, in Vitro Fertilization, and Countertransference

HARRIETTE KALEY

When she first came into therapy, Sally was young, lovely, and starting to disentangle herself from an ungratifying marriage. I was just finishing analytic training and was newly pregnant. It was a hopeful time in both our lives.

Sally was the first by far of my patients to notice my pregnancy. Her alertness to it reflects her own family experience. The oldest of four children, Sally was herself conceived out of wedlock and born when her parents were about 17. They never reconciled themselves to the abrupt ending of their own carefree youth, and the family myth has been that it was having all the children that caused the mother's emotional difficulties years later. A mere 13 months after Sally, her first sister was born. Then there were several miscarriages and ultimately a brother 9 years younger and another sister 12 years younger, both of whom she felt, apparently with much reason, she had to mother. There is little contact these days with the parents, and Sally's willingness to recognize that gaining her parents' affectionate attention is a lost cause is one of the major gains in the therapy.

The tiny upstate New York town Sally calls Dogpatch, where she was born and raised, is part of an area whose emotionally and psychologically deforming provincialism has been impressively documented (Perry, 1982). Because of the early marriage, the father entered the family business; he drank very heavily and was an autocratic, overbearing man with intellectual pretensions. When Sally was growing up, he showed an inordinate amount of cynical interest in her sexuality, conveying to her his conviction that sex, unhappily, made the world go 'round. The mother was a pretty woman, strange and moody, who also drank heavily. She had more recently become drug-dependent, and soon after Sally went off to nursing school, the mother's series of mental hospitalizations began. Needless to add, the household was run haphazardly, and the advantage to Sally of having attractive, youthful parents was offset by their seductiveness to her friends, their alcoholism, their emotional and financial undependability, and the general chaos of their lives.

HARRIETTE KALEY • City University of New York–Brooklyn College, Brooklyn, New York 11210.

With such parents, in such a setting, how could Sally have come to be the functioning, smart, attractive person she was? True, she was in a great deal of personal discomfort, but she was hardworking and successful, well-liked, and intensely involved with the world. The answer must have something to do with the constant presence in her early life of her grandmother, her father's elderly mother. The father and mother hated the grandmother. They made fun of her organized and systematic habits—habits that Sally of course loved—and they tried not to let the grandmother even enter their house, keeping her waiting for Sally out on the back porch. But Sally saw her grandmother every day, and visiting her in her small house right behind the parents' home was the high point of each day. The grandmother seems to have taken genuine and special delight in Sally, listening to her stories, inquiring about her activities, buying her things large and small, taking her on trips to an educated, accomplished maiden aunt in Boston, and sneaking in card games with her on Sundays behind drawn blinds.

When Sally was about 5, she started tiring very easily and falling asleep a lot, even in school. Finally, after long delays and at the school's insistence, the parents took her to a doctor, who diagnosed rheumatic fever and sent her to a cardiologist. The cardiologist was mightily alarmed at her state and prescribed, among other things, what became a year of total bed rest. That illness, the year in bed, and her mother's very ambivalent care of her were decisive for Sally, and her current problems stir up memories of feeling defective, flawed, and excluded from the paradise of her peer group and the anonymity of normality it affords. These memories have fed into her a concern for "looking good," looking as though life is going very well for her, and showing no stigmata of past difficulties.

For several years, the analysis proceeded in predictable ways, fueled by a strong, consistent positive transference.[1] She left her depressed husband even though that meant going to college full time while working double and triple night shifts as a nurse, a profession she hated but the only one really considered possible for women by her family. It was a 3-year period of considerable scrounging and feeling harassed but productive. During that period, she met Dee, the man who is now her husband, and soon their relationship flourished. When they married a year or so after they met, they were happy from the beginning. She and Dee really seemed to like each other, and their sexual intimacy was unparalleled in either one's experience. They were wryly tolerant of each other's often conspicuous foibles, especially his easily evoked anxiety. They shared a remarkably similar vision of the good life, which presupposed a very high level of affluence, and they were delighted when he started making stupendous sums of money almost immediately. He too was in analysis, and it finally looked as though difficulties in that relationship had been worked out. Sally herself was much less anxious and no longer drank to excess or smoked at all, had resolved her conflicting intense feelings about her parents, had finally mourned her grandmother, and had worked through issues of self-concept, assertiveness, and achievement well enough to have changed careers. She no longer had to be solely a "very nice girl." After 7 years of analysis, life looked good.

The picture began to cloud over visibly several years ago. Dee's analyst, a vigorous man in his 50s, died; moreover, he died under circumstances that eerily duplicated

---

[1]Transference is a psychoanalytic concept with technical meaning and many complex implications for treatment. For present purposes, I use it to mean the totality of all the patient's emotional responses to the analyst, both rational and irrational, conscious and unconscious.

those under which Dee's own father had died many years before. This appalling event and its sequelae obscured for a while the fact that after a year or so of dabbling, Sally had that summer gone about in earnest trying to become pregnant, but nothing had happened. Gradually, as the couple tried more and more consistently, even in the face of the by-now-familiar resurgences of marked ambivalence about whether or not they really wanted a baby, it got to be obvious that something was seriously wrong. After months of stress and humiliation, Sally and Dee undertook a complete work-up. I will spare you the details; suffice it that there was at least one attempt at surgical repair of Sally's tubes, and innumerable consultations, estrangements from pregnant friends, tests, doctors' bills, and wild hopeful ups and devastating downs. After about a year or so, the diagnosis, which had been creeping up on everyone, was clear: infertility as an aftermath of pelvic inflammatory disease. Sally later ascertained that the condition was almost certainly the result of an experimental intrauterine device she had used from the time of her divorce until after her marriage.

Sally's feelings of having been betrayed by her doctors and her own body were counterbalanced by her shame and guilt at having brought this on herself. She suffered particularly when people, including her doctor, seemed to assume she had been promiscuous. The charge re-evoked her father's scornful predictions for her sex life, and led her to anguish again over whether something was wrong with her sexuality. She was tormented by how she was marked, by how "different" she would look, by how many aspects of life would now be closed to her.

But the diagnosis, by the time it came, was not entirely unexpected, and Sally and Dee had already begun exploring *in vitro* fertilization programs (IV or IVF programs). Several times they considered adoption, and each time they rejected it. But the demand for admission to IV programs is great, the available openings are few, and Sally's age was close to the cutoff point of 35 for most programs. Thus, the several months that it took to process their application were very troubled.

Sally went on with her life, to all casual appearances, doing good work on her job, pursuing graduate work, being very active in her husband's high-powered new business, and furnishing their new home. But there was a pall over everything, vanquished only temporarily by the trips they took to dream places and by their increasingly expensive and avowedly "preppie" and "yuppie" purchases—both ways of "looking good." Though the money was readily available and their living well would certainly have been expected in any case, the compulsive quality of the shopping during this period was clearly an effort to repair the narcissistic blows.

Finally, several months after applying to IV programs, they got an acceptance from their first choice, and Sally felt as though she'd been accepted for astronaut training. Nevertheless, she and Dee vacillated for a considerable while longer, ostensibly worrying about whether they really wanted to disrupt their lives by this effort, which they had been warned over and over creates great tensions. Several consultants had told them that the stress alone was what limited the number of times most people tried for an *in vitro* pregnancy. But finally they went to the clinic for a 2-day preparatory work-up, and Sally came home jubilant. She found the atmosphere supportive and optimistic; the official statistic was that 90% of all women achieved pregnancy there by the sixth try—a statistic that was touted as better than nature's. She then planned to go there early in the year, the exact date depending on Sally's menstrual cycle.

But as the time drew near, Dee began to have difficulties. His new analyst proposed a month's delay to see if he and Dee could work through Dee's acute anxiety, to moderate what he considered Dee's disengagement and withdrawal from participation in the *in vitro* process. So, literally the evening before Sally was to leave, there was a postponement, and it was more than a month later when they finally went to the clinic. When Sally came back in 2 weeks, she was a basket case.

Just about everything that could have gone wrong had gone wrong. Hormones are administered to trigger superovulation, the eggs being retrieved via laparoscopy—the same surgical technique Sally had previously undergone—fertilized *in vitro*, and then reintroduced, or "transferred," as in embryo transfer. Sally's hormonal levels had remained so low that she fell into the dreaded category of "low responder," a category of women whose chances of achieving an *in vitro* pregnancy is vastly lower than average. Thus, whether or not to "lap" her had become a debate at the clinic. Moreover, within hours after the laparoscopy was done—successfully, as it turned out—Sally went into shock and had to be rushed to the hospital. After she arrived home, the required daily hormone shots caused allergic reactions and abscesses, and the hormones themselves caused a greatly magnified and very unpleasant form of premenstrual tension. When she ultimately learned that she was not pregnant, it had been such an ordeal that the sad news just seemed to fit right in with the downhill run of things.

After that, there was a period of the depression, thrashing about, and consuming involvement with infertility that had been an increasingly prominent part of Sally's life and marriage, side by side with valiant efforts simply to go on with life. Sally and Dee worked hard on the business, and Sally continued to do well on her job. They went to the clinic again in the summer, and this time things went much better. They used slightly different forms of the hormones, in different doses, monitored Sally much more carefully, and the physical processes went relatively smoothly. At home the hormones were given via suppositories rather than injection. But again there was no pregnancy. And still she is a relatively low responder.

The clinic has a rule that each couple may try only twice a year. Sally and Dee are currently in the midst of their third attempt. If they are unsuccessful again, they face the prospect of at least another year and a half before their sixth try—the 90% point—another year and a half of their lives "on hold," as they experience it.

What has happened to the psychoanalysis with all this? Obviously the sense that we were finishing up went by the board. Though Sally struggled mightily to maintain an even keel, many old wounds were reopened. First and foremost, there was resurgence of her sense of being sickly. But it was with much greater intensity this time; now she experienced herself as fundamentally unfit biologically, a basically damaged, weak specimen unsuited for survival except by grace of modern medical miracles. More than that, she came with horror and terror upon the increasing conviction that, when she was sick as a child, her mother had not wholeheartedly wanted her to survive. She has so far acknowledged this awesome conviction without flinching, and has raised some questions about what it did to her, but a full exploration, I think, still lies ahead. Second, there developed a level of anger and narcissistic self-involvement that had not surfaced before; for example, when she caught on that my mother had died and that I was grieving, her sole reaction was fury that, in her eyes, I was not paying enough attention to her. Furthermore, all her personal and social relationships were shaken up, and a great sense of isolation and alienation developed. Though the marriage remained solid through the many anxiety-ridden storms and the many stressful times, Sally worried that the difficulties would ultimately erode even that bond. And overriding everything was a totally revised vision of her life and a vastly undermined self-concept; it had always been somehow understood that, conflicted or not, she would eventually transcend her envy that others had been well cared for in order to care for her own children. Now here was Dee, building a business he ought to be able to leave to his children, but there would be none; and Sally reminded me that, years before, after yet another failed attempt to reach her parents, I had said something to the effect that when she made her own family she would have another chance at the reparative opportunities she longed for. So the bottom line for a while seemed to be that the analysis was doomed to a certain kind of incompleteness.

That, then, is the case history. Now let us turn to questions of the countertransference.[2] What was it like? The very tenor of this chapter reveals much of it. I have had a sense of being with Sally in a state of crisis for over 3 years, with no signs of surcease on the immediate horizon. (Even with an achieved *in vitro* pregnancy, the miscarriage rate is very high.) But why do I call it a *special* issue, a special crisis? After all, long-term crises, if that is not a contradiction in terms, are not unknown in analytic work.

This is a special issue and a special crises for several reasons. For one, the *in vitro* battle against infertility is still new, and the technology is still a marvel and an unknown area to most of us. The first "test-tube baby" was, after all, born only in 1978. Perhaps, some day, *in vitro* fertilization will seem as mundane as such other marvels as VCRs, laser surgery, and space satellites now do, but not now, not yet; it is still a man-made leapfrogging over obstacles that all of human history has accepted as nature's insuperable ones. It is technologically a biological analogue of space flight. Small wonder Sally thought of it as astronaut training.

Because the process is so new, there is little literature and few guidelines for the analyst treating an *in vitro* patient. The special quality of the crisis with Sally is, then, heightened by the paucity of pertinent psychological knowledge. Sally and I have only our own analytic work to help us know what parts of her response are appropriate and realistic, given the situation, and what parts are idiosyncratic and analyzable. It is a lot like trying to figure out what part of a person's reaction to alcohol is due to the drug and what part to his own character structure without knowing anything about the typical effects of the drug.

The medical literature of *in vitro* fertilization and embryo transfer has just begun to publish material on the psychological status of applicants to programs. So far that material focuses primarily on screening to eliminate couples with grossly disqualifying conflicts about pregnancy, and on surveying the applicant population. It finds that population not significantly different from the general population as measured by, for example, the Minnesota Multiphasic Personality Inventory, a well-known paper-and-pencil test (Freeman, Boxer, Rickels, Tureck, & Mastroianni, 1985). However, longitudinal studies of those selected and those rejected, studies of how people respond to selection, rejection, success, and failure, do not exist. One thing is clear, though, even now: The IV teams take it as a given that infertility itself is a stressor, and that the *in vitro* processes are especially stressful. They take it for granted that perfectly normal people will be sorely tried by *in vitro* fertilization. More individualized

---

[2] I use the term *countertransference* in a way that parallels the definition of *transference*. The difference lies only in that countertransference refers to the analyst's emotional responses to the patient. Historically, countertransference has evolved considerably as a therapeutic tool. Initially considered an obstacle in treatment, it is now generally viewed as an inevitable accompaniment in the process and one that, if deftly used, illuminates the nature of the patient's difficulties.

approaches, however, more psychoanalytic reports, reports of the interaction of character structure and the *in vitro* experience do not yet exist. So in the area of the psychoanalytic significance of the experience and the natural history of the personal response, there are no navigational charts.

Then there is also the fact that Sally is a very expressive person, very intense, and when she is not concerned with looking good, there is nothing subdued about her pain. In this special area, there has rarely been a respite from the turmoil. Creating space in which to do the analytic work has itself become an issue, and the constant *Sturm und Drang* has contributed to my sense of being in a long-term crisis. Even when my own defensive needs lead me to move away from the enveloping tumult, as I shall describe later, it is seldom long before an urgent *cri de coeur* from her recalls me to the place of crisis.

But that tumult seems secondary somehow, regardless of how superficially compelling. What seems more important, and more seriously countertransferential, is that I have found myself musing from time to time on the irony that Sally might be denied the symmetry of finishing treatment being herself pregnant, having begun it while I was pregnant. Can the damage done to the fantasy of completing the analysis in a poetically satisfying way not be affecting the work? Sally articulated the fantasy a long time ago, and it seemed not unrealistic at the time; was my grandiosity running rampant? Is it her hubris or mine that is now being dashed? Or is it perhaps something different: Is not the real countertransferential danger that in my sadness for her, I mistake a happy ending for real analytic work, and undermine an authentic termination by replacing continued analytic work with misguided sympathy, thus preventing her completing the analytic part of her progress through life?

Then, of course, there is the fact that Sally's problem speaks to the heart of especially delicate areas of a woman's life, mine as well as hers. Obvious as it is, I think, this is countertransferentially and defensively easy to overlook; she, after all, is over there and I, thank heaven, am over here. Or am I? Sally's infertility has surfaced as my own reproductive years draw to a close. Can that possibly not affect our work? The awareness of the loss of some of life's potentials, the sense of the ending of a set of possibilities—can Sally's struggles with these not resonate for me? It is more than an empathic understanding of what it might mean to be unwillingly destined to childlessness (and I do not think I am romanticizing parenthood—it is a question of lack of choice, not which is the *right* choice). It is that Sally's sharply focused difficulty is a reminder of a more diffuse fact of my own life: the fact that getting older means not having all the options of youth, especially the reproductive ones. This is a sobering truth that I would probably not have to confront so regularly or so frontally were it not for Sally's constant battle for fertility.

In our day-to-day work, what has emerged as the Scylla and Charybdis of the countertransference are outgrowths of these issues and feelings in the forms of defensive detachment and disengagement on the one hand, and overidentification and overinvolvement on the other. In the labyrinth of affects and events that is the analysis, the thread I have found most useful to follow in tracking my contribution is that of where I stand in relation to those two markers. The problem is subtle: It is knowing which side I am leaning slightly toward, for even my countertransferential interactions with Sally get more refined and cunningly concealed with practice. For example, the first session after Sally returned from her first *in vitro* attempt and told what had happened, my recollection is that I mostly listened, feeling great sympathy, concern, and empathy with her sense of dashed hopes. But within a few days, it seems to me now, I had absorbed it, assimilated it to the rest of the complicated story, and was back in there, chin up, ready to work. I now wonder if there wasn't more than a touch in that of denial of the pain that walked into the room with Sally, and, even more, a denial of my own helplessness.

Another example, this time of veering toward the other hazardous rock, the one of overidentification: Sally has typically experienced "looking good" and being the object of much envy and competitiveness as just an aspect of her being, like her extraordinary coloring, that excited jealousy in others through no fault of her own. Since the infertility, it has emerged more clearly as a goal she pursues assiduously and quite effectively, given her natural endowments, her material means, and her devotion to the cause. I think it was because of my sympathy for her, leading to an ill-advised reluctance to undermine one of her few current sources of solid satisfactions, that only recently have we begun, with my prodding, to wonder about the emphasis on "looking good" in all its many manifestations. It turns out that she has never questioned it, imagines it is a universal instinct, and that everyone admires the same emblems of success and achievement that she does, and is amazed and not a little chagrined to find us exploring analytically its various aspects, from the competitive ones through the distancing machinations to the counterphobic behaviors.

A realm in the analysis that is even more important than the countertransferences *per se*, and how I monitor them, is the way all these transferences and countertransferences play themselves out in the treatment, layered upon each other in evolving and mutually transforming ways. The work of various interpersonal psychoanalysts, such as Ehrenberg (1985), Epstein and Feiner (1979), and Greenberg (1986), has been illuminating in this area. Particularly salient are Levenson's (1972, 1983, 1988) descriptions of how patient and analyst interact to transform each other, and of how the heart of the analysis is to break the stranglehold of those transformations and to increase the range of semiotic signs and signals to which the patient responds. Has Sally transformed me? Of course she has. With the help of my own countertransferential reluctance to seem insufficiently sympathetic, she has transformed me into much the same sort of kindly, older woman she knows so well how to be with. She has recreated of me a contemporary grandmother. She acts out with me—or "acts in" the transference—her expectation that a benevolent woman, even one who, like her grandmother, is forbidden to enter her world of action (if not by her parents, as in days of old, then by psychoanalytic restraint) will back her up emotionally in some immensely reassuring way that she seems not to realize is nevertheless enormously infantilizing.

Some of this became clearer as a result of her behavior when she went to the clinic. Despite her teariness and distress at leaving me, and despite her elaborate plans, she did not avail herself of any of the many opportunities to keep in touch. Raising questions about this, and about the complete compartmentalization she reported experiencing when she got to the clinic, reopened the period when she had gone away to nursing school. She had always reported her sense that her parents virtually abandoned her when she left home, in line with the father's dictum that at 18 years of age, the fledglings get pushed out of the nest. Now she realized that she, for her part, had never contacted her grandmother while she was away. She had never written or called her grandmother while she was away at school, had never given her gifts, not even a birthday card (and gifts are very important to Sally), and had in fact never thought much at all about her grandmother's feelings independent of her relations with Sally. Furthermore, it became increasingly clear that she has treated me much as she did her equally well-loved grandmother—that is, as an unending source of good to whom she need give nothing in turn except the very fact of her existence. This material led into Sally's becoming aware that she had been expecting me magically to fix her, as her grandmother had miraculously made things better just by being there. Most recently, it has led to exploring her disguised but massive resistance to deepening and expanding the analytic work instead of merely going around in affectively heavy-laden circles. This is, as I understand it, a way Sally is in the treatment that has many roots and many meanings; one thing it is about, I gather, is an insistence that I love her just as she is. Since her sense of her mother's malevolence requires the antidote of believing in her grandmother's gratification at the mere fact of her existence, it is not surprising that the resistance has been obstinate.

As we explored these materials and their isomorphisms in the transference and countertransference, we moved onto another level from which to address the material. As Levenson (1983) puts it, the helical spiral of engagement between analyst and patient through which understanding develops got kicked up to another, broader level. What I now realized was that not only was I often listening attentively, but also there was simply nothing for me to do. I can't say that I was bored, or even that I felt helpless or impotent; however, I was able to address an aspect of my experience with Sally that I had previously not attended to, not because it didn't exist, but because our transformations of each other had precluded attending to those aspects. Now I started intervening on the basis of my realization that the meshing of my defensive distancing and her demand that people recapitulate with her the paradigm of well-being she developed with her grandmother had transformed me into a patient, benign nonentity. To remain that way would be to help her perpetuate the past forever, and my task now is to enlarge the range of our interactions and thus expand her possibilities for the future.

To illustrate this material and to show how I approached the issues in our actual sessions, here are some data from the last few sessions we had, just before she left for her third visit to the clinic.

Sally had just recently learned that her youngest sister, because of childhood neglect, has a potentially serious heart murmur. She talked about this seriously and intelligently in one session, then in the next few got very engrossed in her plans for vacations after her return. She has felt very deprived by having to use vacation time and money for her clinic visits for the last year and a half; they are, she points out, not very relaxing or pleasant, and her spectacular vacations have played a big part in helping her "look good." Eventually, recognizing that I risked feeling—or even being, or at least being considered—cruel and unempathic, I raised some pointed questions about these plaints, noting particularly that we'd known of these feelings for a long time but knew little more about them now than we'd always known.

A few days later, she dreamed that her husband, whose driving worries her, was driving right on the tail of the car ahead to make it speed up. She yelled at him and even got out of the car. He tried to get her to get back in, but finally he drove off alone and she woke up screaming for him not to leave her. She also dreamed that night of three women with brain tumors, some of whom knew their condition, some of whom didn't. Her associations were to how women at the clinic feel "broken." It makes her nervous about losing her husband, whom she sees as "a good catch." She was glad that she herself was not visibly disfigured, as she feared she might be from the laparoscopies, and had in fact been feeling more normal, even more sexual. I wondered aloud again at the familiarity of this material, and about whether

Dee's need in the dream to speed things up and his ultimately astonishing and horrifying her by leaving her had referred to us as well as to her concerns about him.

That night she dreamed she was in a plane going somewhere on a trip. The pilot came down close to the vegetation and the grasses, to let the passengers see them as part of the educational aspects of the trip. They landed in Russia, and there was a handsome man at the border, a Russian functionary of some sort, who spoke English and was friendly. She tested him by speaking French. There was a fence, but it was really just a series of posts. Beyond it was a new, modern city with beautiful vistas, even though the land she was on was flat.

In working on the dream, she averred her preference for staying with the old; the new modern city did not entice her at all in the dream. We talked about her refusal to move into new territory, or to speak the other person's language, or even a language they had in common. She responded by pointing out that even though at the time of the dream the Russians were defined as friendly, they are in her estimation really the enemy, and their friendly behavior is suspect. It developed ultimately that she was concerned that I had turned on her; avowing that she "can't do it any other way," she doesn't understand what I could be talking about.

Since this was within a few days of her leaving again for the clinic, the temptation was great to smooth over her anxiety, reassure her of my goodwill, and send her off without the added burden of wondering whether or not I would leave her if she resisted speeding things up or moving into new territory. By now I knew that my countertransferential wish to lighten her load led merely to another dead end. It would simply wind up having us again reenact her early drama with her loving grandmother, who nevertheless had no active role in Sally's life outside the charmed circle. So we stayed with the dream material and the resistances in it.

The next session, she reported being awakened by her husband's agitation. He was "beating the drums" again, the more so the closer he got to consummating a crucial business arrangement. She made some discerning comments about his dynamics, and how such frenzy repeated both their experiences with their families and how it served him to keep him from concentrating on his analysis. She felt she should be protected from some of this, that she had a lot of very tough things of her own going on. At the same time, she thought that maybe I'd been saying to her that she herself had been doing that kind of thing, "keeping everything up in the air" wildly, for the last few years; nevertheless, she felt wronged that he was disregarding what was happening to her. To complicate things further, she reiterated feeling that she has to listen to his hysteria about his business because he listened to her about her infertility. But then she seemed to move into new territory.

She began talking about a dawning realization that her way of getting sympathy was to get very "emotional." She thought her emotionality was related to her survival; she realized that her sister's heart problems had been ignored but that hers had not been because the "whole neighborhood could see how sick [she] was." It shows, she said, how the volume had to be turned up high in her experience for anyone to be listened to. This was the first clear recognition so far that her affective expressiveness was anything other than emotional richness. The session ended with an engrossing and promising discussion of how well her grandmother had listened, even without the volume being turned up, but of how impotent she was.

The next session, on the day of the evening she was departing for the clinic, Sally was feeling tense and weepy. She'd had a dream: She was in a hotel, perhaps the hotel associated with the clinic, and was trying to check out but realized she'd left her clothes in the room, and because she had also left her key in the room, she was afraid she couldn't get her clothes back. At the same time, she was saying good-bye to girls from her high school, trying to look brave. But it was also as if she were just going to the clinic, instead of having finished, as in the first part. Then she was getting an injection, realized her menstrual period hadn't even started yet, that she'd "really screwed up," and that maybe they would send her home. It was, she acknowledged, a true anxiety dream. She elaborated: She thought the dream had to do with her feeling that she'd had the key, to her marriage for example—and, I take it for granted, to the treatment—but she now wonders if she's lost the key, or we might add, has locked herself out. The girls are her high school friends; she described herself as trying in the dream to "look like Grace Kelly" but nevertheless signaling her friends secretly to cross their fingers for her—a most un-Grace Kelly indication of concern. Sally spoke of how she had had no contact with her friends after she left for school, in much the same way as she had not maintained contact with her grandmother. She remembered that she had been quite depressed after she came to nursing school, and that had always seemed to her the reason she had not written to her hometown friends or even visited them on her rare visits home. But actually, now it seemed that she didn't want them to know that things were not going perfectly for her in the Big City—that is, she wanted to "look good" to them. As she went on to end the session, she said, "In the last two years, I haven't gotten very involved in anything because I just don't want to just get up and leave [as she might have to at any time when the clinic called]. Right now I don't feel like our relationship is very comforting. . . . I feel I should be serene when I go there. . . . You must be pretty mad at me. . . . Well, at least we didn't waste the last two months talking about infertility. . . . I wish I could go back to just being in love with you."

But that evening, in the therapy group she had been in for several years, Sally began the session by telling the members she was grateful to them for having changed the time of the meeting so she could be there that night. She'd been ambivalent about that, but now she told them her dream and said she realized that she had been so busy looking like Grace Kelly, elegantly cool and unruffled, that she had never again contacted her old high school friends after she had gone off to nursing school. Now she realized she had, after all, let us know about her concerns, even though a part of her imagined she wanted to be, and indeed felt she was, aristocratically reserved. She said she realized the group had responded despite her mixed signals—just as, in the dream, she allowed crossed fingers to show—and that she was really glad of that. She was not particularly intense or dramatic about it, but the group meeting that night went on in a kind of straightforwardness and openness that everyone understood was unprecedented.

What does this material, especially the dreams, say about the interplay of transference and countertransference? Now that Sally has noticed that the web of deforming transformations is no longer so effectively enmeshing, has she responded transferentially by seeing me as the enemy? in disguise? a friendly enemy? Have I, perhaps in some real way, been turned into an enemy? But then, is she not enticing us back into the web by being a good patient and a good student? She knows I have been involved with teaching, and her association to the grasses and the vegetation, the educational part of the dream trip, is to her maiden aunt's elevated but tedious interest in the Audubon Society, and to the field guides she has seen in my office. Is she showing again the lengths she will go to in order to be grandma's wonderful little girl? There is no real barrier to her entering the new foreign territory, just a series of boundary markers, and she knows she'll have a wider and better view from the other side; yet she remains at the border, just talking—and testing by that very talking.

I think she is inviting me to prolonged but guarded negotiations at the border by appealing to our mutual wish, for our own reasons, and for some that grow out of our interaction, not to foist on her still another arduous journey on top of the one she is already embarked on. There is an indication in the final dream that this temptation was avoided: She was anxious and felt she might have locked herself out—of precisely what is not perfectly clear, but considering the role of clothes in her life, it probably had something to do not just with "looking good" as such but with having access to all of life's good things, and of course to the important relationships in her life. In the dream, she felt she had really mistimed something, had angered the authorities, and would be punished by banishment and abandonment. But the next day, as time went on and as a result of our work with the dream, Sally had developed an awareness of her own potential for cutting herself off from support by well-wishers by needing to look regally self-sufficient.[3] Her behavior that same evening in the group showed that allaying her anxiety in her customary ways, usually a top priority with her, had not remained in that position. I think the reason the group responded as it did was that it recognized a less contrived, less princess-y if you will, less double-binding appeal from her than she had hitherto made. For both Sally and the group, the range of signs and signals that was allowed to operate was broader and more complete than before. My hope is that, when she returns, this newly enlarged sense of herself and her relations to the world will not retreat under the buffeting of further real defeats and their attendant pains and anxieties or even under the ecstasy of a successful pregnancy, and that we can continue our voyage into new territory.

To summarize, this material, as a life story, illustrates the profound impact of fertility problems on a woman and her marriage. The resurrection of parts of her past that might otherwise have seemed resolved is particularly striking. Furthermore, as a psychoanalytic case history, the material demonstrates the inevitable engagement of patient and analyst in delicate issues of transference and countertransference. The subtle and varied transferences and countertransferences then fed the processes of our mutual transformations. The termination phase of this analysis really began, I think, when as both a *result* of my participation with the patient, witting and unwitting, and by *means* of that participation with her, we began exploring the interplay between us. That kind of exploration promises to open up the self-perpetuating maze of our reciprocal transformations, to let in more light.

References

Ehrenberg, D. B. (1985). Countertransference resistance. *Contemporary Psychoanalysis, 21*, 563–576.
Epstein, L. & Feiner, A. H. (1979). Countertransference: The therapist's contribution to treatment. *Contemporary Psychoanalysis, 15*, 489–513.
Freeman, E. W., Boxer, A. S., Rickels, K., Tureck, R. & Mastroianni, L. (1985). Psychological evaluation and support in a program of in vitro fertilization and embryo transfer. *Fertility and Sterility, 43*, 48–53.

---

[3]That stance may also have something to do with Sally's identification with me. In the time since the dream was reported, it has occurred to me to wonder if Kelly is a transformation, to stick to my model, of Kaley.

Greenberg, J. R. (1986). Theoretical models and the analyst's neutrality. *Contemporary Psychoanalysis, 22,* 76–86.
Levenson, E. A. (1972). *The fallacy of understanding.* New York: Basic Books.
Levenson, E. A. (1983). *The ambiguity of change.* New York: Basic Books.
Levenson, E. A. (1988). The pursuit of the particular. *Contemporary Psychoanalysis, 24,* 1–16.
Perry, H. S. (1982). *Psychiatrist of America: The life of Harry Stack Sullivan.* Cambridge: Harvard University Press.

Chapter 7
Paternity by Proxy
Artificial Insemination with Donor Sperm

LINDA S. FIDELL AND JAROSLAV MARIK
WITH JOAN E. DONNER, CHRIS JENKINS-BURK, JANIE KOENIGSBERG,
KATHY MAGNUSSEN, CYNTHIA MORGAN, AND JODIE B. ULLMAN

Insemination of women with sperm collected from an anonymous donor—artificial insemination donor (AID)—produced an estimated 5000 to 10,000 births per year in the United States, and another 7000 in Western European countries, Japan, and Australia 10 years ago (Behrman, 1979). In the last 10 years the rate of use of the procedure has probably increased. There are at least 250,000 children conceived by AID currently living in the United States, a number that is very likely underestimated owing to inadequate statistics and the secrecy surrounding the procedure.

AID is used as a remedy for certain types of infertility. Infertility is defined as failure of conception after 1 year of unprotected intercourse and is estimated to affect one couple in six. According to a recent study by Menken, Trussell, and Larsen (1986), however, the rate of infertility may be even higher, affecting 26% of women below 30, 35% of women between 30 and 34, and 44% of women between 35 and 39. Among couples with infertility, between 30 and 40% of the cases are due to male infertility, and 20% due to infertility in both partners.

When the male produces no sperm, has severe inheritable genetic factors, or has Rh incompatibility with his mate, AID is an alternative. When the male produces few sperm or sperm with limited viability, or suffers impotence, premature ejaculation, or hypospadias, insemination of the woman with sperm from her mate, called

---

LINDA S. FIDELL • Department of Psychology, California State University, Northridge, California 91330.   JAROSLAV MARIK • The Tyler Medical Clinic, Inc., Los Angeles, California 90024.   JOAN E. DONNER • Private practice, 1100 Glendon Avenue, Los Angeles, California 90024.   CHRIS JENKINS-BURK • Richard G. Jones, Ph.D., and Associates, and Adjunct Faculty, Psychology Department, Houston Community College System, Houston, Texas 77054.   JANIE KOENIGSBERG • Educational Therapy Programs, 10877 Rose Avenue, Los Angeles, California 90034.   KATHY MAGNUSSEN • Department of Psychology, California State University, Northridge, California 91330.   CYNTHIA MORGAN • Institute for Psychological Development, Thousand Oaks, California 91360.   JODIE B. ULLMAN • Department of Psychology, California State University, Northridge, California 91330.

artificial insemination homologous (AIH), may be tried (Gilbert, 1976). Insemination with sperm from either donor or mate is indicated when the woman has certain anatomic anomalies of the vagina or cervix, or hostile cervical mucus. Both forms of insemination may involve either fresh or frozen (and thawed) sperm, although if the mate's sperm are already compromised they may not survive the freezing and thawing process (Beck & Wallach, 1981). When used with women who are fertile, AID is successful about 70 to 80% of the time (Aiman, 1982).

AID and AIH are most often performed by medical personnel. Anonymous donors make contributions to a sperm bank from which samples are selected that are likely to produce a baby who matches certain characteristics of the woman's mate, or has characteristics that she has specified. The process involves, at a minimum, a donor, a woman, a physician, and, if the process is biologically successful, a child. Usually, but not always, there is also a husband or mate to be considered. If the process is to be psychologically successful, the rights and needs of, and consequences to, all participants must be considered.

But AID is not necessarily a very technically sophisticated procedure. It can also be accomplished with various devices available to nontrained personnel and outside medical practice. This method of producing children is sometimes used in the gay community, although the number of children conceived in this manner is not known.

What are the psychological consequences of use of AID—of cutting the link between procreation and arguably our most human act? How does the public view these activities? Who are the donors and what are the consequences of donation to them? Who are the single women who seek AID and why do they prefer it over more natural methods? Is a marriage disrupted by introduction of a child biologically linked to the wife but not to the husband? What about the child? Is it a problem for a child to be born of an anonymous donor, perhaps long dead? Should the child be told about his or her method of conception? Does the child have a right to knowledge of the donor? Is the child harmed intellectually by the processes of freezing, storing, and thawing sperm?

Psychological Consequences of Infertility

To evaluate the psychological consequences of the use of AID, the consequences of AID have to be weighed against the consequences of infertility. And there is little doubt regarding the adverse psychological impact of infertility, at least among those who present themselves to infertility clinics.[1]

In 1973, Platt, Ficher, and Silver compared infertile men and women with fertile controls on several personality and attitudinal scales. They found that infertile women had increased emotional disturbance on the Group Personality Projective Test, while both infertile men and women saw themselves as less in charge of their lives (external locus of control) and not as similar to their ideal selves as the controls. Bresnick and Taymor (1979) found that infertility was associated with increased guilt, anger, frustration, and isolation. Infertile patients in the study by Rosenfeld and Mitchell (1979) reported sexual dysfunction, fear, anxiety, isolation, depression, inadequacy

---

[1]There are undoubtedly people who are not adversely affected by infertility, and, indeed, some who must welcome it. Because they do not show up at infertility clinics, however, they are not available for research, and the rates of neutral or positive responses to infertility have not been estimated.

of gender role, and external locus of control. Both the latter two groups of researchers concluded that there were beneficial effects of psychotherapy in helping the patients come to terms with their infertility. For a more thorough review of many studies that examined the psychological consequences of infertility prior to 1980, see Berk and Shapiro (1984).

In a recent Swedish study, 30 women with tubal damage and 29 mates reported negative effects on their sexual lives; the women experienced fear and anxiety prior to reconstructive tubal surgery, while the men reported shame and degradation during semen analysis. The period after surgery, if pregnancy did not occur, was particularly stressful (Lalos, Lalos, Jacobsson, & von Schoultz, 1985a). However, personality factors such as neuroticism and extroversion were not affected (Lalos, Lalos, Jacobsson, & von Schoultz, 1985b).

O'Moore, O'Moore, Harrison, Murphy, and Carruthers (1983) found that infertile women were more anxious, tense, introverted, and prone to guilt feelings than female controls. Valentine (1986) interviewed 26 infertile men and women and found that they were sad, depressed, angry, confused, desperate, hurt, embarrassed, and humiliated. They also seemed disorganized, distracted, exhausted, moody, and obsessive—in short, extremely stressed. Link and Darling (1986) surveyed 103 infertile men and women and found that they expressed frustration, isolation, and anger as well as a decline in marital and sexual satisfaction.

Mahlstedt (1985) summarized the reactions of infertile patients as depression, loss, stress, anger, and guilt. In this case, the loss is related not only to the potential child but also to an important bodily function, physical attractiveness, status, prestige, self-esteem, sense of control, and hope. Menning (1980) found that infertile couples experience, in order, surprise, denial, anger, isolation, guilt, and grief—the same sequence experienced by those who are terminally ill. In fact, according to Bernstein, Potts, and Mattox (1985, p. 65s), "infertility is experienced as a loss equal to a death...."

Couples who are participating in programs of *in vitro* fertilization seem to experience the same, if not greater, levels of psychological distress (Fagan *et al.*, 1986; Freeman, Boxer, Rickels, Tureck, & Mastroianni, 1985).

But Is Psychological Stress a Cause of Infertility?

The distress of couples experiencing infertility was noted by previous researchers, and, when no biological cause of infertility was readily apparent, it was suggested that stress might have caused the infertility. Underlying psychological conflict (perhaps of a Freudian nature), emotional disturbance, or neurotic personality configurations were thought to interfere with conception. However, as Hertz (1982) and O'Moore *et al.* (1983) have noted, these speculations may confuse cause and effect. It is just as likely that infertility causes emotional disturbance as that emotional disturbance causes infertility. The evidence is not yet clear as to which direction of causality, if either, is more likely.

Several studies suggest that emotional disturbance is an effect rather than a cause of infertility. Harrison, O'Moore, and O'Moore (1981) found that patients with infertility were under more stress than fertile patients, but infertile female patients who began to ovulate and those who were eventually conceived did not differ in stress levels from those who did not. Similarly, Garcia *et al.* (1985) found that anovulatory women who became ovulatory, and pregnant, when given clomiphene citrate or a placebo did not differ on a number of psychological measures from those who did not. They concluded that there is a placebo effect, but no psychogenic factors, in infertility.

Similarly, Freeman, Garcia, and Rickels (1983) found lower self-esteem and sexual satisfaction but not greater neurosis among infertile women as compared with fertile controls. Brand (1982) found no differences on personality tests between women with functional and organic infertility. Brand, Roos, and van der Merwe (1982) could not distinguish between women with functional (no diagnosed organic source) and organic infertility on the basis of lability in physiological reactions to emotional stress.

Other studies suggest that emotional disturbance can be a cause of infertility. Nijs, Koninckx, Verstraeten, Mullens, and Nicasy (1984) found that women with LUF (luteinized unruptured follicle) syndrome scored even higher on state anxiety scales than women with other forms of infertility, women who have an infertile partner, or fertile women. They conclude that stress either causes or exacerbates this form of infertility, which, in the past, was undiagnosed, and therefore, thought to be a functional or psychological infertility. Morse and Dennerstein (1985) found that, among 30 women who were participating in IVF, those with functional infertility were more neurotic and had lower marital satisfaction than those with organic infertility.[2] Finally, Sarrel and DeCherney (1985) reported that couples with secondary infertility who were given psychotherapy had a higher pregnancy rate than those who did not have therapy, but the samples were very small.

However the causal chain eventually works out (and it will probably prove to be a vicious circle), it is clear that infertility is associated with considerable psychological stress among people who present themselves for treatment at infertility clinics. For a substantial number of these people, AID will turn out to be the only viable option. Is it a good one?

Between 1979 and 1983, we conducted a number of studies of attitudes about AID among the public (Donner and Morgan), among donors and a matched group of nondonors (Jenkins-Burk and Magnussen), and among single women who had requested AID (Morgan). In addition, there was a study of the intellectual level, perceptual-motor abilities, and language development of the children produced by AID (Koenigsberg). Many of the research ideas were initially developed by Marik, and several of the studies were conducted through the Tyler Clinic in Los Angeles. The research designs and analyses were supervised or provided by Fidell. Ullman located and collected a nearly complete set of published articles on psychological consequences of infertility and AID. The remainder of this chapter summarizes this work and integrates it into the published literature on AID.

Attitudes toward AID

Public Attitudes

An early study of the acceptability of AID and AIH was conducted by Greenberg (1951), who found that, among students, 52% approved of AID and 90% approved

---

[2]Marital satisfaction scores were lower in the functional than in the organic group, but still higher than Australian norms for both groups. The researchers also report that the functional group had a more internal locus of control than the organic group, a result that is theoretically hard to understand. In fact, inability to diagnose the reasons for infertility might lead to neuroses.

of AIH. These rates of acceptance were considerably higher than the rates found in a 1970 United States national poll where 26% approved of AID and 55% of AIH (Francoeur, 1970).

In 1979 Morgan and Donner studied the acceptability of AID, AIH, IVF with own ovum, and IVF with donor ovum among 195 college students. The students seemed to have a "live and let live" attitude about use of these techniques: They accepted their use by others (99% approved AIH, 88% approved AID, 93% approved IVF with own ovum, and 85% approved IVF with donor ovum) but had some reluctance to use them themselves, particularly with donor gametes (88% accepted AIH for self, 38% AID, 78% IVF with own ovum, and 38% IVF with donor ovum).

In 1980 Donner and Morgan extended the study of acceptance of AIH, AID, and IVF to the general public by conducting a telephone interview lasting about 10 minutes with each of the 100 randomly selected male and female residents of a residential, light industrial suburb of Los Angeles. The pattern of results was similar to that of the students. There was greater acceptance of use of these techniques by others (89% approved AID, 95% approved IVF with own ovum, and 77% approved IVF with donor ovum) than by themselves (52% approved AID, 90% approved IVF with own ovum, and 77% approved IVF with donor ovum).[3]

These results suggest that it is not the method of conception that is at issue, but rather the question of genetic linkage to the parents. If the genetic linkage to both parents is preserved either with AIH or a couple's own ovum and sperm, then almost all respondents find the techniques acceptable. If donor gametes are used (through AID or IVF with donor ovum) then acceptance is less, but still the norm, particularly when the genetic link is preserved for the mother rather than the father. That is, respondents find AID (where genetic linkage is lost for the father) more acceptable for themselves and others than IVF with donor ovum (where genetic linkage is lost for the mother).

Several legal issues were also addressed during the interview and there was widespread consensus on them. Respondents overwhelmingly believed that a child produced by AID is legitimate (89%), that the mother's husband should be considered the legal father (94%), that the child should not be entitled to inherit from the donor (71%), and that the donor should not be entitled to inherit from the child (83%). Similarly, when IVF is used with donated ova, 90% of the respondents considered the child legitimate and 83% considered the legal mother to be the woman who gestates and gives birth to the child. A total of 89% agreed that receiving donor ova or sperm did *not* constitute adultery. However, the respondents strongly favored (94%) requiring consent from both the recipient and mate before undergoing these procedures.

Respondents were of more mixed opinion regarding who should benefit from these procedures. When asked whether AID should be available to single women, 47% agreed, 16% were neutral, and 37% disagreed. When asked whether AID should be available to lesbians, 41% agreed, 21% were neutral, and 38% disagreed.

Several questions regarding the donors were posed. When asked if donors should be paid, 32% agreed, 29% were neutral, and 39% disagreed. Over half of the respondents (54%) thought children born as a result of these procedures should be told how they were conceived. However, only 28% thought the child should have the right to discover the identity of the donor, and there was nearly universal (96%)

---

[3]Respondents were not asked about the acceptability of AIH for self or others.

disagreement with the notion that the donor should be obligated to support a child conceived through his or her gametes. Thus, although opinions were split about whether a child conceived by AID or IVF should be informed, there was a consensus that the child should *not* have the right to discover the identity of the donor and should not expect any form of support from the donor.

Part of the survey involved questions about the acceptability of experimentation with fertilized human ova. A total of 52% of the respondents found experimentation acceptable (19% were neutral and 29% disagreed); 59% found it acceptable to destroy fertilized ova in the experimental process (16% were neutral and 25% disagreed).

When asked about the role of government in research and regulation of reproductive technology, 61% agreed that "people should be given the opportunity to have children by any method available without government regulation" (15% were neutral and 24% disagreed), but 50% thought the government should provide funds for reproductive research. Regarding the issue of who should make rules and regulations having to do with these methods, 7% thought government, 15% thought doctors, and 4% favored individuals; 74% favored some combination, mostly of doctors in combination with government, individuals, or religious leaders. Clearly, the public felt that physicians should be involved in the decision making, but not as sole agents.

Single respondents were more accepting than married respondents of AID or IVF (with donor ova) for single women, and of experimentation with fertilized human ova in a laboratory. People without children were more accepting than those with children of experimentation on fertilized human ova. Apparently, single people saw more value in preserving reproductive options for those like themselves than did married people, who may place greater value in a two-parent family. Married people and those with children had greater doubt about experimentation with fertilized human ova, although, on balance, they still favored it.

Some attitudes about use of AID were related to religious views. For instance, only about a third of Catholics, compared with over half of members of other religious categories, were willing to use AID (or IVF) if it was the only way to become pregnant. On another issue, Jews and those who professed no religion, as compared with Protestants and Catholics, more consistently thought that children produced from donor sperm or ova should be so informed, although in all religious categories, the majority of respondents thought that children should be informed.

Recent and broad public acceptance of these techniques has also been found in New Zealand (Aickin, 1985) and in a large sample of women of childbearing age in Scotland (Alder *et al.*, 1986).

User Secrecy

Widespread public acceptance of AID contrasts sharply with user secrecy. Virtually all research finds that couples—in England (Ledward, Symonds, & Eynon, 1982), Australia (Clayton & Kovacs, 1982), Sweden (Milsom & Bergman, 1982), and Canada (Berger, Eisen, Shuber, & Doody, 1986)—are very unlikely to tell anyone, even members of their own families, about their use of AID. In these studies, approximately 80% (68% in the Canadian sample) of the couples have kept AID a secret from everyone, including their own parents and especially the child. Once conception occurs, in fact, AID parents often arrange delivery through an obstetrician who is unaware of the use of AID, and who in good faith puts the name of the husband on the birth certificate as the biological father (Curie-Cohen, Luttrell, & Shapiro, 1979).

Although perhaps originally intended to protect the donor, secrecy seems to have evolved as a protection for the husband (Karow, 1982), who fears ridicule if it becomes known that he is sterile; other considerations are avoidance of labels (such as "bastard") for the child, religious proscriptions against AID, and avoidance of legal entanglements with the donor concerning liability and inheritance laws. Miall (1985) argues that infertility is stigmatizing—is a negative condition that represents failure—and that "male infertility is more stigmatizing that female infertility" (p. 383). Men see it as a real threat to masculinity, particularly because it is associated with impotence in the minds of many.

But secrecy may also stem from unresolved conflicts and failure to accept infertility on the part of the couple. Both Berger (1980) and Sokoloff (1987) discuss the potential harmful consequences to the family and the child when there is secrecy surrounding use of AID. Clamar (1980, p. 177) states, "By its very nature, a secret is a potent force, assuming undue proportion and power within the family—an existential fact that remains unspoken, yet controls and colors the lives of the people involved." Elsewhere, Clamar (1984) asserts (without supporting evidence) that AID children often feel that something is wrong. On the basis of experience with adoption, both Clamar (1980, 1984) and Waltzer (1981) argue for an end to secrecy surrounding use of AID.

Donor Attitudes

Largely because of secrecy, very little beyond occupation was known until recently about the men who are donors to sperm banks. Early reports suggested that donors were mostly university undergraduates or graduate students, sometimes of medicine (Corson, 1980; Curie-Cohen et al., 1979; Pennington & Naik, 1977; Quilivan, 1979; Sulewski, Eisenberg, & Stenger, 1978), but other than that, very little was known.

A recent study of Australian donors by Handelsman, Dunn, Conway, Boylan, and Jansen (1985) found that donors were more intelligent, outgoing, adventurous, assertive, extroverted, and independent, and less apprehensive and suspicious than Australian norms.

In 1981 Marik and Fidell designed, and Jenkins-Burk and Magnussen implemented, a study of 39 donors who were at the time of the study contributing to three large sperm banks in the Los Angeles area. Cooperation of donors was solicited to complete a written questionnaire that assessed numerous demographic, motivational, and attitudinal characteristics of the donors. All donors who were currently active in the insemination programs agreed to participate; responses were anonymous.

Donors averaged 28 years of age (range 19 to 48) and 17 years of education (range 14 to 29). Half of the donors were in school and currently working toward a degree (8 toward a B.A., 4 toward an M.A., 3 toward a Ph.D., 3 toward an L.L.D., and 1 toward an M.D.). Twenty-eight of the donors were employed (9 part and 19 full time), 7 were full-time students, and 12 were simultaneously employed and working toward degrees. Six donors were neither employed nor in school at the time. Three donors were physicians, but the remaining 25 employed donors came from a wide range of occupations (e.g., accountant, manager, writer, musician, waiter).[4]

---

[4]In a 1987 survey of 112 donors to a frozen sperm bank in Los Angeles, 78 were undergraduate students, 15 graduate students, and 19 employed. There were no graduate medical students or physicians on the list.

Most donors (25) were single, although 8 were married, 4 divorced, 1 separated, and 1 widowed. In the general population, more men of this age range are married. Among the single donors, 20 planned to marry, 4 did not, and 1 was uncertain. Nine of the donors were fathers other than through AID; 31 reported that they were currently sexually active.

Because some religions do not approve of AID, donors were asked their current religious affiliation. Four identified themselves as Catholic, 8 Jewish, 9 Protestant, 8 other, and 10 did not affiliate with any religious groups. There were more Jewish and fewer Catholic people than found in the population. Religion (but not necessarily a formal religion) was somewhat or very important to 22 donors, although only 12 attended services with any regularity. Altogether, 22 of the donors had maintained the religious affiliation of their parents, while 17 had changed to another religion or no religion.

Donors were asked to describe themselves politically; 7 described themselves as conservative, 15 as middle-of-the-road, and 11 as liberal (6 declined to answer). Sixteen donors shared the political attitudes of their parents, but 14 donors described themselves as more liberal than they perceived their parents to be, while 3 believed they were more conservative than their parents. Thus, donors, on average and like many young people, appear to be more liberal, both in religion and in politics, than were their parents.

Eighteen donors (46%) reported that they had also donated blood to a blood bank. This is a much higher rate of blood donation than the estimated 4% of the general population. Sixteen donors (41%) had signed the card, situated on the reverse side of the California driver's license, that gives consent to use organs for transplantation in case of fatal injury. This percentage is probably also higher than that of the general population.

The characteristics of these sperm donors are similar to characteristics of people who have expressed a willingness to be organ donors (Simmons, Fulton, & Fulton, 1972). Organ donors are more highly educated, higher in income, younger, and more likely to be female (although that characteristic hardly applies here) than the general population. They are less conventional and conservative in religious attitudes, often holding no religious or private religious beliefs; they are also less likely to believe in an afterlife, more likely to want cremation, and less likely to want their body on display at a funeral. They are more favorable in attitudes toward science and transplantation than others, more active in charity work, and more likely to donate blood.

Donors were asked if they had told parents, siblings, or friends about their donations. Sixteen (41%) had told their parents, among whom 12 approved. Fifteen had told siblings, and 24 had told friends, almost all of whom approved. Only 6 of the 9 married donors had told their wives (all informed wives approved), but single donors with an important person in their lives had almost all revealed their donations to that person. Among the single donors who were not currently involved with another person but planned to be in the future, 80% planned to reveal their donations.

Donors were asked to indicate their reasons for donating to a sperm bank. For the primary reason, 29 (74%) listed money, 6 (15%) listed altruism, 3 (8%) listed preservation of genes, and 1 (3%) said he loved kids. Among secondary and tertiary reasons for donating were to facilitate research, to relieve or control sexuality, to determine fertility, to reinforce masculinity, for curiosity, or out of habit.[5] Although money was

---

[5] We had thought that donors might be motivated to donate because of personal knowledge of infertility among relatives or friends, but there was no evidence at all of that in the data.

listed as the primary reason for donation for most donors, 16 (41%) indicated that they would also donate without remuneration.

Sixteen of the 39 donors (41%) stated that they had had second thoughts about donating, but those who donated primarily for money were not more likely to have had second thoughts than those who donated primarily for other reasons. Donors who had had second thoughts were less likely to have told friends about their donations (although not less likely to have told parents or siblings). Donors with second thoughts also appeared (although it could not be statistically verified) to be more often Catholic and more often married. Donors with second thoughts did not seem to differ from donors without them on any other demographic or attitudinal measure.

Altogether 90% of donors approved of abortion upon demand, and 82% favored use of surrogate mothers; 95% favored free access to permanent birth control upon demand for young, single persons, and 85% of donors were willing to adopt a child.

Because there are several parallels, from the child's perspective, between being adopted and being produced by AID, we compared donors' attitudes toward adopted and AID children on several issues. Donors were consistent in their opinions regarding whether single people should be allowed to adopt or to use AID, and whether gay people should be allowed to adopt or use AID. Seventy-seven percent felt that single persons should have the right to adopt, and 74% of the donors agreed to use of their sperm for inseminating single women. Forty-nine percent of donors felt that a gay person should have the right to adopt, and 56% approved use of their own sperm for inseminating lesbians. In the Donner and Morgan study of public attitudes, 47% of respondents had approved AID for single women and 41% for lesbians; therefore, donors were more (or equally) favorable toward insemination of these groups than was the general public. And 79% of donors approved possible use of their sperm for other ethnic and racial groups.

In a study of attitudes of medical students (from whom donors are sometimes drawn), 62% approved AID for single women, 50% approved it for lesbians (Leiblum & Barbrack, 1983). Among these same students, 63% thought recipients should be able to select the donor. Nearly half thought an AID child should be informed, but 72% thought that AID should be kept secret from everyone else.

Opinion is almost evenly split regarding whether to tell a child of the method of his or her conception when AID is used. In the Donner and Morgan study of public attitudes, 54% of respondents thought the child should be informed, while among donors, 49% thought the child should be informed. Because this knowledge might send the child in search of his or her biological father, this rate of agreement among donors is noteworthy.

In fact, when donors were asked whether an AID child should have the right to discover the identity of its father, 49% of donors responded yes (compared with 28% in the general public). Donors were, however, considerably more willing to have an adopted child discover its biological parents (where 82% of donors thought the child should have the right).

Surprisingly, 21% of donors thought they had some responsibility toward an AID child conceived from their sperm. The most commonly endorsed responsibility was to report to the clinic potentially inheritable health problems that appeared after donation, although two or three donors thought they were responsible to provide whatever assistance was required by the child. (Only 4% of those in the telephone survey thought the donors had any responsibility toward the child.) Previous researchers have concluded that donors want anonymity because they do not want responsibility for a child (Annas, 1980; Kovacs, Clayton, & McGowan, 1983), a conclusion that may well be true for many donors, but not all.

Although 90% of donors found it a pleasing idea to have conceived a child through AID, and 69% would like to know if they had fathered a child, only 36% would like to meet such a child (although more might like to see a picture of it), and only 5% thought a donor should have access to an AID child produced from his sperm. Thirteen percent of the donors, in fact, thought that it might upset them to meet a child who was the product of artificial insemination and who bore them a striking resemblance.

When asked, "Did you ever make any connection in thoughts or fantasies to women to whom your sperm was donated?" 28% of donors responded yes. Thirty-eight percent of the donors had had thoughts about the husbands of these women.

Many of these attitudes are similar to those expressed by the sample of Australian donors studied by Handelsman *et al.* (1985). They found that donors were motivated primarily by altruism and by a desire to know about their own fertility (they wanted to know if they were fertile rather than when pregnancy did occur); financial motives were there, but weak. Most donors were willing to have sperm used for IVF and for research; about half were willing to have their sperm used for single women and lesbians. Only about half had told members of their family (other than their wives) or friends about donation. Two-thirds did not want identifying information given to progeny, and 84% did not want it given to the couple.

The donors appeared, on the whole, to be responsible and generous people, liberal in their attitudes toward reproductive issues (abortion upon demand, use of surrogate mothers), and liberal in their attitudes toward use of their sperm (for single women, lesbians, and others). They have been generous with respect to blood donations and possible donations of other organs, as well as donations of sperm. It appears they felt greater responsibility toward AID children than the public feels they have.

There was some evidence that donors did not take their donations lightly. Almost half the donors had had second thoughts about donating, and 13% thought it might bother them to see an AID child who resembled them. In addition, only about half of the donors had told parents, spouses, siblings, and friends about their donations, although the people they had told tended to approve. In response to another question, about half of the donors reported that they hoped to keep their identity secret from potential AID offspring. By the same token, however, the other half did not hope to keep their identity secret.

Donors Compared with Similar Nondonors

In an effort to discover what factors distinguish young men who donate from similar other young men who do not, a group of 39 nondonors was selected by Jenkins-Burk, who matched the donors case by case in occupation and age.[6] For donors who were in professions where lists of such persons in the Los Angeles area were available, three nondonors matched on age were selected to receive a mailed questionnaire with a cover letter soliciting cooperation. For full-time students, or unemployed donors, personal solicitation of cooperation was conducted from suitably aged young men in appropriate locations (e.g., law libraries, unemployment centers). For sales managers

---

[6]We are aware of the dangers of *ad hoc* matching of samples but consider the effort worthwhile as long as caution is used in interpretation of results.

and the like, three similarly aged nondonors were located by telephone calls to appropriate businesses. Three nondonors were matched to every donor. When more than one questionnaire was completed by the three matched nondonors, one was randomly selected to provide the match. Because the cooperation rate was about 33% overall, this problem did not occur often. Physicians gave the most cooperation and accountants the least. Thus, some donors were more easily matched than others.

Despite the fact that attempts to match a group are always risky, nondonors matched donors on years of education, father's and mother's educational levels, rates and types of degrees sought, religion, ethnic background, political attitudes, marital status, sexual preferences, rates of fatherhood, rates of donation to blood banks, and plans to marry and father children. Thus, the nondonors would appear to be a good match to the donors on characteristics beyond occupation and age on which they were deliberately matched. We suspect the same factors that promote cooperation with a survey of this type also contribute to the decision to donate, and that neither group is a representative sample of the population of men of donating age. Thus, differences in attitude between donors and nondonors are probably minimized.

Nevertheless, nondonors differed from donors in some ways. Donors were more favorable than nondonors toward abortion on demand (92% favorable donors vs. 72% favorable nondonors), toward access to permanent birth control for young, single people (97% vs. 82%), and toward use of surrogate mothers (84% vs. 69%). Thus, one difference between donors and nondonors lies in attitudes toward reproductive interventions by others.

Donors also differed from nondonors on attitudes toward use of their sperm for single women (74% vs. 51%), women with different ethnic or racial characteristics (79% vs. 62%), and lesbians (56% vs. 38%). Donors, as a group, have less restrictive attitudes regarding who should receive their sperm than nondonors. Perhaps a willingness to permit AID to a wide range of persons is part of the decision to become a donor.

Last, donors more than nondonors report that they would be pleased with the thought that they might father an AID child (90% vs. 64%) and would more often like to know if such a conception occurred (69% vs. 44%); fewer donors than nondonors felt it would upset them to meet an AID child who resembled them (13% vs. 37%). Donors did not otherwise differ from nondonors in attitudes and characteristics assessed in the survey.

THE SINGLE WOMAN WHO REQUESTS AID

Owing perhaps to an increased acceptability of single-parent families, growing fear of the spread of AIDS, and increased knowledge of the option of AID, medical clinics with sperm banks have experienced an increase in the number of single women who request AID. In 1979 Curie-Cohen et al., found that only 10% of physicians in these clinics were willing to inseminate single women, a number that may well be higher 10 years later[7] although insemination of single women is still somewhat controversial.

Who are the women who seek AID when single? Are they primarily lesbians who

---

[7]See McGuire and Alexander (1985) for a discussion of legal issues involved in denial of AID to a single women or lesbians, as well as for a review of lesbians as mothers.

wish to avoid heterosexual contacts? If not, why have they chosen AID over more natural methods of reproduction, particularly in the climate of greater sexual permissiveness? These and other questions were asked by Morgan of 11 single women who requested AID in 1980 and 1981. In an in-depth, semistructured interview that lasted, on average, an hour and a half, the women answered a variety of questions ranging from routine demographic to questions about their relationships with men and their plans for informing their offspring and others of the mode of procreation. Because of the small sample size, we present these conclusions as extremely tentative.

The women were, on average 33.5 years old (range 27–39). Eight were employed full time (earning, on average, $22,500 per year, compared with a 1979 Los Angeles average for single women of $13,800), two worked part time (one also a student), and one was unemployed and on welfare. One woman owned her own sales agency, one was a computer analyst, one a merchant, and a fourth a school principal; the other six were medical personnel (e.g., nurse, X-ray technician), suggesting that working in medicine may facilitate knowledge of and requests for AID. Five of the women were Protestant, two Jewish, one Catholic, one Mormon, and the other two no religion or "other."

Ten of the women were heterosexual, and one was currently living a lesbian life style although she had been married. Four had been married, two divorced, one widowed, and one annulled. Six women definitely wanted to be married, three possibly wanted to be married, and two did not. Nearly all approved of sex without marriage, although some approved only for adults or in a steady relationship. Seven of the women described their actual relationships with men as disappointing, two found them adequate, and two satisfactory. Nearly all, however, had positive attitudes about men, as reflected in such statements as "a lovable breed," "nice to have around," and "I like them."

Somewhat surprisingly, two of the women had children, five had been pregnant but had had an abortion, and another had miscarried. These women had considerable experience with men, had been sexually active with men in the past, approved of sex without marriage, and had positive feelings about men. Why were they requesting AID?

The overwhelming impression was that their current relationships with men were disappointing, that there were no available and acceptable men on the horizon, and that because of their age, it was "now or never" for a pregnancy. Nine of them expressed the belief that life would not be complete without a child, and they all looked forward to pregnancy. But still, why AID?

There are at least three answers to that question. First, nine of the women expressed the feeling that it was unfair to use a man to produce a child without his knowledge or consent. Thus, although the "one-night stand" was an acknowledged possibility, they felt it was abusive. Second, in many of the answers was a flavor of possessiveness about the child, a desire to have something entirely their own, and a reluctance to share the rights and responsibilities for the child with a man to whom they were not emotionally committed. It is interesting to note that eight women planned to tell the child the truth about his or her conception, a number that is markedly higher than that for couples using AID, and that may be related to the desire to have a child entirely their own.

Third was the genetic background of the child, rated as important by all 11 respondents. Only 1 respondent did not intend to specify hair and eye color, ethnicity, and/or height and weight. Five of them would like to know the identity of the donor,

6 would not. The women believed that the clinics had done a better screening of donors for health and social characteristics than they could achieve themselves, and that the gametes available through the clinics were superior to those available to them elsewhere.

Although the women who were treated at the three clinics in Los Angeles were justified in their beliefs regarding health screening, such faith in screening may, at that time, have been somewhat misplaced nationwide. Both Curie-Cohen *et al.* (1979) and Behrman (1979) concluded that screening for sexually transmitted and genetic diseases among donors in the late 1970s was inadequate. As a result of these conclusions, the Ad Hoc Committee of the American Fertility Society published *Guidelines for Donor Insemination* in 1979, designed to minimize the threat of sexually transmitted and genetic diseases; new guidelines were published in 1986 in specific response to the growing threat of AIDS.

THE AID CHILD

In addition to the belief that donors are screened for genetic and sexually transmitted diseases is the belief that they are screened for high intelligence and other desirable social characteristics, either by physicians or through the process of admission to medical school. And, although the heritability of intelligence is not established and very few donors are medical students, the belief that donors are more intelligent, on average, has led to the belief that AID children are also more intelligent, on average.

In fact, very little is known about AID children. Behrman (1979) concluded that intelligence may be higher and is certainly not lower among AID children, in large part because AID children are wanted and, as often part of one- or two-children families, receive abundant adult attention. On the other hand, Clayton and Kovacs (1982) tentatively reported that there may be a greater prevalence of hyperkinesis among AID children.

Most AID children are produced by sperm that have been frozen and thawed prior to insemination. Although Hammond, Jordan, and Sloan (1986) found no difference in the pregnancy rate with fresh and frozen sperm, both Peterson (1986) and Richter, Haning, and Shapiro (1984), in an excellent within-subjects design, report a higher pregnancy rate with fresh sperm. Although freezing does not seem to affect the fertilizing capacity of X and Y sperm differently (Alfredsson, 1984), motility, penetration, and the potential fertilizing capacity of sperm are reduced by the freezing process. Behrman (1979) summarized at least eight known adverse effects of freezing and thawing sperm. He also reported that sperm samples from about 40% of men known to be fertile do not survive the freezing and thawing process and concluded that there are differences in sensitivity to freezing and thawing. Are these differences in any way related to the intellectual and information-processing capacity of children produced by fresh or frozen sperm?

To answer this question, Koenigsberg gave a battery of psychometric tests to 25 children, ages 6 to 10. Thirteen of these children were conceived through AID using fresh sperm and 12 were conceived through AID using frozen sperm.[8] All children

---

[8]Altogether, cooperation of 40 couples was solicited, among whom 25 agreed to have their children tested. No attempt was made to control for socioeconomic or demographic characteristics of the parents. However, they appeared to represent a cross section of economic status and intelligence, as judged by place of residence and occupation.

were produced with donor sperm. All children were tested in the same surroundings; Koenigsberg did not know the method of conception of the children at the time of testing.

The children were given portions of the revised Wechsler Intelligence Scale for Children-Revised (WISC-R), the Bender Gestalt test, and portions of the Illinois Test of Psycholinguistic Abilities (ITPA). The vocabulary subtest of the WISC-R was used to measure the child's learning ability, richness of ideas, and understanding of word meaning; the block design subtest was used as an indicator of perceptual organization, spatial visualization, whole-to-part perception, and visual-motor control. The Bender Gestalt Test assessed perceptual-motor coordination. The four subtests of the ITPA were used to ascertain language development (the ability to gain meaning from visual symbols, immediate recall of visual and auditory stimuli, respectively, and ability to relate concepts presented visually). These tests and subtests were selected to provide the broadest screening of intellectual abilities in the shortest period of time.

Both groups of children scored comparably on most of the tests, and their performance was higher than expected performance levels based on normative data from the general population. Children produced by fresh sperm scored higher than children produced by frozen sperm on the raw scores of six of the seven tests; however, there was also a small age difference between the two groups, and when adjustments were made for the age difference,[9] most of the differences in raw scores disappeared. After adjustment, only the difference on the ITPA subtest of visual association was statistically reliable, and, although the difference on the vocabulary subtest of the WISC-R also came very close to reliability, the actual discrepancies were minimal.

However, before inappropriate conclusions are reached about these findings, it should be reemphasized that the two groups also differed in age, with the children produced by fresh sperm being 7 months older, on average, than the children produced by frozen sperm. The psychometric tests and the statistical analyses that were used corrected for age differences, but imperfectly. Therefore, the most reasonable conclusions are that AID children are at least of average intelligence, with normal to above normal perceptual and language development, and that there are no important differences between children produced by fresh or frozen sperm.

Effects of Use of AID on Marriage

Marriages of couples who select AID are described as very stable (Ledward et al., 1982). Behrman (1979) reported that the divorce rate of such couples was an astonishingly low 0.5%. The most reasonable explanation for the stability is natural selection—only the most stable relationships withstand the stress of the discovery of infertility and the decision to use AID.

Leiblum and Barbrack (1983) studied attitudes toward AID among 29 infertile couples and found that they were generally quite positive. Kremer, Frijlisg, and Nass (1984) studied 134 Dutch couples who had used AID and found that 98% thought the decision to use AID had been a good one. They did not find it humiliating to have used AID, although the period of decision making and the period during which inseminations occurred were reported to be stressful. They thought their marriages were improved or just as good as before, although like most AID couples they had

---

[9]Adjustments were made through analysis of covariance.

told no one and did not plan to tell the child about AID. These researchers felt that the successful responses of the couples who elected AID were due in part to the 3- to 12-month waiting period for the procedure at their clinic, during which 20% of couples changed their minds about use of AID.

Summary

AID, artificial insemination with donor sperm, is often used by couples as a last resort when all other methods of conception have not worked or are likely to produce a child with an inherited disease. It is chosen by couples who are in distress over their infertility, but whose relationships are stable enough to allow them to make this choice. Once the decision is made, it is regarded as a good one. The child is likely to grow up in a loving and attentive environment and to display average or above average abilities.

Single women seem to request AID because there is not currently an acceptable man in their lives and they feel that their biological clocks are running out. They are reluctant to use a man to become pregnant without his knowledge, and they do not want the entanglements such use could imply. In addition, they trust the screening procedure used by physicians who run sperm banks to select eligible donors for them.

The donors seem to be a generous and thoughtful group of people who have liberal attitudes regarding who should benefit from their donations. They seem motivated by both monetary and altruistic goals and to have a greater-than-expected sense of responsibility toward potential offspring.

The public seems generally accepting of use of AID by others. Although perhaps only 40% or so of those who were asked thought that they themselves would use AID, 80 to 90% have no objections if others use it.

In light of these generally positive findings regarding the psychological consequences of AID, why the secrecy? Neither couples who use AID nor donors are likely to have shared this information with others. Couples do not tell the child or even close relatives; donor husbands sometimes do not tell their wives. Either there are some hidden and dire psychological consequences of use of AID or these attitudes are a holdover from an earlier, more puritanical day. Perhaps other chapters in this volume will provide an answer.

References

Aickin, D. R. (1985). Issues arising from artificial conception practices. *New Zealand Medical Journal*, 8(755) 186–187.
Aiman, J. (1982). Factors affecting the success of donor insemination. *Fertility and Sterility*, 37, 94–99.
Alder, E. M., Baird, D. T., Lees, M. M., Lincoln, D. W., Loudon, N. B., & Templeton, A. A. (1986). Attitudes of women of reproductive age to *in vitro* fertilization and embryo research. *Journal of Biosocial Science*, 18, 155–167.
Alfredsson, J. H. (1984). Artificial insemination with frozen semen: Sex ratio at birth. *International Journal of Fertility*, 29(3), 152–155.
American Fertility Society, Ad Hoc Committee. (1979). *Guidelines for donor insemination—1979*. Birmingham, AL: Author.
American Fertility Society, Ad Hoc Committee. (1986). *New guidelines for the use of semen donor insemination—1986*. Birmingham, AL: Author.

Annas, G. J. (1980). Fathers anonymous: Beyond the best interests of the sperm donor. *Family Law Quarterly, 14,* 1–13.

Beck, W. W., & Wallach, E. E. (1981). When therapy fails—Artificial insemination. *Contemporary Obstetrics/Gynecology, 17,* 113–125.

Behrman, S. J. (1979). Artificial insemination and public policy. *New England Journal of Medicine, 300,* 619–620.

Berger, D. (1980). Couples' reactions to male infertility and donor insemination. *American Journal of Psychiatry, 137,* 1047–1049.

Berger, D. M., Eisen, A., Shuber, J., & Doody, K. F. (1986). Psychological patterns in donor insemination couples. *Canadian Journal of Psychiatry, 31,* 818–822.

Berk, A., & Shapiro, J. L. (1984). Some implications of infertility on marital therapy. *Family Therapy, 11,* 37–47.

Bernstein, J., Potts, N., & Mattox, J. H. (1985). Assessment of psychological dysfunction associated with infertility. *Journal of Gynecology and Neonatal Nursing, 6(suppl.),* 63s–66s.

Brand, H. J. (1982). Psychological stress and infertility. Part 2: Psychometric test data. *British Journal of Medical Psychology, 55,* 385–388.

Brand, H. J., Roos, S. S., & van der Merwe, A. B. (1982). Psychological stress and infertility. *British Journal of Medical Psychology, 55,* 379–384.

Bresnick, E., & Taymor, M. L. (1979). The role of counseling in infertility. *Fertility and Sterility, 32,* 154–156.

Clamar, A. (1980). Psychological implications of donor insemination. *American Journal of Psychoanalysis, 40,* 173–177.

Clamar, A. (1984). Artificial insemination by donor: The anonymous pregnancy. *American Journal of Forensic Psychology, 2,* 27–37.

Clayton, C. E., & Kovacs, G. T. (1982). AID offspring: Initial follow-up study of 50 couples. *Medical Journal of Australia, 1,* 338–339.

Corson, S. L. (1980). Factors affecting donor artificial insemination success rates. *Fertility and Sterility, 33,* 415–422.

Curie-Cohen, M., Luttrell, L., & Shapiro, S. (1979). Current practice of artificial insemination by donor in the United States. *New England Journal of Medicine, 300,* 585–590.

Fagan, P. J., Schmidt, C. W., Rock, J. A., Damewood, M. D., Halle, E., & Wise, T. N. (1986). Sexual functioning and psychologic evaluation of *in vitro* fertilization couples. *Fertility and Sterility, 46,* 668–672.

Francoeur, R. J. (1970). *Utopian motherhood.* New York: Doubleday.

Freeman, E. W., Boxer, A. S., Rickels, K., Tureck, R., & Mastroianni, L. (1985). Psychological evaluation and support in a program of *in vitro* fertilization and embryo transfer. *Fertility and Sterility, 43,* 48–53.

Freeman, E. W., Garcia, C. R., & Rickels, K. (1983). Behavioral and emotional factors: Comparisons of anovulatory infertile women with fertile and other infertile women. *Fertility and Sterility, 40,* 195–201.

Garcia, C. R., Freeman, E. W., Rickels, K., Wu, C., Scholl, G., Galle, P. C., & Boxer, A. S. (1985). Behavioral and emotional factors and treatment responses in a study of anovulatory infertile women. *Fertility and Sterility, 44,* 478–483.

Gilbert, S. (1976). Artificial insemination. *American Journal of Nursing, 76,* 259–260.

Greenberg., S. (1951) Social variables in acceptance or rejection of artificial insemination. *American Sociological Review, 16,* 85.

Hammond, M. G., Jordan, S., & Sloan, C. S. (1986). Factors affecting pregnancy rates in a donor insemination program using frozen semen. *American Journal of Obstetrics and Gynecology, 155,* 480–485.

Handelsman, D. J., Dunn, S. M., Conway, A. J., Boylan, L. M., & Jansen, R. P. (1985). Psychological and attitudinal profiles in donors for artificial insemination. *Fertility and Sterility, 43,* 95–101.

Harrison, R. F., O'Moore, A., & O'Moore, R. R. (1981). Stress and artificial insemination. *Infertility, 4,* 303–311.

Hertz, D. G. (1982). Infertility and the physician-patient relationship; A biopsychological challenge. *General Hospital Psychiatry, 4,* 95–101.

Karow, A. M. (1982). Family secrets: Who is to know about AID? (Letter to the editor). *New England Journal of Medicine, 306,* 372.

Kovacs, G. T., Clayton, C. E., & McGowan, P. (1983). The attitudes of semen donors. *Clinical Reproductive Fertility, 2,* 85–90.

Kremer, J., Frijlisg, B. W., & Nass, J. L. (1984). Psychosocial aspects of parenthood by artificial insemination donor (Letter to the editor). *Lancet, 17,* 628.

Lalos, A., Lalos, O., Jacobsson, L., & von Schoultz, B. (1985a). Psychological reactions to the medical investigation and surgical treatment of infertility. *Gynecologic and Obstetric Investigator, 20,* 209–217.

Lalos, A., Lalos, O., Jacobsson, L., & von Schoultz, B. (1985b). The psychological impact of infertility two years after completed surgical treatment. *Acta Obstetrica et Gynecologica Scandinavica, 64,* 599–604.

Ledward, R. S., Symonds, E. M., & Eynon, S. (1982). Social and environmental factors as criteria for success in artificial insemination by donor (AID). *Journal of Biosocial Science, 14,* 263–275.

Leiblum, S. R., & Barbrack, C. (1983). Artificial insemination by donor: A survey of attitudes and knowledge in medical students and infertile couples. *Journal of Biosocial Science, 15,* 165–172.

Link, P. W., & Darling, C. A. (1986). Couples undergoing treatment for infertility: Dimensions of life satisfaction. *Journal of Sex and Marital Therapy, 12,* 46–52.

Mahlstedt, P. P. (1985). The psychological component of infertility. *Fertility and Sterility, 43,* 335–346.

McGuire, E. A., & Alexander, N. J. (1985). Artificial insemination of single women. *Fertility and Sterility, 43,* 182–184.

Menken, J., Trussell, J., & Larsen, U. (1986). Age and infertility. *Science, 233,* 1389–1394.

Menning, B. E. (1980). The emotional needs of infertile couples. *Fertility and Sterility, 34,* 313–319.

Miall, C. E. (1985). Perceptions of informal sanctioning and the stigma of involuntary childlessness. *Deviant Behavior, 6,* 383–403.

Milsom, I., & Bergman, P. (1982). A study of parental attitudes after donor insemination (AID). *Acta Obstetrica et Gynecologica Scandinavica, 61,* 125–128.

Morse, C., & Dennerstein, L. (1985). Infertile couples entering an *in vitro* fertilization programme. A preliminary survey. *Journal of Psychosomatic Obstetrics and Gynecology, 4,* 207–219.

Nijs, P., Koninckx, P. R., Verstraeten, D., Mullens, A., & Nicasy, H. (1984). Psychological factors of female infertility. *European Journal of Obstetrics, Gynecology, and Reproductive Biology, 18,* 375–379.

O'Moore, A. M., O'Moore, R. R., Harrison, R. F., Murphy, G., & Carruthers, M. E. (1983). Psychosomatic aspects in idiopathic infertility: Effects of treatment with autogenic training. *Psychosomatic Research, 27,* 145–151.

Pennington, G. W., & Naik, S. (1977). Donor insemination: Report of a two-year study. *British Medical Journal, 1,* 1327–1330.

Peterson, E. P. (1986). Artificial insemination by donor—A new look. *Fertility and Sterility, 46,* 567–570.

Platt, J. J., Ficher, I., & Silver, M. J. (1973). Infertile couples: Personality traits and self-ideal concept discrepancies. *Fertility and Sterility, 24,* 972–976.

Quilivan, W. L. G. (1979). Therapeutic donor insemination: Results and causes of nonfertilization. *Fertility and Sterility, 32,* 157–160.

Richter, M. A., Haning, R. V., & Shapiro, S. S. (1984). Artificial donor insemination: Fresh versus frozen semen; the patient as her own control. *Fertility and Sterility, 41,* 277–280.

Rosenfeld, D. L., & Mitchell, E. (1979). Treating the emotional aspects of infertility: Counseling services in an infertility clinic. *American Journal of Obstetrics and Gynecology, 135,* 177–180.

Sarrel, P. M., & DeCherney, A. H. (1985). Psychotherapeutic intervention for treatment of couples with secondary infertility. *Fertility and Sterility, 43,* 897–900.

Simmons, R. G., Fulton, J., & Fulton, R. (1972). The prospective organ transplant donor: Problems and prospects of medical innovation. *Omega, 3,* 319–339.

Sokoloff, B. Z. (1987). Alternative methods of reproduction. *Clinical Pediatrics, 26,* 11–16.

Sulewski, J. M., Eisenberg, F., & Stenger, V. G. (1978). A longitudinal analysis of artificial insemination with donor semen. *Fertility and Sterility, 29,* 527–531.

Valentine, D. P. (1986). Psychological impact of infertility: Identifying issues and needs. *Social Work in Health Care, 11*(4), 61–69.

Waltzer, H. (1981). Anonymity and donor insemination. (Letter to the editor). *American Journal of Psychiatry, 138,* 262.

Chapter 8

Psychological Implications of the Anonymous Pregnancy

APHRODITE CLAMAR

Since the dawn of civilization, humankind has been admonished to be fruitful and multiply. Religious, cultural, social, and economic values set a premium on fertility. Early religions are rife with rituals worshipping the phallus and/or the goddess of fertility; magic and incantations promised relief from the sorrow of childlessness and solace for despair (Darlington, 1969). Many of these attitudes and values still affect—consciously or unconsciously—those who wish to conceive but cannot do so. For some couples the biological facts of their infertility acquire different meanings and different responses. Some forego parenthood and choose a different life-style; others seek to adopt an infant or a child, substituting someone else's birthchild for their own; still others seek help from the rapidly expanding array of sophisticated drugs and innovative surgery, while others use the donated sperm of an unknown male to achieve conception. This chapter will focus on the latter procedure—donor insemination (DI).

The first instance of human donor insemination is credited to John Hunter of England, who in 1785 inseminated a woman with her husband's semen (Kleegman, (1967). In the United States in 1866 Marion Sims performed 55 inseminations in six women, again with their husband's semen. Only one became pregnant. Dr. Robert L. Dickinson, a pioneer in birth control, sex education, marriage counseling, and family mental health, first performed donor insemination in 1890 (Feingold, 1976). Dr. Dickinson not only taught all the earliest practitioners but was most responsible for its growing practice and acceptance.

Today DI is available to married couples, unmarried couples, single women, and lesbians, although the latter two groups may still have some difficulty finding a physician who will provide such a service. The focus of this chapter will be on the use of DI by couples—married and unmarried—as a means of having a family.

For most couples, DI is a last resort, a decision that is reached usually after 3 to 5 years of frustration, of "trying," of fertility work-ups and perhaps surgery, of family and social pressures, and of feeling alone and lost in a maze of medical decisions, anxieties, and fears as time passes and there is no baby. A survey published

---

APHRODITE CLAMAR • Private practice, 162 East 80th Street, New York, New York 10021.

in the *New England Journal of Medicine* estimates that each year between 6000 and 10,000 children are born in this country as a result of artificial insemination (Berman, 1979). An estimated 12,000 to 15,000 couples request this procedure annually. It is believed that at least a quarter of a million children have been born as a result of this medical intervention over the past 20 years.

Infertility in men—whether due to oligospermia (low sperm count), azoospermia (lack of sperm), improperly formed sperm, or low motility sperm—is generally unresponsive to treatment. (DI is also used when the male is a known carrier of a genetic disease, and when there is the need to eliminate RH incompatibility.)

Although it is known that male infertility is responsible for one-third of all cases of infertility, until recently the major emphasis on fertility research has been on detecting and correcting abnormalities in women. When men are asked to provide a semen specimen during the course of a fertility study, a frequently observed response is one of disbelief. This attitude may be grounded in a biblical tradition that makes references to barren women but none to barren men.

The first recorded laboratory investigation of male fertility appears in Genesis when Sarah, who was childless, urged Abraham to impregnate their servant Hagar. The outcome of this experiment may well have reinforced what may be described as the prevailing belief in the infallibility of male fertility.

Yet many factors affect male fertility. Mumps at puberty may lead to damage of the sperm-producing cells; gonorrhea and other bacterial infections may scar the reproductive passage; herpes—a virus disease—may cause infertility; common pesticides, anticancer drugs, toxic poisons, and compounds such as alcohol, tobacco, drugs, and marijuana may change the sperm's shape, kill it, or reduce its ability to propel itself to union with an egg. According to the Washington, D.C., Fertility Center, sperm counts in healthy men are falling "alarmingly"—a phenomenon that could lead to increased infertility among men and even affect the availability of potential donors for DI who meet the minimal standards for sperm quantity and quality ((*American Health*, 1982; *New York Times*, 1988).

The discovery of infertility in the male is likely to precipitate a life-crisis for the man individually, and for the couple as a unit (Mazor, 1978). To successfully overcome this psychological crisis, the couple must undertake these steps (Sawatzky, 1981): (1) recognize and express their feelings about fertility; (2) grieve for their loss of a genetic child; (3) evaluate their reasons for wanting a child—separating their own desires from those of family, peers, and society; (4) make decisions about their future—remain childless, adopt, or try DI?

These tasks parallel the sequence postulated by Kübler-Ross (1969) in her work on death and dying: denial, anger, bargaining, depression, and, finally, acceptance. Experience with childless couples indicates that this sequence should be allowed to complete its course before DI is begun.

A fertile woman who wants a baby even if she has an infertile mate has three choices: to take a new husband, to take a lover, or to bypass her mate's infertility medically (Wilson, 1979). DI thus becomes a way of conceiving without actually changing one's mate. However, the emphasis on genetic ties as defining fatherhood is eliminated; the patrilineal bond is achieved through the process of claiming, naming, and legitimizing the offspring of one's wife and an unknown man.

Having chosen DI, the couple will find that medically it is a simple, painless, and totally asexual procedure. With a syringe, 2 to 5 cubic centimeters of semen—usually obtained from a sperm bank—are injected into the woman's vagina. A small plastic cup or plug is placed on the cervix to keep the semen in place; after a few hours the cap is removed. There is some disagreement among fertility specialists as to whether fresh or frozen sperm is more effective, but with the rising danger of acquired immune deficiency syndrome (AIDS), the argument has become moot; freezing is imperative to destroy the AIDS virus.

As a rule, the physician cautions the couple to keep the fact that they are using donated sperm a secret. The identity of the donor is never revealed. In almost all cases, the physician himself does not know the identity of the donor, since the sperm comes from a medical laboratory, which does not identify the donor except for his physical characteristics; these are matched by the physician to those of the husband.

An overall success rate of 57% is reported, with conception occurring after an average of 3.7 inseminations. However, if no pregnancy results after 4 or 5 inseminations, the chances of achieving pregnancy drop sharply.

The reasons for failure of DI are not known. It is believed that psychological factors may play a significant role: The couple becomes "distracted" by anxiety, by fear of never achieving their goal, by obsession with temperature charts, by the stress of scheduling everyday life around ovulation, fitting in appointments, and the inevitable discouragement at the onset of the menses, betokening another "failure" (Denber, 1965). Research on female infertility has documented the influence of emotions and ambivalence in suppressing ovulation. There are reports of women ceasing to ovulate as a result of the stress of infertility examinations and treatment. There may also be undetected fertility problems in the women.

Certainly the success rate reported in veterinary medicine using DI suggests that the pregnancy take in humans should be higher than it is. With this concern in mind, the psychological characteristics of 58 women attending the DI clinic were examined (Reading, Sledmere, & Cox, 1982). The women were assessed prior to treatment on a number of attitudinal measures, as well as by completing personality and marital adjustment inventories. Following an interval of 6 months the women were reassessed.

Asked to evaluate their mental state at the time of the insemination, the women all but unanimously said they lived in a state of high anxiety. Moreover, when asked to identify the single factor that most influenced the outcome of the insemination procedure, both those who achieved pregnancy and those who did not cited their psychological state at the time. In terms of the impact of DI on the marriage, both partners agreed that the relationship came under intense strain; one couple separated following failure to conceive. On the other hand, several women reported that one result of experiencing the stress of DI together with their husbands actually strengthened their marriage.

Personality traits of women who undergo DI suggest a conforming personality type, with particular emphasis on behaving in socially sanctioned and acceptable ways. This characteristic may serve as an impetus to continue the insemination procedure and preclude extramarital sexual relations as a way of conceiving. All subjects agreed that psychological preparation for DI would have allayed many of their fears and helped them realistically face the prospect of failure—thus reaffirming the need for medical staff to be sensitive to the psychological needs of the patient.

At the insemination itself, many physicians encourage the husband to be present. Some may even allow him to do the actual inseminating. Still others instruct the couple to "go home and have intercourse, so you will never really know whose child it is" (Feingold, 1976). The latter, however, is a questionable practice that distorts and denies reality and contributes to a sense of mystery and confusion about the child's identity.

DI is a relatively expensive procedure, dependent on donors willing to sell their sperm. How healthy the donors are and how honest or candid they are about their genetic background are two of the controversies surrounding DI (Beck, 1976). There is no general procedure for screening potential donors to guard against the transmission of genetic diseases or mental problems. Another criticism of the donor system is that a particularly fertile donor might "father" a large number of children (especially in a small town), increasing the possibility of incest among half-siblings when they reach adulthood. The *New England Journal of Medicine* (Berman, 1979) observes: "A single donor may make a large contribution to a local ethnic community. Intermarriage within such a community would result in increased inbreeding due to artificial insemination. In fact, several half-sibling matings have nearly occurred already, and our data further suggest that inbreeding may be more frequent than expected." Thus, divorced from the procedure yet essential to it, sometimes accused of "reproduction without responsibility," the donor remains unremarked and undefined—certainly an individual worth more attention than the few studies available to date.

One study by Handelsman, Dunn, Conway, Boylan, and Jansen (1985) provides data on the personality profile and related attitudes of 75 sperm donors. The data suggest that the sperm donor population is distinct in certain personality traits from the general population—especially on such variables as intelligence, risk taking, and boldness. The authors speculate that these characteristics reflect the donors' desire to perform a socially useful but not fully sanctioned task.

This personality profile is consistent with a study of Australian volunteers screened as prospective sperm donors (Nicholas & Tyler, 1983). Personality characteristics of 50 consecutive donors using the Eysenck Personality Inventory were assessed. Test results indicate that this population was emotionally stable and moderately extroverted. Reasons for volunteering were primarily altruistic; financial remuneration was a poor inducement. Many of the married men in the study had discussed their decision to donate with their wives, who in most cases encouraged their husbands to donate because they empathized with the women's desire to experience motherhood. The authors suggest, from the latter finding, that one way to recruit potential donors might be through female—rather than male-only—sources.

Members of both the general public and the medical community have assumed that donors are a reluctant and secretive group who wish to remain anonymous. Rowland and Ruffin (1983) studied 67 donors at the Queen Victoria Hospital in Melbourne, Australia. Through questionnaires and structured interviews, donors were asked a series of questions to determine their socioeconomic status, reasons for donating, attitudes toward the infertile couples receiving their sperm, attitudes toward the selection of couples, the possibility of revealing identifying information about themselves, and how they would feel about meeting their DI offspring.

The results of this study reveal that some stereotypic views about donors are not justified. They do not donate primarily for monetary reasons and they do represent a cross section of the work force. Furthermore, the majority of the men in the study would not object if information about them (excluding their names) were given to the couple to pass on to the child, and over half would be willing to meet the child after it was 18 years old. The donor's desire for anonymity, the study found, stemmed from fear of potential legal liability for child support and inheritance rights. These are two areas that require legal clarification and nationwide laws that uniformly protect donors from such liability. At the same time, it would appear, the medical establishment might well rethink its rush to destroy records while attitudes and expectations about anonymity are in flux.

Another finding in the Australian study concerned information about the sexuality of the donors. It has generally been assumed that donors were heterosexual; Rowland found that a number of the donors were homosexual—unfortunately, she does not cite the percentage.

Unknown are the responses of the donors who discover, as a result of donating, that their sperm count is at an unacceptable level. Does rejection from such a program lead to depression? An altered sense of self? Is it comparable with the impact of a diagnosis of infertility? Perhaps these men should be offered counseling services to help cushion the impact of their rejection from a donor program.

Equally unknown are the personal feelings of the physician who carried out the DI procedure. Seymour and Koerner (1936) reported finding that DI physicians often see themselves as playing a parental role, bringing happiness to the patient. Yet many are uneasy about the legality, morality, and ethics of their role (Souval, 1959). Of primary importance, however, is the emotional tone generated by the physicians and their staff. Is there concern, patience, willingness to answer questions and deal with patients' worries and fears, and an ability to resist playing God, or do they unconsciously signal their own ambivalences—even misgivings—about the procedure? Perhaps physicians should be encouraged to share their feelings about DI among themselves, with their patients, and at fertility self-help groups. Airing these feelings might make them more sensitive to the psychological needs of the couples who come to them for DI.

Research on the psychological conflicts and stress engendered by DI is hampered by the secrecy that surrounds both the procedure and the couples who undergo it. Subjects are difficult to find, and most research consists of follow-up questionnaires sent by physicians to former patients, or after-the-fact reconstructions by therapists who see such people in treatment. The results are often contradictory and limited in scope and applicability.

Farris and Garrison (1954) studied 38 successful DI couples who had chosen the procedure over adoption. A summary of the couples' motivations, as revealed by the study, appears in Table 1.

This study surveyed middle-class, college-educated parents. Significantly, the most frequent reason given for the husband's preference for DI was a belief that a closer relationship would exist with the child. Among the women, the largest number (but less than one out of four) indicated that their primary consideration was a desire

Table 1. Reasons for Choosing DI over Adoption

	Wife	Husband
Desire to experience pregnancy	23%	16%
Dissatisfaction with adoption procedure	21%	25%
Derive benefits from maternal heredity	20%	22%
Closer relationship to child	15%	32%
Conceal infertility	8%	6%
Faith in selection of donor	2%	3%

to experience pregnancy. The authors acknowledge that their survey did not tap anxieties over legal, religious, and moral issues. All 389 couples, however, indicated that they desired another DI child.

Two follow-up studies of DI parents (Harvey & Harvey, 1977; Levie, 1967) report generally successful results. In these studies a high percentage of the couples who received questionnaires responded, and almost 90% of them reported that having a DI child strengthened their marriages. Nevertheless, the question remains: What percentage of couples must encounter emotional difficulties before a procedure is considered psychologically risky? And if it is designated as harmful, what is the nature of the stress involved?

There are also articles by psychotherapists about patients who were discovered to have used DI in the past (David & Avidan, 1976; Gerstal, 1963). In these studies the patients' symptoms were attributed to DI; it was therefore concluded that the procedure precipitates psychological problems. These conclusions appear too far-reaching, however, in light of the small number of patients studied. Moreover, retrospective theorizing makes it difficult to pinpoint the role of DI in the etiology of the patients' symptoms.

A study of 16 DI couples revealed that over 80% exhibited definite signs of symptoms that suggest the presence of conflict when the man was discovered to be azoospermic (Berger, 1980). After learning they were infertile, a number of the husbands experienced a period of impotence of at least 3 weeks' duration; they became depressed, preexisting medical conditions were exacerbated, and some entered into extramarital affairs, leading to divorce in several cases. Many of the women reported feelings of rage toward their husbands upon learning that their mates could not sire children. Other reported dreams in which their husbands were violently injured or killed.

Those couples that had taken the longest time between the discovery of the husband's infertility and the decision to have a DI baby did considerably better psychologically than those who acted with less patience. The author suggests that the couples in the study that had problems had not successfully resolved the conflict over infertility and the decision to take the DI route. Another reason offered was that the secrecy that surrounds DI obstructs resolution of that conflict.

In another study, Rubin (1965) compared a group of mothers who had children through natural insemination with a group of DI mothers. He found little significant difference in terms of the women's own childhood development and their eventual feminine roles. Nor were their pregnancies or child care methods appreciably different. However, there was a significant difference in their fantasies about whom the child resembled after birth. The DI mother evinced a strong need to dissociate from thoughts and concerns about the meaning of the donor to them, resorting to suppression, denial, repression, and intellectualizing defenses.

Typically, DI parents tend to be socially middle to upper class, well educated, and achievement-oriented (David & Avidan, 1976). Desirable personality characteristics include flexibility and an openness to new ideas, and the ability to cope with frustrations and handle the loss of direction over their lives, and the capacity to share their sadness and grief over the failure to conceive through natural means. According to this study, it is particularly helpful if DI couples have confronted the failure of their hopes and dreams for immortality through their own offspring and have come to terms with these feelings before the DI child is conceived.

Critics of DI raise the possibility that "the child may serve as a constant reminder of the husband's incapacity, intensifying feelings or resentment" (Dianes, 1968). The power balance between the spouses may be tipped in the wife's favor, making her feel stronger at the expense of the husband's loss of power and status. Other possible psychological results include erotic fantasies that the wife may develop for the donor or project onto the treating physician, a special bonding between mother and child that excludes the father, or resentment of the child by one or both parents.

The husband may consent to DI either out of a strong wish to satisfy his wife's desire for a child or out of fear that she will leave him or have an affair (Czyba & Chevret, 1979; Dianes, 1968). Her ensuing pregnancy may bring him pride and help hide his infertility from society. Nevertheless, he will feel deeply his lack of genetic input and may feel guilty over it. He may worry that he is less than an adequate role model for the child if it is a male. He may develop anxiety over incestuous feelings if it is a girl, since the incest barrier does not apply to this father–daughter relationship. Or he may see himself as inadequate because he cannot do what is expected of him—impregnate his wife—while allowing his wife to be violated by another man (a primitive, ancient fear of men) with his consent and at his expense.

There are three times when the DI husband experiences emotional turmoil: at the time of the initial DI decision; when his wife becomes pregnant and the reality of the method of conception becomes a fact; and at the time of the approaching birth, when his insecurities and fears about his masculinity and parenting role are rekindled (Currie-Cohen, Luttrell, & Shapiro, 1979).

Stewart, Daniels, and Boulnois (1982) recommend that prospective DI parents undergo a thorough psychosocial assessment, an approach that goes counter to the prevailing attitude that every couple is entitled to have children with little or no concern for their suitability as parents. As a result of this increased media attention to infertility and the extraordinary technological advances achieved to date (with more still to come), the authors recommend that physicians and clinics begin to implement nonjudgmental guidelines before a couple is accepted for DI.

The four areas for evaluation proposed by the authors are duration of marriage; psychological functioning of each partner; social functioning of the couple, including the extent of the support network available to the prospective parents through friends, family, community, and work; and insight into the ramifications of DI, particularly the effect on their family if they choose to tell or not tell them about the method of conception.

But if the prospective couple fails to "pass" the test, does the physician have the right to withhold donor insemination from them? Is the physician not then truly playing God? The moral and ethical dimensions of DI are serious; thus far, however, the medical profession has apparently ignored them.

Another subject virtually ignored to date is the effect of telling one's offspring that he or she is a DI child. Nor are there any guidelines or accumulated wisdom one can offer to parents on the question of to tell or not to tell. Yet we do know that a commitment to secrecy can be a strong factor in determining the type of relationship DI parents will have with their child. By its very nature a secret is a potent force, assuming undue power within the family—an existential fact that remains unspoken yet colors and controls the life of each family member. Conscious effort to "forget" a secret only reinforces it, separating those who know (the parents) from the one who does not (the child) (Bok, 1982). To maintain the secret, the parents must of course deceive the child and society; in so doing, they deceive themselves as well by altering the reality they know to be.

Secrecy as a fundamental aspect of DI serves to protect the three parties involved: the recipient couple, the donor, and the offspring. This secrecy has been consistently supported by the medical profession—presumably because of its own fears about legal liability and because of what it considers to be binding commitments of anonymity with both donors and couples.

In recent years, however, the principle of secrecy in DI has been challenged, in part because the traditional approach in a related field—adoption—is now being widely questioned. Historically, secrecy was the watchword in adoption. This secrecy caused some adult adoptees to experience "genealogical bewilderment"—that is, confusion and uncertainty about their identity as adults who had no knowledge of their heritage (Sants, 1964). For some adoptees, it became imperative that they find out who their biological parents were and identify their ethnic and cultural roots. While the requirement of secrecy in adoption grew out of social taboos attendant to illegitimacy, in recent years strong pressure exerted by adoptees (and to a lesser extent by adoptive parents) and biological parents have brought about major changes in adoption practices today. Most adopting couples are given extensive information on the child's birthparents and are counseled to tell the child of his or her adoption at an early stage. How-to books, support groups, and search networks abound. Research in adoption has indicated that this is a psychologically healthier situation for all concerned (Clamar, 1978; Sorosky, Baran, & Pannor, 1978).

Sants (1964) observed that "conscious acceptance of the known facts, intolerable though they may appear to be, tends to improve rather than worsen relationships." Children and adults are less upset by what are presumed to be unpalatable facts than by the deception that is designed to protect them from the facts.

Why do DI parents maintain secrecy at such a high psychological toll? Primarily, it would appear, as a means of hiding the husband's infertility. Because society equates fertility with virility in men, there is the concomitant assumption that infertility is more devastating to men than to women. No evidence exists to support this assumption, yet countless women are prepared to pretend that they are infertile rather than to expose their husband's problem. It may be time for men to take the lead in changing society's definition of their value as based on their ability to impregnate women. Acceptance of infertility is a process, not a static state. Ongoing discussion with mate/friend/counselor will help to ameliorate the pain and regret of infertility—especially as the man reaches various transition and passage points in his life. To deny his reality is to lessen his stature as a man, not to enhance him.

DI parents anticipate social disapproval and seek to protect their children from social rejection. They feel that there is something "not quite right" about using DI. Unfortunately, the continuing secrecy about DI reinforces the taboos and negative attitudes toward it. Society teaches us that anything you have to hide must be inherently wrong or unclean.

DI parents also fear that their child will respond negatively to being told about its DI origins, fearing that the child will reject its nonbiological father—another effort to protect the husband. However, adoption literature shows us that such a strongly negative response to information about one's background is more likely to come from an adolescent who "accidentally discovers" his or her origins than from a child who grows up knowing the truth and having a caring father.

The experience of one person conceived through DI, and who was told of that fact, may be instructive. Lillian Atallah (1976) described her feelings upon being informed of her DI origin at the age of 19. Knowing about her origin, she writes, "did nothing to alter my feelings for my family. Instead, I was grateful for the trouble they had taken to give me life. And they had given me such a strong set of roots, a rich and colorful cultural heritage, a sense of being loved. With their adventure in biology, my parents had opened up the fairly rigid culture they had brought with them to this country. The secret knowledge of my 'differentness' and my sister's may have helped our parents accept. . . . the few deviations from their norms that we argued for."

Perhaps the reason DI parents hesitate to tell their children about the method of their conception is that there are no scripts for them to follow. We have no literature that they can turn to, no mentors for them to consult, and no support groups that will encourage them to seek their identity. Instead, we have a culture that imposes a double standard on sexuality. On the one hand, sexual exploits and explicit sexuality are the common coin of the realm, pervading every aspect of life. On the other hand, infertility is still whispered about, and visits to the fertility clinics have the same aura that a trip to the abortionist did a generation ago.

Still another issue arises if the offspring is told of its DI background. Inevitably, questions will arise about the donor parent. However, if semen banks and physicians continue to destroy records, the questions will only give rise to frustration. If the penchant for secrecy is lifted, registration centers could be established that would permit identification of the donor, thus enabling parents (or the grown offspring of DI families) to learn who the biological father is.

In their aptly titled book, *Lethal Secrets*, Baran and Pannor (1988) point out that "the donor father was never perceived as anything but a donor of sperm who enabled the couple to become parents. He does not have any role of nurturing or parenting. His importance in the total equation lies in the genetic and historical connection he offers the child. To complete that role, he should be available to his offspring if and when necessary."

As America enters the 21st century, society's definition and understanding of family is changing. Technology and genetic engineering are rapidly altering the meaning of conception, pregnancy, and parenthood. With these changes will come, I believe, a new respect for, and recognition of, the rights of the child who is conceived through such methods. There will develop a new appreciation of DI offsprings' right to know of their genetic origin and religious, social, and ethnic background—and thus have access to information that defines their biological heritage. Society cannot much longer put off reevaluating the secrecy issue, especially in view of the increasing recognition of its psychological and moral implications. As one donor commented (Rowland & Ruffin, 1983), "I made a contract with the couple that we would never meet, but the child made no such contract."

Surely the psychological impact on the husband, wife, child, donor, donor's wife or girlfriend, the couple's family and friends, the physician—and the implications for the legal profession, religious leaders, professional counselors, and therapists—are profound and far-reaching. Far too many people are affected by DI for it to be allowed to stay in the closet any longer. The more DI is explored and discussed, the more DI and infertility become a matter of public interest, the more effective it can be in helping couples to have the psychologically healthy children they want to raise in a psychologically sound family.

The opportunity exists to evolve new relations between parents and the DI offspring, to ask new questions and rethink old ideas about the role of genetics in parenthood and the meaning of biological fatherhood.

References

American Health (1986, Sept./Oct.). Medical news. Vol. VI, p. 15.
Attallah, L. (1976, April 18). Report from a test-tube baby. *New York Times Magazine*, pp. 44–53.
Baran, A., & Pannor, R. (1988). *Lethal secret*. New York: Warner Books & Amistad Press.
Beck, W. W. (1976). A critical look at the legal, ethical and technical aspects of artificial insemination. *Fertility and Sterility*, 27 1–8.
Berger, D. M. (1980). Couples' reactions to male infertility and donor insemination. *American Journal of Psychiatry*, 137, 1047–1049.
Berger, D. M., Eisen, A., Shuber, J., & Doody, K. F. (1986). Psychological patterns in donor insemination couples. *Canadian Journal of Psychiatry*, 31, 818–823.
Berman, S. J. (1979). Artificial insemination and public policy. *New England Journal of Medicine*, 300, 40–49.
Bok, S. (1982) *Secrets*. New York: Pantheon.
Clamar, A. (1978) *A comparative study of selected personality characteristics of 8- to 12-year-old adopted and non-adopted girls*. Unpublished doctoral dissertation, New York University.
Currie-Cohen, M., Luttrell, L., & Shapiro, S. (1979). Current practice of artificial insemination by donors in the United States. *New England Journal of Medicine*, 300, 585–590.
Czyba, J. C., & Chevret, M. (1979. Psychological reactions of couples to artificial insemination with donor sperm. *International Journal of Fertility* 24, 240–245.
Darlington, C. (1969). *The evolution of man and society*. New York: Simon & Schuster.
David, A., & Avidan, D. (1976). Artificial insemination: Clinical and psychological aspects. *Fertility and Sterility*, 27, 528–532.
Denber, H. C. B. (1965). Psychological aspects of human artificial insemination. *Archives of General Psychiatry*, 13, 121–129.
Dianes, A. (1968). Artificial donor insemination: Perspectives on legal and social change. *Iowa Law Review*, 54, 253–269.
Farris, E. J. & Garrison, J. (1954). Emotional impact of successful donor insemination. A report of 38 couples. *Obstetrics and Gynecology*, 3, 19–20.
Feingold, W. J. (1976). *Artificial insemination* (2nd ed.), Springfield, IL: Charles C. Thomas.
Gerstel, G. (1963). A psychoanalytic view of artificial donor insemination. *American Journal of Psychotherapy*, 17, 64–77.
Handelsman, D. J., Dunn, S. M., Conway, A. J., Boylan, L. M., & Jansen, R. P. (1985). Psychological and attitudinal profiles in donors for artificial insemination. *Fertility and Sterility*, 43, 95–101.
Harvey, B., & Harvey, A. (1977). How couples feel about donor insemination. *Contemporary Ob/Gyn*, 9, 10–17.
Kleegman, S. J., (1967). Therapeutic donor insemination. *Connecticut Medicine*, 31, 705–709.
Kübler-Ross, E. (1969). *On death and dying*. New York: Macmillan.
Levie, L. H. (1967). An inquiry into the psychological effects on parents of artificial insemination with donor semen. *Eugenics Review*, 59, 97–105.
Mazor, M. D. (1978). *The woman patient—Medical and psychological interfaces*. New York: Plenum Press.
New York Times, (1988). Increased male infertility puzzles researchers, February 10, p. 1.
Nicholas, M. K., & Tyler, J. (1983). Characteristics, attitudes and personalities of AI donors. *Clinical Reproduction and Fertility*, 2, 47–54.
Reading, A. E., Sledmere, C. M., & Cox, D. N. (1982). A survey of patient attitudes towards artificial insemination by donor. *Journal of Psychosomatic Research*, 26, 429–433.
Rowland, R. (1983). Attitudes and opinions of donors on an artificial insemination by donor (AID) programme. *Clinical Reproduction and Fertility*, 2, 249–259.
Rowland, R. & Ruffin, C. (1983). Community attitudes to artificial insemination by husband or donor. *Clinical Reproduction and Fertility*, 2, 195–206.

Rubin, B. (1965). Psychological aspects of human artificial insemination. *Archives of General Psychiatry, 13,* 121–132.

Sants, H. J. (1965). Genealogical bewilderment in children with substitute parents. *British Journal of Medical Psychology, 37,* 133–141.

Sawatzky, M. (1981). Tasks of infertile couples. *Journal of Gynecological Nursing (10),* 132–133.

Seymour, F. I., & Koerner, A. (1936). Medicolegal aspect of artificial insemination. *Journal of the American Medical Association, 197,* 1531–1534.

Sorosky, A. D., Baran, A., & Pannor, R. (1978). *The adoption triangle.* New York: Anchor Press.

Souval, P. A. (1959). Artificial insemination: Review of opinions on its moral validity. *Medical Arts Science Review,* 119–125.

Stewart, C. R., Daniels, K. R., & Boulnois, J. D. (1982). The development of psychosocial approach to artificial insemination of donor sperm. *New Zealand Medical Journal, 95,* 853–856.

Wilson, E. A. (1979). Sequence of emotional responses induced by infertility. *Journal of the Kentucky Medical Association,* 229–233.

Chapter 9

Who Becomes a Surrogate
Personality Characteristics

JOAN EINWOHNER

The conceiving and bearing of a child for another person or couple would not be likely without the historical events and the scientific progress in reproduction that have occurred since the 1960s.

The Supreme Court's ruling in *Roe* v. *Wade* that allowed women the legal right to control their bodies' reproductive functions was a landmark decision. By recognizing a woman's right to choose whether or not to bear children, the Supreme Court paved the way for surrogate motherhood as an option.

The new social philosophy emanating from the women's movement and the changed attitudes toward sexuality were major factors in providing the background for surrogacy. With the lessening of moral and social stigma attached to unwed motherhood, motherhood itself became more of a social and economic choice than a moral or biological imperative. A woman, married or not, could choose to bear a child for herself or someone else.

Surrogate motherhood in the United States began about 12 years ago in Michigan, with a lawyer named Noel Keane. A friend of Mr. Keane approached him with the idea of paying for someone to bear a child because his wife was unable to. Mr. Keane, himself a Catholic and father of a sizable family, appreciated his friend's wish for a child. He agreed to the concept. After placement of an ad for a volunteer and the selection of a suitable person, money was put in escrow for the surrogate mother and for handling the expenses. The arrangement was successful and became a specialty in Noel Keane's practice.

Traditionally, the one in six couples who wanted, but were unable to have, children turned to adoption. However, abortion and the use of birth control have reduced the number of unwanted children, and a more accepting social climate has permitted many unmarried women to keep their babies. In less than 20 years, the number of white babies available for placement in adoptive homes has dropped so much that some adoption agencies report a 5-year waiting period before a couple can hope to receive a child.

JOAN EINWOHNER • The Infertility Center of New York, New York, New York 10022.

This waiting period becomes a deterrent, if not a barrier, to parenthood. Couples often postpone families for careers or economic reasons. When ready to rear children, they are at an age when fertility has declined. They often try for years to become pregnant. Then there are years of medical procedures before couples are certain that they cannot conceive. Given these long delays and a lengthy waiting period, many couples pass the age limits set by many adoption agencies.

The only children available to adoptive couples in this situation may be orphans outside the United States, handicapped or older children, or children of different or biracial backgrounds—which present complex problems a couple may be unwilling or incapable of handling.

Surrogate motherhood, then, presents a viable, reasonable means of obtaining a wanted child. It is estimated that 500 children in the United States have been born in the past 12 years through surrogate mothers.

Some couples see advantages to surrogate motherhood over adoption. Half the genetic background of the child is from a member of the couple, which can be an important psychological factor. The couple has a choice in the selection of the person contributing to the genetic makeup. They can try to ascertain beforehand that the surrogate is mentally stable, intelligent, and physically healthy, with no habits of substance abuse or history of known genetic defects. They are reassured that their child will receive good prenatal care. And, unlike adoption, they can participate in the planning for the child and be present at its birth.

The use of artificial insemination from donor men to women married to infertile husbands has become routine in recent years. When preconception legal procedures are followed, 20 states now accept a child born by this method as legal issue of the marriage. Single women can also employ artificial insemination from a donor male without problems of parental rights.

The most common procedure with surrogate motherhood is for the surrogate's ovum to be fertilized through artificial insemination with the intended father's sperm. According to the agreement, the baby is given to the biological father and his wife.

A less common procedure is that of removing the fertilized ovum from a woman unable to carry to term and implanting it in the surrogate's uterus for the rest of the gestation. It is also possible, though rare, for a surrogate to donate an ovum fertilized by the intended father's sperm and have it implanted into the womb of the infertile mother, who can then experience pregnancy and birth. It boggles one's mind to realize that a child can have five "parents": an ovum donor, a sperm donor, the birth mother, and the two people the child knows as mother and father.

After 30 years as a clinical and school psychologist, I entered the field of surrogate counseling in 1982 and became a consultant with the Infertility Center of New York in Manhattan. Since that time I have seen approximately 100 volunteers. I provided counseling and psychological screening to assess their suitability for surrogate mothering.

The data for this article are from a sample of the first 50 volunteers to be surrogates who gave informed consent to be research subjects. Data were obtained over a 4-year period of psychological screening.

The screening consisted of a semistructured interview and psychological testing—the Roschach Inkblot Test, the Minnesota Multiphasic Personality Inventory, and the Ammons Quick Test. Each provides a different kind of information about the person being investigated. Training and experience are necessary to interpret the results of these tests.

The Rorschach is a series of standardized inkblots in which the person "sees" different forms, much like "seeing" objects in cloud formations. There are no right or wrong answers, since the way each person interprets the blots is indicative of his or her personality, attitudes, and characteristic ways of handling situations.

The Minnesota Multiphasic Personality Inventory (MMPI) is a list of many statements, which the person sorts into two groups, depending on whether the statements apply. Since the person can choose whether to admit to particular feelings or actions, the test is designed to reveal when a person is not being honest.

The Ammons Quick Test is a brief measure of verbal intelligence. Subjects were also asked to Draw A Person and provide a written description of the drawing. This projective test reveals some of a person's self-image and awareness.

The group ranged in age from 18 to 38 and had an average IQ of 99.8 (ranging from 82 to 116). Most had completed high school and many had gone to college. Only a few had graduate degrees. One had three master's degrees.

Eighty percent had had successful pregnancies, which they characterized as easy. Those with children averaged two. Of the five without children, three had had one or more abortions. Ninety-six percent had experienced pregnancy. Knowledge of the realities of pregnancy also came from growing up in larger-than-average families.

Early in my work with surrogates, I was particularly concerned with the dangers of exploitation and the potential for abuse. I was worried about the possibility of someone's dominating a woman and using her body for a selfish purpose, as in pornography. Therefore, it was important for me to question volunteers carefully, to find out whose idea it had been, where they had learned about surrogacy, and why they wished to be surrogates.

Generally, they were women who valued children and felt fortunate that they were mothers. They felt great sympathy with couples unable to have children, spoke of the sadness they felt when observing childless women at family gatherings or at baby showers. One reported a sister-in-law who always cried, and another said her husband's sister had committed suicide because she was unable to conceive. Many mentioned a relative or a friend who had had severe difficulties in conceiving.

Most had learned about surrogacy from magazine or newspaper articles or television. Some reported they were attracted to the idea even before they were married and found it more attractive after having children of their own.

Only one in the initial group said the suggestion had been initiated by her husband. Forty-three (86%) reported that the husband or lover approved of the plan or felt it was a course of action that a woman should decide for herself. He would support her if she so decided. One husband said his wife was never as beautiful or as energetic as when she was pregnant.

The first meetings between the couple and the potential surrogate are essentially mutual interviews. Initially, the couple knows a great deal about the surrogate from the biographical sketches they have received. The surrogate, although very interested in the couple, the quality of their marital relationship, and the kind of home they will provide, has been given little information about the couple. Sometimes she needs help to determine if the couple are people with whom she can enter into a long-term commitment involving a child.

Part of my function as counselor is to help elucidate important issues. For example, in one case I noticed from the Rorschach test that the surrogate had more than average religious concerns. From her interview I learned she'd had a strong Christian fundamentalist upbringing, often telephoned her minister, and had attended a Christian fundamentalist college. I asked her, "Would you want the child you bear to be raised in a Christian home?" She replied, "Yes, absolutely." She had not been aware that the couple was of another faith since she had not asked about the couple's religion.

Other issues might be whether there is to be contact or communication between the couple and the surrogate after the child's birth, whether amniocentesis should be performed to detect possible abnormalities, and whether the surrogate would be willing to abort a defective child. Such topics must be discussed and resolved. The contract always stipulates that a handicapped child is the responsibility of the infertile couple.

The surrogate has more control than is usually exercised by the birth mother in adoptions. Some surrogates place importance on a good relationship between spouses, others seek economic security in a home. In one instance, a surrogate became troubled when she saw the couple fighting and discerned that the husband was domineering and difficult. She withdrew and became a surrogate for someone else.

Mary S. initially declined to have a child for a single man who had been accepted as a client. She felt a child should have two parents. If the single father died, who would raise the child? Her own experience had left her with negative feelings. She had had two children, the first given up for adoption when she was a naive 14-year-old. The 18-year-old father had denied paternity and offered no support, even when she had given him a picture of the child that showed the resemblance to himself. Her parents, too, were divorced when she was 19, which had made her more aware of the importance of a child's having both parents.

When she expressed her concerns to the prospective father, he explained that he had a sister living nearby who would care for his child while he was at work. He described the large extended family that the child would have. His warmth, sincerity, philosophy of childrearing and yearning for fatherhood reassured her that he would provide for a nurturing, loving environment. She decided to have his child.

Many surrogates welcome the wife, less often the husband, in the delivery room so that the birth experience can be shared. They want the intended mother to bond to the infant as early as possible. Participants have reported the experience to be exciting. Surrogates have spoken of the look of joy on the intended mother's face as they hand the baby to her. They regard this as a consolation for any sense of loss they may feel.

What kind of woman is willing to conceive a child by a man not her husband, carry it within her and feel it move, go through the effort and pain of delivery, and then give it to relative strangers for love and care?

From my experience, surrogates tend to be down-to-earth, practical, decent people who assume that others are also. Most are not worriers; they tend to be optimistic. They want to experience and enjoy the pregnancy without the responsibility of raising the child. Money is a major factor, but rarely is it the sole reason. Money is put in escrow and changes hands only after the baby is born.

Only one of the surrogates, in my experience, has wanted the child back. Of the approximately 500 children in the United States born of surrogate mothers, maybe 1 in 100 has chosen to keep the child. In the other situations, the decision of the birth mothers was not opposed by the couple. Baby M was the first instance where the intended parents decided to go to court for custody.

Let me describe some surrogates and their backgrounds. Mrs. Masone was representative of the larger number of volunteers. She was an emotionally responsive and expressive young (24) mother of an 18-month-old daughter. She was soft-spoken and poised, yet conveyed a capacity for playfulness. She'd met her husband while both had been in the armed forces, he working in a technical, skilled area of engineering, she doing clerical work.

I felt that her husband was quite caring. He had traveled a long distance with their daughter to meet his wife in my office. He was concerned about her being in this large, unfamiliar city for the first time.

Mrs. Masone came from a close family with six children. Family life for her had been filled with pleasure and good times. Mother, grandmother, sisters, and grandchildren lived as neighbors. Long before she was married or had a child of her own, she had heard about surrogate motherhood on television and thought, "It's the nicest thing one can do for somebody."

Concerned about many different social problems, she was especially empathic with the pain and distress of infertile women. "I know how I felt when I wanted to have a baby and didn't conceive." Having enjoyed a feeling of exceptional well-being during her pregnancy, she looked forward to repeating the experience. She did not worry about separating from the infant. She thought only of the couple she was helping.

Fourteen months later, Mrs. Masone delivered a daughter and gave it to the couple without hesitation. By prior agreement, she was to receive news of the child from time to time through the agency. She has reported that her own life is going well, and after having another child for herself she may again volunteer to help another infertile couple.

Although she appreciated the money to be paid, and planned to use the fee as a down payment on a home, I feel that altruistic, idealistic feelings and her pleasure in pregnancy were her primary motives. She exhibited and spoke of enhanced feelings and of self-worth as a consequence of contributing to the happiness and well-being of others. She accepted the couple's desire to maintain separateness and to rear their child without outside pressures.

Separateness can be an important issue. Couples vary in their desire and need for privacy after receiving the child. Some want total separation; others wish to report milestones to someone with a special interest in their child. One couple named their child after their surrogate. In her nightly prayers, the child would say, "God bless the other Patricia." The same surrogate is providing a sibling so that Patricia will not be an only child.

And then there is the "family reunion" described by a surrogate mother at a public hearing conducted by State Senator Mary B. Goodhue of New York. She and her children meet the child she had borne and the parents at a family gathering once a year in an atmosphere of mutual affection. Feeling her life so enhanced by her participation as a surrogate, she plans to have another child for this couple.

To some surrogates, contact with the family is an important part of the recognition of their contribution. Surrogacy, however, is not without its disappointments.

Casey, a 25-year-old secretary, married with one child, had borne a baby for a couple. They had expressed great excitement, appreciation, and joy for what she had done and wanted to maintain contact. "I felt I did something really worthwhile," Casey said. Surrogacy gave her a special feeling of being valued. Her husband and her mother had been quite supportive.

Casey looked forward to a repetition of a rewarding experience when she volunteered again. Her mother was against the second surrogacy. She accused her daughter of having a child only for the money. She seemed unaware of her daughter's deep emotional needs for self-worth. Casey had long been ambivalent toward her mother, who was very sharp-tongued. Casey vividly remembered that when she was an adolescent, her mother had said to her, "You will never amount to anything." The pain of that remark had retreated with the sense of having done an exceptional thing when she bore a child for the first couple, who had remained in contact with her.

The second couple, however, was different. Casey felt the husband was domineering and self-centered. She didn't like his manner. The tension between them was increased by the daily headlines of the Baby M case. The couple feared she might not honor the agreement. Casey was barely out of the delivery room when the father presented her with legal documents. Also, he refused to have any contact with her after she returned home from the hospital. His wife did call a few times, and Casey liked her but felt disappointed and cheated. Moreover, she was offended and angry with him for thinking her capable of reneging on her promise to them.

Casey herself was confused. She'd always loved children, had even wanted to be a pediatric nurse. As a teenaged baby-sitter, she had been told she was surely going to have a huge family because of her delight in being with children.

Counseling provided by me and paid for through the Infertility Center helped her to sort out her feelings and become aware that she had expected too much from the second surrogacy. She was also able to face her need to prove to her mother that she was worthwhile and realize that her mother's criticisms stemmed from a fundamental lack of respect for her maternal and nurturing needs.

She also needed to work through her feelings that her husband was reluctant for them to have another child of their own. Eventually, she prevailed. He accepted her need for another child of her own, and she became pregnant. Casey seems to me representative of generative women who experience deep satisfactions in creating life and being with children.

A more unusual case needed ongoing help because the surrogate's feelings evolved as she participated in the program. Shelley was 33 and married. She wanted to experience pregnancy and childbirth. "I feel the female body is set up for it and should do it if it can," she said. A former dancer and actress, she wanted to "get fat and ugly and pursue an experience that didn't place such superficial value on the figure."

Shelley had deep fears about having children of her own to rear. She'd grown up in a large and troubled Catholic family with alcoholic parents. The father was passive, the mother was overwhelmed, and the children were often out of control. There were many painful reminders of her tumultuous childhood.

By joining a very stable commune, she'd eventually found the closeness, affection, and security missing in her family. Indeed, part of her fantasy was that of giving a child the loving family she wished she'd had. Realistically, she knew that rearing a child would require sacrifices and place a burden on her that she felt unable to handle. Furthermore, she wanted to study nursing to become a nurse practitioner providing community service. The surrogate fee would fund her education. If at some time she desired her own child, she felt that a prior pregnancy would increase the odds of successful childbearing at a later age.

After trying five times to conceive, Shelley still was not pregnant. Since insemination must be synchronized with the fertile times of a woman's menstrual cycle, it generally takes 3 months to a year before conception is achieved. Ultimately, however, Shelley withdrew. Worried about the child's growing up in someone else's home, she could not dismiss her feelings of responsibility toward the child.

Motivations for surrogates can be quite varied. Two women volunteered as a treatment for endometriosis. They'd been told by physicians that the condition, which incurred extreme pain daily, is in remission during pregnancy. Neither, however, felt able to support more children. (One had three children, the other two.) Both had undergone surgery for the endometriosis, which had then recurred. Pregnancy was for them a means of temporarily relieving their pain and at the same time providing a child that would be cherished.

Health, also, was behind the surrogacy of Priscilla, a 23-year-old physical education instructor in a health club. Slim, petite, very alert, and fresh-faced, she was an attractive, healthy-looking young woman. However, Priscilla had a history of severe anorexia that had been overcome through intensive psychotherapy. She feared that her prolonged starvation might have had a long-term effect on her ability to conceive. She wanted to reassure herself of her body's ability to function normally, especially after having had an abortion.

Engaged to marry a man with many interests similar to her own, she planned to use the fee to buy land in another state and breed dogs. Her affection for animals had been long-standing, and she had rescued many from neglectful situations.

She did expect to undergo some postpartum depression and said, "I know how hard it is for me to separate from my dog, my family, or my fiance." Despite this expectation, and the lack of enthusiasm from her fiance, a year later she gave birth to a healthy infant and was able to part from the child without regret.

A small percent of the surrogates volunteered for altruistic reasons. One wished to bear a child for an infertile cousin. A woman from South Africa has carried and borne triplets for her infertile daughter, which has made her both biological mother and grandmother.

Ann, 23, offered to be a surrogate for her older sister. Attractive and ambitious, she had a responsible position in an insurance company and had been given several promotions. Marriage and a family for her was sometime in the future, possibly around age 30. She had attended parochial schools and had lived a sheltered life in a traditional family. She had experienced little adolescent rebelliousness or experimentation. Nor had she been involved in any romantic or sexual relationships.

"I never imagined myself being pregnant until now. Nine months is a long time but not that long in terms of a lifetime," she said. "I know how much my sister and her husband want a child. They're happy; it's such a good marriage. She's done a lot for me throughout my life. They've been very giving, and it's my opportunity to really help them and give something back."

Personally, I'm uncomfortable with total altruism. Unless the experience is going to be satisfying in itself, I feel that altruism is not enough to guarantee inner satisfaction. Too much sacrificing is an unhealthy situation. There should be mutual benefit. If the act itself earns its own reward, people are more likely to persevere, and there is less burden on other people, less likelihood of disappointment.

In Ann's case, I was uneasy and suggested she move very slowly. I felt her to be so innocent, so inexperienced. Although surrogacy might have provided her with rewarding feelings, I worried if she could make an informed decision because of her lack of life experience. After the death of her father, Ann had become very close to her mother. In fact, her sister felt Ann had difficulty separating from their mother and lacked independence.

As of this writing, I do not know if Ann became a surrogate. However, this case particularly highlights problems with volunteers who have never been pregnant. They are unable to know how pregnancy will affect them, even if they come from large families with frequent births and they assume there will be no problems.

On the other hand, women who have had children can anticipate the feelings of pregnancy and birth. Indeed, re-experiencing pregnancy without the responsibilities of rearing a child brought into the world is one of the major motivations women express. Some feel a special excitement as they experience life quickening inside themselves. Many state they physically never felt better than when pregnant. Most volunteers state that for them childbirth has been easy. One young woman worried about the hospital's being an hour away from her home because she usually gave birth in 30 to 40 minutes.

Although surrogates often voice sympathy for childless women and a desire to help them, many view surrogacy as an attractive way to supplement their income. They often have important plans for the money. Starting a small business, a college fund for their children, or a down payment on a home have been mentioned.

One young wife saw surrogacy as a way of contributing to the family income while enjoying staying at home with her preschool children. Her pregnancies had been comfortable, the births easy. She knew that if she worked at an outside job, much of her earnings would go for child care, and she distrusted day care centers. She felt there would be no problem in separating from the child because "It's not my husband's. It belongs to someone else."

A surprising number (20%) had no immediate use for the money. They planned to bank it for their own children's future. No one turns money away, not even the three surrogates who said they would gladly volunteer even if no money were offered.

Nevertheless, 20 people (40%) in this study said that their foremost reason for volunteering was the $10,000 fee. Almost never, however, is money the sole motive. Almost all mentioned other feelings, such as sympathy for the emotional deprivation they believed childlessness brought to a marriage. These women enjoy their own children and feel happy in their home lives.

Of the volunteers I have counseled, only three women were on welfare. Two were black and one was Puerto Rican. Very few surrogates experience significant economic hardship. One welfare mother of two children, Mrs. Rivera, longed to complete college. Though her father had promised to pay for college, he refused to help when she became pregnant by a married man shortly after graduation from high school. He was rigid in his adherence to Christian fundamentalist beliefs and could not accept her behavior. When she was a small child, their lives had revolved around daily church attendance. She had been tightly overcontrolled by her parents, particularly by her father.

Indeed, some of her life choices seemed to have been the result of the need of an adolescent to break away from oppressive parental domination. But her rebellion seemed superficial. She felt most secure in a narrow, familiar environment, and she tended to isolate herself from others and from outside influences. In childhood, she had defensively withdrawn into personal fantasies.

At 24, she was still living with the man and their two children in a common-law arrangement. He was divorced but had been disabled in a construction accident. She refused to marry him, although he was very supportive of her in the care of their children.

By her own efforts and loans, she managed to attend college for 2 years but did not have the means to continue. She volunteered as a surrogate in order to pay off the loans and continue in school. "I expect to feel glad when it's over because I will have done my part and will be compensated," she said, but added, "I like the idea of helping people to have children because it would be sad to be unable to have any."

Ms. Rivera was sensitive and imaginative, and though self-centered, she lacked insight into herself and others. She was quick to volunteer, to be giving and helpful, without anticipating the effort required. She was vulnerable to mood swings, alternating between periods of depression and euphoria. Her lack of stability, combined with excessive fantasy, led me to feel she would not be a reliable surrogate.

I discussed these issues with her in detail and recommended that she obtain therapy to gain greater insight into her motives, to work out her feelings about her parents and her childhood, and to explore her relationship with her common-law husband. A few weeks later, I received a letter from her stating that she intended to ask her son's school psychologist for a referral to a therapist.

The statistical analysis of the psychological tests revealed that the majority of surrogate volunteers in my study were intelligent, self-aware, stable adults, motivated by idealism and a variety of personal motives. Given careful counseling, they were capable of entering into and fulfilling surrogate contracts freely.

The concept of surrogate motherhood, however, is controversial. Critics cry that surrogate mothers are being "exploited" and "dehumanized." They fear that surrogacy might result in emotional deadening. However, the surrogates do not report feeling deadened during pregnancy, nor do they seem to experience an emotional strain. Nonetheless, research is currently being planned. Surrogates will be contacted to see what the long-term consequences are or if some individuals have more regrets than they had anticipated.

I do agree that there are stresses upon the surrogate. More important, the surrogate must adjust to bodily changes and will have emotional reactions to the quickening of life within her. Finally, she will experience the physical strain of birth, and in a heightened hormonal and emotional state, must give over the infant and separate from it.

There are also complex interpersonal adjustments. She must cope with the reactions of husband, relatives, family, friends, employers, and those of the infertile couple. Most relatives' reactions are reported to be positive. However, it must be remembered that the surrogates are young adults who make their own choices and live their own lives. They often do not say anything to relatives who might be critical. Some stated frankly that, because they lived far away from parents, they would simply not tell them. Another, currently pregnant, stated that she would consider being a surrogate again only when her mother moved to another state because she liked being pregnant but found it difficult to cope with her mother's pressures to stop having babies and pursue a career instead. This young woman already has three children of her own; her husband has had a vasectomy because they do not want the burden of raising more.

Some conservative groups feel it is presumptuous for individuals to plan and choose for themselves when and how to have children rather than resigning themselves to the "will of God." The *New York Times* reported that a brief by Catholic bishops, filed with the New Jersey Supreme Court, states, "In surrogacy, a child is conceived precisely in order to be abandoned to others and his or her best interests are the last factors to be considered. . . . There is great potential for psychological injury in the child when he realizes that he was born, not of a loving relationship but from a cold, usually financial, relationship" (1987, July 19, p. 28).

Some critics expect the children to feel rejected and abandoned by their birth mothers. Others believe a child will be damaged by knowing that the birth mother was paid. On the other hand, the child may feel quite cherished when he or she learns of the effort and desire that went into the birth. Moreover, it is unlikely that money will be mentioned to the surrogate child any more often than adoptive parents discuss financial details with their adopted child. Adoption often entails considerable medical and legal expenses as well as recompense to the birth mother.

In the end, the critical factor in the satisfaction or dissatisfaction a child feels is the quality of the relationship with the parents. It is my opinion that social acceptability of surrogacy will also be a crucial determinant influencing the child's reaction. I feel that, unlike the rigid social atmosphere that used to shun and stigmatize children of unwed mothers, the climate is currently favorable in many places. Criticism may abate as surrogacy ceases to be novel.

In addition, I feel that surrogacy may enhance the infertile couple's marriage. An infertile wife often feels inadequate, guilty, and depressed at not being able to have the child she wants and because of her sense of frustration and failure in being the infertile partner. Her maternal impulses are frustrated. These feelings, of course, have an impact upon her husband. Surrogacy may diminish these negative feelings. In most instances, there are good feelings between the wife and the surrogate mother because it is most often the wife who is in contact with the surrogate during the pregnancy.

Moreover, surrogacy reinforces the husband's message to his wife that she is cherished, that he believes she is a good partner and will be a good mother for his child. He is expressing his determination to prevent her biological incapacity from coming between them. By making it a joint endeavor, the husband and wife are deeply involved in the planning and implementing of the agreement with the surrogate.

The history of mankind has been to control events that better ensure the survival of our species. Surrogate parenthood is another way to overcome obstacles to reproduction and to bring children to the parents who desire them.

ACKNOWLEDGMENT. I gratefully acknowledge the skilled assistance of Helene Kylen in the preparation of this manuscript.

Chapter 10
Contemporary Adoption
A Cooperative Enterprise

DOROTHEA S. MCARTHUR

BASIC PREMISE

The author of this chapter is an adoptive mother currently participating in the Cooperative adoption* for her adoptee daughter. She is also a clinical psychologist and a writer with a keen interest in relationships and the feelings gained through interpersonal experience. This author offers two premises.

1. An adoptee, whenever possible, should be allowed the chance to have some individually tailored contact with his or her birthfamily to resolve feelings of loss, rejection, and blame. A cooperative adoption aids the adoptee in creating a whole, independent, self-determined adult.

2. Cooperative adoption, if handled with reasonable appropriateness, may be more complex, challenging, rewarding, and psychologically healthy than traditional closed adoptions for all members of the adoption triangle.

This chapter will consider the issues, advantages, and disadvantages of allowing an adopted child a nonparenting relationship with members of her birthfamily. The notion of cooperative adoption is a relatively new way of handling adoption in the United States and is contrary to some of the beliefs that fostered traditional sealed-records adoptions.

DEFINITION OF TERMS

Before cooperative adoption is examined, a few terms used throughout this chapter need to be defined. The *adoptive family* is the family that has become the legal guardian of a child but is not genetically related (Rillera & Kaplan, 1985). The *birthfamily* is genetically related to the adoptee but has relinquished legal guardianship of the

---

*© Rillera & Kaplan, 1985.

DOROTHEA S. MCARTHUR • Private practice, 2362 Cove Avenue, Los Angeles, California 90039.

child. The term *members of the adoption triangle* refers to adoptive mother/father, adoptee, and birthmother/father.

There are many different kinds of adoptions now taking place in the United States and the world. The concerns and issues in this chapter apply to all of the different kinds of adoptions, including the following:

Agency Adoption. This is an adoption coordinated by a social service agency.

Relative Adoption. This term applies to an informal or legal transfer of guardianship within the family structure from the biological mother to a relative such as a mother, grandparent, aunt, uncle, brother, or sister.

Fertilization Adoption. This kind of adoption includes artificial insemination, surrogate, embryo transplant, and *in vitro* fertilization. An egg and/or sperm are donated to an infertile couple through informal or legal custody transfer. Frequently, one fertile genetically related parent is able to participate in the reproduction process.

Independent Adoption. This is an adoption that is arranged privately outside of a licensed adoption agency between the birthparents and the adoptive family, often with the help of a lawyer or a physician.

Closed Adoption. This describes the legal transfer of an adoptee from birthfamily to adoptive couple with the agreement that there will be no contact between the two parties. Records are legally sealed so that it is difficult to reestablish contact without showing "good cause" in a court hearing.

Open Adoption. Such an adoption is one in which there remains some limited contact between the birthfamily and the adoptive family. This may involve yearly exchange of letters and photographs, addresses kept current with a mediating lawyer, and/or a few meetings between the adoptee and the birthmother when the child reaches adolescence.

Cooperative Adoption. This involves an ongoing relationship between members of an adoptive family and a birthfamily. This relationship is created and maintained mainly for the adoptee, although other members of the adoption triangle may also benefit. The adoptee's feelings, both verbal and nonverbal, are always consulted and considered even when the adoptee is very young. The adoptee assumes increasing responsibility in the decisions affecting the amount and quality of contact between the two families. Beyond this definition, it is difficult to describe cooperative adoption because it is different for each adoption triangle, and it undergoes changes over time.

The essence of cooperative adoption is defined beautifully in the opening pages of a handbook by Rillera and Kaplan (1985).

> Cooperative adoption represents possibilities. . . . Cooperative adoption adds options and extends family relationships. (p. 1) If the child has access to both families, (s)he does not lose anything, and both sets of parents by the nature of the relationship will have continued access to each other. . . . (p. 1)
>
> Cooperative adoption requires an understanding that all relationships are continually renegotiable. None of us stay the same and all our dreams, needs, and

> relationships change with time, maturity and experience. In a Cooperative adoption the child must be seen as having progressive participation in his/her own life and in the relationships established by adoption. . . . (p. 2)
>
> Cooperative adoption is what you make it. It is continually evolving. . . . (p. 2)

This kind of adoption has been customary within a number of cultures (Eskimo, Hawaiian, Irish) but has recently blossomed in some parts of the United States. For example, a cooperative adoption group was started in Southern California approximately 3 years ago with only a few families. The group has expanded to over 100 with participants traveling for many miles to learn and question this new way of relating.

A cooperative relationship can start before the baby is born and continue indefinitely. Cooperative adoption can also begin late in life after the search is completed to unlock sealed records. Cooperative adoption may happen for only the period of time until the needs of the adoptee are satisfied. It is never too late to start a cooperative adoption. However, it does require the permission of all parties involved. Any member of the adoption triangle has the right to refuse or close down a cooperative adoption.

This new kind of adoption requires that society rethink what is best for the adoptee. The secrecy of traditional adoptions creates losses and unknowns that may not need to be present. Advocates of sealed-records adoption, although perhaps unintentionally, present the uncomplimentary assumption that adoptees cannot handle or integrate information about two families. Perhaps the real issue is that professionals, adoptive parents, and birthparents are afraid of the complexity that enters adoption relationships when there is full knowledge.

The advent of surrogate adoption has helped to bring the issues of cooperative adoption into focus. It usually takes approximately 6 months to conceive a surrogate child. Therefore, the adoptive couple and the surrogate family know each other for a minimum of 1½ years before a baby is born. Both the adoptive and surrogate families have worked hard with each other and have reason to challenge the necessity of totally cutting off a relationship after the baby is born.

Sealed Records Adoption

> Secrets are powerful. They are powerful producers of curiosity, action, guilt, rumor and panic. They cause people to feel worthless. They demean and shame people. They haunt people and obsess people. The impact of secrets is jolting and far reaching. (Martin, 1980, p. 213)

Since the 1930s, professionals and society subscribed to the notion that if we did not tell the truth about adoption, everyone would be spared a lot of pain and difficulty. If we withheld information from adoptees after they were adopted, they would not know about the preexisting bonding between themselves and their birthmothers. Adopted parents hoped that if they did not talk about adoption, they could feel like biological parents. Birthmothers hoped that if they did not know where their children were placed, the pain of relinquishment would decrease.

Unfortunately, all parties are unable to put aside the transfer of a child from one family to another. No one can pretend that such an important departure from the norm did not happen.

There were additional reasons why the sealed records movement became established in the 1930s. First, society was much more negative about unwed mothers during this time. Birthmothers were encouraged to give up their children with the understanding that the records would be completely sealed and their adoptees would never contact them later in life. Social workers did not want the adoptee to carry the stigma of being "illegitimate." Sealed records hid birthfamily traits that might or might not be inherited. Professionals felt that the adoptive parents should have sole parenting rights when they opened their homes to these children. Agencies also wanted the privacy so that unwanted children might have an increased chance of being placed (Lasnik, 1979).

In the process, adoptees have continued to be treated as children who have to get permission to do anything about their constitutional right to recover their heritage. The literature reports that a vast majority of birthmothers do wish some contact with the adoptee (Johnston, 1984; Lasnik, 1979; Martin, 1980; Sorosky, Baran, & Pannor, 1978). Debate continues regarding the necessity for adoptees to be presented with regulations and obstacles against contacting his or her birthfamilies.

We now understand the deleterious effects of secrecy. The American Adoption Congress and over 370 search-and-support organizations over the country help professionals and members of the adoption triangle to lift the veil of secrecy (Kaplan, 1987).

Attachment

John Bowlby (1969) defines attachment behavior as "seeking and maintaining proximity to another individual" (p. 194). He continues by saying: "No form of behavior is accompanied by stronger feelings than is attachment behavior. The figures toward whom it is directed are loved and their advent is greeted with joy" (p. 209). "So long as a child is in the unchallenged presence of a principal attachment-figure, or within easy reach, he feels secure. A threat of loss creates anxiety, and actual loss, sorrow; both moreover are likely to arouse anger" (p. 209).

We have learned that pregnant mother and unborn fetus establish a bonding relationship with each other during the last 2 to 3 months of pregnancy (Verny, 1981). They establish the same sleeping patterns. An unborn fetus increases bodily movements when the pregnant mother is upset. A baby who is psychologically rejected by a mother during pregnancy may turn its head away from her breast when born (Verny, 1981). An adoptee may have had a disturbing intrauterine experience if the biological mother was in pain about the planned relinquishment and would know when a new mother takes over. Infants adopted on the first day of life often come to their new home clinically depressed. Some of them have nightmares for the first few months of life. Although they may not remember consciously, their unconscious minds apparently have records of the transfer. Birthmothers may choose, because of life circumstances, not to raise a child, but the longing for attachment and love are not relinquished so easily. The pain about the loss may be carried for a lifetime.

For the adoptive couples, adoption cures childlessness but not infertility. Adoptive couples do not forget their infertility and the pregnancy that was not shared with their adopted child.

The Adoption Triangle's Response to Adoption

Responses to adoption are not stereotypical for any member of the adoption triangle. Some adoptees speak directly at an early age about their adoption experience.

Others may not speak directly about the transfer from one attachment figure to another but show instead the impact of adoption through their behavior. Many adoptees show psychological distress around moving. One little boy sometimes requested to take a cookie in a plastic bag when he went out for his morning walk with his adoptive mother. He would save some of his lunch at school until he saw his adoptive mother come and pick him up. Then he gulped down the remaining bits of food. Was he protecting himself in case he lost another attachment figure? Changing teachers at the beginning of the new school year may be a painful experience for an adoptee because it feels like another adoption. Other children drop an inquiry too subtle to be noticed easily. Still other children display their pain openly in defiant or limit-testing behavior. There are some children who do not seem to experience much curiosity or pain about their birthfamilies. Often adoptees initially shoulder these events and feelings alone because no one understands or believes that they have some memory of the psychological pain from the loss of the original attachment figure, a memory that surfaces over and over again (Johnston, 1983, Krementz, 1982, Nerlove, 1985).

Birthmothers, too, show a wide variation in their response to an adoption experience (Arms, 1983). A few birthparents do abandon their children; others have children taken away from them without their choice. Most give up their children because they feel unable to provide adequately as parents. Some think about their relinquished child every day of their lives, while others do not appear to give the adoptee much thought.

Adoptive parents should be a more uniform group in terms of their response because they have all been through a similar screening process. However, some adoptive couples are superb parents and some are poor parents. Some parents embrace the difference between adoptive parenting and parenting a natural child, while others deny it (Johnson, 1983).

It is commonly known that adoptees, in the absence of accurate and specific information, know that something went wrong. They blame themselves for the loss of a relationship with a birthmother: maybe the adoptee was bad, or maybe the adoptive parents stole the adoptee from the birthmother (Stein, 1979). Whatever happened leaves the adoptee feeling angry and unresolved. However, it takes many years of development, both cognitive and emotional, for the child to understand the complexities of adoption (Phillips, 1969, Melina 1986, Lindsay, 1987). The question becomes how we as a society can best help an adoptee to come to terms with a birthmother attachment that came to an end before it barely began and adoptive attachments that started late.

Adoption Is a Different Form of Parenting

In the past, adoptive families have been encouraged by professionals to regard their family unit as "just the same as a biological family." One of the problems with this attitude was that society did not believe it. To accommodate this problem, professionals then advised hiding the truth from society. The message was changed slightly to read, "Take your adoptee home, love him or her as your own. There is not a difference, but don't tell anyone about adoption, including the child." At that time, we began to understand the damaging impact to the adoptee of such a major lie that was certain to be discovered later on. Next, adoptive families were encouraged to say "Love him as your own. There is no difference, but tell your adoptee about adoption." The prescription to tell about adoption was followed perfunctorily because adoptive couples had no guidance on how to do it well. Also, "Tell about adoption, but there is no difference" is a contradiction in terms (Johnston, 1984). Adoption is different from parenting a natural child.

1. Adoption pulls apart the ties that bind birthparents and adoptee, taking away the adoptee's lineage and heritage.
2. Adoption denies access to birth records.
3. Adoption denies inheritance and insurance benefits to an adoptee unless specifically stated in a will (Kirk, 1981).
4. Adoption produces a role handicap. This means that adoptive families have to assume a life role without assuming all of the role expectations (Kirk, 1981). For example, an adoptive mother is not a mother in the traditional sense. Instead she is one of two mothers without a 9-month pregnancy.
5. Adoption is a "fundamental life altering event with intergenerational repercussions" (Kaplan, 1987), leaving every member of the adoption triangle with seven psychological core issues to work through. These issues may be briefly summarized to include continuing fears regarding loss; separation; intimacy and rejection; shame and guilt; grief; identity confusion; and concern about mastery and control (Kaplan, 1987).

Perhaps we will move forward in our thinking to a new prescription: "Adoption is different for all members of the adoption triangle. Tell your adoptee about it as soon as he or she asks. Let the birthfamily help the adoptee understand and minimize the sense of loss."

If the adoptive family can experience the losses, accept the difference in adoption, accept all of the parents and children as they are, then this family stands to gain in intimacy and life experience. Kirk (1964) labeled this process "shared fate theory." Professionals and society at large need to grant members of the adoption triangle the education and freedom without criticism to share with each other as a part of accomplishing this task (Johnston, 1984).

Considering a Cooperative Adoption

Statistics are not well established, but it is estimated that there are approximately 50,000 new adoptions per year in the United States. Approximately 70% of all adoptions remain closed, while 15 to 20% are open adoptions and 1 to 5% are cooperative.

There are three reasonable concerns that need to be addressed regarding cooperative adoptions.

1. What if one or more parties may be unable to handle a cooperative adoption? What if someone does not want it? What if one party has a history of criminal, antisocial, mental or drug problems?

Of course, a cooperative adoption can be attempted only if all of the parties involved wish to participate. If a member of the adoption triangle is unprepared, do not assume that that person will not become ready at a later time. The invitation to participate in a cooperative adoption and a noncontrolling open-door policy is a valuable offer. Some people take a long time to become prepared.

Society tends to stereotype birthfamilies as people who have made a mistake. They are classified as people with lives in too much disarray to parent a child appropriately. Sometimes this is indeed true. More often, birthmothers are adoptees themselves, working out their unresolved conflicts with adoption by becoming pregnant. Other birthmothers are just people who got caught making a mistake that others got away with. Many birthmothers proceed to do a creditable job with life, creating their own new families and choosing a profession. Birth and adoptive family members with difficulty with other aspects of their lives have successfully come together to negotiate a relationship for an adoptee.

2. *Aren't we taking a risk that the birthmother will take the child back?*

It is important to remember that adoptions well underway have already been through the legal system. It would be kidnapping for the birthfamily to remove the adoptee from the adoptive family unit.

Second, most birthmothers feel the loss, the pain, and the longing but generally continue to believe that relinquishment was the correct decision; otherwise they would not have given up a child in the first place. They do not want to try to parent a child that has already been partially raised by someone else. They do, however, want to know that their relinquished child is doing well on an ongoing basis. They want to know what the adoptee looks like, and to know the people who are raising their child. There is no one who knows better the wrenching pain of losing a child, and if the birthmother knows and respects the adoptive parents, she feels reluctant to impart such pain to them.

3. *Isn't a relationship with the two families overwhelming for an adoptee and therefore psychologically disturbing?*

Of course there is pain for each member of the adoption triangle as they negotiate a cooperative adoption. However, the pain of reality is generally easier to bear than the secrets, fantasies, doubts, misconceptions, or lies in the absence of concrete information.

It is important to design the cooperative adoption so that it is not psychologically overwhelming for the child. Cooperative adoption families do this by slowly, carefully, and openly considering the child's feelings. Events shared with the birthmother are carefully planned, with time in between to absorb and process reactions.

The questions presented are valid indeed, but they can also become a cover-up for underlying feelings of threat, jealousy, and competition involving the adoptive family, the birthfamily, and the professionals.

> Along with guilt and shame, fear emerges. The adult adoptee fears he won't like what he finds out about himself or he fears a second rejection from the birthparent. The birthparents fear the blame their son or daughter will have for what they have done. The adoptive parents fear the loss of their child to another set of parents. The adoption agencies fear criticism for what they have done and for what they have tried not to do. (Martin, 1980, p. 219)

The reality is that the adoptee is likely to validate his strengths through seeing his birthfamily. The birthparents can be forgiven for what they did because an adoptee is given a chance to understand the reason for relinquishment, and has hopefully had a reasonable adoptee upbringing to appreciate. If the birthparents can be honest, the adoptee will learn something about mistakes and how they are corrected. If the adoptive parents have faithfully put in the quality time necessary to parent appropriately, they will have little to fear. As part of the working through of the experience of adoption, the adoptees may have periods of time when they request special time with the birthfamily. There are also times when the adoptive parents will not be perfect parents, just like all parents, and the adoptee may temporarily turn to the birthfamily for advice and an assessment of what happened. Such an opportunity could be an advantage for both. But in the last analysis, any adoptee knows that the person who provides the day-to-day care is the *real* parent.

There has been little research done on adoption. The work of Sorosky, Baran, and Pannor (1978) on adoptees who had opened sealed records reveals four significant facts: 1. Forty-one of 50 adoptees who searched were female. 2. Most adoptees (90%) were glad they had attempted a reunion. 3. Almost half of the adoptees developed a meaningful relationship with their birthparents. 4. Adoptive family relationships were not damaged as a result of the reunion between adoptee and birthfamily.

Creating a Cooperative Adoption

Adoptive couples who are successful with cooperative adoptions have some common characteristics. They have a solid sense of who they are, a belief that people are basically well-intentioned, a good sense of humor, and a support system. They have other sources of mastery and pleasure besides children. They would like to be parents but do not have to have children to maintain their self-esteem (Kaplan, 1987).

The easiest and most successful form of cooperative adoption occurs when the adoptive parents and the birthparents decide to create this form of relationship from the very beginning of their contact with each other. The adoptive and the birthparents then have a chance to get to know each other before the adoptee is born. During this time, ground rules are laid that form the structure of a long-term relationship. Decisions are made about the frequency of contact and the role that each person will have within a cooperative adoption. It is clearly established that the adoptive parents maintain the parenting role. The birthfamily fits most closely into the position of an aunt and an uncle. If the birthmother has children of her own, the adoptee acquires half-brothers and sisters who might be visited as frequently as cousins are seen. This can be especially advantageous for adoptees who are only children. The two families may schedule time to see each other and may even share portions of some holidays or vacations together.

A cooperative adoption may also be created out of an open, independent, or agency adoption. The adoptive couple and the birthmother may have had contact with each other before the child was born but cut off the relationship after the birth or after the adoption became final in court. They may have decided just to exchange letters and photographs and an occasional phone call. The adoptee may activate his or her adoptive parents to arrange a meeting with the birthfamily because questions arise that are difficult to answer in the absence of current information. Another member of the adoption triangle may introduce the possibility of a more cooperative adoption. The members of the adoption triangle meet with professional help. If all parties agree, plans are made to introduce the adoptee slowly and gradually to the birthmother through a series of letters, photographs, phone calls, and/or cassettes or videotapes, culminating in a face-to-face meeting. It takes emotional work to reestablish contact with each other, but the result can bring both relief and reward.

A search when the adoptee reaches adulthood may uncover the essential details in a closed or sealed-records adoption and result in a cooperative adoption. The unknowns and risks are much higher in this situation. The adoptee's search may be long, painful, and fraught with dead ends, disappointments, and underlying conflicts. Infrequently, birthparents may not welcome contact and may refuse to acknowledge their former relationship. On the other hand, the birthmother may have already initiated contact herself and is eagerly awaiting news of the child she surrendered long ago.

Cooperative adoption may exist briefly or for a lifetime. There may be periods of time when one member of the adoption triangle needs to take a break from a cooperative relationship; absence from time to time may be part of the working through of conflictual issues. However, the structure and the work has been done to renew the relationship as needed.

One fact remains constant across all successful cooperative adoptions. This extended family is formed primarily to meet the needs of the adoptee, although other members of the adoption triangle also benefit. The adoptee assumes progressively more control over the amount of contact as he or she matures.

Advantages to Cooperative Adoption for the Adoptee

There has been little theoretical literature devoted to the psychological aspects of adoption for an adoptee. Much of the adoption literature is of a "how to" nature or is a narrative of the adoption experience. Society has not considered adoption as an experience with attachment, loss, and separation because they thought that the child was too young to know that a separation had already occurred. A good example of this notion occurs in John Bowlby's (1969, 1973, 1980) major contributions to psychology, his three volumes on attachment and loss. There is no mention of adoption in the entire work!

However, we are learning that adoption presents an adoptee with a psychological handicap. Losing a relationship with a birthmother affects an adoptee's basic self-concept. This handicap can be taken on as a challenge and an opportunity to build strength or as a justification for compromised living. Some adoptees are raising feelings about adoption through behavior or words as early as age 3; the various books about adoption for children are written for toddlers and latency age children. Cooperative adoption provides a direct arena for the child to experience and articulate the feelings, doubts, questions, and fantasies about the adoption experience. Cooperative adoption minimizes the sense of total loss and gives the child the chance to feel noncompetitive, deserved love and attachment from a birthmother as well as from the adoptive parent. The adoptee is allowed to experience the ongoing concern that the birthmother has regarding the welfare of her relinquished child.

Daniel Stern (1985) and Thomas Verny (1981) give infants more credit than do previous researchers for observing the differences between the baby itself and other people and having relationships with others. We can speculate that an infant is able to sense the change between birthmother and adoptive parents. Since children are able to hear inside the womb, they certainly have a sense of the voice of the birthmother.

Adopted children must also experience a birthmother's distress as she makes the decision and cries about giving up her child. One birthmother had to find a second adoptive couple shortly before the birth of her child. When she met the new couple, she spoke about her anguish during the past weekend and the physical discomfort she felt as her unborn child moved more restlessly than usual in her uterus.

In independent adoptions, the birthmother is allowed a period of time after the birth to decide whether she is going to legally relinquish her child. During this period of decision making, the child is usually already placed with the adoptive family. The adoptive parents must begin to bond to and love this child while facing the underlying reality that they may have to return the baby to the birthmother. There is no way around the fact that this is a compromising situation for the adoptive family and the adoptee, and it affects the loving that goes on between them. The situation is hardly a normal one, and the infant must feel the complexity of emotions.

A 3-year-old adoptee spoke to his parents about being sent home from the hospital to his new family. He said, "I was very sad, but when I got there I was very happy." He spoke about crying while he was in the hospital.

The birth and adoptive parents were puzzled by this comment because it was clearly impossible for him to consciously remember the second day of his life when he left his birthmother and met his adoptive parents. Neither set of parents had seen him cry during his brief stay in the hospital. Therefore, no one had given him a story to remember about crying. The birthmother noted only that he seemed to recognize her voice because he would whirl his head around when she spoke to the nurses in the nursery.

Clearly this child did not know what had happened. He sensed enough, however, to ask his adoptive mother directly, "Are you my mother?"

Adoption is a complex phenomenon involving many personalities and circumstances. It will take any adoptee many years to understand. Cooperative adoption provides the children with some reality to observe the birthfamily, their coping with life, and their feelings about the adoptee. This reality is worth a thousand conversations about why the child was given away. The adoptees can see for themselves that there were reasons for the adoption that began long before birth. The adoptees can *see* that they were not to blame.

Finally, a birthfamily that is able to invest in the adoptee by providing a cooperative adoption is a birthfamily that cares. The adoptee does not have to face a complete rejection; the sense of loss is decidedly minimized. Instead, the adoptee can begin to build the birthfamily relationships necessary to ask those tender and delicate questions about the reasons for relinquishment. The birthmother comes to know the adoptee well enough to speak with the child in the optimal way to provide understanding. She knows and is respected by the adoptive family well enough so that she feels less embarrassment in talking about the home she could not provide. The adoptee gets the experience of seeing the birthmother as a thoughtful outside support system.

Every person strives for a sense of self and a sense of wholeness. Perhaps it is life's toughest challenge. We need to integrate all the pieces of our lives to accomplish this. We compile a memory bank of all of the important relationships we have had. That includes knowing the history of the family that came before us. An adoptee is entitled to the same rights. Only then can adoptees truly decide who they are and what they wish to do with life.

> Donna was adopted shortly after her birth. She was raised by an adoptive family who were scientifically talented, and short and stocky in build. She was artistic by nature, very tall and slim. She felt "dumb" and "skinny" until she met her birthfamily. Then she discovered them to be artistic and tall and slender in build. This information aided her tremendously in her decision to become a dancer.

Society challenges adoptees' ability to manage a cooperative adoption. However, we know that children are inherently wise and incredibly skilled at intuiting what is really going on between people. We know that children learn our vulnerable points and play on them at a very young age. Therefore, they can also accurately sense when to trust or not to trust a birthmother. When we are socialized and taught to be polite, we lose some of our innate capacity to accurately judge an interpersonal situation. Children still have this capacity and use it wisely, especially when their judgment is respected. In giving adoptees a chance to participate in the decisions inherent in cooperative adoption, we encourage the development of self-determination (Rillera & Kaplan, 1985).

Advantages to a Cooperative Adoption for a Birthmother

In my consultations as a psychologist I have never met a birthmother who wanted to give up her child. Instead, many birthmothers willingly insist upon saving an adoptee's life by refusing abortion and taking on society's condemnation of giving birth to a child without assuming the parenting responsibilities. Most birthmothers decide that adoption is the responsible action to take for themselves and the adoptee, but they feel wrenching pain, grief, and guilt in doing so. Once birthmothers have made a decision, most are not prone to change their minds. They fantasize that seeing the child will minimize the pain, but they know better. They would like the pain to go away, and they would like to know that the adoptee is alive and well.

Birthmothers and their extended families in closed adoptions worry about what has happened to the adoptee. They wonder, when in a public place, whether they have just passed by their surrendered child. They speculate about whether they would recognize the adoptee.

A birthmother decided to place her child in an open adoption situation. Therefore, she had met the adoptive couple several times before the birth of her child. After the adoption was final, the adoptive couple insisted for a time that their open relationship continue only by letter. During this time, the birthmother feared driving through the town the adoptive couple lived in on her way to work. She was afraid to go to the shopping mall or grocery store in that area because she didn't know what to do if she accidentally met her adoptive couple with the child. On the one hand, she felt that she would be intruding if she acknowledged the relationship, but she also longed to see how the child she gave away was growing up. The couple was able to initiate a cooperative adoption when the child became older. The birthmother's longings were greatly minimized with this new relationship.

Some birthmothers frequently wonder how the adoptee is managing. They may intuit an accident or illness on a particular day but have no way of checking with the adoptive family. Many feel resentful that they cannot know.

The birthmother's ongoing relationship or a renewed relationship with the adoptive family reduces the sense of total loss of a blood relative because the child is still allowed a nonparenting relationship with her. On the other hand, the experience of a cooperative adoption forces a birthmother to clarify her role as a birthmother who has relinquished parenting rights. This situation requires her to grieve the loss of the parenting attachment and resolve as much as possible the guilt related to allowing her child to be raised by someone else. Although she has relinquished parenting responsibilities, she is still able to demonstrate love in a way that actively helps her minimize her guilt and helps the adoptee to resolve feelings of basic rejection.

Perhaps society has chosen to punish birthmothers with silence and darkness for choosing not to raise a child. Does punishment help a person to grow and to fill in the parts that feel incomplete? Are our energies better spent in helping her to feel less pain and to make a contribution to the psychological health of the adoptee? Can a birthmother be allowed to take pride in saving a life of an unborn child and giving an infertile couple the important opportunity to have a family?

> An adoptive mother asked her birthmother whether she was going to have any more children. The birthmother responded, "No, I have given birth to three children and made two families. I am proud of what I have done."

Birthmothers feel that no one could love their child the way they do, and adoptive parenting is a necessary compromise. In most adoptions, however, the birthmother is able generally to approve of the adoptive parenting the adoptee receives and to appreciate the hard work that goes into raising a child responsibly. Unfortunately, adoptive couples are sometimes poor parents. Direct experience with the adoptive parents and a thriving adoptee can go a long way toward reassuring a birthmother and reducing the feelings of guilt about placing a child.

Advantages of Cooperative Adoption for the Adoptive Parents

An ongoing relationship with members of the birthfamily forces a lifting of any denial regarding the fact that the adoptee will always have two mothers who have participated in the growth of a child and have earned the right to care.

> An adoptive mother, in a cooperative adoption, spoke with another adoptive mother, participating in a closed adoption, about the experience of cooperative adoption. The adoptive mother with the closed adoption cut her off quickly by saying, "We would have no use for such a relationship. My son is completely my son and that is all there is to it. Our birthmother is gone and my son is just fine. He never talks about her and has no need to."

This adoptive mother is likely denying reality, making some false assumptions about her child's thinking, and perhaps closing doors for her family, especially her adoptee. What will this mother do if she is approached by the birthmother for a meeting with her adoptee?

Most adoptive mothers feel some guilt in participating in another woman's relinquishment of a child. This is especially true for women for whom the specific cause of infertility remains unclear. It is a painful experience to participate in causing the grief of a birthmother. However, if there is an ongoing relationship with the birthmother, the guilt is attenuated. First, an adoptive couple has not taken the child away completely. The birthmother has been freed to go on with other aspects of her life that may be critical to her survival and development, while the adoptive couple gets to see how she uses this gift of freedom. Of course, in every healthy relationship between a birthmother and an adoptive mother there will be a mixture of some competition and cooperation as they figure out how to be with each other. When feelings of threat and competition surface, both parties need to step back and consider what is needed for the adoptee. Then a resolution frequently comes into focus. A friendship often develops between birthmother and adoptive mother, easing the pain for both parties.

Family relatives may live far apart from each other. Adoptive families and birthfamilies may not be near their relatives for holidays and celebrations. A cooperative adoption creates a more extended family. Celebrations and holidays have the potential for becoming richer and more meaningful. As one adoptive mother said to her toddler adoptee, "Some children have four parents, some children have three, and some children have two parents. Other children have one, and some children have no parents. You happen to have two mothers who care about you and one father. You are lucky in many ways to have all that caring." (This toddler had yet to raise questions about the birthfather.)

Finally, it is gratifying for an adoptive couple to take a real risk for their child and have it be meaningful and helpful. It makes an adoptive couple feel a sense of heightened wholeness, a sense of self-determination, stolidity, and individuality in the face of societal pressure to do otherwise.

Parenting Issues for the Adoptive Couple

The obligation to parent well is heightened because the adoptive parents are accountable to the birthfamily. It is interesting to note that a number of birthmothers, in their writing about cooperative adoption, wish that the adoptive parents would be more strict with the adoptee (Rillera & Kaplan, 1985). When an adoptive mother feels overwhelmed, tired, careless, or frustrated with parenting responsibilities, sometimes it helps her to gain the necessary control of the situation by thinking, "Our birthmother would not like me to behave this way."

Adoptive parents have been through so many interviews and evaluations to become parents that they sometimes have the feeling that they should be superhuman in raising children. If the birthmother selected them to parent, they had better do it right. It is a relief to see that the birthmother does not regard an occasional lapse in discipline as a reason to go back to court! In fact, the birthmother is relieved that the adoptive parents are not superhuman.

Cooperative adoption forces early basic training in some very important parenting issues.

1. *Adoptive parents need to allow their children to have other important relationships without sabotaging them.*

As time goes by children turn to more and more people outside of the home for nurturance, training, and experience. Teachers, baby-sitters, Boy/Girl Scout leaders, ministers, counselors, and, finally, dating relationships all contribute to the growth and independence needed for a child to successfully leave home. Sharing the adoptee with the birthfamily is excellent basic training for handling the gradual emancipation of a child into the larger world.

2. *Adoptive parents need to observe, recognize, and enjoy the physiological and personality differences between the adoptee and the adoptive parents.*

One of the ways to appreciate physiological and personality differences is to have contact with the birthfamily. Then it is easy to see that "Jane has her mother's eyes." "Jimmy looks just like his brother when he runs." These differences can be clarified, supported, and developed as the adoptee acknowledges his or her genetic roots.

3. *Adoptive parents observe and support the emergence of adoptees' intellectual abilities, talents, and strengths, rather than predicting or dictating them.*

We all have hopes and wishes for our children. Perhaps we are all guilty, at times, of directing our children to behave in certain ways to enhance us as parents. Sometimes we want our children to be like us, or to do what we did, only better. It is harder to make these demands on an adopted child because we can't make the assumptions about capabilities and talents as we tend to do with our biological children. The adoptive parents can say, "Alice seems to have a talent in music. I think we should ask her if she would like lessons," rather than, "My kid will go to Harvard and be a scientist just as I did." Adoptive parents have to wait to see what emerges, a stance that gives adoptees more freedom than natural children to decide for themselves.

4. *Adoptive parents give the adoptee choice and reasonable measure of control over their lives and relationships with others.*

Young children, when their opinions are respected, make reasonable decisions in relation to cooperative adoption. They are able to ask when they have a need to see the birthfamily, and to say when they need time away from the relationship. They keep their birthmother at a distance until they feel they can trust her, and they relate to other members of the birthfamily first.

An adoptive family, in the process of establishing a cooperative adoption, scheduled a luncheon in which the birthfamily, including interested relatives, came to their home. Wendy, their 3-year-old adoptee, would meet her birthgrandparents for the first time. The adoptive family had been warned that the birthgrandparents might be understandably emotional since they had not supported the adoption in the first place. The grandparents drove into the driveway. While the adults stood motionless, trying to decide what move to make next, Wendy ran out to the car. She opened the door and said, "You must be my Granddaddy." Before Granddad could utter anything, she ran around to the other side of the car and said, "And you are my Grandma." Grandma reached down and scooped up this child to give her a big hug. Then they walked hand in hand to the porch where the adults still watched motionless and speechless.

5. *Adoptive parents need to deal with important adoption issues in a way that is congruent with the adoptee's readiness and motivation.*

There is so much to say to an adoptee about adoption. It is tempting to want to get it all out on the table right away and be done with it. But there is some information that the child cannot understand until much later. Cooperative adoption helps to provide information naturally and gradually. There are more people to help the child deal with it. It is an unfolding story told not so much in words, but with the actions of many complex characters. The adoptive parents and the birthfamily learn more about the complexities, too.

6. *Adoptive parents have to learn that they cannot rescue children from pain, only help them go through it.*

Our children's struggles will, we hope, be different from ours. We cannot create an environment with pain, and if we could, it would not be healthy. Cooperative adoption does not take away the pain for anybody; it simply provides an arena with a set of ongoing activities and interactions that each person can make use of to settle an unresolved conflict, heal a vulnerability, or learn something new. We can help our children to articulate the pain they do feel, respect it, and aid them in finding a resolution.

The Birthfather

The birthfather is most often the important character left out of this gathering together. If he has an ongoing relationship with the birthmother, then he is much more likely to want to be included in a cooperative adoption. However, if the birthfather is a casual relationship of a brief duration, then he is apt to go on his way and perhaps not even be available to sign necessary relinquishment papers. Therefore, a cooperative adoption frequently involves the birthmother, her extended family, her new boyfriend or husband, and any children she may have had before or since the adoption. The need for a birthfather to participate in a cooperative adoption may appear less intense because there is not the bonding to a fetus during pregnancy. However, some birthfathers do care and want to know what has happened to the children they have fathered. Adoptees care about who their birthfathers were, although their interest in this person usually follows their primary need to know about their birthmother.

The adoptive father provides valuable moral support to both the adoptive mother and birthmother, who tend to do the front-line negotiations regarding activities and feelings. The adoptive father can also provide a quiet, steady perspective that keeps adoption triangle members from despairing during difficult times.

Society's Response to Cooperative Adoption

Society tends to feel skeptical about cooperative adoption. There are reasons for this, some better than others. When a belief system has been established, such as closed adoptions, people make an emotional commitment to that principle and are slow to change their opinion. We tend to look at something new with a cautious eye. Friends and colleagues quickly raise many of the questions already addressed at the beginning of this chapter.

In addition, there is another feeling that rarely, if ever, is directly addressed. Members of the adoption triangle are a minority—people to look down upon. Their behavior is questionable. Birthmothers have made a most serious mistake, and adoptive mothers should have managed to become pregnant. Therefore, they deserve punishment by isolation. They shouldn't really talk with each other, let alone have a healthy, meaningful relationship. If they can come together successfully, that somehow minimizes the minority status.

However, there is an interesting precedent that is helping those involved with adoption. An increasing number of articles are being written on stepfamilies and their ability to share children openly within the new blended family constellations. Dads and stepdads are showing up together for a child's graduation, concert, or birthday. Divorced couples are maintaining a congenial parenting relationship for their children. Children no longer have to have a primary allegiance to one set of parents. Stepchildren are doing better psychologically with a continuing relationship with all of their parental figures.

Difficulties

Cooperative adoption, when done with care, is a rewarding and expanding experience. That does not mean that occasionally there are not times of confusion, jealousy, competition, and insecurity. Any major project has difficult times when it seems impossible to make it through to a satisfactory conclusion. This goes for writing books, building houses, and raising children, adopted or not.

Rewards

Some adoptees, in the absence of information and dialogue, unconsciously decide to start a pregnancy and give the baby up for adoption. That is certainly one way to see how their birthmother must have felt. A secondary, or psychological, infertility may be the result, depending on how traumatic the relinquishment experience may be. Then the adoptee has to become an adoptive mother herself in order to have her own family. Thus, the cycle is complete; she has become every member of the adoption triangle. It is not unusual to find a history of adoption in the background of anyone involved with adoption. Perhaps cooperative adoption will make these painful extra life steps unnecessary.

The adoptive family and the birthfamily obtain a loving relationship with the adoptee defined through shared knowledge, truth, respect, and independence rather than with secrets, lying, lack of information, and exclusivity. This is a good model to carry forward to other relationships.

A birthmother wrote a letter to her adoptive family after 8 months of cooperative adoption involving a 3- to 4-year-old adoptee. They had met six to seven times, and exchanged letters and phone contact as needed. They had shared birthdays and the Thanksgiving holiday, and were planning time together at Christmas. The birthmother wrote the following paragraph to her adoptive parents. "You know, I am so glad you let me see Danny. I feel so much more at peace now just knowing he is okay and being able to *see* so for myself. It's nice not to have a hole in my life anymore. Thank you so much."

The adoptive couple added, "It simply is not necessary to discount our birthfamily in order for us to be a family together. In fact, we feel like more of a family when we come together to include them and consider our feelings about them. We feel cheapened when we isolate them because they gave us something so important. Excluding them means we don't trust them or what they gave us."

Perhaps we can negotiate a cooperative adoption more peacefully if we remember the poet Kahlil Gibran, *On children:*

Your children are not your children
They are the sons and daughters of life's
    longing for itself.
They come through you but not from you.
And though they are with you, yet they belong
    not to you.

References

Arms, S. (1983). *To love and let go.* New York: Alfred A. Knopf.
Bowlby, J. (1969). *Attachment and loss, volume one: Attachment.* New York: Basic Books, Inc.

Bowlby, J. (1973). *Attachment and loss, volume two: Separation, anxiety and anger*. New York: Basic Books, Inc.
Bowlby, J. (1980). *Attachment and loss, volume three: Loss, sadness and depression*. New York: Basic Books, Inc.
Johnston, P. (1984). *An adoptor's advocate*. Fort Wayne, Indiana: Perspectives Press.
Johnston, P. (1983). *Perspectives on a grafted tree*. Fort Wayne, Indiana: Perspectives Press.
Kaplan, S. (1987, August). *A retrospective look at adoption in America. Screening for successful adoptions*. Presentation at the American Psychological Association Convention.
Kirk, D. H. (1964). *Shared fate*. New York: Free Press.
Kirk, D. H. (1981) *Adoptive kinship: A modern institution in need of reform*. Port Angeles, Washington: Ben Simon Publications.
Krementz, J. (1982). *How it feels to be adopted*. New York: Alfred A. Knopf.
Lasnik, R. (1979). *A parent's guide to adoption*. New York: Sterling.
Lindsay, J. (1987). *Open adoption: A caring option*. Buena Park, California: Morning Glory Press.
Martin, C. (1980). *Beating the adoption game*. La Jolla, California: Oak Tree Publications.
Melina, L. (1986). *Raising adopted children*. New York: Harper & Row.
Nerlove, E. (1985). *Who is David?* New York: Child Welfare League of America, Inc.
Phillips, J. L. (1969). *The origins of intellect*. San Francisco: W. H. Freeman & Co.
Rillera, M. J., & Kaplan, S. (1985). *Cooperative adoption. A handbook*. Westminster, California: Triadoption Press.
Sorosky, A., Baran, A., & Pannor, R. (1978). *The adoption triangle*. Garden City, New York: Anchor Press/Doubleday.
Stein, S. (1979). *The adopted one*. New York: Walker & Company.
Stern, D. N. (1985). *The interpersonal world of the infant. A view from psychoanalysis and developmental psychology*. New York: Basic Books, Inc.
Verny, T. (1981). *The secret life of the unborn child*. New York: Dell Publishing.

Chapter 11
Artificial Insemination by Donor
Yours, Mine, or Theirs?

BONNIE R. ARONOWITZ AND JOSEPH FELDSCHUH

In this chapter, brief interview data from donor insemination recipients, consisting of married couples, single heterosexual women, homosexual women, and from donors themselves are complemented by authors' commentaries regarding artificial insemination from medical and psychological vantage points. The intent is to highlight clinical interviews with pertinent psychodynamic and physiologic correlates of the procedure insofar as they suggest appropriate areas for further investigation. Such research concerns include the compilation of representative subject populations and control groups studied longitudinally and the delineation of biopsychosocial interaction variables in predicting general outcome and in identifying individuals at risk for negative sequelae.

MEDICAL ASPECTS OF ARTIFICIAL INSEMINATION BY DONOR

Until the early 1970s, human frozen sperm was believed to be less effective in artificial insemination than was fresh sperm, despite the fact that frozen sperm had been widely utilized in the animal industry. In 1971, however, IDANT Laboratories of New York City developed a technology that permitted the freezing of the majority of human sperm with effective sperm recovery. The technique involved staged freezing coupled with the use of a cryoprotective agent (Keel, Webster, & Roberts, 1987). This allowed for storage of semen for periods exceeding 15 years with limited loss of viability and enabled sperm collection from a broad spectrum of donors. It thus became possible to obtain donors whose genetic and biological

---

BONNIE R. ARONOWITZ • Ferkauf Graduate School, Yeshiva University–Einstein College of Medicine, Bronx, New York 10461; Neurological Institute and Anxiety Disorders Clinic, Psychiatric Institute, Columbia Presbyterian Medical Center, New York, New York 10302. JOSEPH FELDSCHUH • Cornell Medical College, New York, New York 10021; Montefiore Hospital, Bronx, New York 10467; and IDANT Laboratories, New York, New York 10022.

characteristics more closely matched those of the sterile father. An additional revolutionary aspect of the technique related to the woman's fertility cycle and the donor's availability during that period. In the past, a candidate's availability to produce sperm during future ovulation periods had been a major criterion in donor selection—a factor that greatly decreased the number of potential donors. The novel technique, however, completely eliminated this restrictive criterion. As a result, frozen and fresh semen are now being used for artificial insemination with comparable frequency.

Technique Description and the AIDS Virus

Typical of most viral infections is bodily recognition of the invading virus, with subsequent manufacture of antibodies which generally remain for a lifetime and prevent reinfection of the initial invading virus. In contrast, one of the insidious peculiarities of the AIDS virus (HIV-1) is that it attacks and invades specifically those bodily cells that provide the immune defense system, without host recognition of the invasion. The virus, instead, produces an antibody ineffective in preventing reproduction and spread. It is the lack of a blocking antibody that enables the AIDS virus to progress, unimpeded, and ultimately destroy the host. When no measurable antibodies to the AIDS virus have been manufactured, individuals may have active, transmittable AIDS, yet fail to evidence positive physical or laboratory findings of the virus. Currently, no simple tests detect the presence of the virus in blood or in tissues. The standard test—the ELISA test and its variants—developed in 1986 detects only the presence of antibodies to the AIDS virus.

Public awareness of the potentially fatal aspects of AIDS and consequent demands for safe sperm have been major factors in promoting the transformation to the more complex, yet safer technique of frozen sperm storage (Ball, 1986).

Frozen semen is preserved in liquid nitrogen at −321° F, which may then be transported to all parts of the world. Semen stored under these precisely monitored conditions loses virtually no viability after 15 years. It may ultimately be demonstrated that sperm can be kept viable for periods in excess of 100 years, and thus, it is theoretically possible that an individual may father offspring 50–100 years after he has been deceased. Frozen semen offers the additional advantage of enabling testing for the presence of infection, such as AIDS. AIDS and disease protection occurs through the freezing and quarantining of semen for a minimum of 3 months, thereby allotting time for the donor to be retested for AIDS. Should results be negative, the 3-month-old semen may be reasonably assumed to be AIDS-free. The Centers for Disease Control has, indeed, recommended a 3-6-month semen quarantine with subsequent donor retesting for AIDS antibodies, and the utilization of frozen sperm for artificial insemination has now been officially endorsed (Peterson, Alexander, & Moghissi, 1988; American Fertility Society, 1988).

Psychological Concomitants of the Infertility Work-up

Approximately 10% of the population is sterile and another 10% has serious fertility difficulties that impede conception. The incidence of infertility is approximately equally distributed between the sexes. However, assessment of male infertility is facilitated relative to female infertility owing to the ease of examination of a semen sample. Typically, infertile couples are initially referred to a gynecologist. In the past, this process has frequently resulted in the woman's undergoing extensive evaluations and testing prior to the male's undergoing even the most basic of semen examinations. Fortunately, this practice is less frequently encountered at the present time.

As couples make the initial transition from the avoidance of pregnancy to permitting pregnancy to occur, anxiety and emotional trauma escalate, with successive futile attempts at planned pregnancy. The invariable result is negative psychological sequelae for both partners. Discovery of infertility encompasses a broad spectrum of emotional responsivity. For example, since conception occurs within the woman, the tendency is for both partners to implicate the woman as the originator of the difficulty. The intensity of the emotional trauma is dependent upon multiple factors. One such factor is the time at which the true cause of infertility is discovered. For example, a couple that waits many years prior to undergoing evaluation may initially experience prolonged periods during which negative attention is focused upon the woman as the cause of the infertility. In contrast, a couple that undergoes a relatively early evaluation—i.e., less than 1 year of attempting pregnancy—may possess a more realistic or balanced view of the problem. In the authors' experience, it is typically the female who bears the initial burden of causality for infertility, as she fails to become pregnant over a specific time period. When she is confirmed as the cause of infertility, her "infertile attitude" has usually antedated the specific evaluation of the problem. In contrast, males who suspect themselves to be the cause of infertility are often reluctant to undergo appropriate testing for verification. Thus, the temporal relationship between suspicion of infertility and confirmation via semen analysis in the male may be quite brief relative to the female's discovery of her own infertility. Therefore, the discovery of infertility in men is typically unexpected, may be extremely traumatic, and is quite psychologically disorganizing.

Psychological Intervention

Brief-term psychotherapy for the sterile father should address the inevitable intermingling of potency and fertility inherent in the male psyche. Males, upon discovering their infertility, occasionally develop serious secondary potency and relationship difficulties. Crisis intervention reinforces the concept that masculinity and potency are essentially exclusive functions. Excluded from this group are a small percentage of males with organic, as opposed to dysfunctional, potency problems, which may be corrected by proper treatment—e.g., males with testosterone deficiency who may show significant improvement following treatment with testosterone injections.

It should likewise be stressed to the father, and to the couple, that artificial insemination by the use of frozen banked semen provides the opportunity to have a child genetically similar to the one the father would have naturally sired. Since counseling emphasizes genetic similarities between the donor and the sterile father, blood types should almost always be matched to the father. Emphasis should likewise be placed upon the naturalness of the insemination process—namely, that the sole artificial aspect is the insemination process itself. Once inserted into the vaginal canal, a sperm moves through the cervix to meet the egg in the fallopian tubes, where conception occurs and an embryo is formed. The embryo moves down the tubes to the uterus, where implantation occurs on approximately the fourth or fifth day following conception. It should be stressed that conception occurs normally and that the embryo develops in a completely natural manner, assuming no other preexisting genetic or developmental embryonic problems.

Partners should be informed that approximately 25% of all conceptions result in a spontaneous abortion or a miscarriage. However, this rate is identical with the rate of miscarriage risk in sexual intercourse. Moreover, children born through AID have no higher rate of birth defects than those conceived through intercourse. Statistical evidence suggests an actual lower malformation rate due to the selectivity of the sperm that results from the freezing process.

Among the problems that partners face is their reaction to a child who, while genetically similar to the sterile father, is not genetically identical to him. The female requires reassurance in order to provide support to her partner in the acceptance of the idea of conception by a donor. Often a partner reveals in an individual counseling session that he or she has accepted artificial insemination but believes that the respective mate has not truly been reconciled to the idea. Skillful intervention aimed at enhancing communication between the partners often yields great rewards in terms of acceptance. Conversely, although initial individual consultation may be indicated, in order to provide a forum for discussion by each partner of secretive feelings, it is guaranteed to yield diminishing long-term results. Counseling should focus on encouraging the couple to openly discuss hidden concerns in the presence of a counselor. Counselors may be physicians, psychiatrists, psychologists, or other qualified professionals trained in the specifics of infertility counseling.

Often one partner may request AI without informing the other; e.g., a woman may indicate that her husband could not accept AI or that his defective sperm should be mixed with donor semen. Similarly, males have often made requests regarding only partial disclosure to their partners. In most instances, both individual and couples treatment resolves the conflict. While experiencing great empathy for the altruistic motivations underlying such requests, we consider the collusion with an individual partner, exclusive of the mate, to be essentially unethical. Instead, extensive and, if necessary, prolonged psychotherapy is recommended to bring conflictual concerns into accord. For example, religious couples of certain denominations, such as orthodox Jews and Catholics, accept AI with the father's concentrated sperm inseminated directly at the cervical os, but they may not accept AI with an anonymous donor. While we respect these religious and moral convictions, our refusal to comply with one partner's request for incomplete disclosure to the other is based upon its inherent unethicality. Treatment in these situations includes referral to additional and supportive religious or secular sources appropriate to the couple's denominations in addition to supportive therapy.

Rarely has a couple with initial apprehensions about AI later regretted a decision to undergo the procedure at the laboratories where our interviews were conducted. However, marriages have occasionally been broken owing to communication difficulties and lack of successful conception during fertility treatment. It is difficult to ascertain whether infertility served as a nonspecific trigger for antedating relationship problems or as an independent and unique relationship stressor.

Since the fertility period occurs during a limited phase of the month, a couple should be encouraged to engage in their typical frequency and variety of sexual activity that preceded the discovery of infertility. Since approximately 15 to 20% of our couples treated are not sterile but are semisterile, they may successfully be treated with the male's semen. Thus, excessive or planned sexual activity may lead to exacerbated sexual dysfunction and/or diminution of pleasure associated with spontaneity. Therefore, continuation of usual sexual activity during the nonfertile phase is essential. Indeed, Rantala and Koskimies (1988) cautioned against interfering with and excessively monitoring a couple's sexual activity. Seibel and Taymor (1982) suggested that stress factors, such as infertility investigation, may change hormonal balance. Androgens, catecholamines, prolactin, adrenal steroids, endorphins, and serotonin each affect libido, ovulation, sperm production, fallopian tube activity, and gamete transport.

Animal Analogues, Hormones, and Behavior

Testosterone is the most potent sexual stimulant for both sexes. Chimpanzee studies demonstrated that the dominant monkey had the highest testosterone level. When displaced through physical combat, testosterone levels dropped to levels comparable to the remaining monkey group. Human studies are lacking that would investigate the effect of self-discovery of infertility on testosterone levels. A theoretical link between environmental stressors and sperm production has been proposed, with only equivocal evidence that stress may elicit immature cell exfoliation from the testes (Amelar & Dubin, 1977; Steinberger, 1978).

Depression has been correlated with lowered testosterone levels. However, mechanisms by which environmental or psychological/emotional stressors induce testosterone shifts have not been delineated. Certain cases of spontaneous fertility that occur following patients' acceptance of their own infertility may be related to sexuality being psychologically separated from procreation. It is similarly unclear whether improvement is in the male, in the female, or is in both partners. Restoration of sexuality as an activity separate from procreation may result in the lifting of an underlying depression in some infertile men. In turn, mood shifts may result in an improvement in the cascade of pituitary and gonadal hormones, such as testosterone, required for sperm reproduction. This mutually interactive cyclic pattern of biophysical influence requires further research.

Anabolic steroids, which are analogues of testosterone, produce psychological alterations, which, in extremes, are manifested in a form of aggression known as "steroid rage." Discontinuation of the use of anabolic steroids will reverse alterations in behavior in both sexes. Chimpanzee studies provide a model of potential human behavioral responses to severe environmental stressors. Situational factors may thus produce secondary hormonal changes, which, in turn, may produce tertiary behavioral changes. The authors hypothesize that the marked drop in testosterone levels has significant survival value. In the case of the dominant monkey, typically displaced by combative means, survival is best ensured by reverting to a form of semisubmissive behavior. This nonfatal submissive behavior as a normal form of adaptation is readily observed in almost all animal species and in humans.

Infertility may likewise result from environmental factors, exacerbated by the infertility itself. This may lead to a vicious cycle, disrupted when the couple ultimately embarks upon a properly counseled program of artificial insemination with a donor. The male is reassured that he can have a child with his partner via artificial insemination, and both consciously and unconsciously, relative confidence in his masculinity is restored. The fact that the child is genetically similar to him, but is not necessarily identical to him, serves as a major form of reassurance. It should be emphasized that no child is genetically identical, in reality, to either parent and that a sterile female who, in turn, accepts the genetic similarity of the donor will aid her partner in breaking the psychological equation of impotence-infertility and masculinity. Frequently, this type of intervention has led to serendipitous improvements in couples' intimate and sexual relations that antedated the delicate issue of infertility. This finding is unsurprising considering that infertility is but one biopsychological marker of couples' interaction patterns, and more generally of communication.

To date, the general status of the literature regarding psychological aspects of artificial insemination and sequelae is, at best, tentative and methodologically unsound. The novelty of artificial insemination as a viable fertility option and the secrecy surrounding the procedure present difficulties in obtaining objective case studies. Thus, sparse clinical lore, unidimensional case reports, and unvalidated assessment of adjustment and sequelae from a longitudinal standpoint severely limit inferences about the psychological aspects of donor insemination. Psychoanalytic accounts of AI tend to stress such inevitable psychodynamic formulations for the male as castration anxiety, depression, and unconscious competition with the donor. The emotional sequence involved in the discovery of infertility has been likened to that involved in natural mourning—e.g., surprise, denial, anger, isolation, guilt, grief. We introduce concepts which may overlap with mourning reactions but which are qualitatively distinct from typical mourning.

Reactions to the discovery of infertility and AI appear to encompass a broad spectrum of responses and are as varied as the characterological structures and defenses of the interviewees. The following are excerpts extracted from interviews with 13 heterosexual couples, 2 homosexual couples, 7 single heterosexual women, and donors themselves. All informants were Caucasian, in the age range of 25 to 35, of middle to upper middle socioeconomic status, with a mean education level of 3 years of college. Incomplete compilation of data is due to informants' almost uniform insistence upon the utmost secrecy and confidentiality in dissemination of interview data. While we have addressed certain psychodynamics of the infertile couple, comparably little attention has been paid to the problem of donor recruitment and donor attrition, owing to certain hospital or clinic staff's insensitivity to the psychological vulnerabilities of the donor. Sparse concern for the psychological and emotional needs of donors appeared to be reflected in interviewee's narratives. Daniels (1986) has suggested that comprehensive service needs, including consideration of psychosocial issues, be provided for semen donors.

Interviews with potential donors who experienced the aforementioned staff insensitivity took place in the public waiting room of a large New York City hospital, where donors were specifically evaluated for infertility. This setting should be contrasted to a donor recruitment program, where donors are specifically counseled and their specific needs are addressed.

Potential Donor 1. You could say we all felt like incompetents. We're staring at each other in the room [laughs anxiously], and everyone knows what they're there for. It is a little embarrassing, especially when you had to go into this room and give a specimen. Over here, you don't get to bring your specimen with you. You have to do whatever you have to do over there and it's very embarrassing. I went five or six times. The doctor was very good—microsurgeon, but after a while I just couldn't take the embarrassment anymore. It was like mass production. You're here for this, and everybody knows about it. You gave the specimen alone, of course, but I remember one instance when the nurse came out and said in front of everyone, "You have to give more specimen." You walked out and bowed your head down and walked into the room again, and when you come out everybody is looking at you. They know what you did.

Potential Donor 2. It is not fair to call everybody "disabled." I shouldn't even say that—"other subfertile people," you think to yourself. Thank God you're not the only one. There are a lot of other people with the same problem. I guess it hasn't been as widely acknowledged or publicized as it has been recently.

Potential Donor 3–6. You know, nobody talks to anybody else in that waiting room. I know they definitely felt the same way I did. Very strange . . . embarrassing. There wasn't even a cough [laughs anxiously], just dead silence. That was probably the worst part and so tough.

In contrast, the proper program is one where donors are counseled and are screened privately and provided with appointments to further ensure patient privacy and confidentiality. The following is an excerpt from an interview with a donor who initially presented to various large hospital and clinic facilities, but who later became a donor at our laboratories.

Potential Donor 7. It was so much better at IDANT, where it was more private. You got to be in a room with all different types of patients, so nobody knew what anyone else was there for. There were some guys in wheelchairs, etcetera. Plus, in those places, the nurses made you feel excellent. It's hard to put into words, but that kind of thing is very, very important, so you didn't feel that bad. The easiest time was then, when everyone was pleasant. I had no qualms. The staff became like family to me. I commend them. A lot of them took a lot of time out of their own lives to make us feel more comfortable.

A husband expressed his attitude toward fertility injections.

I went twice a week for several years while I was working thirteen hours a day in a very physical job. The physical pain of the shots wasn't the worst part. The worst part was the side effects. I walked around like a stiff because it caused me stiffness in my back from the injections. There were times when you couldn't even talk to me. I was so stressed. My wife and I always took a couple of days away, through the years. That helped.

The issue of secrecy in married women with infertile husbands was raised.

It's nobody's business. I don't feel it should be public. That's just the way I feel. Nobody knows anything, and we don't want anyone to ever know. Anyway, we're from a close-minded family and I don't know what they would think. . . . We're keeping it secret because of our concern about the way they might treat the baby. They're immigrants, second generation and very old-fashioned, and they have ideas of what it means to be a man and masculine. That's why they couldn't understand why there was something wrong with my husband. They really think he can have kids. They believed at first there was something wrong and we corrected it by injections.

A homosexual female couple, each simultaneously inseminated by different donors, spoke of the experience.

Most of our gay friends know and they're extremely supportive, and we've given them the idea of insemination by our example. We're both really very excited about it. Otherwise, it's our secret, and we give nobody the opportunity to make value judgments about our decision.

The following is a compilation of interview excerpts from inseminated single women.

It's not anybody's business what I do—not friends, not anybody. What is good for me is good for me and what is good for them is good for them. . . . We don't exchange what we do personally. Personal feelings like this, our secrets, our business, my baby. I worked for it and it is a private event. . . . I don't know yet what I'll tell my daughter about how she was conceived. I'll have to make that decision when the opportunity presents itself. Right now is how I live and right now it's not a concern.

Two married couples voiced their attitudes about AI, following multiple futile attempts over 4 years of testing and fertility work-ups.

Husband. I built my business up from scratch. If you make a mistake, you make a mistake. You learn from experience. Smack yourself in the face and go on to the next step. That's the attitude that I have. It's a challenge. You ride the waves from day one. We're determined and you gotta set a goal for yourself and that's it. There's no other way. . . . We went through hell. I went to a microsurgeon and it cost a lot of money, and I don't regret a penny of it. I don't think I wasted any time. I took time off. I cancelled appointments, but I don't regret anything I did.

Wife. At first, I felt "my poor husband," and I felt so sorry for him that I could do something he couldn't, and I said, "Don't worry. I'll stand by you in whatever it is." We were both depressed we couldn't have a baby, but we were determined to find a way. I've been through everything and I'm a very determined person, so I did anything I could. I never look back. It doesn't work and it doesn't pay. What we accomplished in our lives, the ups and downs—we already had a lot of practice, and it was always accomplished. A father is one thing and to father a child is another, and my husband is the father. He treats my daughter well; so as far as I'm concerned, he's the father and just the sperm doesn't mean anything. We never disagreed and stayed together on artificial insemination one hundred percent. I'm sorry if it sounds too perfect to you. We consider it an extreme miracle.

The following is an example of how counseling and matching of genetic characteristics to the father have yielded excellent results. We excerpt some couples' attitudes regarding matching of physical appearance of the donor to the father.

Wife. My child mostly resembles my husband. He was matched to my husband. I love it. I forgot all about it—that it's not really his. I never had any doubts. I don't wish he resembled me more, because [laughs] my husband is better-looking than I am.

Husband. My daughter is my daughter and nobody can change that. The first words out of my mouth when I saw my daughter in the delivery room were "She looks just like me." But whether she looked like me or not, it didn't matter.

Several themes emerged both across the literature and in interviews. For example, some authors believe that the issue of total secrecy itself detracts from the working through of infertility conflicts and AI (Berger, 1980, 1982; Clamar, 1980; Czyba & Chevret, 1979; Karpel, 1980; Milsom & Bergman, 1982). Certainly most interviewees, despite their acceptance of AI both during the procedure and in retrospective accounts, have a general commitment to anonymity. Longitudinal follow-up research assessing the effects of this clandestine attitude on the AI child and on subsequent AI generations is a prerequisite for determining long-term psychological sequelae of artificial insemination by donor, both for parents and for children conceived by the procedure.

The issue of matching the physical appearance of the couple to that of the donor and the blood group of at least one of the future parents was emphasized (Amnon & Avidan, 1976). Indeed, artificial insemination patients unanimously agreed upon the benefits of this procedure and the enhancement of attachment and of bonding afforded by matching of donor to the father's genetic characteristics.

Moreover, the attitudes of paraprofessionals, M.D.'s, and psychologists exert a significant impact upon patient attitudes (Amnon & Avidan, 1976; Karpel, 1980; Menning, 1980; Ledward, Symonds, & Eynon, 1982; Nijs & Rouffa, 1975). Owing to the novelty of the procedure, the burden of responsibility falls upon professionals to shape, from the initial encounter, healthy and open attitudes about artificial insemination, to maximize the naturalness of the process, and to open avenues for communication. Most of the literature is confirming of the fact that AI sequelae are positive— e.g., that hardly any couple regrets the decision to bear children by this method (Kraus & Quinn, 1977; Milsom & Bergman, 1982; Reading, Sledmere, & Cox, 1982; Sokoloff, 1987); and that the initial quality of the relationship in the case of couples is of paramount significance in traversing intrapsychic conflict in AI (Nijs & Rouffa, 1975; Stewart, Daniels, & Boulnois, 1982).

The largely positive sequelae of AI, which we reported, may be an artifact of the excellence of patient care provided by physicians and staff through virtually every stage of the insemination process at the particular clinic at which interviews were conducted. In contrast, donors at a large public hospital reported more negative sequelae. Thus, the context in which insemination occurs must be taken into account in assessing patient outcomes.

Paulson, Haarmann, Salerno, and Asmar (1988) examined the psychological assessments of infertile women in comparison with the general population of women. Scores on a total of 41 test variables showed no significant differences between the groups. Moreover, means and standard deviations were "remarkably similar" for all variables. The authors concluded that singificant emotional disturbance is no more prevalent in infertile women than in the general population of women.

Some individuals, such as homosexual or feminist women, who opt for artificial insemination are in all likelihood less conventional in their attitudes when compared with their adopting or childless counterparts, since they have essentially "gone against nature," as one recipient declared. These individuals undergoing artificial insemination may thus be a select group in terms of liberality, who have already made a political statement regarding the negation of traditional sex-role stereotypes. In this population, largely positive sequelae may be partly attributable to lack of sex-role conflict owing to nontraditional attitudes, of which artificial insemination is just one additional facet. Such subgroups provide rich attitudinal information in comparison with other AID recipients and subgroups in terms of adjustment.

Largely positive sequelae in AI may be expected to result from a properly constructed counseling program, and characterological variables, in the individuals undergoing AID, that are consonant with acceptance of the procedure. Moreover, further longitudinal research should identify both biopsychosocial interaction variables in artificial insemination by donor and those individuals psychologically at risk for negative sequelae.

REFERENCES

American Fertility Society (1988). Revised new guidelines for the use of semen-donor insemination. *Fertility and Sterility*, 49, 2, 211.
Amelar, R. & Dubin, L. (1977). Other factors affecting male fertility. In R. Amelar, L. Dubin, & P. Walsh (Eds.), *Male fertility* (p. 74). Philadelphia: W.B. Saunders.
Amnon, D., & Avidan, D. (1976). Artificial insemination donor: Clinical and psychologic aspects. *Fertility and Sterility*, 27, 528–532.
Ball, G. D. (1986). Acquired immune deficiency syndrome and the fertility clinic. *Fertility and Sterility*, 45, 172–174.
Berger, D. M. (1980). Couples' reactions to male infertility and donor insemination. *American Journal of Psychiatry*, 137, 1047–1049.
Berger, D. M. (1982). Psychological aspects of donor insemination. *International Journal of Psychiatry in Medicine*, 12, 49–56.
Clamar, A. (1980). Psychological implications of donor insemination. *American Journal of Psychoanalysis*, 40, 173–177.
Czyba, J. C., & Chevret, M. (1979). Psychological reactions of couples to artificial insemination with donor sperm. *International Journal of Fertility*, 24, 240–245.
Daniels, K. R. (1986). Psychosocial issues associated with being a semen donor. *Clinical Reproduction and Fertility*, 4, 341–351.
Karpel, M. A. (1980). Family secrets: I. Conceptual and ethical issues in the relational context. II. Ethical and practical considerations in therapeutic management. *Family Process*, 19, 295–306.
Keel, B. A. Webster, B. W., & Roberts, D. K. (1987). Effects of cryopreservation on the motility characteristics of human spermatozoa. *Journal of Reproduction and Fertility*, 81, 213.
Kraus, J., & Quinn, P. E. (1977). Human artificial insemination—Some social and legal issues. *Medical Journal of Australia*, 1, 710.

Ledward, R. S., Symonds, E. M., & Eynon, S. (1982). Social and environmental factors as criteria for success in artificial insemination by donor (A.I.D.). *Journal of Biosocial Science, 14,* 263–275.

Menning, B. E. (1980). The emotional needs of infertile couples. *Fertility and Sterility, 34,* 313–319.

Milsom, I., & Bergman, P. (1982). A study of parental attitudes after donor insemination (A.I.D.). *Acta Obstetrica et Gynecologica Scandinavica, 61,* 125–128.

Nijs, P., Rouffa, L. (1975). A.I.D. couples: Psychological and psychopathological evaluation. *Andrologia, 7,* 187–194.

Paulson, J. D., Haarmann, B. S., Salerno, R. L., & Asmar, P. (1988). An investigation of the relationship between emotional maladjustment and infertility. *Fertility and Sterility, 49* (2), 258–262.

Peterson, E. P., Alexander, N.J., & Moghissi, K. S. (1988). A.I.D. and AIDS—Too close for comfort. *Fertility and Sterility, 49,* 209–210.

Rantala, M. L., & Koskimies, A. I. (1988). Sexual behavior of infertile couples. *International Journal of Fertility, 33,* 26–30.

Reading, A. E., Sledmere, C. M., & Cox, D. N. (1982). A survey of patient attitudes towards artificial insemination by donor. *Journal of Psychosomatic Research 26,* 429–433.

Seibel, M.M., & Taymor, M. L. (1982). Emotional aspects of infertility. *Fertility and Sterility, 37,* 137.

Sokoloff, B. Z. (1987). Alternative methods of reproduction. Effects on the child. *Clinical Pediatrics, 26,* 11–17.

Steinberger, E. (1978). The etiology and pathophysiology of testicular dysfunction in man. *Fertility and Sterility, 29,* 481.

Stewart, C. R., Daniels, K. R., & Boulnois, J. D. H. (1982). The development of a psychosocial approach to artificial insemination of donor sperm. *New Zealand Medical Journal, 95,* 853–856.

Chapter 12

Infertility and the New Reproductive Technologies
Speculations from a Psychodynamic Perspective

RANDY MILDEN

INTRODUCTION

For women of childbearing age today, reproductive biology is one among many determinants of destiny. Women may choose to act on their biological capacities and have children. They may choose to delay or reject childbearing in framing their life plan. The subjects of this chapter, infertile women, find their wish to bear children countermanded by their bodies. They do not have the option of realizing a biological procreative potential. For many infertile patients, biology is a painful limitation on destiny.

I will discuss the psychological impact of this limitation. I will first review the literature on the psychology of infertility, up until now a psychology of loss and mourning. I will the suggest that this psychology requires redefinition in the wake of the recent and extraordinary advances in reproductive technologies that can manufacture *in vitro* what was impossible *in vivo*. Offered the possibility that science may override biological limits, infertile women must now manage their grief at their own underlying sense of damage or deprivation, along with the elation that accompanies a new prospect of restitution.

REVIEW OF THE LITERATURE

The literature on the psychology of infertility sketches the response to a medical problem about which there was, until recently, a dearth of scientific knowledge and a consequently poor prognosis. Less than 20 years ago, most infertility problems could

---

RANDY MILDEN • Dean's Office and Departments of Psychology and General Programs, Haverford College, Haverford, Pennsylvania 19041. An earlier version of this chapter was delivered as part of a symposium "Psychoanalysis and Childbearing: Is Biology Still Destiny?" at the annual meetings of the American Psychological Association, Los Angeles, August 26, 1985.

not be diagnosed, and only a small percentage successfully treated. The absence of information offered a blank screen onto which infertile women might project internal feelings and fantasies about their inability to conceive. The corresponding low rate of successful treatment framed an affective portrait of hopelessness and despair. The psychological literature on infertility has these feelings as its focus.

There is great debate in the literature about whether infertile women manifest more distress or disturbance than fertile women and whether psychological problems that are observed in infertile women have etiological significance (Benedek, 1952; Benedek, Ham, Robbins et al., 1953; Berger, 1980; Bos & Cleghorn, 1958; Bresnick & Taymor, 1978; Denber, 1978; Deutsch, 1945; Eisner, 1963; Karahasonoglu, Barglow, & Growe, 1972; Mozeley, 1976; O'Moore, O'Moore, Harrison et al., 1983; Rutledge, 1979; Seibel & Taymor, 1982; Singh & Neki, 1982; Walker, 1978; Wilson, 1979). The specifics of these long-standing controversies have changed over the years to reflect current fashions in psychiatric thinking. Today's proponents of psychogenic infertility comment not on the etiological significance of a woman's unconscious rejection of femininity but on the impact of stress mediated by her neuroendocrine system. To date, however, we are still left with no conclusive answers when we consider questions of incidence and etiological significance of emotional problems in this population.

There is, on the other hand, ready agreement among most writers when they consider the consequences of infertility. Most report that a significant sense of loss and narcissistic injury are almost inevitable psychological sequelae. The specific features of these reactions may vary according to a woman's history and personality. (Goldfarb, Rosenthal, & Utian, 1985; Rosenthal, 1985). For many women, the loss taps unresolved psychosexual and object relational issues, evoking strong feelings of sadness, anger, and guilt. For some women, oral themes predominate in their fears of abandonment by a fertile spouse, isolation from friends who have children, or a desolate aloneness without a baby as a symbiotic object (Mazor, 1978). Other women feature Oedipal conflicts, consciously or unconsciously viewing infertility as punishment for past (often sexual) fantasies and behaviors (Mazor, 1978, 1984; Menning, 1980). Oedipal competition and sibling struggles may come to the fore as these women respond to the fact that they are denied what their mothers, sisters, and friends have. These reactions can be powerful. In the book of Genesis, when Rachel discovered her infertility, she "envied her sister and said unto Jacob, 'Give me children or else I die.'"

The depression and envy of infertile women often has a prominent narcissistic core (Keye, 1984; Kraft, Palombo, Mitchell, Dean et al., 1979; Mazor, 1978, 1984; Rosenfeld & Mitchell, 1979; Seibel & Taymor, 1982). This is, after all, not a loss of a real object but a loss of something that is part of the self, the representation of a fantasied object (Daniels, Gunby, Legge et al., 1984; Menning, 1980). One patient quoted in the literature characterized the diagnosis of infertility as "the death of a dream: the loss was somehow unreal, confusing, because it was a loss not of something concrete, but of something potential. . . . No one had died, no one was sick, everyone looked the same, yet everything had changed" (Mazor, 1978, p. 155). The assault on sense of self and self-worth is complex. In the words of one patient quoted in the literature, "I feel empty. It's like within me where a uterus ought to be, there is a 'black hole' of space. I feel mutilated" (Mazor, 1978, p. 148). The feelings of fragmentation and violation stem not only from the medical problem but also from the assessment and treatment (Berger, 1980; Riddick, 1982). In the words of another patient, "there is no inner recess of me left unexplored, unproved, unmolested" (Menning, 1980, p. 315). The sense of damage may more broadly characterize the sense of self as female, particularly insofar as the capacity to bear children has a central role in a woman's feminine identity (Daniels et al., 1984; Kraft et al., 1979, Mazor, 1984). This feeling may be generalized to nonreproductive and non-gender-defined aspects of the self as well. It is not uncommon for infertile women to feel at times unattractive, unlovable, and incapable of other meaningful personal or professional accomplishments. There may be a sense of falling short of one's ego ideal, accompanied by a glorified fantasy of one's life with children (Mazor, 1978, 1984). Using a semantic differential scale, Platt, Fischer, and Silver (1973) found that infertile women rated their real selves as more discrepant from their ideal selves than did fertile women. There is a loss of a sense of omnipotence among these patients. They feel out of control and helpless. They had always imagined that they could, when they were ready, become pregnant. Now they discover that, in contrast to other well-ordered aspects of their lives, childbearing is not something they can plan and accomplish (Daniels et al., 1984; Mazor, 1978; Menning, 1980). In the words of one patient, "I'm not used to finding things I can't surmount" (Kraft et al., 1979, p. 621). Administered measures of locus of control, infertile patients, not surprisingly, harbor a perception of external rather than internal control of their lives (Platt et al., 1973).

Although the narcissistic vulnerability of these patients is described in some detail, writers in this area have paid less attention to the defenses and coping mechanisms marshaled to bind the narcissistic injury. These patients tell you that the experience is not one of unremitting pain. The narcissistic assault is warded off or coped with in different ways, at different times, with different degrees of success. While one would expect a wide range of strategies in managing these feelings, prominent in the defensive efforts would certainly be narcissistic defenses. Rather than feeling damaged and helpless, one feels perfect and in control. Efforts at narcissistic restitution may be laced with expressions of the original insult. A striking example is an infertile patient in the literature who described her anguish at letting down her family because she could not carry on the family line: "I think I know how Princess Soraya felt when she could not produce an heir of the Shah of Iran" (Mazor, 1978, p. 154).

Some writers describe a progression of response to infertility over time as the feelings are worked through. This dynamic framework is an improvement on those writings in which emotions are viewed as passively endured, reactive, and static. Unfortunately, however, the patterns of change described have not been conceptually elaborated or empirically demonstrated. Drawing loosely on the models from other literature (death and dying, stress response syndrome), a number of authors describe the patients' reaction to their infertility in a psychologically stylized series of linear stages. A number of "characteristic" patterns are proposed (Goldfarb et al., 1985; Kraft et al., 1979; Mazor, 1984; Menning, 1980, 1982; Rosenfeld & Mitchell, 1979; Rosenthal, 1985; Wilson, 1979). For example, the patients first experience a sense of narcissistic injury, then mourning, and finally consideration of alternatives to childbearing (Mazor, 1984). In a second scheme, the patients feel, in order, surprise, denial, anger, isolation, guilt, grief, and resolution (Menning, 1980, 1982), and in another disbelief and denial; depression, anger, and altered self-concept; optimism; desperation; depression; and, finally, acceptance (Wilson, 1979). Some writers, pointing to a nonlinear pattern of reaction, observe monthly cycles of hope and then, with the onset of menses, disappointment, or midcycle and premenstrual anxiety, followed by depression when menstruation begins (Kraft et al., 1979; Mazor, 1978, 1984).

REFORMULATION

Infertility in 1988 is a significantly different medical phenomenon than it was even 10 years ago. With the extraordinary developments in the assessment and treatment of these problems, we should expect corresponding changes in the patient's psychological experience. As psychoanalytic psychologists interested in the impact of biological limits and potentials, it is time to take a new look at this area.

I have described the bleak state of medical expertise in the field of infertility in the past. Infertility in 1988 is a different medical phenomenon offering a new and changing basis for psychological response. Today, physicians are able to diagnose 85% of their infertility patients, with 50% of these patients successfully treated. Many of the pregnancies in these patients occur through elaborate medical procedures. The most basic diagnostic work-up for infertility today is extensive, including basal body temperature records, semen analysis, postcoital tests, endometrial biopsy, laparoscopy and hysteroscopy (tests to visualize the reproductive organs), and hysterosalpingography (a test of tubal patency in which radio-opaque dye is injected into the uterus) (Bernstein & Mattox, 1982; Kredentser & Schiff, 1984; Riddick, 1982; Speroff, Glass, & Kass, 1983; Thompson, 1984). Along with the continued use of conventional surgical and hormonal therapies, there has been a veritable explosion of high technology treatments. Artificial insemination by donor is neither new (the first reported artificial insemination by donor occurred in this country in 1884) nor particularly high in the high tech reproductive hierarchy. What is new and dramatic are recent advances in the technology of freezing tissue, as a result of which it is estimated that the use of artificial insemination by donor has doubled in the last 3 years. There are other advances as well, such as uterine insemination, in which biochemically treated sperm are injected into the uterus, and gamete intrafallopian tubal transfer, in which treated sperm mixed with newly harvested eggs are inserted into the fallopian tube.

Probably the most extraordinary new development in reproductive technology is *in vitro* fertilization, which was first accomplished in 1978 at Kershaw's Cottage Hospital in Oldham, Lancashire, where the first IVF baby, Louise Brown, was born. In the 10 years since that time, worldwide estimates of the number of babies born who were conceived through *in vitro* fertilization are in the thousands. There are now more than a hundred *in vitro* fertilization programs in the United States.

In normal *in vivo* conception, an egg is ovulated into a fallopian tube, where it is fertilized. The fertilized egg remains in the tube for 2 days, growing to four to eight cells—an embryo—and then enters the uterus, where it implants and develops over the 9 gestational months. *In vitro* fertilization artificially performs the functions of the fallopian tube in the laboratory (Seibel & Taymor, 1984). Specific details of the procedure vary across centers. The description I will present is a general model. The women undergoing *in vitro* fertilization are given injections of a fertility drug, Perganol, to stimulate egg production. They are followed with daily ultrasounds and hormone levels to monitor the growth of the follicles. As the eggs approach maturity, the patients are given an injection of a hormone, HCG, to stimulate ovulation, and the egg or eggs are retrieved through laparoscopy. Sperm collected from husband or donor are united with the egg or eggs in a culture dish, labeled by one poetic physician the "extra corporeal antechamber of the womb" (Selzer, 1982, p. 161). After 48 hours in the dish, the embryo or embryos, anywhere from 4 to 16 cells, are released into the uterus through a catheter threaded through the cervix. For 14 days after the transfer, the patient self-administers daily intramuscular injections of progesterone to facilitate implantation. The percentage of pregnancies per egg retrieval is estimated across centers to be 25%, with an approximate 20% rate of spontaneous abortion, yielding a figure for live births per egg retrieval of roughly 20%. For most women, this procedure will need to be repeated multiple times before a pregnancy and birth can be expected, at a cost per cycle of anywhere from $3000 to $5000.

In discussing the psychology of infertility in the era of the new reproductive technologies, I will concentrate on *in vitro* fertilization, the method that, in its transposition of conception and early gestation from the body to the laboratory, has changed the face of reproduction more dramatically than any other. In sketching a new psychological portrait, I will draw on reports that are just beginning to appear in the literature and observations by clinicians working with these patients, and suggest some preliminary thoughts that might provide a springboard for clinical and empirical elaboration.

First, I want to emphasize the inestimable benefits of IVF for couples who could probably not otherwise have a biological child. In grateful testimonials, successful patients exclaim that their IVF baby was worth all the physical and psychological stress of the procedure and more (Singer & Wells, 1985). We want to be careful, in spelling out some of the more complicated emotional aspects of these new procedures, to steer clear of doomsday pathologizing. It is important that we do not follow the example of Gerstel (1963), who more than 20 years later remains somewhat notorious in the scanty psychoanalytic literature on infertility. Observing conflicts in patients undergoing artificial insemination by donor, she concluded, "while its more ardent proponents frequently refer to artificial donor insemination as 'therapeutic' insemination, I would question the psychological benefits to be derived from the procedure for even the most normal individuals. . . . I believe that a decision to participate in artificial donor insemination, in itself, is indicative of emotional disturbance." There are those who revile today's new reproductive technologies (Kass, 1972; Tiefel, 1982; Walters, 1979). The critics believe that "this new holy war against human nature," where the "course of action is deduced simply from the possibility of action," must be halted (Kass, 1972, pp. 20, 27). I disagree, advocating responsible scientific advancement on medical, ethical, and psychological grounds (Singer & Wells, 1985). We should champion progress; at the same time we should address and, to the best of our clinical abilities, curtail its inevitable costs. In its promise of extraordinary, biologically liberating benefits, *in vitro* fertilization also engenders emotional upheaval, which we must try to understand and mitigate.

The empirical literature on the psychological aspects of IVF is scant and perplexing (Applegarth, 1986; Fagan, 1986; Fagan, Schmidt, Rock et al., 1986; Freeman, Boxer, Rickels et al., 1985; Garner, Kelly, & Arnold, 1984; Haseltine, Mazure, Greenfield et al., 1984; Mikesell & Falk, 1984; Stewart, 1986). On standardized psychological tests, IVF patients appear hopeful, psychologically healthy, displaying not only low anxiety but less anxiety than normal. Are these people, indeed, as sanguine as their test responses suggest, the obvious major stressors in their lives notwithstanding? Are our measures not sensitive enough to normal subjects who are less ready to endorse items derived from clinical populations? Are these people consciously masking negative emotions in an effort to impress mental health professionals whom they, correctly or not, view as gatekeepers to IVF programs? Are we seeing a less consciously motivated denial, a defensive response to conflict? It is certainly plausible that this is a nonclinical sample who, consciously or unconsciously, want to look good. Mazure

(1986) offers empirical support for this view, showing that a substantial number of IVF patients who score low on the Taylor Anxiety Scale score high on the Marlow-Crowne Social Desirability Scale.

I would add another possible explanation of these unexpectedly problem-free portraits. In redefining a high tech psychology of infertility, we must take care not to discard all that we have learned about infertile patients in the past. We should not throw out the baby with the bath water (or petri dish solution). I would suggest that the "super" testings are the narcissistic flip side, as it were, of the sense of depletion and depression that was observed in many of these patients before the high tech era.

In vitro fertilization patients are infertility patients until now unsuccessfully treated. As I have described, the sense of loss and narcissistic injury can run deep in the patients, warded off by defenses and coping strategies mobilized against these assaults, including, for some women, narcissistic defenses. In procedures like *in vitro* fertilization, capable of, if not creation *per se*, then of dramatic interventions that effect creation where it had been humanly impossible, these internal narcissistic defenses find a compatible external reality.

In vitro fertilization releases women from biological impairment. They can escape from a sense of damage and loss of control. *In vitro* fertilization promises intactness and omnipotence. Emotions of grief and envy can be erased, with an elation that accompanies participation in involving, extraordinary, even, it may feel, magical procedures. What was human and flawed is restored in the perfect and uncontaminated laboratory. Patients, previously helpless, are now narcissistically allied with the dazzling possibilities of modern reproductive endocrinology, merged with the grandiose technology object. They can create the world of their experience. The limits of reality are erased by a fantasy of restitution, and they are not, in fantasy, broken any longer. They are bionic, not defective, their reproductive system functioning, with its high tech extensions, better than normal. In fantasy, they are superwomen. There may be an accompanying androgenous fantasy, in which this penetrating new technology is the idealized penis that makes them complete (Fast, 1979). Selzer (1982) offers a fanciful portrait of the glow that IVF can engender: "will the artists of some future day, moved by adoration, paint their versions of The Harvest, and Fertilization, and Implantation? Instead of an archangel holding a lily and whispering, they will show a masked gynecologist holding a laparoscope; instead of Mary kneeling in ecstasy, a covered glass dish; instead of sunlight streaming through a window, no window at all through which germs might permeate. For it will be sterility rather than purity that is painted here."

The narcissistically resistive fantasies that may underlie the disavowals of psychological distress may be nurtured secretly or expressed indirectly. Implicit in the fantasy may be the notion that thoughts are wordlessly shared with physicians, who are the focus of projected qualities of godlike omniscience. These fantasies are observable at particular stages of the IVF cycle. The procedures that are the most elaborate, quintessentially high tech, elicit a particularly "electric" affective response, an inflated set of expectations that are openly verbalized. Some patients attribute magical therapeutic properties to some of the diagnostic procedures, experiencing, for example, the exquisitely precise tracking of follicular growth as protecting the maturing eggs, guaranteeing rather than monitoring outcome. The presence of the fantasy also becomes apparent when it is challenged. Descriptive clinical teams are puzzled when some patients respond with unbounded optimism to education and multiple informed consents, read and duly signed, emphasizing the low probability of success. They "mis-hear," insisting they were told that there was an 80% success rather than failure rate. Transformed into gamblers, they believe that, even when they hear the odds, they will beat them. The odds apply to other patients: "I hear what you're saying about a twenty percent chance of getting a baby, but I know in my heart I'll be in that twenty percent." A small number of these patients, told that a pregnancy is unlikely, make major life changes in preparation for the success that they feel is, for them, assured, setting up a baby's room or quitting a job in anticipation of full-time motherhood.

For most patients, the pregnancy test is the reality jolt that breaks through the illusions. There are some reports of patients who refuse to believe a negative pregnancy test, continuing to inject progesterone, and repeating the test at another clinic. For most patients, however, the negative result is immediately devastating, bursting the narcissistic bubble in which a wish is tantamount to its achievement. The narcissistic depletion they may have experienced before they began the *in vitro* fertilization program can return, in some cases with renewed intensity and bitterness directed at themselves and at others, particularly the doctors onto whom they projected their narcissistic claims and who did not deliver what was, in their defensive distortions, promised. It is emotionally dangerous to have such high hopes when that hope is not supported by realistic expectations. Infertility patients are, by virtue of their medical problem, more or less narcissistically vulnerable. One might ask if high tech/low success reproductive options pose special psychological risks for those infertility patients who have particular difficulty accepting narcissistic limits or losses. When the IVF cycle fails, 80% of the time, the depth of despair can be profound. Some choose to stop what they term this "roller coaster," preferring to accept their infertility and live their lives without biological progeny. They move on to explore the options of adopting children or remaining childless.

Others describe how hard it is to stop. Another aspect of the limitlessness implicit in these technologies is the message that it might work during next month's cycle or in a few months or years, when there will be a new procedure. In the "old days" gynecologists labeled infertility cases "closed" after the handful of limited interventions were tried unsuccessfully. Today, as this season's new technological advance makes headlines and last season's innovation has already become established as standard gynecological practice, the case marked "closed" is the exception. Looking toward an anticipated future of continued scientific progress against the backdrop of a recent past that saw such unprecedented change, physicians feel obliged to tell a 38-year-old woman who has not been able to achieve a pregnancy in 1988 that the treatment that will help her might become available in 1989 or (too late for her) 1998, or never. In one sense, hope is positive. In another, it's not. I noted earlier that infertility is difficult to work through, in part because it is the loss of something potential rather than real (Mazor, 1978). The difficulty is made more complex when that potential is never absolutely lost. Mourning and resolution are elusive, when there is always a promise that, if not today, then tomorrow, technology and not biology will be destiny.

ACKNOWLEDGMENTS. The author wishes to extend thanks to the following colleagues for their help with this manuscript: Drs. Dennis Smith, Miriam Rosenthal, Judith Ballou, Susan Bram, Irene Fast, Malkah Notman, Vivian Halfin, Cynthia Austin, Judith Evans, and Ms. Sandra Stewart. This work was done with the support of the Department of Reproductive Biology, Case Western Reserve University School of Medicine, and MacDonald Hospital for Women, Cleveland, Ohio.

References

Applegarth, L. (1986). *Coping and problem-solving in in vitro fertilization patients.* Paper presented at the Conference on Psychosomatic Obstetrics and Gynecology, Philadelphia.
Benedek, T. (1952), Infertility as a psychosomatic defense. *Fertility and Sterility, 3,* 527–541.
Benedek, T., Ham, C., Robbins, F. P., et al. (1953). Some emotional factors in infertility. *Psychosomatic Medicine, 15,* 485–498.
Berger, D. M. (1980). Infertility: A psychiatrist's perspective. *Canadian Journal of Psychiatry, 25,* 553–559.
Bernstein, J., & Mattox, J. H. (1982). An overview of infertility. *JCGN Nursing,* 309–314.
Bos, C., & Cleghorn, R. A. (1958). Psychogenic sterility. *Fertility and Sterility, 9,* 84–98.
Bresnick, E., & Taymor, M. L. (1979). The role of counseling in infertility. *Fertility and Sterility, 32,* 154–156.
Daniels, K. R., Gunby, J., Legge, M., et al. (1984). Issues and problems for the infertile couple. *New Zealand Medical Journal, 97,* 185–187.
Denber, H. C. (1978). Psychiatric aspects of infertility. *Journal of Reproductive Medicine, 20,* 23–29.
Deutsch, H. (1945). *The psychology of women* (Vol 2). New York: Grune & Stratton.
Eisner, B. G. (1963). Some psychological differences between fertile and infertile women. *Journal of Clinical Psychology, 19,* 391–395.
Fagan, P. (1986). *Sexual functioning and psychological evaluation of in vitro fertilization couples.* Paper presented at the Conference on Psychosomatic Obstetrics and Gynecology, Philadelphia.
Fagan, P., Schmidt, C., Rock, J., et al. (1986). Sexual functioning and psychological evaluation in in vitro fertilization couples. *Fertility and Sterility, 46,* 668–672.
Fast, I. (1979). Developments in gender identity: Gender differentiation in girls. *International Journal of Psychoanalysis, 68,* 443–453.
Freeman, E. W., Boxer, A. S., Rickels, K., et al. (1985). Psychological evaluation and support in a program of in vitro fertilization and embryo transfer. *Fertility and Sterility, 43,* 48–53.
Garner, C. H., Kelley, M., & Arnold, E. S. (1984). Psychological profile of IVF patients. *Fertility and Sterility, 41,* 57S. (Abstract)
Gerstel, G. (1963). A psychoanalytic view of artificial donor insemination. *American Journal of Psychotherapy, 17,* 64–77.
Goldfarb, J. M., Rosenthal, M. B., & Utian, W. H. (1985). Impact of psychologic factors in the care of the infertile couple. *Seminars in Reproductive Endocrinology, 3,* 93–99.
Haseltine, F. P., Mazure, C. M., Greenfield, D. A., et al. (1984). Psychological testing of couples in the in vitro fertilization program suggested dysphoria among the males and high-anxiety component in the couples. *Fertility and Sterility, 41,* 57S. (Abstract)
Karahasonoglu, A., Barglow, P., & Growe, G. (1972). Psychological aspects of infertility. *Journal of Reproductive Medicine, 9,* 241–247.
Kass, L. R. (1972). New beginnings in life. In M. P. Hamilton (Ed.), *The new genetics and the future of man* (pp. 15–63). Grand Rapids: William B. Eerdmans.
Keye, W. R. (1984). Psychosexual responses to infertility. *Clinical Obstetrics and Gynecology, 27,* 760–766.
Kraft, A. D., Palombo, J., Mitchell, D., Dean, C., et al. (1980). The psychological dimensions of infertility. *American Journal of Orthopsychiatry, 30,* 618–628.
Kredentser, J. V., & Schiff, I. (1984). Infertility: An overview. *Resident and Staff Physician, 30,* 55–66.
Mazor, M. D. (1984). Emotional reactions to infertility. In M. D. Mazor & H. Simons (Eds.), *Infertility: Medical, emotional, and social considerations* (pp. 23–35). New York: Human Sciences Press.
Mazor, M. D. (1978). The problem of infertility. In M. T. Notman & C. C. Nadelson (Eds.), *Sexual and reproductive aspects of women's health care* (Vol. 1, pp. 137–160). New York: Plenum Press.
Mazure, C. M. (1986). *Methodological issues in the psychological study of IVF participants.* Paper presented at the Conference on Psychosomatic Obstetrics and Gynecology, Philadelphia.
Menning, B. E. (1980). The emotional needs of infertile couples. *Fertility and Sterility, 34,* 313–319.

Menning, B. E. (1982). The psychological impact of infertility. *Nursing Clinics of North America, 17*, 155–163.

Mikesell, S., & Falk, R. (1984). The utilization of assessment of marital satisfaction and interpersonal perceptions with in vitro fertilization couples to develop intervention strategies to reduce the psychological impact of the stress of infertility. *Fertility and Sterility, 41*, 58S. (Abstract)

Mozeley, P. D. (1976). Psychophysiologic infertility: An overview. *Clinical Obstetrics and Gynecology, 19*, 407–417.

O'Moore, A. M., O'Moore, R. R., Harrison, R. F., et al. (1983). Psychosomatic aspects in idiopathic infertility: Effects of treatment with autogenic training. *Journal of Psychosomatic Research, 27*, 145–151.

Platt, J. J., Fischer, I., & Silver, M. J. (1973). Infertile couples: Personality traits and self-ideal concept discrepancies. *Fertility and Sterility, 24*, 972–976.

Riddick, D. H. (1982). Sexual dysfunction: Cause and result of infertility. *Female Patient, 7*, 45–48.

Rosenfeld, D. L., & Mitchell, E. (1979). Treating the emotional aspects of infertility: Counseling services in an infertility clinic. *American Journal of Obstetrics and Gynecology, 135*, 177–180.

Rosenthal, M. (1985). Grappling with the emotional aspects of infertility. *Contemporary Ob/Gyn*, 97–104.

Rutledge, A. L. (1979). Psychomarital evaluation and treatment of the infertile couple. *Clinical Obstetrics and Gynecology, 22*, 255–267.

Seibel, M. M., & Taymor, M. L. (1982). Emotional aspects of infertility. *Fertility and Sterility, 37*, 137–145.

Seibel, M. M., & Taymor, M. L. (1984). In vitro fertilization. In M. D. Mazor & H. Simons (Eds.), *Infertility: Medical, emotional, and social considerations* (pp. 207–216). New York: Human Sciences Press.

Selzer, R. (1982). *Letters to a young doctor*. New York: Simon & Schuster.

Singer, P., & Wells, D. (1985). *Making babies: The new science and ethics of conception*. New York: Scribner's.

Singh, J. R., & Neki, J. S. (1982). Psychogenic factors in some genetic and non-genetic forms of infertility. *International Journal of Gynecology and Obstetrics, 20*, 119–123.

Speroff, L., Glass, R. H., & Kass, N. G. (1983). *Clinical gynecologic endocrinology and infertility*. Baltimore: Williams and Wilkins.

Stewart, S. P. (1986). *Expectations and coping of patients undergoing in vitro fertilization*. Unpublished master's thesis.

Thompson, I. E. (1984). The medical workup: Female and combined problems. In M. D. Mazor & H. Simons (Eds.), *Infertility: Medical, emotional, and social considerations* (pp. 3–12). New York: Human Sciences Press.

Tiefel, H. O. (1982). Human in vitro fertilization: A conservative view. *Journal of the American Medical Association, 247*, 3235–3242.

Walker, H. E. (1978). Psychiatric aspects of infertility. *Urologic Clinics of North America, 5*, 481–488.

Walters, L. (1979). Human in vitro fertilization: A review of the ethical literature. *Hastings Center Report, 9*, 23–41.

Wilson, E. A. (1979). Sequence of emotional responses induced by infertility. *Journal of the Kentucky Medical Association, 77*, 229–233.

Chapter 13

Amniocentesis
The Experience of Invasion and the Ambivalence of Foreknowledge

ALICE EICHHOLZ

We waited 5 weeks for the amniocentesis results. It's hard to believe those 5 weeks were fraught with as much anxiety as they were.

We'd read everything we could about the pros and cons of amniocentesis. Having decided it was the prudent thing to do since this was my first pregnancy and I was 37, we prepared ourselves for the experience. Most of what is written prepared us for the technical aspects of the procedure. But we could find nothing written that prepared us for the emotional aspects of it. We found ourselves approaching the date with great anticipation. It became the pivotal point in the pregnancy. From that day on it was real. We had "seen" the baby.

It began early in the morning. We joked about its being a "dry run" to the hospital. Upon our arriving at X-ray, 20 minutes early, the usual hospital forms and red tape needed to be filled out. Our obstetrician had not yet arrived, but the X-ray technician led us to the ultrasound room. We had expected a sterile hospital atmosphere, but it was relaxed and informal. My husband was offered coffee while I was directed to the lavatory down the hall to change into a paper gown and empty my bladder. The technician was not too pleased with having fathers present. But our OB had previously guaranteed that fathers could be there. We decided not to press the issue until the OB arrived.

At exactly 7:30 he did arrive, and my husband was permitted entry to the ultrasound room. I was already on the table, far different from the usual X-ray table. This one had a soft pad and a terry cloth cover, which was not at all uncomfortable. The technician had already covered my abdomen with baby oil, which left a warm moist feeling. She was moving the transducer, a microphone-like appendage to the ultrasound machine, across my abdomen. As she manipulated the keyboard attached to the machine, she explained that it was taking sound "pictures" of different segments of my abdomen.

I had to stretch my neck up to the right to see from my supine position. At that,

---

ALICE EICHHOLZ • Vermont College of Norwich University, Montpelier, Vermont 05602.

I couldn't really tell what I was seeing without her explanation. I was disappointed not to be able to distinguish more of what the picture supposedly showed. She zipped back and forth on the tic-tac-toe-like grid superimposed on the screen, continuing her search for the appropriate place where the most amniotic fluid would be available. Each button on the keyboard signaled the sound wave to a different square on the grid. It seemed like an elaborate computer game, especially when one button sent a dotted line at different angles across the screen. That line indicated the path for the needle to follow to reach the fluid. I could see my husband straining as much as I was to "see" our baby on the screen.

The technician found what seemed the most appropriate spot, verifying with the OB that the fetus was using my bladder as a pillow. As the procedure began, the OB described the appropriate details. Just a little novocaine for the spot where the needle was to be inserted. My previous apprehension about a 5-inch needle entering my abdomen and "intruding" into the baby's precious space was hard to defend against psychologically. But my defenses were mustered up because I trusted my OB, and it gave me a chance to try and relax by using the breathing techniques I'd learned in prenatal exercise class.

The novocaine felt like a small prick, much less than a blood test and similar to getting novocaine at the dentist. There was an immediate numbing, cooling sensation. Next, he said I would feel a lot of pressure in my abdomen as the needle was inserted. I did. It wasn't really pain, but discomfort pressure like heavy, unrelenting gas.

Fluid quickly filled up the tube that was fitted to the end of the needle. Although I couldn't see, he told me the fluid was nice and clear. I knew that was important.

Then after he switched tubes, the fluid stopped flowing. The technician ran the transducer across my abdomen again. Both the fetus and the fluid had moved and my bladder was filling up again. The needle was removed because another tap would have to be done after I emptied my bladder. But before I got up from the table for the trip down the hall to the lavatory, we were treated to a most incredible experience.

I was still feeling discomfort and tension from the tap. Then the technician changed machines from the one-dimensional ultrasound, which made it very difficult for the untrained eye to distinguish form in the sound waves, to a machine with an unbelievably appropriate name—the Real Time Machine. More baby oil and the same transducer were used, but this time the image on the new screen bounced two-dimensional sound waves clearly, providing the first view of the baby. Immediately the fetus became a real person with a profile that my husband recognized immediately as like his grandfather's. Arms swimming, hands boxing and turning, and a heart rapidly beating were all clearly visible, leaving an image that would be indelibly imprinted in our memories.

I was dumbfounded. So much movement inside me that I hadn't yet felt! How could it be so real? It seemed surrealistic to me, and absolutely fantastic to my husband.

It wasn't easy to get up from the table and walk down the hall to the bathroom. I was still feeling shaken from the tap and reeling from the vision on the screen of what was inside of me. As I emptied my bladder I was able to sit and contemplate, for a few moments, what had just happened. I felt an overwhelming sense of confusion and excitement, but mostly disbelief. How could all that movement—that person—be inside of me? How could technology see in me so much life that I hadn't felt?

But a few minutes later, I was back on the table ready for it all to happen again—

a small prick for the novocaine in a different spot, the cooling-numbing sensation, the heavy pressure of the needle. Again the baby moved right up front, making a tap very difficult. Our OB reluctantly tried a third tap, knowing I was hurting and finding it very hard to hold still. When the third one didn't provide any more fluid, he decided the lab would have to use what he'd already gotten, hoping it would be enough. Once more, the Real Time Machine was connected for the two-dimensional pictures, and we saw our baby.

The trip home was hard. New York potholes added to my physical discomfort. But my husband's new exuberance about being an expectant father made me feel relaxed and less in a daze about what I had seen and experienced. Once at home, I slept most of the day and woke to call family and friends, at my husband's urging, to share the experience with them. While it did help to incorporate it into my life, it wasn't until I myself started to actually feel the baby move that I could really do that. The process of seeing the baby inside me made me realize that a part of myself was going to be set aside forever, to make room for another individual. At the same time as I was realizing how connected I was emotionally to this new individual, I missed the me I had come to know comfortably. The time for new beginnings was a time for old endings, and I didn't even know whether I could give up this connection with the new life if something was wrong.

Ten days later, just when we expected to have the results, our OB called late at night. I was glad not to answer the phone because I emotionally couldn't have heard what he had to convey. The lab was having trouble getting enough cells to grow and analyze. There was a possibility the amniocentesis would have to be done again.

Initially I was very angry and upset. I felt defeated. I hadn't realized the whole experience had generated quite so much anxiety. What I heard was my worst fears, "no good," instead of the real message, "not enough." My husband insisted I have a positive attitude and kept reassuring me that this did not mean there was something wrong with the baby. But it really didn't help; the part of me that sat in the bathroom in disbelief found that some of the anxiety came from thinking I'd seen only one leg, or a combined one, on the swimming creature in the pictures from the new technology. The amniocentesis wouldn't pick up that kind of "wrong." By then I was already attached to the baby but struggling with the not uncommon feelings during pregnancy that the baby wouldn't have all its fingers and toes or in some way would be not quite whole. The psychologically trained part of me knew that the issues were about my own sense of damage and inadequacy. That did not help me from being dragged down by the images I thought I'd seen on the screen.

Despite the fact that the OB said we could wait a few days to see if enough cells would be generated, I gathered up my optimism and asked to have the retap scheduled immediately. This was a healthy new pattern for me—to be active in confronting anxiety and overcoming denial by gathering as much information as quickly as possible. The prospect of adding more time to the waiting was not comforting. I wanted life to go on and not have to sit in the hiatus of anxiety that was being generated by the possibility of having to give up my already strong attachment to this new person.

Next morning, our OB rechecked the lab, which reiterated that not enough cells had come up in the fluid yet, and although they would not make a commitment as to whether or not to do it again, both the doctor and I agreed not to wait any longer.

I since have learned that doing the procedure twice is not that unusual, something none of our reading had conveyed to us. Laboratories play a highly critical role in the emotional aspects of the procedure, something which I am convinced they clearly don't understand. One senses that to the "scientists" lab tests are simply routine chemistry tests without real people attached to the bodily products that come their way.

The following morning, back at the hospital, we figured we were experts at dealing with amniocentesis. This time things went very smoothly and quickly. Having already felt the baby's movements and the strong bond developing, I excused myself to the lavatory for a conversation with this new being before entering the ultrasound room. "OK, little baby, you and I have got to do a good job this morning" was my assertion, though I think I felt a little silly talking out loud to someone inside me. Whatever, it worked. I used breathing and concentrated on contracting the muscles in my hands while relaxing the lower part of my body. The tap took 2 minutes with little discomfort, and we again saw our baby. This time, it was apparently hiding in a corner of my uterus, away from the path of the needle. There wasn't as clear a total image as the last time, so I never really got to check out my fears about deformity. The movement I could feel for myself somehow helped to quell those concerns more and more during the pregnancy.

Even the trip home was easier. We figured out that if I brought a pillow to recline on and dropped the seat back all the way, the potholes didn't have quite the same devastating effect. A few months later we discovered that part of the car ride problem was a result of the gas station's having overloaded the air pressure in the tires, making the shocks dysfunctional. But I did feel much more positive about the results and much less disoriented than at any other point in all of the 5 weeks of waiting.

During the last 3 of those 5 weeks, I anxiously responded to every ring of the phone. If I had been able to know exactly which day the results would be ready, it would have been better. I still find it hard to believe that labs can't be more specific about when results will be available. I tried to rationalize it by reminding myself that since I wouldn't know when labor would begin, this would be good practice for that waiting. The rationalization never really worked well. With labor you could be sure that a few hours, even a day later, you would have a baby as a result. Now waiting meant that I did not know whether to psychologically prepare for a baby or the possibility of an abortion. This psychological hiatus in the second trimester runs counter to the preparations that are usually necessary during those weeks in order to accept the pregnancy and reality of a new person. The daily wonderful feeling, of the baby moving, kicking, somersaulting, reminded me constantly of how possible it was for my lifelong desire to have a baby to finally come to fruition. My own sexist reaction to seeing such an active baby was that it was probably a boy, but my husband and I didn't share those aspects of our thoughts with each other. Regardless, instead of anxiously waiting, I wanted to be out shopping for baby things, finishing up our apartment, making space in our lives for a third person.

Five weeks from the first tap and 3 weeks from the second, I felt I couldn't wait any longer. Our OB had told me to feel free to call him to check regularly, although he had assured me he would call the moment he knew. He had been checking with the lab regularly, reminding them of the time constraints involved. We were right on the edge of time as to whether an abortion, if necessary, would be done without inducing labor.

We had been told the culture was growing and there were plenty of cells to analyze. I wanted to call the lab myself, feeling I'd have a little more control over the anxiety. Finally, the calls produced an answer. We were going to have a normal, healthy baby!

Pounds of anxiety dropped from my shoulders, and I breathed a cleansing sigh of relief.

We had already told the doctor we definitively wanted to know what sex the baby would be. My response had always been, if the lab and the doctor knew, I wanted to know. The thought of these people outside of myself knowing something so important and me not was an unacceptable situation. There was no question that I wanted to know. We were already referring to the baby as Cady or Jason. It didn't seem appropriate to use either when one was the right name.

I called my husband right away to tell him to hurry home and "give me and Cady a big hug." At first I thought he might be disappointed if it wasn't Jason, because having a son had seemed to be important to him. But I could tell from the intonation of his response, "Really?!", he was more pleased that we could *finally* get to the fun of being pregnant, and equally happy about having Cady. It was going to take some getting used to not having all that anxiety floating around.

"I want a feisty girl," he said. "Next time it will be Jason," I replied. We obviously both had our own reactions to seeing the moving pictures. What I felt about having a daughter was thoroughly reassuring. I was genuinely pleased because I knew I would feel more confident about being a "good enough" mother for a girl for the first baby than I would if it had been a boy. I had spent a good deal of energy understanding myself as a woman, and I could see the connections between childhood and adulthood for a girl. I had a harder time seeing that for a boy, then.

I also felt more confident about my husband's being a "good enough" father for a girl. He would love her like a princess but still get her involved in the things he would for a boy. It just seemed a generally easier option to be having a girl first. But even more important, knowing the baby was healthy made it possible to shed much of the anxiety from the weeks of waiting. I also had to admit that it made me feel secure in my own family as well. My parents already had two grandsons. I knew they would love a granddaughter.

Other people, particularly my mother, didn't want to know the sex. She was the only holdout in the family. She represented, to me, the flip side of some of the wonders of technology. She wanted the surprise. She welcomed the not knowing. It was a pattern of relating with which she felt comfortable, though I have to admit it seemed a little like denial to me. She kept referring to the baby as "Baby X." It seemed impersonal and I told her so. To accommodate me, she switched to "Baby Eddy." But eventually, even she wanted to know the sex, but not the name. She needed some kind of surprise with which to greet the birth. So until the day she was born, her grandmother called her "Little Miss Eddy." I knew it was a hopeless battle to suggest "Little Ms. Eddy!"

What if it had been a boy? I asked myself that question and tried to answer it honestly. It would have been fine. I know I would have felt a little less confident, but what seemed most important to me was that this person whom I had been introduced to on the monitor and whose facial features were so clearly recognizable to me, whom I had felt swimming and somersaulting in me, needed an identity. It just wasn't an "it" any longer. She was a part of our lives long before she quietly peered at me from above my abdomen and took her first breaths on her own.

It has been 8 years since that day and since the journal entries were written that recorded much of the above. The marriage has ended. There haven't been any more children. Amniocentesis is a common practice for women over 35. There are many more of us who have had that experience of meeting our children for the first time on a monitor, knowing the sex of our babies before they are born, though having the procedure done just for that is not appropriate. A few of us had to decide whether to have an abortion as a result of the knowledge gained from the technology, or prepare for a baby who would need a different kind of welcome.

Cady and I started our relationship with that first vision on the ultrasound monitor. We both thrive and are equally enthralled and cautious with technology. Without the human responses from our OB and the exuberant response to the pregnancy by her father, the technological advance would have been shallow and distant. Human beings focused on their relationships with us, which made all of the technology used during my experience with pregnancy and childbirth an aid, and not the center stage.

Today, Cady and I were watching a cartoon on another instrument of technology. The moral of the story was an important one to consider when technology plays such a critical role in human relations: Don't let a deception become your reality.

The picture on the monitor screen and my initial fears about it weren't the real person. She is ever so much more complex, spirited, and delightful. I never even thought to see if all her fingers and toes were there when I first met her in person. It wouldn't have mattered. The real was so much better. Being her mother is a privilege and a challenge. With the help of the people and technology involved, we both got the best of what was possible, even if not perfect.

Chapter 14

Gender Selection and Society

JODIE B. ULLMAN AND LINDA S. FIDELL

The preference for boys in general and firstborn boys in particular crosses the boundaries of time and culture. Almost every major study reveals a preference for boys, from the writings of Aristotle (Nentwig, 1981) to the present, and around the globe, from the developing societies of India, Morocco, and rural Bangladesh (Bairagi & Langsten, 1985) and the Asian societies of China (Goody, Duly, Beeson, & Harrison, 1981) and Korea (Arnold, 1985) to Europe and the United States. Within this country, preference for boys is found among both men and women (Fidell, Hoffman, & Keith-Speigel, 1979; Gilroy & Stienbacher, 1983) and among people from all walks of life. It finds concrete expression in the requests of middle-class Americans for boys to adopt, and in the abortion of female fetuses in China (Nentwig, 1981).

Preference for girls is rare. Cross-culturally, it is found in simple agricultural societies, such as Thailand and Ghana, where there is a matrilineal system of inheritance (Goody *et al.*, 1981). In this country, girls are more popular for adoption among older couples and among white couples adopting racially mixed children (Culpepper, 1981).

Except for female infanticide, gender selection has until now been left solely to nature. Recent technological advances, however, make fulfillment of the preference for boys a realistic possibility. Selection techniques are becoming increasingly more accurate and readily available. Some of them are "do-it-yourself," others require medical intervention; some are used prior to fertilization, others after.

The simplest do-it-yourself method involves the timing of sexual intercourse to correspond to a woman's ovulation. This capitalizes on functional differences between female and male sperm. When intercourse takes place 36 to 48 hours prior to ovulation, the conception rate of girls is as high as 80% (Nentwig, 1981). Some report that conception of boys is heavily favored when intercourse takes place the day of ovulation. Reported probabilities of conception of boys range from slightly over 50% to as high as 75% (Nentwig, 1981). The trick is, of course, to predict the time of ovulation.

Manipulation of vaginal pH balance is another do-it-yourself method that capitalizes on differences in sperm. Male sperm are adversely affected by acidity, so if a mildly acidic substance (e.g., vinegar) is introduced into the vagina prior to inter-

---

JODIE B. ULLMAN AND LINDA S. FIDELL • Department of Psychology, California State University, Northridge, California 91330.

course, conception of a girl is more likely. Through manipulation of the vaginal environment and positioning to maximize placement of sperm, girls are said to be selected with a success rate of higher than 80% (Nentwig, 1981).

More sophisticated methods use antibodies that are produced by ova in the presence of either male or female sperm. These antibodies are injected into the woman to counteract one type of sperm and facilitate conception of a baby of the other gender (Nentwig, 1981). Female and male sperm can also be separated by centrifuge and used in conjunction with artificial insemination to select the gender of the fetus.

First- and second-trimester abortions are sometimes used to ensure gender preference as well. Amniocentesis was developed to evaluate genetic defects, but it also reveals fetal gender. It is suspected that some second-trimester abortions following amniocentesis are not solely for genetic reasons. In China, for instance, the Anshan aspiration technique, which reveals fetal gender in the first trimester of pregnancy, is used in conjunction with first-trimester abortion to select a boy 93% of the time (Nentwig, 1981).

But who has this preference and why do they have it? Is the preference different among people who support the goals of the women's civil rights movement? And what will happen if a substantial segment of the population arranges to have boys, particularly firstborn boys?

In 1979, Fidell *et al.* found a strong preference for boys in a large sample of university students drawn primarily from middle- and working-class backgrounds. If these 710 students have their way, they will have a total of 1681 children, 919 (55%) boys and 762 (45%) girls, confirming their overall preference for boys. But they also wanted children born in a certain order; fully 85% of them wanted a boy born first and 73% a girl born second. This pattern of preference was the same for men and women and for people of all different religious and ethnic backgrounds. The only factor that moderated the preference was belief in the goals of the women's civil rights movement. Among those who were strongly in favor of the movement, and, curiously, among those who were strongly opposed to it, there was a lessened preference for boys and firstborn boys.

But nearly 15 years have passed since these data were collected, and feminism seems to have become a stronger, more socially integrated force than it was 15 years ago. Have family preferences changed? We collected data again from students attending the same university to find out.

A total of 361 students, 31% men and 69% women, specified, among other things, their ideal family composition. Politically, 24% of the students said they were conservative, 42% were middle-of-the-road, and 34% liberal. Two-thirds of the sample were Caucasian, 4% Black, 13% Hispanic, 14% Asian, and the rest "other." Among religions, 34% were Catholics, 19% Jews, 18% Protestants, and the rest "none" or "other" (some members of Eastern and Mideastern religions and some Christians who did not consider themselves Protestant or Catholic).

There were several interesting differences between responses in 1979 and in 1987. The average number of children desired increased slightly from 2.4 in 1978 to 2.53 in 1987. A total of 3% of the students wanted no children, 6% wanted one child, 48% wanted two children, 26% three children, and the remainder up to eight children. Respondents would also wait another year to begin a family; in 1979 they wanted to be, on average, 25.5 years old when the first baby was born, compared with 26.5 years in 1987.

If these 361 students have the children they want, they will have 867 children,

448 (52%) boys and 418 (48%) girls. Thus, the overall preference for boys is lower than 15 years ago. Further, only 70% of the students wanted a firstborn boy and 65% a secondborn girl, compared with 85% and 73%, respectively, 15 years ago. It is interesting to note that the preference for boys disappears after the second child: 46% wanted a boy and 46% a girl for the third child and subsequent children. Thus, among these students, there is still a slight overall preference for boys, and a somewhat stronger preference for firstborn boys and secondborn girls, but the preference has reliably declined in the last 15 years.

In 1979, the only factor that reduced the preference for boys was strong belief in the goals of the women's civil rights movement. At that time, 76% of the students reported that they were in favor of the movement. By 1987, 96% of the students said that they support the goals of the women's civil rights movement. It appears that one of the gains of feminism has been a reduction in the preference for boys. However, there also appears to be a lag; students have changed their minds about wanting boys and firstborn boys. There is no way to tell if the trend will continue.

Almost half of the students (48%) wanted two children, and, among these, 56% wanted the boy-girl combination. A multiway frequency analysis was done to see if preference for this pattern was related to gender of respondent, the student's own birth order, political affiliation, or ethnicity.[1] There were two reliable two-way relationships: Men were more likely than women, and politically conservatives more likely than liberals, to want a firstborn boy and a secondborn girl. The more conservative the respondent, the more likely the desire for the boy-girl combination. Among conservative men, 92% want a firstborn boy.

The students were reasonably familiar with the various methods of choosing the gender of children. Two-thirds knew about separating sperm for use with artificial insemination; half knew about timing intercourse with ovulation and about use of abortion for gender choice. Hormonal and chemical interventions were less familiar (roughly a quarter of the sample had heard of them). Would the students use any of these methods to ensure their desired family pattern? A total of 63% of the sample said "No, not at all," while 37% of the sample said "Yes"; 8% of the sample would spend "a great deal" of effort, and 20% "a moderate amount" of effort to ensure their chosen family pattern. Half of them would use timing of intercourse, about a tenth hormonal or chemical interventions; less than 1% would use abortion. Interestingly, it appears that in both 1979 and 1987 only about a third of university-educated people would consider using sex-choice technology, although they have heard of it, and most would only consider methods that are used prior to fertilization.

What type of people are willing to go to "a great deal" of effort to have their desired family pattern and what pattern do they choose? Almost 80% of them want a firstborn boy and 62% a secondborn girl (many want only boys). Sixty percent of them were men, although men were only a third of the entire sample.[2] They were also more conservative, more Hispanic or "other," and more Catholic than the rest of the sample. Additionally, this group was not as strongly in favor of women's civil rights as was the full sample. These people were more willing than others to use all of the methods for selection of gender of children, although timing of intercourse was still the most popular of currently available methods.

[1] For a variety of statistical reasons, we could not test for relationships between belief in the women's civil rights movement or religious affiliation and preference for boy firstborns.
[2] Because the burden of use of sex-choice methods falls on women, these men will need the cooperation of women if they intend to use the methods.

Table 1. Reasons for Selection of Gender of Firstborn

Reasons	Gender preference			
	1979[a]		1987	
	Boy	Girl	Boy	Girl
For the firstborn child				
To provide the child with practical or psychological advantages of firstborn status	26%	20%	4%	7%
For the younger sibling	11%	20%	35%	12%
To provide protection for younger sibling	2%	0%	17%	0%
To provide instruction for younger sibling	3%	7%	2%	1%
To help care for younger sibling	2%	13%	7%	3%
To provide social instruction for younger sibling	4%	0%	2%	0%
To provide a role model for younger sibling	Not included		3%	5%
Other	Not included		4%	3%
For the parents	39%	27%	44%	65%
To carry on family name/tradition	4%	0%	11%	3%
To replicate family pattern of respondent's family	3%	3%	4%	8%
To have a family pattern opposite of respondent's family	Not included		2%	3%
Parental ego needs or pleasure	23%	7%	19%	31%
To provide an "easy" child to raise	9%	17%	6%	19%
To raise "harder" child first	Not included		2%	1%
For "no special reason"	25%	33%	16%	15%

[a] From Fidell, Hoffman, and Keith-Spiegel (1979).

We also asked the students *why* they selected the gender they did for firstborn and secondborn. The reasons given by the students for selection of the gender of the firstborn child are seen in Table 1. In 1979, 39% of the students wanted a firstborn boy for the parents' sake (for their own ego needs or pleasure), while 26% knew there were advantages to firstborn status and wanted to give those advantages to a boy. Only 11% were thinking about the younger sibling when selecting a boy. That pattern is different in 1987. Almost half wanted a firstborn boy for the parent's sake, a third were thinking about the younger sibling, and only 4% wanted to give the advantages of firstborn status to a boy.

In 1979, the dominant reason for selecting a girl first was for the parents' sake (primarily to have an easy child to raise), followed by consideration of the younger sibling (where the girls could help raise the younger child) and to give advantages of firstborn status to a girl. In 1987, a firstborn girl was wanted by almost two-thirds of the sample for the parents' sake (for their ego needs and pleasure as well as to have an easy child to raise). The younger sibling was considered less often.

In 1987, respondents were less interested in giving the advantages of firstborn status to either boys or girls. Either they were less aware that there are advantages or they were less eager to give them to a child of a specific gender. Indeed, in 1987 (as in 1979, but much less so), the students were thinking primarily of their own needs and aspirations when they made their gender selections.

Gender Selection and Society

Given the presence of sex-choice technology, the preference for boys and firstborn boys, and the willingness of perhaps a third of the population to use some forms of this technology, it is important to examine the potential societal implications of the use of it. As in most things, we judge some consequences as positive and some as negative[3]; some are associated with production of more men than women; and some with confounding gender with birth order.

One result of the employment of these techniques is a numerical shift in the balance between men and women so that there are fewer women. The size of the shift depends on the preferences of the proportion of the population that actually uses the technology successfully. We consider first the consequences of a society with fewer women than men and then the consequences of confounding gender with birth order.

The natural birthrate is not even; there are more boys conceived and born than girls, but, owing to higher infant mortality among boys, the gender ratio is about even by the end of the first year of life and stays even through the first two decades. Then, owing to the greater male accident and, eventually, illness rate, the ratio favors women increasingly into middle and late years. Women over 65 far outnumber men. One positive consequence, then, of the birth of more boys might be a more even male–female split in later years, with an attendant drop in the loneliness often encountered by older heterosexual women.

A second positive consequence of the use of this technology is a reduction in the number of "wrong"-gender children born. It is unknown the extent of damage done to a child who knows that she is "wrong"; however, any reduction in this syndrome is likely to be positive. In discussing birth control, Planned Parenthood has used the phrase "every child a wanted child" (cited in Chico & Hartley, 1981). Those citing the advantages of gender selection technology have applied the slogan to this technology. But what damage is done to the woman who knows she was wanted, but wanted second?

Third, anecdotal accounts and research on the "stopping rule" indicate that people often continue to have children until a desired gender ratio is achieved. With gender ratio assured through technology, parents would be free to have smaller families. This could lead to a reduction in family size wherever the technology is employed, and an increased ability of women to continue their careers and personal growth once the desired family is achieved.

However, these benefits are likely to be realized only among middle- and upper-middle-class women who can afford and have easy access to medical advances. Lower-income women are often denied access to new medical advances (e.g., infertility treatment). It seems unlikely that sex-choice technology would be any more readily available to these women than would any other gynecological advance. The use of sex-choice technology could, therefore, lead to a society with more women born into poverty to women who are unable to escape from poverty.

Williamson (cited in Steinbacher, 1981) suggests that use of sex-choice technology would give women more control over their bodies and their reproductive decisions. The historical use of chastity belts, clitoridectomy, and footbinding and, more recently,

---

[3]Because both authors accept the goals of the women's civil rights movement, we judge consequences as positive when they foster, or at least do not hinder, equality of opportunity between women and men; consequences are judged negative when they interfere with the goal of equality of opportunity between the sexes.

the overzealous use of mastectomy, hysterectomy, and Cesarean section suggest that gains in control of women over their own bodies are desirable. If, indeed, sex-choice technology fosters greater control, then this is another benefit of the technology. However, it could also lead to less control, as discussed below.

Some have speculated that women would have higher value in a society with fewer of them. It is indeed possible that women would be treated better and valued more highly if they were scarce. However, it is also possible that women would be given superior treatment in a manner similar to the special treatment given a prize heifer—valued more highly, but primarily as human incubators. Women choosing not to have children or those unable to bear children might be ostracized by society. If women become a truly scarce resource, there may be cloistering of women, the formation of purdahs, and polyandry, all developed to reward the dominant males in society (Postgate, cited in Powledge, 1981; Steinbacher, 1981).

In such a situation, women could be denied opportunities of career and education in favor of maximal childbearing. Traditionally female-dominated careers, such as nursing, secretarial work, assembly-line work, and teaching, could experience shortages. The shortages could serve to increase the value, prestige, and salaries of currently female-dominated fields, with a likely consequence that men would move into them.

Currently, many governments control a woman's right to abortion. If women become scarce through use of sex-choice technology, further governmental control might follow. It is possible that governments would seek to exercise quantitative control of population by regulation of this technology, thus removing any control a woman hoped to gain over her body from this technology.

Religion is often considered the moral backbone of a country and women are usually the backbone of organized religion. If fewer women are born, organized religions may suffer. Many social programs and much of the charitable work done through religious organizations and others could be lost or severely curtailed. Governments that rely heavily on religious and other organizations to provide volunteers for numerous social programs might find that they have to fill the void with more numerous governmental agencies and increases in taxation.

And what are the consequences to men of too few women? Competition among men is a dominant force in society now, widely regarded as linked to circulatory and other health problems that men suffer in excess over women. What would happen if, in addition to everything else, a man had to compete not just for the girl of his dreams but for any girl at all? What would happen if lots of men had to look forward to a life largely bereft of female companionship?

Men are responsible for the majority of violent crime and aggression in our society, and, as the number of men increases, so may crime and aggression. If women become scarce, there could well be an increase in all types of sex-related crimes, such as rape, molestation, and pornography (Cavin, cited in Connors, 1981). Homosexuality would increase along with certain types of sexually transmitted diseases. Society could develop an ongoing "locker room" mentality.

The overall consequences, then, of the use of sex-choice technology to produce more boys than girls are not likely to foster equality of opportunity for women. Society is likely to become rougher if men find that their access to women is limited. Women might well enjoy the benefits of increased value for their conjugal and reproductive functions, but at a stiff price to personal growth and independence. But these consequences derive from numerical imbalance, and people might well choose to have more girls if the imbalance became large, thereby redressing it.

Unfortunately, numerical imbalance is not the most likely, or potentially most damaging, result of use of the technology. People would also confound gender with birth order to have firstborn boys and secondborn girls, with attendant psychological and physiological consequences.

Much psychological research addresses the effects of birth order on the development of children. Reasons for birth order effects have been linked to such factors as biology (Boroson, 1984; Stone & Rowley, 1966), maternal behavior (Palmer, 1966; Sears, Maccoby, & Levin, 1957), behavior and number of older siblings (Falbo, 1981), and intellectual composition of family at each child's point of entry (Zajonc, Markus, & Markus, 1979). Although the causes of the differences are not clear, the results are: There are consistently found advantages and disadvantages to both firstborn and secondborn status.

A firstborn child of either gender has better mental health (Abraham & Prasanna, 1983), is more achievement-oriented, has higher self-esteem, and is more competitive (Falbo, 1981), ambitious, conscientious, self-confident (Boroson, 1974), creative (Lichtenwalner & Maxwell, 1969), verbal (Rosenberg & Sutton-Smith, 1966), intelligent (Belmont & Marolla, 1973; Falbo, 1981), self-controlled, serious, and adult-oriented (Arrowood & Amaroso, 1965; Becker, Lerner, & Carroll, 1966; Carringan & Julian, 1966) than laterborns. Firstborns are also more likely to attend college and are overrepresented in academic and professional eminence (Boroson, 1974; Warren, 1966).

On the negative side, firstborn children of either gender tend to be less accepted by peers, to exhibit more disturbed behavior (Baskett, 1985), to be more self-centered and introverted (Klein, 1984), and to be more conforming, susceptible to social pressure, affiliative, dependent (Schachter, 1959; Sears, 1950; see also Conners, 1963, for a reversal of this finding; Vats, 1986), and anxious (Schachter, 1959) than laterborn children.

Firstborn women have been found to be more politically conservative than their corresponding male counterparts (Heingartener & Wetherell, 1982). Thus, if people use sex-choice technology to produce the boy-girl combination, there would be fewer politically conservative women. Other research has shown that firstborn men are less accepting of women as managers than laterborn men, particularly when they have a younger sister (Beutell, 1984). Thus, overproduction of firstborn men would make it even less likely that a woman could succeed in a managerial role.

Secondborn status has some advantages. These children are reported to be more cheerful, easygoing, talkative, popular, practical, and action-oriented (Boroson, 1974) than firstborn children. They are also more likely to seek help and adult approval and are more talkative than their firstborn counterparts (McGurk & Lewis, 1972). On the other hand, secondborn children tend to display more nervous habits, and have a greater need for affiliation, if not greater expectation of affiliative rewards (Conners, 1963).

Adults, whether or not they are parents, have differential expectations about children according to their ordinal position (Baskett, 1985). Firstborn children are expected to be outgoing, dominant, leaders, obedient, responsible, secure, self-confident, and undemanding. Because the oldest child is expected to be better behaved, he or she is more likely to be criticized. Laterborn children are expected to be likable, sociable, popular, followers, less obedient, and lower in achievement motivation (Baskett, 1985).

It is critical to realize that the characteristics and expectations of first- and secondborn children correspond almost exactly to sex-role stereotypes for men and women. Firstborns of either gender tend to display masculine sex-role stereotypes while secondborns of either gender tend to exhibit feminine sex-role stereotypes. Therefore, if use of sex-choice technology actually confounds ordinal position with gender, stereotypical sex-role behavior is likely to be exacerbated. If society is working toward the goal of equality of opportunity for men and women, this is clearly counterproductive. If women are selected to be born second, the second-class status of women is confirmed *de facto* (Steinbacher, 1981). The ramifications to women of knowing that they were "wanted," but second, can hardly be beneficial.

There are also physiological consequences to women of being born second. The current trend in the United States is to delay childbirth. But as childbirth is delayed, both mother and child are at higher risk. Chromosomal deficits leading to such diseases as Down's syndrome are directly related to maternal age at time of pregnancy. As a result of increased risk, older women must often submit to medical tests, such as amniocentesis, which may themselves be injurious to the fetus. Couples may plan to have a girl after the boy, but as they age, their fertility declines. Therefore, couples may find that while they desire a girl, they are no longer able to produce one. A final ramification of women born to older parents is that the parents may be unable or unwilling to take as active a role in the development of the second child as they did for the first.

While many of these implications have the flavor of science fiction, it is important to consider all the consequences of a technology whose use could substantially alter society. It is promsing that there has apparently been a reduction in the desire for a firstborn boy; however, the preference is still there, as is the willingness among some to use technology to determine the gender of a child. As Powledge (1981, p. 196) so aptly stated, "we should not choose the sexes of our children because to do so is one of the most stupendously sexist acts in which it is possible to engage. It is the original sexist sin." Social education is necessary to shed this antiquated bias and allow us to strive toward a more balanced, androgynous society.

REFERENCES

Abraham, M., & Prasanna, K. C. B. (1983). Child's age and ordinal position in the family as factors of mental health. *Asian Journal of Psychology and Education, 11*(4), 45–51.

Arnold, F. (1985). Measuring the effect of sex preference on fertility: The case of Korea. *Demography, 22*(2), 280–288.

Arrowood, A., & Amaroso, D. (1965). Social comparison and ordinal position. *Journal of Personality and Social Psychology, 2,* 101–104.

Bairagi, R., & Langsten, R. L. (1985). Preference for sex of children and its implications for fertility in rural Bangladesh (Abstract). In C. B. Lloyd (Chair), *Preferences for the sex of children: Implications for fertility.* Symposium conducted at the annual meeting of the Population Association of America, Chapel Hill, NC.

Baskett, L. M. (1985). Sibling status effects: Adult expectations. *Developmental Psychology, 21,* 441–445.

Becker. S. W., Lerner, M. J., & Carroll, J. (1966). Conformity as a function of birth order and type of group pressure: A verification. *Journal of Personality and Social Psychology, 3,* 242–249.

Belmont, L., & Marolla, F. A. (1973). Birth order, family size, and intelligence. *Science, 182,* 1096.

Beutell, N. J. (1984). Correlates of attitudes toward American women as managers. *Journal of Social Psychology, 124,* 57–63.

Boroson, W. (1974). Firstborn—Fortune's favorite? *Readings in Human Development '74/'75* (pp. 134–138). Guilford, CT: Harper and Row.

Carrigan, W., & Julian, J. (1966). Sex and birth order differences in conformity: Function of need affiliation arousal. *Journal of Personality and Social Psychology, 3,* 479–483.

Chico, N. P., & Hartley, S. F. (1981). Widening choices in motherhood of the future. *Psychology of Women Quarterly, 6,* 12–25.

Conners, C. K. (1963). Birth order and needs for affiliation. *Journal of Personality, 31,* 408–416.

Connors, D. (1981). Response. In H. B. Holmes, B. B. Hoskins, & M. Gross (Eds.), *The custom-made child? Women-centered perspectives* (pp. 205–207). Clifton, NJ: Humana Press.

Culpepper, E. E. (1981). Sex preselection discussion moderator's remarks. In H. B. Holmes, B. B. Hoskins, & M. Gross (Eds.), *The custom-made child? Women-centered perspectives* (pp. 213–214). Clifton, NJ: Humana Press.

Falbo, T. (1981). Relationship between birth category, achievement, and interpersonal orientation. *Journal of Personality and Social Psychology, 41,* 121–131.

Fidell, L., Hoffman, D., & Keith-Spegel, P. (1979). Some social implications of sex-choice technology. *Psychology of Women Quarterly, 4,* 32–42.

Gilroy, F., & Steinbacher, R. (1983). Preselection of child's sex: Technological utilization and feminism. *Psychological Reports, 53,* 671–676.

Goody, J. R., Duly, C. J., Beeson, I., & Harrison, G. (1981). Implicit sex preferences: A comparative study. *Journal of Biosocial Sciences, 13,* 455–466.

Heingartner, A., & Wetherell, C. K. (1982). Birth order, sex, and socio-political orientation in college students. *Psychological Reports, 51,* 891–896.

Klein, S. (1984). Birth order and introversion-extraversion. *Journal of Research in Personality, 18,* 110–113.

Lictenwalner, J., & Maxwell, J. (1969). The relationship of birth order and socio-economic status to the creativity of preschool children. *Child Development, 40,* 1241–1247.

McGurk, H., & Lewis, M. (1972). Birth order: A phenomenon in search of an explanation. ERIC, Ed 067156.

Nentwig, M. R. (1981). Technical aspects of sex preselection. In H. B. Holmes, B. B. Hoskins, & M. Gross (Eds.), *The custom-made child? Women-centered perspectives* (pp. 181–186). Clifton, NJ: Humana Press.

Palmer, R. D. (1966). Birth order and identification. *Journal of Consulting Psychology, 30,* 129–135.

Powledge, T. M. (1981). Unnatural selection in choosing children's sex. In H. B. Holmes, B. B. Hoskins, & M. Gross (Eds.), *The custom-made child? Women-centered perspectives* (pp. 193–199). Clifton, NJ: Humana Press.

Rosenberg, B. G., & Sutton-Smith, B. (1966). Sibling association, family size, and cognitive abilities. *Journal of Genetic Psychology, 109,* 271–279.

Schachter, S. (1959). *The psychology of affiliation.* Stanford: Stanford University Press.

Sears, R. R. (1950). Ordinal position in the family as a psychology variable. *American Sociological Review, 15,* 397–401.

Sears, R. R., Maccoby, E., & Levin, H. (1957). *Patterns of child rearing*, Evanston, IL: Row, Peterson.

Steinbacher, R. (1981). Futuristic implications of sex preselection. In H. B. Holmes, B. B. Hoskins, & M. Gross (Eds.), *The custom-made child? Women-centered perspectives* (pp. 187–191). Clifton, NJ: Humana Press.

Stone, F. B., & Rowley, V. N. (1966). Children's behavior problems and mother's age. *Journal of Psychology, 63,* 229–233.

Vats, A. (1986). Birth order, sex, and dependence proneness in Indian students. *Psychological Reports, 58,* 284–286.

Warren, R. (1966). Birth order and social behavior. *Psychological Bulletin, 65,* 38–49.

Zajonc, R. B., Markus, H., & Markus, G. B. (1979). The birth order puzzle. *Journal of Personality and Social Psychology, 37,* 1325–1341.

Chapter 15

Woman's Shifting Sense of Self
The Impact of Reproductive Technology

DONNA BASSIN

INTRODUCTION

The title may imply that this chapter has a psychic hold on what may be the "greased pig" issue of contemporary feminist thought. It has not. The effect of reproductive technology on women's psychological development and sense of self is of critical import for the creators, administrators, and users of these interventions. As such, there has been much concern from the feminist community regarding its potential exploitative and destructive impact on women.

Barrett (1987) has defined science as the exhibition of the power of the human mind. Science and its offspring, reproductive technology, have become both evidence of and a vehicle for our freedom. It is possible that as we become less tied to nature and biology there will be more opportunities for both men and women to transcend gender roles. But science has its dark side. Too large a departure from our physicality has far-reaching ramifications. To be able to create birth through science suggests that we may also be able to deny death as well. In some distant or not so distant age when all desires are fulfilled by technology and all losses are compensated by science, we may very well lose the need to create the compensatory psychological representations and symbols that comprise culture, art, and dreams.

While I am quite aware of the problematic aspects of reproductive technology, I am also critical of its simplistic portrayal as a new form of patriarchal domination. In this chapter, I will argue that while the use of reproductive technology can be a situational trauma for a woman, it need not have destructive symbolic meaning for her. The need to rely on something outside of oneself to become pregnant or to carry a baby to term can, of course, be traumatic. The dependency on technology can be a temporary insult to a woman's narcissism in that it interferes with her expectation of the natural unfolding of a life process within her body. Reproductive technology can, however, be stressful without being symbolic. That is, the use of technology need neither carry unnecessary psychological weight nor take on destructive sub-

---

DONNA BASSIN • Institute of Psychoanalytic Training and Research, New York, New York 10028.

jective importance to her sense of self. Unfortunately, for many women, the need for reproductive intervention often brings the additional burden of being a sign of incompetence, victimization, or pervasive defects and deficiencies. Ideally and optimally, reproductive technology can facilitate conception and birth and provide opportunities for biological motherhood to those who might have otherwise remained childless. The use of these interventions can, in fact, be a facilitating tool and provide a woman with more autonomy and control over her body and her life. The specific reactions will vary, depending upon the strength of the woman's bodily integrity, her early identifications, the stability of her female identity, her developmental history, the nature of the intervention, attitudes of the medical personnel, environmental supports, and the chance of a positive outcome. I will discuss in this chapter some of the variables that impinge upon a woman's reaction to reproductive technology. In particular, I will focus on the development of an optimal female bodily self, the obstacles and vicissitudes of its realization, and its relationship to biological motherhood and inner subjectivity.

In my attempt to turn the sonogram back on itself, much remains dark and formless. There are many problems that this chapter does not address, such as the issues related to class and race and the long-range effect on the children of these interventions. In addition, as cultural changes infuse and affect individual development, sociological concerns regarding the effects of reproductive technology on equal rights and the division of labor must be thoroughly addressed. However, I will limit my discussion to the perspective of the individual.

While my orientation is primarily psychoanalytical, it is also shaped by the feminist critique of the early basic psychoanalytic assumptions of women's development. Freud's theory of gender development is essentially based on the theory of sexual phallic monism, the belief that all children acknowledge only the existence of one sexual organ, the penis. Freud admitted that he knew or understood little about female psychology and based his theories of femininity on the masculine experience. This excessive, phallocentric perspective contributed to the negative perception of psychoanalytic theory in the early stages of the women's movement and tended to obstruct the possibility of using psychoanalytical tools to examine a woman's psyche. In my perspective, psychoanalysis is useful as a theory of inquiry that offers access to the unconscious but nevertheless controlling templates that we use to view the world. To the extent that psychoanalysis does not proscribe gender roles, it offers the possibility of freedom through self-understanding. It need not define women in any particular way, but can instead illuminate our unconscious fantasies, which remain powerful when we do not understand them.

Many of the earlier formulations on female development have recently been reappraised. Many theorists are now reframing Freud's observations about anatomical differences within a perspective that reflects the more recent developments in ego psychology, object relations theory, and infant observation, and hence more accurately captures female development. Thus, some of the basic psychoanalytic assumptions can be reconceptualized in light of differences in parental handling and early childhood experiences, and can provide us with some powerful tools for understanding.

I have begun my inquiry with a brief overview of the historical meanings that a woman's body has had for women and for society at large. Despite a specific feminist argument that we need to move away from the historical emphasis on a woman's body, reproductive technology has thrown us back into this spotlight. In my opinion, the new focus should move away from an emphasis on a woman's body as seen by others, i.e., an emphasis on preoccupations with beauty and youth, and toward a view of the woman from within.

SOME FEMINIST PERSPECTIVES ON WOMEN'S BODIES AND THE EFFECT ON SELF AND CULTURE

Every child constructs a representation of the self that includes some notion of gender and sexuality. Although children have genitals at birth and thus a biological sex, according to many theorists gender is established slowly through the developmental cycle. Various theorists have argued as to how gender develops within each child. It is difficult to speak with certainty about any characteristic that defines sex difference, other than reproductive functioning. In fact, the feminist movement itself is far from agreement about the role of biology in women's psychological development.

Biology, especially the function of motherhood, has historically been used to perpetuate inequality in social situations. Women have been treated as objects for use or nonuse by men, children, and each other. Woman as sexual object is the most familiar role. We are all aware of the erotization of the female body in religion, art, literature, and popular culture. In fact, women's sexuality is usually defined in relation to, or in contrast to, men rather than in relation to themselves. Woman is also viewed by society as a vehicle for procreation and perpetuation of the species whose own needs and desires are easily dismissed for the sake of her offspring.

Reproductive technology has contributed to feminists' concerns about women's object status in their role as mothers. Many feminist theorists view women's biological functioning and motherhood in particular as oppressive forces, keeping them bound to reproduction and restrictive maternal functioning. Some of these theorists believe that gender differences tied to reproduction should be eliminated. Simone de Beauvoir, for example, saw transcendence of animality as the springboard for liberation. In her landmark book *The Second Sex*, de Beauvoir recognized the gains made for women who are free of biologically determined reproductive service. In contrast, other feminist theorists see motherhood as the wellspring of psychological development that brings with it autonomy and creativity. Thus, changes that impinge on women's biology, such as those associated with reproductive technology, may seem either threatening or liberating, depending on one's view of the origins and ramifications of sex differences. Further, those who take a more or less essentialist position may assert that reproductive technology can further alienate women from their biological authenticity and exacerbate women's already problematic stance vis-à-vis ownership and intactness of their bodies. From still another position, reproductive technology can be seen as a means of liberating women from both the limitations of their bodies and the need for heterosexual relationships. Each of these positions captures an aspect of the problems, yet minimizes or excludes real differences between women. It is only fair to point out, however, that in my attempt to summarize these positions I do an injustice to their complexity. Janet Sayers (1982) has written a comprehensive overview of the place of biology in explanations of sexual inequality for those interested in a more detailed historical perspective.

THE ESSENTIALIST POSITION

One position often referred to as biological essentialism by its critics argues that women need to regain access to their own bodies and to develop a language with which to speak about their bodies that reflects something inherent and essential within the female herself rather than define her in terms of what is not male. According to the so-called "essentialists," women are essentially dissimilar from men on the basis of biological and anatomical differences. Those who represent this position may argue that biology has given women a particular psychology from which they have become alienated because they live in a male-dominated culture. This perspective does not imply that women should stay home and raise children, but rather that the nature and structure of work must be reoriented to reflect two definitions, a male and a female one, of work, thinking, and knowing. Feminist literature and art have also attempted to deconstruct male-generated images of women and to construct images that more closely approximate some inherent feminine essence. During the 1970s this position was common to such diverse movements as the French "writing of the feminine" ("*écriture féminine*") and the American imagery of female body parts in the arts. I have argued (Bassin, 1982) that like phallic activity and its representations, women's early experience of inner space seems to contribute to the construction of a category of experience that serves as a structure of knowing and creating the world. I demonstrated that the images and metaphors in some women's unstylized poetry illuminated the existence of a bodily schema for productive inner space that goes beyond maternal and reproductive functions.

Now, however, many who subscribed to the 1970s' position, that of recovering the biological essence, see it as outdated or sentimental. Nevertheless, it has had the very necessary function of helping women to begin to celebrate their uniqueness and examine their attitudes about their bodies and their bodily functions. As long as women allow themselves, as women, to be unwritten, they remain amorphous and vulnerable to attributed and ascribed meaning. Also emerging from this position was an attempt to find a language in which women could express their own sexuality instead of being a sex object or a reactive to a male gaze. No longer would women be content to be the sex without the penis. All this actually contributed greatly to women's ability to reclaim their "body as a whole" and not a "body with a hole." Unfortunately, in an attempt to achieve a positive consciousness, I believe this position went too far, idealizing women in a way that simply reversed the rampant sexism. Women were seen as claiming the superior position. In a sense, the extreme flaunting of what "we women got" was no different from the domination of phallic imagery that they were attempting to level out. This articulation of women's bodies also neglected the difficulties with, and obstacles to, pure celebration that women experience in and with their bodies, such as menstrual pain, childbirth, fears of genital harm, and damage to their reproductive processes. Bernstein (1986) has recently attempted to understand the role of specific female genital anxiety in psychic development. She underscores the importance of a girl's integration of her genitals into her body ego. To ignore these psychobiological realities is to neglect a crucial force in women's sense of self. The increased reliance on natural childbirth may have begun as a positive trend but subsequently placed undue pressure on women to select this method despite, in some instances, risk to mother and baby and/or incredible pain and suffering. Some women experienced an incredible loss of self-esteem regarding bodily competence and "being a natural woman" if they had cesarean sections or asked for medication. A woman may not be able to help comparing her personal experiences with the ideals of various ideologies, which, in turn, results in feelings of guilt and inadequacy.

The Antibiology Position

Other feminists argue that there is no such thing as biologically generated femininity and therefore no inherent differences between the sexes. Although this position has many postures, it basically argues that socialization—or the way boys and girls are treated differently by their parents and society—is responsible for all male and female differences and inequalities. Thus, some theorists believe that freedom from biologically determined reproductive services would be the way to transcend sexual differences and inequality. Some have gone so far as to argue that nature itself is just an invention of human subjectivity. Although this assertion is exhilarating and promises revolutionary changes, it smacks of grandiosity. For better or worse, the idea of transcending the body is an illusion. The trend toward disregarding the biological as a factor in sexual differentiation is erroneously based on an overdependence on rationality.

The Social Constructionist Position

The social constructionist point of view is more interactional and critical of any conception of psychological development that doesn't take into account the effect of culture on biology. This position, best exemplified by Sherri Ortner's work in 1974, argues that women's oppression is based on social attitudes toward women's biology. The social constructionists assert that biology is socially constructed within any particular society. Ortner argues that women have historically been associated with nature because of their reproductive functioning; women have been devalued because the task of culture is to gain control over nature. The culture at large views the menstruating women as taboo, dangerous, or dirty and reflects this belief in many cultural rites and rituals.

Women have been affected by these attitudes in very real ways. A woman's sense of her body is certainly passed on from generation to generation by the way significant others in her life respond to their own bodies and handle her body. In addition, many women do suffer real pain or discomfort because of their menstrual cycle. This physiological process is not simply the result of social attitudes or of a woman's attitude toward her body. Social views do affect women's conceptions of their bodies and may mediate some changes, but not all of biology is amenable to modification. Conversely, biology does affect women's psyches in definite ways. The way that biology affects women is shaped by cultural and family influences, as well as by inner representations of our bodies, which are themselves subject to development throughout the life cycle.

Those involved with the constructionist position ask whether there is such a thing as women's bodies or women's sexuality outside of categories of experience or historical representation created by a dominant male culture. The attempt to excavate and find an original or untainted femininity is improbable; any notion of essence is unreachable since sense of our bodies becomes mediated through representations, images, and languages. The body, as experienced psychologically, is processed and channeled through personal and cultural symbols. At the same time, however, language and culture are determined in part by early body experiences and bodily relationship with others.

Women's Body Ego and the Obstacles to Its Integrity

Women's concerns about bodily inferiority, inadequacy, and incompetence have historically been read by some members of the psychoanalytic community as a symptom of penis envy and castration anxiety. According to traditional orthodox psychoanalytic position, normal development for a girl includes awareness of her anatomical shortcomings and the gradual transformation of age-appropriate penis envy into a wish for a baby from the penis. The theory overestimated the traumatic effects of the awareness of the lack of a penis, and along with it the reason for a girl's repression of her active aims, feelings of bodily defect, difficulties with achievement, and wishes for a child. Deutch (1933) has argued that the awareness of genital deficiency becomes generalized to a pervasive sense of inadequacy. Lampl-de Groot (1927) has commented that some women try to compensate for their bodily inferiority by competitive professional activity. At the same time, according to Lampl-de Groot the woman gives up her own feminine sexuality.

Thus, from this traditional psychoanalytic perspective, the girl is psychologically doomed without a child to compensate for her lack of penis. Emotional difficulties that a woman might experience as a result of reproductive problems and the subsequent need for technological intervention can superficially appear to be either an example of or a revocation of this basic psychoanalytic assumption of innate bodily inferiority. However, the overarching and limited definition of penis envy and castration anxiety as the female child's awareness of real anatomical lack has negatively encapsulated and reduced psychoanalytic understanding of women's potentially richer normative development. The entire construct of penis envy is now being questioned and reexamined in regard to its overall role and significance in women's development.

There have been many attempts to understand the very real vulnerabilities and obstacles in women's development that undermine optimal psychological growth. The idea of pre-oedipal developmental complications, such as a girl's problem during the separation–individuation phase, has been suggested by Chassaquet–Smirgel (1970) and Edgcombe (1968). Recently some theorists have addressed the specific problems facing the female child during the crucial developmental phase. During separation–individuation, the child must come to terms with psychological separation from the mother as well as develop her own autonomous functions. Boys as indicated by current research observations appear to separate more cleanly and fully from their mothers than do girls. In addition to the boy's anatomical distinction from his mother ("I have a penis, I am not like mother"), he is seen as possessing greater motor activity and pleasure in aggressive activity than the female child. These differences are believed to help the male child compensate for the loss of the illusion of oneness with his mother, as well as facilitate individuation. Chodorow (1978) has argued that the mother's identification with the child of the same sex makes separation–individuation more problematic for the female child. The daughter is seen by her mother as more continuous and less separate than her brother.

Kaplan (1978) has also suggested that an experience of object loss, such as emotional abandonment by a significant person in the child's life, can make a girl more vulnerable to the narcissistic blow of anatomical differences. Edgcombe et al. (1968) stated that a lack of well-being and a lowered self-esteem in the girl may include elements derived from oral deprivation and inadequate mothering. Applegarth (1976) has argued that what is referred to as penis envy is in fact a condensation of many interpersonal and intrapsychic experiences of what should be a temporary awareness of differences and acceptance of a limit. Fast (1984) has claimed that both boys and girls are overinclusive in their original gender experiences, and that boys must also come to terms with their reproductive limitations. All of this suggests that much more attention is needed to understand both normative and problematic development in the female child.

Bernstein (1986) has forcibly argued that girls have their own bodily and relationship anxieties that are constructed from their own specific bodily experiences. Specifically she describes the dangers to the female's body integrity to be access, penetration, and diffusivity. In a similar vein, I believe that the pervasive feelings of inadequacy and overall incompetence that may arise for some women in response to difficulties with reproductive functioning reflect problems in the development of an optimal female body ego and in the body ego's evolution into adaptive and generative psychological structures. These adaptive and generative psychological structures provide inner subjectivity where good contents reside regardless of stressful situations. Optimal female development relies on its own specific bodily schemata for relating to self and others and not on the birth of a child to compensate for the lack of penis. Motherhood is much more than the culmination of a narcissistic process to reclaim a penis. Identifications and interactions with significant males and females before, during, and after the Oedipal period allow the female to fill in the specifics of her female self. Ideally, the body ego provides a developed sense of subjectivity, intentionality, instrumentality, positive identifications with a maternal figure, and the ability to receive pleasure and direct inner genital needs and sensations. The body ego is the psyche's representation of inner and outer bodily sensations formed in interaction with the infant's touching and exploration, parental holding, and sensitivity to inner and outer stimuli. General knowledge of the world, as well as how one can affect the world, initially comes from bodily experiences. For example, the child learns about gravity by throwing toys and objects from its highchair. It learns about space by trying to fit itself into nooks and crannies, and it learns about time by tossing and retrieving. The child's body is the first source of information about what will later be called a self. Action and its different consequences generate the first distinctions between self and non-self during the separation–individuation process. Activity is as well the basis of bodily competence that contributes to self-esteem. Grand (1982) has argued that a well-developed body ego enables the child to recognize itself as an initiator of actions in the external world. The ability to experience oneself as an agent of one's actions provides the crucial sense of intentionality and instrumentality necessary for an intact sense of body integrity and capability.

The body does not simply serve our instinctual needs for survival and reproduction; it also has a role in the organization of our experiences. As such it serves as the prototype for our imaginative and symbolic capacities. The child not only learns about material reality through its bodily experience, it also defines inner realities through its bodily relationship with self and others. Winnicott has argued that a positive and crucial result of the separation–individuation process with a mothering figure is the development of what he calls "potential space." This "potential space" refers to the internal state in which creativity, play, and the ability to be alone are made possible. An intact sense of a body self with the accompanying sense of agency, competence, intentionality, self-esteem, and the belief in the integrity of one's creations is crucial for optimal female sexuality and identity.

It is beyond the scope of this chapter to delineate the specifics of the development of a proactive or primary female self, i.e., a self built on the female's bodily experiences and relationships rather than on a response to her lack of a penis. The interested reader should consult the most recent work of Benjamin (1988), Bernstein (1986), and Mendell (1988). Benjamin, in developing her theory of "intersubjectivity" and its relevance to the development of the female child, has argued that "having an inside" and "holding oneself" provide authority and authenticity for the female self. Specifically, she contends that it is not physical organs per se which do or do not enable a woman's desire and activity but rather the totality of a girl's relationship with her father. She argues for the importance of "recognition" between self and other self. Bernstein, on the other hand, has argued that girl's have their own unique developmental attempts at mastery of their unfocused, open, and penetrable genitals, which contribute in part to the development of female object embeddedness. Mendell has also made an important contribution to the theoretical understanding of the development of the female child through her revised look at the girl's psychosexual stages. Her articulation of the girl's psychosexual stages includes many of the most relevant revisions of original Freudian theory, and current clinical and observational data on the female developmental cycle.

A woman with optimal development will take reproductive difficulties in stride. If childbearing is not possible or feasible she will of course feel loss and mourn. However, she will be able to accept this limit of infertility (see Shapiro, 1988, for further discussion of infertility) without it stimulating pervasive psychic feelings of sexual undesirability, inadequacy, castration, or fears of a lack of a generative inside.

On the other hand, motherhood can be reparative. Benecek (1960) has suggested that parenthood allows adults to re-experience and master early developmental states as they go through them with their children. In addition, for some women the act of creation and the process of motherhood facilitates a reidentification with the positive aspects of their own mother which they denied during earlier attempts to separate from her. The powerful bodily experiences during conception, pregnancy, delivery, and nursing do impact on a woman's sense of self, but they are by no means necessary for creative female functioning. Anatomy is a reality upon which our inner world develops—men can't bear children, women can't inseminate. However, these specific early anatomy realities can be transcended in our symbolic world. For example, Mendell (1988) has suggested that a girl's ability to identify with her father later enables her to empathize with the phallic sexuality of her lover. Early rigid lines of gender and the sex-specific identifications can be erased, and more inclusive psychological states can be experienced.

I do not mean to suggest an idealized or overly sanitized view of the psychic reality of women. Rather, I am arguing for the necessity of providing women who have reproductive difficulties with the opportunity for working through the "symbolic obstacles" by legitimizing them as part and parcel of many women's development, and not as a function of patriarchal control or an inherent lack in women. Perhaps with increased articulation regarding the psychophysical vicissitudes of the female life cycle, women will be able to normalize their reproductive experiences and develop their opportunities for further self-exploration and growth.

Reproductive Technologies: Their Positive and Negative Potentials

I have participated in many conversations and read a good deal of literature that focuses on the potential dangers of reproductive technology. The users of this technology are frequently portrayed as victims of overmedicalization and colonization of women's pathological reproductive systems. The concern expressed is that women will lose control of their basic biology as science and technology increasingly control and use their reproductive systems. Benjamin (1980) has suggested that there is widespread fear of the scientific and technological power to destroy nature. This romantic critique of male rationality, she argues, has grave limitations for women's reappropriation of mastery. However, I do not believe that these opponents necessarily believe that reproductive technology is inherently or intentionally dangerous to women, but only potentially dangerous, depending on how it can be interpreted and manipulated. For example, Pollack–Petchesky (1987) has discussed how the antiabortion movement has abused reproductive technology to make improbable claims about the fetus. The movement's propaganda utilizes films from sonograms to portray a fetus seemingly sensing its doom and moving in response to the pain of the abortion. Margaret Atwood's recent best-selling novel, *The Handmaid's Tale*, illuminates the danger of patriarchal control over women for their reproductive capacities. She describes a future fearful society in which women are essentially enslaved within reproductive brothels. In Atwood's novel, breeder women who are unable to bear children are punished by death.

Some critics are suggesting that carried to its extreme, reproductive technology will reduce women into separate reproductive parts. Those parts will be appropriated or women will become obsolete as reproduction more frequently occurs outside of their bodies. In fact, eggs, uterus, and sperm are already shared, rented, and sold. Concerns about the exploitation of women and whether we have the right to determine whether we can share or sell body parts or whether we need society to protect us are not dissimilar from ongoing debates about prostitution and pornography. All of these issues are related to the question of whether women are simply making use of what they have or instead are being exploited for what they have. One's position on this question depends in part on whether the locus of control is perceived to be within the woman or outside of her. It is also historically significant that men have milked and sold their sperm. We have only recently reexamined the bioethics of such behavior in light of the technologies that allow for "renting a uterus" or sale of eggs. Perhaps the new concerns are tied to the fact that we all implicitly sanction men's distance from reproduction and parenting while accepting that women's role in motherhood should not be tampered with. As Pollack–Petchesky (1987) has recently pointed out, the fetus has increasingly been represented as independent from the mother, who becomes absent or peripheral to the reproductive process. The fear has been voiced that given women's historical lack of power in society, how much more of a choice will women really have? How much further will the public sphere invade the private one?

A recent *New York Times* article has described how medical personnel have utilized the court system to force mothers to cooperate with hospital interventions. Since 1981 there have been 21 cases in which hospitals have used the courts to override the wishes of a pregnant woman by detaining her, treating the unborn fetus inside her womb, or forcing a cesarean section. In all but 3 of these cases, the courts ruled in favor of the hospital decision to do what they thought was best to protect the unborn. Of course, this is a complicated issue. One could argue that society needs to protect its future and that regardless of parental opinion or belief every child has the right to the best possible opportunity for life, including the best medical care. The dark side of this position, however, has to do with how far a woman's rights concerning her body and her unborn extend. At what point is the fetus still a part of her body and at what point does it become autonomous and a separate member of society? Some have argued that a woman's right to self-determination and privacy is violated by compelled treatment. This issue is central to the conflict between the pro- and anti-abortion forces. Of course, most parents do whatever they can to optimize the development of a healthy child. Amniocentesis, *in vitro* surgery, and sonograms, for example, provide positive tools for prevention and intervention. In some cases, however, an assumption is made that a problem exists until amniocentesis or sonogram proves otherwise. This assumption can delay parental attachment to the unborn until the test results are known 4 months into the pregnancy. The desire for healthy offspring that have the best possible biological opportunities can become inseparable from a narcissistic search for perfection and/or a preoccupation with damaged creations.

Many would argue that the new technology represents a legitimate and new vehicle for men to gain mastery over the unknown and feared female body and, by extension, the frightening mystery of birth and death. In other words, by gaining scientific control over the essential act of reproduction, we can as well delude ourselves that we have finally conquered Mother Nature. This represents both the wish to create and the fear that the creation will be a Frankenstein's monster. Karen Horney (1937) suggested that part of the difficulty between the sexes is related to men's envy of the womb and women's procreative powers. I believe that some men have great longings to create children, which are based on their early identification with their mothers. The desexualization of the male wish to have a baby, if it is not paralyzed by conflict, can lead to male creativity. Of course, in most men, this wish is repudiated and excluded from consciousness along with many other feminine identifications. These repudiated longings contribute to some men's difficulties with women. The need to disavow their connectedness with a female self and with their mothers can also inhibit their capacity for empathy.

Reproductive technology allows increased access to, and increased demystification of, procreation and women's interior. What was once obscure is now accessible. The psychological meaning of the disruption of the interior private space by the external public world will of course vary from woman to woman. The notion that this inner space of woman, the center of procreative potential, can be tampered with may very well deprive us of the awe and supernaturalness of reproduction associated with the magical mother of our early childhood. Kestenberg (1968) argues in her understanding of the battle of the sexes that women remind men of their infantile selves who were once subordinate to mothers. She argues that men associate the inside of the body with femininity, and thereby externalize their anxiety around bodily sensation onto women. This may very well be a necessary psychological step that allows boys to disconnect from the inside and cathect to their external penis. This shift from inside to outside in men has mythological expression. In the story of Adam and Eve, God took a rib from Adam's body and made it into woman, thus enabling man to see what was inside of himself. The exploration of his inside, via Eve, became associated with the notion of original sin in the Garden of Eden. Adam lost both his innocence and his immortality as Eve taught him about sex and the reality of the body. Man was then compelled to leave the magic kingdom and conquer nature. The so-called eternal enigma of woman, falsely associated with Freud's attempt to describe ideal femininity and its relationship to inner space, still remains the unsolved psychoanalytic riddle.

There are, as well, dangerous aspects of some women's intense focus upon their inner world, or interior, which may be a function of their own genital anxiety. For some women this anxiety becomes focused around fears of penetration and intrusion from the outside or may manifest itself in difficulties integrating this inner space with the external world. Mediating the balance between inner and outer space or internal and external world is a struggle for both men and women. Some individuals tend to rely protectively to a greater extent on either one or the other, utilizing one psychic residence, so to speak, to ward off the frightening aspects of the other. For example, whereas the schizophrenic lives in a self-created inner world that is preferable to the pain of reality, the workaholic can be seen as constantly creating tasks and activities in the external world that leave little time to focus inward. The need to shut off one's womb, or interior space, can become as compelling as the fear of confronting the contents of the inside.

In my clinical practice I have found that many women find it easier than men to enter treatment, to explore their inner world, to talk about their feelings, and to generate insight. But many of these very women then have difficulty translating these inner changes into real-life activity. I think this difficulty is not only the result of inadequate environmental support and encouragement but also the reflection of some women's fear of opening themselves to view. I have worked with many women artists who consciously struggle with issues of visibility. Now this conflict partly concerns the notably difficult politics and economics of the art world, but another aspect for some of these women is related to more personal fears of putting outside what could ruin or spoil the artists' perceived special internal contents. On the other hand, many men struggle with the fear of giving expression to their inner life for fear it will affect their competence outside. Of course, these problems are those of people who seek treatment, and I don't presume that they affect all men and women. Certainly not all men and women manifest conflicts around genderized problems of identity and bodily integrity. Optimal male development requires an acceptance and tolerance of the inside. Only immature male genitality is completely phallocentric and externally oriented. Similarly, optimal female development, in my perspective, also reflects an integration of the masculine and feminine aspects of early identifications with both mother and father.

As I mentioned earlier, for those who have overidealized the "natural woman," reproductive technology may represent more invasion by male scientific control, and therefore the instinct to return to less invasive childbirth practices undoubtedly has an appeal. For many women, however, natural childbirth, without the aid of medication and without a long cultural history and enabling childbirth practice, was extremely painful, a violation of the body self. For some women it required or led to a state of depersonalization. The return-to-nature movement of the 1960s and 1970s so affected some women's psyches that they experienced anything less than a totally pure delivery as a defeat. Even the wish for some relief during the difficult moments of childbirth or the hateful feelings aroused toward the birthing baby or the spouse during childbirth were experienced as a betrayal of their true authentic selves, which should be in ecstasy during this experience. In fact, for some of these women, difficulties during childbirth became symbolically associated with defeat or a demonstration of their bodily inadequacies.

I am not focusing on the efficacy of medical technology in this chapter because I think there are not yet sufficient data to determine how helpful they actually are. There is a widespread belief that the fascinating tools of medical technology have been overused in individual cases while, at times, medical personnel have been insensitive about the psychological implications of looking inside and insensitively categorizing a reproductive problem. I certainly believe that the medical establishment has an obligation to educate itself. From the perspective of a psychologist, some medical personnel have a relatively primitive understanding of the potential effects of language and representation on their patients' functioning. In one case, a woman was told that her problem in conception was that her vaginal mucus was a hostile environment, that her mucus was in fact killing her husband's sperm. The psychological effect of feeling as if a part of one's body is in an adversarial relationship with the rest and with her conscious desires to support the sperm should be obvious. I believe that this condition could have been more accurately described as sperm–mucus incompatibility, which does not attribute negative psychological intent to the woman. Feminist critics are concerned that the objective scientific systems may supersede a woman's own sensorium in connecting with the growing fetus. Rosalind Pollack–Petchesky (1987) has stated that when the fetus is visualized and therefore constructed by means of such media as ultrasound and electronic heartbeat, the mother becomes invisible and is, in fact, severed organically from the fetus. The fear of disconnection of mother from fetus—that is, the mother who is without—can also be reinforced by the unconsciously derived body experience of a lack or void created by the cultural idealization of the phallus.

For some women, specific interventions can be very positive. For single women and lesbians, reproductive technology offers alternative vehicles for motherhood. Contrary to the Pollack–Petchesky (1987) suggestion about the disconnecting effects of a sonogram, many women report a sense of connectedness and reassurance after seeing and hearing their babies through ultrasound and electronic heartbeat machines. A patient of mine who had difficulty conceiving found that her observation of her husband's sperm swimming actively through her mucus restored her faith in her own reproductive process. In this instance and others like it, the medical technologies become a part of the creative process, a link or facilitating environment that supports the woman rather than controls her. The interpersonal vision of collaboration, interdependency, and mutuality are experienced. The outside assistance provided during pregnancy by amniocentesis, *in vitro* fertilization, electronic fetal monitoring, and fetal therapies certainly has positive effects for some women by allowing them to conceive and support the healthiest possible babies. For these women, who view themselves as essentially creating the baby, albeit with some support, nothing has really changed. However, for other women, who may have deep anxieties and conflicts about their bodies, pregnancy and motherhood, feelings and beliefs about technology may serve as a projection or displacement of their own internal issues. One woman patient reported that her faith in the technology enabled her to avoid her personal psychological conflicts about conception and motherhood. Her conscious feeling was that she could wait to have a baby because science would enable her to do so whenever she wanted. This woman was quite aware that she was denying a piece of reality, her own biological clock, and idealizing the medical profession. Her idealization of technology reflects her unconscious dependence and belief in the omnipotent power of the parents of her childhood, which she had transferred to the medical profession. Her faith in the technology resulted in her evasion of her very real conflicts about becoming a mother and the intactness of her body.

For some women, the idea or the ideal of reproductive technology can delay the mourning process or acceptance of limitations that some women and/or couples will have to face. The belief that there is still one more intervention to be tried can extend the uncertainty about reproductive success. The months or years invested in the wish for biological parenthood can pay off if the intervention is successful. But if it is not, how does a woman internally negotiate the investment of time, money, and psychological involvement in a failure? I think there should be some concern that these so-called failures not further contribute to extreme feelings of inadequacy and incompetence in the women who experience them. I also believe that the failure of a needed reproductive intervention may stir up guilt for women who have delayed childbirth for other goals.

In sum, the greater a woman's earlier developmental obstacles involving the integrity of the body ego and its development into a stable effective subjective, the more likely she will be to perceive the necessity for reproductive technology in irrational, archaic terms. Thus, it is not reproductive technology per se that causes the difficulties for some women but rather that what is assumed to be a normal, natural progression of mature female physicality—conception, pregnancy, and a healthy normal baby—is questioned and interrupted. The need for intervention highlights this and may stir up more archaic anxieties about bodily deficiencies, mastery, and the goodness of the body and its products. Furthermore, to the degree that self-esteem, self-reliance, and mastery are tied to inner fantasies of absolute control and independence, reproductive intervention will take on painful symbolic meaning. Medical personnel must take cognizance of the fact that even a "simple" reproductive intervention may carry complex psychic meaning for the female user. These meanings are still yet to be discovered as more and more women turn to technology for assistance and begin to articulate their experiences. These "meanings" are connected to women's intrinsic bodily anxieties and conflicts, their specific relations with mother and father, and their developmental history and as such requires the continuation of our exploration of "women's dark continent."

References

Applegarth, A. (1976). Some observations on work inhibitions in women. *Journal of the American Psychoanalytic Association*, 24, 25.

Barrett, W. (1987). *Death of the soul*. New York: Anchor Books.

Bassin, D. (1982). Women's images of inner space: Data towards expanded interpretative categories. *International Review of Psychoanalysis*, 9, 191–203.

Benedek, T. (1960). Parenthood as a developmental phase: A contribution to the libido theory. *Psychoanalytic Study of the Child*, 15, 60–76.

Benjamin, J. (1980). Bonds of love: Rational violence and erotic domination. *Feminist Studies*, 6, 144–174.

Bernstein, D. (1983). The female superego: A different perspective. *International Journal of Psychoanalysis*, 64, 187.

Bernstein, D. Female genital anxieties: Conflicts and mastery modes. Paper presented at the meeting of the Division of Psychoanalysis of the American Psychological Association, Mexico, February 1986.

Chasseguet-Smirgel, J. (1970). *Female sexuality: New psychoanalytic views*. Ann Arbor: University of Michigan Press.

Chodorow, N. (1978). *The reproduction of mothering: Psychoanalysis and the sociology of gender*. Berkeley: University of California Press.

Deutsch, H. (1933). Motherhood and sexuality. *Psychoanalytic Quarterly*, 2, 476.

Edgcombe, R., Lundberg, S., Markowitz, R., and Salo, F. (1968). Some comments on the concept of the negative Oedipal phase in girls. *Psychoanalytic Study of the Child, 31,* 36-61.

Fast, I. (1984). *Gender identity: A differentiation model.* Lawrence Erlbaum Associates, New Jersey.

Gallop, J. (1982). *The daughter's seduction.* Ithaca, NY: Cornell University Press.

Grand, S. (1982). The body and its boundaries. A psychoanalytic view of cognitive process disturbances in schizophrenia. *International Review of Psychoanalysis, 9,* 327-341.

Horney, K. (1933). The denial of the vagina. *International Journal of Psychoanalysis, 14,* 55-70.

Kaplan, L. (1978). *Oneness and separateness: From infant to individual.* New York: Simon and Schuster.

Keller, E. F. (1982). Feminism and science. *Signs, 7,* 589-602.

Kestenberg, J. (1968). Outside and inside, male and female. *Journal of the American Psychoanalytic Association, 16,* 457-520.

Lampl-de Groot, A. (1927). The evolution of the Oedipus complex in women. *International Journal of Psychoanalysis, 9,* 332.

Mendell, D. (1988). Early female development: From birth to latency. In J. Offerman-Zuckerberg (Ed.), *Critical psychophysical passages in the life of a woman: A psychodynamic perspective* (pp. 55-70). New York: Plenum Press.

Ortner, S. (1974). Is female to male as nature is to culture? In M. Z. Rosaldo & L. Lamphere (Eds.), *Woman, culture, and society.* Stanford: Stanford University Press.

Pollack-Petchesky, R. (1987). Fetal images: The power of visual culture in the politics of reproduction. *Feminist Studies, 13,* 259-262.

Sayers, J. (1982). *Biological politics: Feminist and anti-feminist perspectives.* London: Tavistock.

Shapiro, S. (1988). Psychological consequences of infertility. In J. Offerman-Zuckerberg (Ed.), *Critical psychophysical passages in the life of a woman: A psychodynamic perspective* (pp. 269-290). New York: Plenum Press.

Part III
The 21st Century
Futuristic Patterns, Concerns, and Issues

In Part III of this book we look into our crystal ball and test our psychic powers. This is the world of AIDS, the 20th-century plague, the disease that is affecting sexual practices on this planet, on every level. We are learning to bear the unbearable and ultimately, perhaps, our humanness may deepen (Goldman). Against this horrific backdrop, our options continue to increase: Lesbians are proudly parenting (Martin); couples are voluntarily choosing to remain childless, without guilt, in increasing numbers (Bram); and the surrogacy issue continues to evoke debate, controversy, and psychological discomfort. This discomfort, arising out of divided loyalties, is understood and explored (Lichtendorf). It is further examined from a legalistic point of view (Taub); the discomfort and outrage is felt and the complexity of the issue expressed by a feminist-sociologist (Rothman) and responded to by the surrogacy advocates, who reason with the irrational terror evoked by surrogacy itself and attempt to differentiate between reality and fantasy (Schmukler and Aigen).

Psychobiological history is being made. It is a wondrously miraculous time of new choices, new freedoms, and new anxieties. New concepts of masculinity and femininity are being forged (Eichholz), and more questions are asked than answered.

Chapter 16

Divided Loyalties
Ongoing Reactions to Baby M

SUSAN S. LICHTENDORF

Baby M didn't just happen in an office where a surrogacy contract was signed, or in a clinical setting where new life began, or in courtrooms where control of that life was contested—it happened in the powerful mass media beamed full blast at all of us.

Somehow it has been forgotten that we— the members of the public—have been the living, breathing audience to the drama of Baby M. A sensitive audience, stirred to rapt attention and personal response.

As members of the public, reporters have asked for our opinions about who is right and who is wrong, what we think about the complexities raised by this landmark case. But far fewer questions have been asked about our feelings, the points of emotional contact, the impact of Baby M on our inner selves.

And impact there has been.

"For months I have thought about this case, these people, this child," novelist Mary Gordon confessed in a published essay (Gordon, 1987). "Every woman I know seems obsessed by it."

Speaking for myself, I know that I was whirled by fury. I read news report after news report, as if I could not read enough. I felt betrayed, betrayed in ways that I could hardly put aside my anger to assess. It was only when a psychologist friend offered analytic insight (to be discussed below) that I could begin to put my subjective reaction into context and to raise, as a journalist, some more probing questions than were being asked.

I wanted to know what it is about the drama of Baby M that makes us care so much, and just who stirs us to response. Is it Baby M? Her warring parents? Her siblings? Is it the actual people of Baby M with whom we identify or people whom we carry within, the people who are the pillars of our own sense of identity?

It seems to me that these are very crucial questions to ask, most particularly in this volume seeking to gauge the psychic impact of 21st-century biological technologies and alternative social options. The unconscious may be unchanging and timeless—

SUSAN S. LICHTENDORF • Medical Science Journalist, New York, New York 10128; Member, National Association of Science Writers; Author's Guild.

but times are changing rapidly in ways that can't be ignored. In the troubled reaction to Baby M, there is an example of the clash between high tech advance and slowly evolved humanity that is well worth study and reflection.

The purpose of this chapter is to put that example forward by (1) giving a brief cross section of the vast media coverage that brought Baby M to public consciousness and then (2) presenting quotes from a series of personal interviews done in 1987-1988 open to interpretation in terms of themes of the unconscious.

THE BABY M MEDIA BLITZ

> Struggle for Baby M, Fierce Emotions and Key Legal Issues. (*New York Times*, August 23, 1986)
>
> Mothers Urge Ban on Surrogacy as Form of "Slavery." (*New York Times*, September 1987, p. A13)
>
> Baby M's Mother is Pregnant out of Wedlock, Lawyers Say. (*New York Times*, November 1, 1987, p. 50)
>
> Court Bans Hired Moms: Jersey Rules "Baby M" Deal Illegal. (*New York Daily News*, February 4, 1987, p. 1)
>
> 2 Moms for Baby M: Sterns Keep Tot but Mary Beth Can Visit. (*New York Post*, February 4, 1987, p. 1)
>
> Parents in Baby M Case Clash on Visiting Rights. (*New York Times*, March 28, 1988, p. B3)
>
> Baby M's Mother Wins Broad Visiting Rights. (*New York Times*, April 7, 1988, p. 1)

From the early reports of the conflict between the Sterns and Mary Beth Whitehead (as she was then named) in the summer of 1986, through 1987—when Baby M was ranked as a top story of the year ("Beyond Words," 1988), on a par with the war in Nicaragua, AIDS, the Iran-Contra affair, and the stock market crash—into 1988, when a lower court ruling was overturned and broad visitation rights granted to Whitehead-Gould, public attention was grabbed by headline after headline as the drama of Baby M. unfolded. In one 3-month period at the start of 1987 there was almost daily coverage.

From the screens of televisions, from the front pages and magazine covers, image after image pressed into our awareness. And the images were indeed striking:

- Images of Whitehead-Gould dismally weeping, triumphantly laughing; Whitehead-Gould demure in a white-collared mother/daughter dress matched to one worn by her daughter, Tuesday; flamboyant in a striped maternity top carrying off Baby M.
- Images of William Stern grinning as he carried Baby M, thankfully resting his head on his wife's forehead after a lower court ruling in their favor. Images of Elizabeth Stern, timidly smiling but more often serious and still.
- Images of Baby M, bundled up against the northeastern cold, an apple-cheeked toddler with yarn bows tied in the bunches of her soft hair.
- Images of a chorus of women, black and white, demonstrating against surrogacy, carrying aloft a placard reading, "Woman Are Not Dogs for Breeding" (*On the Issues*, 1987).

- An image on the cover of *Ms.* Magazine (1988) of a mother shielding and pressing her baby to her breast, with the question "Endangered?" stamped across their bare, vulnerable bodies.

Whatever the market served, specialized media found a way to custom-tailor the Baby M story. *Discover* magazine, for example, a magazine aimed at those interested in science, came up with "The Baby M Case: Pregnancy & MS" (1987).

Influential women's magazines as different as *Ms.* magazine (Gordon, 1987) and *Mademoiselle* (Harrison, 1987) tackled the subject of Baby M.

The story was carried by mass market news magazines like *Time* and *Newsweek* and by periodicals appealing to narrower, more elite audiences, such as *Maclean's* (Gray, 1987), *Commonweal* (Garvey, 1987), and the *National Review* (Gallagher, 1987).

And the media exercised a variety of professional techniques. For example, just as instant replay and clips of other games stir and keep alive excitement in coverage of a sports event, the sensational news value of Baby M was kept alive by splashy parallel stories—for example, this cover story blurb from *People* magazine (Levin & Reid, 1987): "A Mother's Love: Their story has made headlines around the world—how a 48-year-old woman served as surrogate mother for her daughter's triplets, giving birth to her own grandchildren. Here is the touching human drama—and the extraordinary family behind those headlines."

Even this brief survey gives a sense of the extraordinary media coverage of Baby M. The effects of that swamping of the public have been rapid and profound.

In a brief span of time, Baby M became part of our language, a recognized symbol of surrogacy, encapsulating in two words what it requires many, many words to adequately describe. Note that to begin this chapter I needed only to say Baby M, confident that you, my reader, would instantly know what I was talking about and instantly summon up the complexities and principals involved.

Strangers at first, William and Elizabeth Stern, Baby M, Mary Beth Whitehead-Gould, her family, all have become people familiar to us. We know their names and personalities, their strengths, their weaknesses, the clothes they wear, their finances, their raw emotions of love and hate.

Like people whom we know in real life, like people in compelling artificial life, the people of a continuing soap opera, we have moved forward in time with them. We have lived through their past, and, knowing that, we have a deeper sense of their present. We may not have seen Whitehead-Gould pregnant with Baby M, but we have known her long enough to see her pregnant again. We have watched her stand with her husband during much of the struggle for Baby M and leave him soon after. We may call Baby M "Baby," but having watched her as we might watch a baby grow in our own families, we know that she is not a baby anymore.

The people of Baby M are people real to us. They make us angry, they make us unsettled, they draw deep from our reserves of empathy. Were we to meet them on the street we might expect them to greet and know us because we indeed know them. This is a phenomenon that actors in soap operas have reported in encountering members of their audience in real life, and it shows the effect of deeply felt drama brought into the home and one's emotional life over time.

The door to our privacy was opened by one of the most potent influences of our time, the mass media. But we are the ones who invited the conflicts and passions of Baby M in.

However adept at elevating awareness and molding opinion, the mass media can do only so much. We do the rest. It is within us that a sensational news story finds points of contact so that we make it ours, so that we react in terms of who we are. This does not happen with all top news stories. That it happened with Baby M is evident in the visceral feelings evoked:

> Buying a baby is so gross, it makes me sick.
>
> That tape of what she [Whitehead-Gould] said about killing herself and the baby hit me so hard I was in shock.

In the passion stirred:

> I hate her [Whitehead-Gould]. . . . I just hate her. . . .

In the willingness to talk about the case. While there were many reactions to Baby M, "no comment" wasn't one of them.

Reactions to Baby M

A series of interviews done in 1987–1988 shows a surprising range in the points of emotional contact with the people and issues of Baby M. It should be noted that these interviews were done specifically when the controversy was in the realm of news, before the first televised miniseries, shown on national network television, WABC, May 22—23, 1988, and before the anticipated publication of a book by Whitehead-Gould. Journalistic reporting can project a point of view in the way that a story is covered and the images selected to be transmitted, but daily news breaking over time is very different from a professionally sculpted network TV dramatization or a polished bestseller giving the public persuasive scripts of what to think.

The information gathered here does not reflect a scientific sample screened for bias, nor does it attempt to speak for all reactions to Baby M. Rather, it indicates what some individuals, mostly women, felt about this landmark case at the time that it was actually happening, before Baby M could be totally assessed or individual reactions reworked as social and legal issues are resolved.

The major finding of this series of interviews was that reaction to Baby M had more to do with the people questioned than the actual principals in the case. While I was told in one of the first interviews, "This is a case where you focus on the sensational, it's not something you can identify with," the very opposite proved to be the rule. The drama of Baby M seemed to provide something for everyone: There were those who talked only about Whitehead-Gould; there were those who responded to the person and plight of William Stern; there were those who suffered the feelings of Baby M and Whitehead-Gould's other children; there were those who chose Elizabeth Stern as the subject of primary focus.

If there was one aspect of Baby M that drew common reaction, it was paid surrogate motherhood. Even those who were harsh toward Whitehead-Gould and adamant in their feeling that she had signed a contract and was obligated to fulfill it, people who noted—

> She was a conduit, nothing more.
>
> She's the one who got herself into it.
>
> It infuriated me that she voided a contract; it showed that if you have a cute lawyer who can be trickier than the next one, the law and honor of a contract doesn't matter.

Any time you sign a contract now, you are going to have to wonder how valid it is.

—felt that the contract between Whitehead-Gould and the Sterns was in its essence, repugnant:

It's buying and selling babies. That's what we're talking about, nothing more, nothing less.

It was as if another kind of contract, one pledged between the members of the human family to keep everyone secure, had been broken.

This touching on basic human beliefs and needs seemed to be at work in individual reactions to Baby M, which, for the purposes of discussion, can be grouped under the headings of (1) Reactions to Whitehead-Gould: Good Mother, Bad Mother, or "Whore"? (2) Empathy for William Stern, The Mystery of Elizabeth Stern; (3) Identifying with the Children in Baby M.

REACTIONS TO WHITEHEAD-GOULD:
GOOD MOTHER, BAD MOTHER, OR "WHORE"?

No one was neutral about Whitehead-Gould.

In terms of my own reaction, the question—How could she!—screeched furiously in my mind.

How could she do something so incredibly stupid just when women are fighting so hard to be recognized and respected for who they are, free to be all they can and want to be? How could she betray women by providing ammunition for bias; how could she set women backwards by in effect saying, I am a womb, a womb with no brains or purpose on earth, except to be used? How could she sell out those who value being mothers by putting a price tag on conception and birth?

Having worked myself into a feminist rage, I was stunned when some admirable advocates of women's rights took up Whitehead-Gould's cause. They would have me see her as victim, defenseless woman, besieged mother. They would have me extend my deepest compassion. I couldn't; I was too angry.

I held onto my anger even as I wondered what was the matter with me. Where were my loyalties? Hadn't I always fought for women's rights to do as they please with their bodies and their lives? Hadn't I always been able to stretch empathy across the cultural and socioeconomic gaps that separate women of different backgrounds with limits on their options?

It was only when I discussed my continuing anger with a psychoanalyst friend that clarity for me set in.

"How could she?" was indeed the question in my mind, but it wasn't the question I described above. Rather it was this: How could she agree to become pregnant, to carry a living fetus within her body and spirit, to give her baby, her child away?

In my conscious mind I flailed against Whitehead-Gould as a betrayer of women's progress; in my inner mind I desperately fought against her because I experienced her as a rejecting mother, a woman who chose and was chosen specifically to be a mother, who chose to give her child away.

The concept of a rejecting mother is cruel, hard to take. I understood why my normal balance and compassion were burned to a cinder by rage.

With insight, fury dissipated. If Whitehead-Gould represented rejecting mother to me, I was curious to discover what she represented to those who were eager to talk about her.

Identification with the Self

Of the women interviewed, no one could identify with Whitehead-Gould in being totally willing to be a surrogate mother. While one woman ventured,

> I think I could imagine giving up a baby if I was able never to regret it,

there were many echoes of this statement:

> I couldn't do it. I wouldn't have it in me to carry a child and give it up. I can't relate to her.

There appeared to be identification of a kind in feelings that some of the women interviewed projected onto Whitehead-Gould, as in these comments:

> Maybe she was caught by the idea of being thought to be so valuable to someone else.
>
> What were her initial motives beyond the money she was promised? She didn't do it out of love or affection. Maybe because she had some need to continually bear children.
>
> Maybe she thought that she was doing something useful.
>
> She's just like girls I knew in high school who've gone on to have child after child, getting their whole sense of worth out of that.

There was a sense of common humanity—something that could happen to anyone—reflected in remarks like these:

> Maybe it turned into something worse than what she thought she was getting into.

And there was sympathy:

> At first I thought that she was crazy, manipulating everyone for what it is worth. But you know, she did herself a lot of harm too.
>
> There is a natural tendency to side with her.

The visible and audible image of Whitehead-Gould that the media conveyed was vividly and variously interpreted:

> I followed the case in the newspapers and on TV and the picture I got of Mary Beth was of a flake. She named her kid Tuesday; she had an affair and divorced her husband. And what she did—the whole thing is weird.
>
> There are a lot of stereotypes about Whitehead-Gould as an angry woman, therefore not feminine, giving, caring. In the pictures of her, she looked angry, which is unfeminine and turned people off.
>
> That tape of what she said about killing herself and the baby . . . she has to be unbalanced to make threats like that.
>
> You don't have to be friends with a client. As a lawyer, if Mary Beth came tooling into my office to have me represent her, I wouldn't be thrilled basically because we've seen her to be a person who changes her mind. It is difficult and frustrating to represent someone like that.

A flake, an angry woman, unbalanced, an impossible client—while Whitehead-Gould was seen in these terms of personality characteristics, she was most intensely perceived in the role of mother. And by mother, those interviewed seemed to mean good mother or bad mother.

Good Mother/Bad Mother

It can be argued that Whitehead-Gould's determined fight to keep the infant she bore reflects fierce motherly impulse, but those questioned were strained to see her as a good or what social science calls the good-enough mother.

"What is she like as a mother?" was a question that drew a great deal of response:

> I am not clear that she loves her child, though she may think she does.
>
> What is she like as a mother—she threatened to kill that baby.
>
> What is she like as a mother? I think it's a form of child abuse to name a kid Tuesday.
>
> She's nasty, mean, and manipulative. What kind of a mother can she be?
>
> She is an unfit mother who abducted and kidnapped that baby. We've seen that she is not a sufficient parent to her own children; essentially what she has taught them all along is how to manage poorly in life. Now, because of her, that little girl is living in a circus being pulled in two directions, being subject to two different kinds of discipline.

What, then, constitutes a good mother? From these comments it would appear that she is someone who loves and does not endanger her child; someone who is kind, who teaches a child well. Earlier it was noted that Whitehead-Gould appeared as an angry woman, unfeminine, not caring or giving. These "feminine" qualities figure strongly in this description of a good mother:

> She [Whitehead-Gould] has never shown the motherly instinct, the willingness to be unselfish, to sacrifice herself. I know that this is not the 1930s or the 1950s, and things have changed, but to me—and I am a woman who is a mother today—a woman who cares about herself primarily is unmotherly. That's not what being a mother is about.

That good motherly qualities are not purely "feminine" was expressed by a man who said:

> As a father I don't want to hear about her parental rights, that isn't what makes a parent male or female . . . it's parental responsibilities that are important and is she meeting them.

Although, as one woman put it, "There is a natural tendency to side with her," or as a man noted, "Even though the whole thing is wrong there certainly is her side to it," many felt it was "harmful, even dangerous to give her visitation rights, especially now when the girl is so young."

It is the bad mother who is dangerous to her own, who might harm more than her own, who makes people afraid. That Whitehead-Gould, as bad mother, represented such negative power and stirred elements of fear appeared to be reflected in these remarks:

> Because of her no one is safe. What if I were artificially inseminated and had a child I wanted very much and loved and some day some surgeon or internist who donated sperm when he was a hospital resident showed up and demanded my kid?
>
> What can adoptive parents do? Do they always have to be afraid? This has the potential to upset all the adoption and custody laws, and Mary Beth has certainly shown us what a contract is worth.

Good mother, bad mother—Whitehead-Gould also was a paid mother, which added another dimension to her identity.

The Price of Being a Paid Mother

In terms of motive, there was a general belief that Whitehead-Gould quite literally did it for the money.

> She didn't do it for love or affection; she did it for the money. . . .

> For a woman like that, $10,000 is a lot of money; I might not think so, you might not think so, but she thought so.

> It's very simple, she wanted money. She started the big fight because she didn't think she had gotten enough. The Sterns really blew it. Right away, when she wanted the baby back, they should have said, "Fine! Take her; we never want to see you again. From this moment you are fully, totally, financially responsible." That would have stopped her. And what about now, do you think she is using any of the money she has gotten out of this for the kid?

> It was the money not the child. She created the atmosphere of a marketable product, only the Sterns didn't pay her enough. What if they had upped the price?

Other products and services can be bought and sold, but when a woman or a man use their bodies in the market place, specific terminology is applied:

> She wants to take the kid to go whoring to get as much money as possible out of her. Look what she has gotten out of her already.

Whitehead-Gould also was described as "promiscuous" because she became pregnant out of wedlock during the time of the Baby M controversy.

While William Stern was not condemned for paying for Whitehead-Gould's services—similar to the general societal lack of condemnation for the "John" who buys a prostitute's services—the fact that Whitehead-Gould agreed to be a paid surrogate added a shaky moral tinge to the ambivalence about her as a good mother.

EMPATHY FOR WILLIAM STERN, THE MYSTERY OF ELIZABETH STERN

Among those questioned there was empathy, particularly for William Stern:

> People have to acknowledge that fathers make good parents too. Just because they don't give birth doesn't mean that they shouldn't be fully recognized. To tell the truth, I was against this whole surrogacy thing, then I read a story in one of the big newsmagazines about a man who had an adopted baby and how much he loved it and it was incredibly moving. It made me rethink my attitude.

> You have to understand the desperation. I'm a man with two kids so I can't speak for myself, but I have a nephew whose wife had a hysterectomy when she was 27 and they paid $25,000 for a baby. I can tell you this, they would have paid $100,000, they wanted that baby so much.

> The Sterns aren't all good, and basically I am against surrogacy, but I know I might feel very different if I couldn't conceive.

In many ways, Elizabeth Stern, who tended to be restrained and silent, was the forgotten woman of the Baby M Media splash. Nonetheless, she made an impression. For reasons that remain open to interpretation, several women chose specifically to talk about her.

> I am extremely confused about Elizabeth Stern. I have less sympathy for her than I did at first because she concealed the fact that she had MS. It wasn't true that she couldn't have kids. Still it had to be very hard on her—the reality of surrogacy—can you imagine seeing another woman physically carrying your husband's child?
>
> I have an image of her as vague, careful but no saint.
>
> I don't know why I keep thinking about her; I guess I keep thinking about the invasion of privacy, and she seems such a private person.
>
> She is a fine woman with an excellent reputation in the scientific community.

Elizabeth Stern was seen as wife, career woman, but not as mother. Perhaps, despite all the recent change in the social roles of women, mother is still internally perceived as a separate identity.

Identifying with the Children in Baby M

With all due deference to the point that those who reacted to Whitehead-Gould as mother or William Stern as father were dredging up childlike feelings, it is necessary to give separate space to those who instantly felt as one with the children involved in Baby M. Psychology's teaching that our sense of worth is forged on the anvil of our parents' caring would appear to be echoed in these comments:

> I keep thinking about her [Whitehead-Gould's] other kids. If it were me, and my mother was willing to have a baby and give it away, I'd have to wonder what I was worth.

There also were feelings of loss:

> It has to be very troublesome to have a sister who you'd never really have as a sister.
>
> Whatever the outcome of the Baby M case, and someday we'll see what kind of a kid she'll turn out to be, biologically she is a sibling to Mary Beth's other children and they are already old enough to know. The whole thing has to be pretty horrible for them.

A heartfelt comment came from a 12-year-old girl:

> All the adults are so selfish about their own needs they are forgetting about the baby's needs. She [Whitehead-Gould] has got two other kids but she has to have whatever she can get. She doesn't care about how do her two other kids feel when she runs off and takes that baby to Florida. They also forget that Baby M is a person.

Conclusion

Baby M didn't just happen in an office where a surrogacy contract was signed or in a clinical setting or in a courtroom; it very much happened in one of the most pervasive forces of our time, the mass media. Because it did, because of the compelling nature of the issues involved, Baby M happened to members of the general public who had to grapple with the human impact of 21st-century biotechnology. That this encounter was not an easy one was evident in remarks like this:

Right now there is nothing but a lot of pain.

But what of the future? It is interesting to note that in the series of interviews done for this article, some people interviewed at a later time than others reported an easing of attitude whether it was to Whitehead-Gould:

> I started out thinking no way, she signed a contract and she's trying to get out of it. I didn't have the ability to see that maybe Mary Beth had a point. You shouldn't have picked me because my viewpoint has changed, softened a little.

or to change itself:

> It's a bizarre, inhuman kind of technology, but I guess the final goal is basically a good purpose.

The biotechnology of the present and the future is not likely to go away; neither is the age-old desire for biological children. Yet when paid surrogacy was tried in the instance of Baby M, turmoil and misery was the immediate result—even for those not directly involved.

In considering some of the reactions I gathered—and certainly they are open to other interpretation and there are many studies yet to be done—I could not help but wonder, What if? What if Whitehead-Gould could have been seen as a good mother? What if the image of Baby M was not of a child in danger, but of a child greatly loved? What if we were satisfied that no one was being abandoned? What if Elizabeth Stern made us believe in her fighting determination to be a good mother?

We of the late 20th century have come to understand that parents can still be parents even when they are divorced, that children can accept half- and step-siblings. In our best moments, we are proving the point that if inner needs for love and caring and firm support are there, the new, the radical, can become an acceptable norm.

It would appear that the adults of Baby M did not convince us of that:

> I feel that the parents and lawyers and the experts and the media are a bunch of sharks who don't really care about the best interests of the child.

Baby M challenges us to do better if surrogacy is to be part of the future.

ACKNOWLEDGMENTS. This article would not have been possible without the willing cooperation of people who agreed to be interviewed on the condition that they remain anonymous. To them I am extremely grateful, as I am to Dr. Joan Zuckerberg for her expert guidance.

References

Beyond words: Recollections of 1987. (1988). *New York Times*, January 3, Section 4.
Chessler, P. (1987). Women, mothers, and motherhood: An interview. *On the Issues: The Journal of Substance for Progressive Women, 8*, 4.
Endangered? (1988). Cover of Special Mothers Issue, *Ms., 16* (May), 11.
Gallagher, M. (1987). Womb to let. *National Review, 39* (April 24), pp. 27–30.
Garvey, J. (1987). Contracting anguish. *Commonweal, 114* (April 24), p. 232.
Gordon, M. (1987). Baby M: New questions about biology and destiny. *Ms., 15* (June), pp. 25–26.
Gray, M. (1987). A battle of ethics, money, and blood. *Maclean's, 100* (January 26), p. 44.
Harrison, B. G. (1987). Surrogate mothers: No way to treat a baby. *Mademoiselle* (June), pp. 93–96.

Hoffman, M. (1987). Merle Hoffman on the issues. *On the Issues: The Journal of Substance for Progressive Women, 8,* 3.
Levin, E., & Reid, S. (1987). Motherly love works a miracle. *People, 28* (October 19), pp. 39–43.
The Baby M Case: Pregnancy & MS (1987). *Discover, 8* (June), p. 13.

Chapter 17
Feminist Tensions
Concepts of Motherhood and Reproductive Choice

NADINE TAUB

Now well past the exuberance of early revelations and early victories, feminists in the United States today are again struggling with questions faced by earlier generations in the women's movement. At times, these seemingly perennial questions have led to deep and debilitating divisions within the feminist community over particular issues. At other times, individuals experience the tensions in terms of personal ambivalence or inconsistency. One of the sharpest debates within the feminist legal community in recent years has concerned the significance to be accorded women's unique role in reproduction. In the work context, the debate has focused on the desirability of laws that attempt to ensure greater job protection and benefits for pregnancy-related disabilities than for other types of temporary incapacities.[1] In the reproductive

---

[1] "Special treatment" advocates accept, and in fact welcome, such classifications where they benefit women. For example, a law that prohibits the firing of disabled pregnant women but permits the firing of other temporarily disabled workers would be endorsed under a special treatment approach. "Equal treatment" advocates, on the other hand, doubt that laws that appear to accord pregnant women preferential treatment will ever really benefit women. They see such laws as likely to jeopardize the hiring of women in view of the potential increase in costs to the employer, likely to engender resentment of male co-workers, and to reinforce the notion that women's maternal role is primary. Instead, proponents of the equality model would require pregnant workers to be treated like other workers who are equally able or unable to work. This requirement allows women to share in benefits already accorded males and to encourage individuals of both genders to see similarities in their experiences, thereby diffusing the narrow focus on motherhood, which has had such a limiting effect on women's societal participation to date.

A major criticism of the equality approach from the special treatment perspective is that it fails to take account of a real difference in the sexes' physical makeup. Proponents of special treatment postulate that by analogizing pregnancy-related disabilities to other temporary disabilities the equal treatment approach ignores a physical fact that must be accommodated in order to achieve equality. Special treatment advocates thus call for legislation ensuring in-

---

NADINE TAUB. • Women's Rights Litigation Clinic, Rutgers University School of Law, Newark, New Jersey 07102-3192. © Copyright 1989 by Nadine Taub; all rights reserved. Used by permission.

technologies context, debates over the need to recognize women's unique contribution are heard most sharply in discussions of the determinants of parenthood.

In the conventional biological family, fathers are both genetic and social parents, while mothers are genetic, gestational, and social parents. Adoption and other mores have long permitted the formation of families in which either or both sexes are social parents without being biological parents. For men, the introduction of artificial insemination in the last hundred years or so has provided an additional way of separating genetic and social parenthood.[2] Now, technology has made it possible to separate genetic from gestational mothering, and society is once again being called upon to determine who will have the rights and responsibilities of parenthood. Like rules governing the treatment of pregnancy in the workplace, the debate over the definition of motherhood has ramifications that extend well beyond the immediate issue, and in debating the question, feminists must be alert to the consequences of various approaches for all areas of reproduction choice. What are the consequences of defining as mother the woman who donated the egg, the woman who carried the fetus, or the woman who raised the child?

Though the necessity for determining parenthood can arise in a variety of situations, the situation of the so-called surrogate mother—who may or may not have contributed the egg—has received a great deal of attention in the wake of the Baby M case. In that case, of course, Mary Beth Whitehead was both the genetic and gestational mother. Yet in analyzing her claim to parental ties and custody, most feminists have gone beyond the particulars of the Baby M case to consider situations in which the gestational mother is not the genetic mother. Much of the ensuing discussion has centered on the question of who is the real mother in surrogacy conflicts.

For many feminists who side with Mary Beth Whitehead and her sisters, the gestator's role is crucial. They emphasize the physical reality of pregnancy and the special contribution the woman makes in nurturing the fetus. To ignore that reality and contribution is, in their view, to devalue women. If gestation becomes a service for hire, they foresee that the meaning of the gestational relationship will be devalued, not just for the women who allow their services to be hired but for all pregnant women. Once gestation is regarded simply as a service subject to contract, rather than a unique aspect of life, it seems more acceptable to require pregnant women to conform to the demands of others, and it thus becomes easier to impose limits on the behavior of all pregnant women. They are concerned that stressing either the relationship the rearing mother establishes after birth or (in cases of donated eggs or embryos) the genetic ties between the donating women and the resulting child, and minimizing the contribution of gestation, will reduce motherhood to fatherhood.

---

come replacement, job security, and similar benefits for women disabled by pregnancy, whether or not other temporarily disabled workers received such benefits. Equal treatment advocates agree that their approach is inadequate without positive programs that recognize and accommodate the needs of pregnant women but seek to meet those needs in the context of meeting the needs of all workers who are temporarily unable to work. Both camps do, however, agree on the need for positive programs, such as guaranteed leaves with income replacement to facilitate parenting activity.

[2]The widespread introduction of artificial insemination by donor into the United States in the 1950s and 60s seems to have been viewed with horror initially. Bans on the procedure were proposed in a number of states; however, none was adopted. State legislative action over the years has instead focused on identifying the legal father of the child, usually by designating the consenting husband of the sperm recipient (Andrews, 1987).

Women will be equated with men, and given the realities of male dominance and the demands of childbearing, women will be regarded as second-rate men at best.

On the other hand, some feminists are concerned about focusing on gestation as the crucial aspect of motherhood. They fear that glorifying pregnancy in this way will serve to limit options available to women. Women, they are concerned, will be seen and see themselves primarily as baby-makers. The life-chances they are afforded and they allow themselves will be constrained by this view of their primary role. Male willingness to share in childrearing and female ability to allow men to do so will be limited by the glorification of pregnancy. Moreover, to value pregnancy above other contributions to reproduction or above other nurturing relationships will increase the pressure on women to bear children.

The privileging of the gestational contribution over the genetic and social aspects of parenthood can take different forms. In objecting to the term *surrogate mother* as applied to a woman who carries and bears a child she intends to relinquish, some feminists express the view that at birth, the birthmother—as opposed to the egg donor (if any) and the prospective adoptive mother—is "the real mother."[3]

The same view is also expressed in debates over the desirability of permitting such arrangements. Barbara Katz Rothman, for example, argued in testimony before the New York State legislative committees considering legislation to legalize and regulate surrogacy that one way to stop the nightmare visions she sees as the inevitable consequences of "hiring" pregnancy is to reject "the very concept of 'surrogacy' for motherhood" that forms the underpinnings of contract parenthood.

In her formulation, "A surrogate is a substitute. In some human relations, we can accept no substitutes. Any pregnant woman is the mother of the child she bears. Her gestational motherhood establishes her motherhood. We will not accept the idea that we can look at a woman, heavy with child and say the child is not hers" (Rothman, this volume). Thus, she argues for legislation that recognizes that "the gestational mother is the mother . . . regardless of the source of the egg or the sperm" (Rothman, this volume). With that recognition, paying the gestational mother to relinquish the child must be viewed as a variation of baby-selling, which is both undesirable as a matter of policy and illegal under present law (Rothman, this volume).

The primacy of gestation also comes up in attempts to resolve competing claims for custody where the birthmother changes her mind about giving up the child to the contracting parents. Some feminists who wish to see custody go to the birthmother in all such cases focus on the unique position the birthmother occupies as a result of pregnancy. They stress two, possibly inconsistent, aspects of this position: the physical identity of the woman and the fetus, and the emotional relationship that the woman forms with the fetus during pregnancy.[4] Ruth Hubbard, for example, argues:

> At birth, we must make a clear distinction between the birthmother and the sperm donor (or the egg donor, if she is not also the birthmother). Whether or not she

---

[3] It is, of course, important to be clear that not all arguments in favor of preferring the gestational mother in surrogacy cases rest on the claim that the gestational mother is *the* mother.
[4] The notion of a relationship implying two entities would seem to negate the notion of physical identity. To the extent that arguments for abortion rights turn on claims of physical identity, they may be undercut by such relational claims. On the other hand, to degrade the fetus to a non-entity is to deny many women's experience. The struggle to maintain the right to choose abortion therefore must involve the struggle to explain the fetus as a developing entity that only later emerges as a being distinct from the woman's body.

> has provided the egg, a birthmother has gestated the baby. At birth, the baby is literally her flesh and blood. Until moments before, it was part of her body and nourished like her own organs. To have provided a sperm or egg is trivial by comparison. Although the birthmother may decide to give her child up, it is hers in a way quite different from that in which it is the sperm and/or egg donor's. In ordinary procreation, both biological parents become their child's social parents and, once the baby is born, the father's contribution to its growth and development can be equivalent to or, indeed, greater than the mother's, if they arrange it that way. In that case, the difference between them that exists at birth can soon become insignificant as parents and baby become attached. But such an equivalence between parents cannot exist at birth. It takes time—and parental effort—to establish. Therefore I would argue that a father acquires parental rights by parenting his children. Birthmothers have parental rights when the child is born and may subsequently relinquish them. (Hubbard, 1987, p. 71; see also Chavkin, Rapp, & Rothman, 1987).

For Hubbard, the gestator has a superior claim to custody at birth because "at birth the birthmother is in a special position to be the 'real' parent" (Hubbard, 1987, p. 72). Thus, she argues, surrogacy-related custody disputes should always be resolved in the gestator's favor.

Beliefs about the relative significance of genetic, gestational, and social ties do not account for all reactions to surrogacy arrangements. There are, of course, many other considerations at play: concerns about the commodification of human life and the potential for sex, class, and race exploitation to name a few. But there is little question that the different consequences attributed to gestational process and differing perspectives on the desirability of prizing that process go a long way in accounting for the different views of the practice and different approaches to custody disputes that it may produce.

I do not try to sort out the surrogacy puzzle here. Rather I seek to explore the consequences of attempting to resolve the problems posed by surrogacy by identifying the primary parent or the mother by reference to women's unique role in reproduction. My point is simply that according a birthmother the status of *the* mother is likely to have ramifications in other reproductive contexts and that there is a need to think through those ramifications. If gestational ties are elevated above genetic and social links in a way that denigrates those other links, what will be the impact on the general climate for reproductive choice? What will be the fallout for reproductive choice in the area of gamete donation, embryo transfer, abortion, and genetic screening?

Approaches that risk fostering a mystique about pregnancy may constrict women's procreative choices. While the reality of pregnancy—with its joys and difficulties—cannot be denied, glorifying pregnancy makes it harder for women to choose to forgo childbearing by making other types of relationships appear far less attractive, and makes the inability to experience pregnancy seem more painful. Defining the birthmother as *the* mother cannot help but imply that a woman who does not undergo pregnancy is not a real mother. Though Hubbard, Rothman, and other feminists suggest that both men and women can later establish relationships with children, in their portrayal, social mothers—be they adoptive mothers, stepmothers, or something less formal—inevitably become something less than real mothers. The process of justifying the primacy of gestation is likely to involve rosy images of pregnancy as uniformly poignant, as unremittantly rewarding, and as crucial to fulfilling relationships with children. Images of this sort are all too reminiscent of the official versions of motherhood that feminists correctly point out are used, in Gena Corea's words, to "structure a woman's will to be a mother" (Corea, 1988, p. 88). Like the repetition of those official versions, the process of privileging birthmothers is likely to heighten the pressure on women to undergo *in vitro* fertilization and other technologically intensive routes to motherhood, particularly as other relationships are rendered less attractive.[5]

The mystification of pregnancy may also have other detrimental effects. Women who do not experience gestation as bonding during pregnancy may come to question their adequacy as women. Moreover, emphasizing the primacy of gestation in assigning motherhood may make it harder for fertile women to exercise the choice to forgo conventional motherhood. The "choice" to give birth may be weighted unduly by the fear of missing out on life's most meaningful relationship, one that cannot be matched by becoming an adoptive mother, let alone an aunt, godmother, or other honorary kin.

Just as the privileging of gestational mothers over potential social mothers may constrain women's choices, so too the failure to afford sufficient recognition to the genetic mothers' contribution may constrict reproductive freedom. Abortion is an obvious area in which women's reproductive choice is linked to the value placed on genetic ties. Woman's right to choose abortion has been justified in large measure by her right to bodily integrity: She cannot and should not be forced to sustain fetal life within her own body. This justification has limited value, however, in situations where fetal life may be sustained outside her own body either by artificial means or as a result of transfer to another woman's body. Thus, for example, requirements that postviability abortions be performed by means designed to result in live births so long as there is no additional risk to the woman's health do not interfere with a woman's bodily integrity. Nor when, as is likely, technology regularly permits successful embryo transfers early in pregnancy, would a requirement that a woman seeking a previability abortion have her embryo transferred to another woman.

Though genetic ties should not be overvalued any more than gestational ties, in justifying a woman's right to defeat choice of method requirements and choose a true abortion, the genetic contribution and sense of responsibility it brings for women must be recognized. As Nan Hunter has argued:

> What it means to be a parent is more than physical risk taking or radical alteration of daily life or the assumption of financial obligation or even the impact of lost options such as not finishing a degree. To bear or beget a child is to bring into being another human life, to project further into the future a genetic continuity, and to create a physiological kinship bond regardless of by whom the child is raised. Each of these considerations is profound. Forcing parenthood upon the unwilling individual is an awesome degradation of the self. The impact of knowing that one has a child continues long after even a successful adoption. For many birth parents (and adopted children), the knowledge that a parent-child relationship exists creates an issue that may never be fully put to rest and a sense of responsibility which always feels undischarged.

Nor are the consequences of contributing to bringing a child into this world sex-blind. Women have traditionally been expected to bear that responsibility and have

---

[5]Of course, the pressure to have one's own genetic children is also important here, but, as Michele Stanworth (1988, p. 22) has suggested, that factor may be more important for men than for women.

in fact borne it day in and day out (see, e.g., Center for Constitutional Rights, 1986; New Jersey Coalition for Battered Women, 1982). Their sense of responsibility endures even after adoption, perhaps because of the gendered expectation that women will meet the burdens of childbearing.

Arguments from bodily integrity simply do not suffice in the late abortion and embryo transfer context. An appreciation of the moral and emotional baggage that attends genetic parenthood for women thus appears essential to protecting abortion rights.[6] Yet denying the importance of the claims and responsibilities that attend the genetic component of parenthood in the surrogacy context makes it more difficult to assert the importance of such concerns in this context.

The relative devaluation of genetic ties that may limit women's reproductive freedom may have an unfortunate impact on women's health and autonomy in other respects as well. According to the press, egg banks and egg and embryo transfers have become a reality (see, e.g., Clinic Plans Variation, 1957; Rising Use, 1988). The major source of eggs in the past has been extra eggs produced by women undergoing *in vitro* fertilization. However, since it is increasingly possible to freeze these eggs, women have begun to save them for their own future use. The search for new sources has led to requirements that women find their own donors, to recruitment by advertisement, and to use of tubal ligation patients. Donors are subjected to risks resulting from hormone stimulation used to increase egg production and invasive techniques used to retrieve the eggs.

The notion that genetic ties are unimportant and that egg donors, like sperm donors, have no claims on their offspring and few legal responsibilities in relation to their offspring suggests that egg donation is a step that may be taken lightly. Indeed, women who are reluctant to donate may be considered selfish. Arguments that focus exclusively on the danger and invasion donation entails may be of limited value now in cases involving tubal ligation where the women is already undergoing certain risks. These arguments may carry even less weight in the future as the technology improves. Women's ability to choose freely between donating or resisting pressures to do so depends, then, at least in part on society's recognition of genetic links. This may be particularly important where medical professionals are involved in obtaining the eggs or fertilizing them (as in the case of "extras"), and the tendency to deny woman any say in the disposition of eggs or embryos they have produced is exacerbated.

While freedom to make the decision to abort or not to donate relies in large measure on the importance of the right not to engender a human life, the right to have one's genetic line continue becomes equally important in the context of genetic screening. Reproductive freedom requires that prospective parents are able to determine freely whether or not to beget and bear a child in view of what is known about the consequences of their genetic makeup. Barriers to exercising that freedom may include restraints on contraception and abortion and lack of access to necessary testing, resulting in involuntary childbearing on the one hand or undue pressure to abort in the face of certain test outcomes on the other. In either event, society's willingness

---

[6]Some might argue that it is the woman's pregnancy rather than her genetic link that brings the weight of society's expectations upon her. But it is more likely that her sense of responsibility, shaped as it is by society's gendered expectations, is triggered by the fact that she is contributing to the creation of another being—that is, by both elements. It does not seem probable that eliminating one element, e.g., by terminating her pregnancy through embryo transfer, would relieve her burden.

to recognize the progenitor's right to make the choice whether or not to beget a child depends on an appreciation of the part a genetic parent plays in producing a child and on the understanding that one bears responsibility for a life whose potential is determined by one's genetic contribution whether or not another has undertaken to gestate or rear the child. Thus, to ignore or denigrate the role of the genetic parent by focusing single-mindedly on the gestational parent in the surrogacy context may diminish genuine choice in this context.

This is not say that in all contexts we can avoid the necessity of determining who has the superior claim. Baby M must live somewhere after all, and joint custody is hardly a realistic alternative. It is to say that we should strive to recognize the importance of all relationships and that, above all, we should seek ways of deciding competing claims that avoid pronouncements that one particular relationship constitutes true parenthood.

Feminists as a group seek approaches to expand the definitions of family relationships (see, e.g., Taub, 1984–1985), and as Barbara Katz Rothman has said, "The new technology offers us another opportunity to work on the definitions of motherhood, fatherhood and children" (Rothman, 1982). But, as she adds, "Reproductive technology will not make social change. As long as our social definitions remain the same, the technology will be used to support those definitions." If, in attempting to confront the challenges posed by an alternative mode of reproduction, such as surrogacy reproduction, society generally and feminists in particular rely on those old definitions—on the need for one and only one mother, for example—choice will be constrained. If, on the other hand, society heeds her broader vision, choice can be expanded.

> We do not have to be "donors" and "hosts" and "surrogates"—we can be mothers and fathers and aunts and uncles. We can take away the gender assignments and leave the relationships. We are coming to understand this with social parenting, that several people, including fathers and other men, can "mother" a child. Perhaps we will learn the lesson for physical parenthood too. . . . (Rothman, 1982).

But here, as elsewhere, it is not immediately apparent how this goal can be served at the point where conflicts must be resolved. Finding the appropriate way to resolve surrogacy-related custody conflicts is not an easy matter, and thoughts rather than definitive solutions are offered here. Feminists have been struggling for some time and in a variety of contexts with the problem of resolving competing parental claims.[7] In wrestling with these difficult situations, feminists have attempted to devise approaches that are fair to women and meet children's needs. Feminists generally wish to view parenthood in terms of responsible and caring relationships rather than exclusive ownership (see, e.g., Bartlett, 1988; Rothman, 1987). Disagreements among feminists often reflect differing opinions about what women stand to gain from efforts to encourage male involvement as well as differing views about the ways it may come about (cf. Bartlett & Stack, 1986; Polikoff, 1982).

Given the dual focus on women and children, the time frame for determining conflicting claims is not always clear in feminist discussions. From the child's perspective, the question is a forward-looking one: What physical and emotional care will

---

[7]Much of the concern has focused on custody disputes at the time of divorce. Feminists have also debated the rights of unmarried fathers to forestall adoption without their consent and sperm donors' rights to maintain contact with their offspring. Feminists appear to have paid less attention to the states' attempts to terminate parental rights, particularly of poor women.

be forthcoming and what relationships—including ties with the past—will meet the child's future needs? Fairness from the woman's perspective may involve both recognition of the contenders' past contributions and estimates of the likelihood of their future efforts. At times, feminists attempt to meld the two temporal perspectives by citing past performance and/or current relationships as a basis for predicting future performance. That may well be what Barbara Katz Rothman and Ruth Hubbard have in mind when they seek to resolve competing claims in surrogacy cases by reference to the birthmother's gestational contribution and existing relationship with the child.[8] But existing relationships and past contributions, though often more helpful than expressions of intent, may not always be accurate predictors of future behavior. Nor will invariably giving primacy to past efforts and current relationships do much to build on any sense of relationship or responsibility felt by the various participants in the reproductive process. Moreover, decisional rules that focus exclusively on current bonds may be used to defeat the parental claims of vulnerable mothers in other contexts—as, for example, in cases where poor women have placed their children in foster care temporarily or women in transition have temporarily left their children with their father.

Much of the pressure for absolute preferences comes from the dangers feminists correctly perceive in the use of open-ended decisional rules in custody and other parental disputes. Like all parental disputes, surrogacy-related custody conflicts are likely to be permeated by sex and class bias (Polikoff, 1982; Sheppard, 1982). But rigid preferences have their dangers too. Seeking ways to identify and correct for that bias (see, e.g., Women's Rights Litigation Clinic, 1988), and trying to minimize the occasions for conflict by maximizing the situations in which multiple relationships can be tolerated may thus be the best tack in trying to chart a course between the romanticization of pregnancy and the reduction of woman to vessel.

REFERENCES

Andrews, L. (1987). The aftermath of Baby M: Proposed state laws on surrogate motherhood. *Hastings Center Report,* 31 (October/November).
Bartlett, K. (1988). Rights and responsibilities: From an exchange of views to an expressive view. *Yale Law Journal,* 98, 291.
Bartlett, K., and Stack, C. (1986). Joint custody, feminism and the dependency dilemma. *Berkeley Women's Law Journal,* 2, 9.
Center for Constitutional Rights. (1986). Brief Amici Curiae. In *Thornburgh v. American College of Obstetricians and Gynecologists,* 476 U.S. 747, 106 S.Ct. 2169.
Chavkin, W., Rapp, R., Rothman, B. K. (1989). Third party reproduction: Dissenting voices and questions. In S. Cohen & N. Taub (Eds.) *Reproductive laws for the 1990s.* Clifton, NJ: Humana.
Clinic plans variation on fertility techniques. New York Times, July 19, 1987, Section E, p. 26.

---

[8]It is not clear that everyone who would give absolute superiority to maternal claims in custody disputes is focusing on future performance. Even among those who would not always honor such claims, some may have their focus on past contributions. Linda Gordon, for example, writes: "Some feminists argue the absolute superiority of maternal claims in all custody disputes; I do not. It is not a question of the equal contribution of egg and sperm but of the difference between a genetic and a gestational relation to a future child. The latter is a far more burdensome and personal commitment and deserves greater recognition, although other factors might supersede it in some cases" (Gordon, 1987).

Corea, G. (1988). What the king cannot see. In E. Baruch, A. D'Adamo, Jr., & J. Seager (Eds.), *Embryos, ethics and women's rights*.

Gordon, L. (1987). Reproductive rights for today. *The Nation*, September 12.

Hubbard, R. (1987). A birthmother is a birthmother is a. . . . *Sojourner: The Woman's Forum*, September.

Hunter, N. (1989). Time limits on abortion. In S. Cohen & N. Taub (Eds.) *Reproductive laws for the 1990s*. Clifton, NJ: Humana.

New Jersey Coalition for Battered Women. (1982). Brief Amici Curiae. In *Right to Choose v. Byrne*, 91 N.J. 287. (Reprinted in *Women's Rights Law Reporter, 7*, 285.)

Polikoff, N. (1982). Why are mothers losing: A brief analysis of criteria used in child custody determinations. *Women's Rights Law Reporter, 7*, 235.

Rising use of donated eggs for pregnancy stirs concern. *New York Times*, January 18, 1988, Section A, p. 1.

Rothman, B. K. (1982). How science is redefining parenthood. *Ms.* (July/August).

Rothman, B. K. (1987). Surrogacy: A question of values. *Conscience* (May/June), *8*(3).

Sheppard, A. (1982). Unspoken premises in custody litigation. *Women's Rights Law Reporter, 7*, 229.

Stanworth, M. (1988). The deconstruction of motherhood. In M. Stanworth (Ed.), *Reproductive technologies*. Minneapolis: University of Minnesota Press.

Taub, N. (1984–1985). From parental leave to nurturing leaves. *New York University Review of Law and Social Change, 13*, 13.

Women's Rights Litigation Clinic, Rutgers Law School (1988). Brief Amici Curiae. *In the Matter of Baby M*, 109 N.J. 396.

Chapter 18

On Surrogacy
Constructing Social Policy

BARBARA KATZ ROTHMAN

The first thing to bear in mind is that surrogate motherhood is not a new reproductive technology. The booming business in "surrogates" has nothing to do with scientific progress, and everything to do with marketing. The reproductive technology used is artificial insemination. Artificial insemination with donor sperm (AID) has been used in human beings for over a hundred years. The "technologies" involved are the technology of masturbation and of the turkey baster or its equivalent.

It is important to remember that fact, because we are sometimes overwhelmed with the developments of the new reproductive technology, as with our other technology. Sometimes we think—and sometimes we are encouraged to think—that there is nothing we can do to halt "progress." If science can produce "test tube babies," how can we ever stop it? And if our new knowledge gives us these new powers, should we even want to stop it?

These are important questions. But they are not the questions of surrogate motherhood. Surrogate motherhood was not brought to us by the march of scientific progress. It was brought to us by brokers, by people who saw a new market and went after it. And the market is something we know we *can* control and often *should* control.

When artificial insemination was introduced, it was used to support the traditional family structure, husbands and wives having and raising babies. In earlier times, when couples were unable to start a pregnancy, it was most often assumed to be the fault of the wife, and in some cultures husbands had the recourse of divorce. With expanding knowledge, infertility was shown to be sometimes a problem in the husband's body. Wives were not given the recourse of divorce under these circumstances, and artificial insemination became a way of maintaining the intact husband-wife unit. Wives were not encouraged to take a "surrogate," a substitute lover, but rather doctors used semen, given anonymously, to impregnate wives.

BARBARA KATZ ROTHMAN • Department of Sociology, Baruch College, New York, New York 10010. This chapter is based on the testimony by the author before the joint hearings of the New York State Senate and New York State Assembly Judiciary Committees on Surrogate Parenthood and New Reproductive Technology, October 16, 1986.

The process was undertaken with the greatest of secrecy. According to some accounts, the wife herself in one of the first American uses of artificial insemination was not told what was done to her. Certainly, no one outside of the couple and the doctor was told—artificial insemination has been shrouded in silence. This enabled men to be the social fathers of the children their wives bore.

Social fatherhood is a key issue here. What makes a woman a mother has always been quite obvious. But what makes a man a father has been subject to some question. The formula our society, along with many others, has arrived at is that fatherhood is determined by the man's relationship to the child's mother. A man married to a woman is the recognized father of her children. This way of reckoning fatherhood builds on two things: The obvious and unquestioned nature of biological motherhood, and the traditional patriarchal relationship of men and their wives. This is a way of acknowledging parenthood that is based on relationships: The relationship of the woman to her baby as it grows within, and the relationship of the man to the woman.

And so it stood for over a hundred years: Artificial insemination was a way of managing male infertility that kept the family intact, that allowed children to be born to a couple, children who would be truly theirs, to bring into the world together, to raise and to cherish together.

So what changed? For one thing, infertility appears to be on the increase: More and more couples are facing infertility problems. For another, the supply of babies available for adoption has dropped dramatically. Young women, faced with unwanted pregnancies, have been given choices: The choice of abortion and the choice of raising a child without a husband. Infertile couples can no longer benefit, no matter how innocently, from the tragedies of young mothers. A second change was that our attitude toward infertility has also changed—and this may indeed be an indirect result of scientific progress. Progress against infertility has become a newspaper and television reporting staple. Remember the excitement that surrounded the first *in vitro* baby, the first American *in vitro* baby, the first *in vitro* twins, and so on. The idea began to be generated that infertility was curable, if only a couple tried hard enough, saw enough doctors, went through enough procedures. The reality is something quite different. Only 10% of those couples attempting *in vitro* fertilization will have a baby. There is a 90% failure rate with that technology.

What we have done is to create a population of desperate, heartbroken infertile people, people who cannot find babies to adopt, who have "tried everything" and cannot get pregnant, people who have devoted years of their lives to trying, one way or another, to get a baby.

The medical technology has enabled the couple to sort out "whose fault" the infertility is. When it is the husband who is infertile, artificial insemination with donor sperm remains a solution, enabling the couple to have a pregnancy and the much-wanted baby. When it is the wife who is infertile, the pressures mount on the woman to feel guilt at not being able to "give her husband" a child. A baby is what they want more than anything. And he could have one, if not for her.

It is in this context that the marketing of "surrogate" motherhood developed. Brokers entered the scene, telling the couple that they could indeed have a baby, and it would be "his" baby. "Surrogate motherhood" was sold as a solution to the tragedy of infertility, and a way of resolving women's guilt at their own infertility. For couples who have spent untold thousands of dollars on medical treatments, the thousands more for surrogacy contracts may have seemed a bargain. For people without these many thousands of dollars, infertility remains unsolved.

With this new use of artificial insemination, the relationships of the parties involved changed totally. The relationship of the mother to her baby within her no longer counts. The baby has become a commodity, something a woman can produce and sell. She is encouraged to think of the baby as no more hers than a factory worker thinks of the car he works on as his. The relationship of the father to the mother no longer counts: It will cease to exist as motherhood is made anonymous, handled by brokers and doctors. The relationship that will count is that of the father to his sperm donation, and the market relationship: The contracts and the fees. What makes a man a father is not his relationship to the mother, we are told, but that it is his sperm and his money.

The brokers tell us that this is not baby-selling: How can a man buy his own baby? they ask. And true enough, how can someone buy something that is already his? But what makes the baby his? His sperm donation? Surely not. If a sperm donor in the more traditional use of artificial insemination came upon the couple a year later and said he had had an accident and was now infertile, and would like to have their baby, he would have no right to it. If he offered them money, he would not be buying that which is his, but that which is theirs: Producing a semen sample does not make a man a social father, does not make that his baby. Is it then his intention that makes the child his? The fathers in the surrogate cases do not donate their sperm. The are not donating or giving or selling. They are buying. Then how is this different from any other example of baby-buying and selling? And the answer is: It is not.

If we legalize surrogacy arrangements, then to buy a baby one will need sperm and money. Couples—or just men—who have both can buy babies. But what of men without adequate sperm? Many cases of infertility involve both partners. What of a couple desperate to have a baby, in which the wife cannot carry a pregnancy and the husband has insufficient sperm, or carries a deadly disease? Sperm too is for sale; we literally have sperm banks. If we permit surrogate motherhood for the situation of men who produce their "own" sperm, then what of the men who must buy sperm? If he buys the sperm, then it too is his, and cannot he too use it to buy a baby? We are going to find ourselves selling babies in "kit" form, purchasing the pieces and services separately. This is of course a "slippery slope" kind of argument—once you permit some people to buy some babies under some conditions, it is very hard to justify any given person's not being allowed to purchase a baby under other circumstances.

And what would be wrong with simply opening up a market economy in babies? Others have argued eloquently what the problems are with baby-selling, and we have as a society accepted those arguments. Some things, we have felt, should simply not be sold—and certainly not people. One of the strongest arguments against baby-selling is that we know that if we allowed babies to be sold, some people would be put under great pressure to sell their babies. This is the same reason that we do not allow organs to be sold from living people, even when we know that lives might actually be saved. If we allowed some people to sell, say, a kidney, we know that some might feel forced to do so. And so now and again someone with much money dies for lack of an organ that he or she was willing to buy, and someone else willing to sell, because such a sale, such a contract, even if arguable in the best interests of the parties involved, would be against the best interests of the society as a whole.

I believe that "surrogacy" presents a parallel situation to organ-selling, and the same arguments apply. The fetus exists in its mother's body, a part of her, and selling that part is comparable to selling other parts. The "allowing" quickly turns to "forcing" for people in dire economic straits.

I began by saying that surrogacy is not a result of new reproductive technology but must be understood entirely as a marketing strategy. Let me now amend that slightly. Most of the surrogate motherhood cases that we see reaching the courts, and the media, are based on the old technology of artificial insemination. But some are using a newer technology. We must consider what the developments in reproductive technology will mean for the future of surrogacy contracts.

The new technologies are varied but share in common the use of genetic material from one woman to create a pregnancy in the body of another woman. There are several ways this can be done. An egg from one woman can be removed, fertilized *in vitro* (in glass), and put into the body of another woman. Some *in vitro* fertilization clinics are doing this for women who want to become mothers but cannot produce eggs. Other women, who produce "extra" eggs, donate those eggs for the use of infertile women who cannot produce their own eggs. This is the situation most closely analogous to artificial insemination with donor sperm, when used with a heterosexual couple. Genetic material from outside of the couple is used to enable a woman and her husband to have a pregnancy and share in the birthing and rearing of a baby, just as happens with artificial insemination with donor sperm.

Another way that this same thing can be accomplished is by allowing fertilization to take place within the body of the woman who is donating the egg. A fertilized egg, what some call a preembryo or preimplantation embryo, is removed from the donor and is placed in the woman who will be the mother. This too is much like artificial insemination. Some months later we seee a pregnant woman and her husband, expecting their child. In these situations of embryo transfer or egg donation, like the situation of artificial insemination with donor sperm, genetic material from outside of the couple is used to create the pregnancy, but the social parenthood, from the point of early pregnancy on, is shared within the couple.

That, then, is the technology. And what of the marketing? Like the marketing of artificial insemination, egg donations can also be turned around, used to create a pregnancy not within the family but in a hired woman, leading to the ultimate purchase of a baby.

With this technology, it is not necessary for the "surrogate" mother to be genetically related to the baby she bears. So one marketing strategy is to hire a woman to carry a pregnancy for a woman who can produce eggs but not carry a pregnancy herself. Now something challenging happens to our thinking: We are forced to confront the question of what makes a woman a mother. Is it the egg or it is the pregnancy? In the cases mentioned above, where a woman is unable to create an egg, the transfer of egg or embryo left the pregnant woman the social mother; it was the pregnant woman who intended to be the mother, who would not only bear and birth the child but intended to raise the child. But if we hire a woman to carry the pregnancy, who then is the mother? Is it the egg donor or the pregnant woman?

In one court decision involving such a case, the egg donor was named as the mother, and the name of the pregnant woman—the *gestational* mother—was not put on the birth certificate. This is of course analogous to the marketing of surrogate motherhood with the old technology of artificial insemination. Relationships are discounted, and the genetic tie, along with the exchange of money, is given primacy. We are asked to accept the idea that the mother is the person who donated the egg and paid for the services, just as we were asked to accept the sperm donor who hired the surrogate as the father.

This opens up an enormous new profit potential for the brokers in the surrogacy market. The technologies of egg and embryo transfer, were surrogate motherhood contracts made enforceable, can be used to drive costs down and keep profits up for the baby brokers. The numbers of couples who are infertile is high and growing. As it stands now, the brokers are limited in their use of surrogate mothers. Because the women are genetically related to the babies they produce, the father-purchasers want only certain kinds of women: Intelligent, attractive, and most assuredly of the same race as the couple. Since it is predominantly white couples who have the $25,000 and up that the brokers charge, and since it is particularly white babies that are in scarce supply for adoption, what brokers need are intelligent, attractive, healthy white women to act as "surrogates." In our society, such women can command some money for their services—not enormous sums compared with what, say, corporate executives get for their work—but at this moment the going rate is upwards of $10,000.

But what will happen if we legally recognize surrogate motherhood contracts and the new technology allows brokers to hire women who will not be genetically related to the babies that are to be sold? Like the poor and nonwhite women who are hired to do other kinds of nurturing and caretaking work, these mothers can be paid very little, with few benefits, and no long-term commitment. Poor, uneducated, third-world women and women of color from the United States and from outside, with fewer economic alternatives, can be hired more cheaply. They can also be controlled more tightly. With a legally supported surrogate mother contract and with the new technology, the marketing possibilities are enormous—and terrifying. Just as Perdue and Holly Farms advertise their chickens on the basis of superior breeding and feeding, the baby brokers can begin to advertise their babies: Brand-name, "state-of-the-art" babies produced from the "finest" of genetic materials and an all-natural, vitamin-enriched diet.

The implications of this commodification of gestational relationship, of "hiring" pregnancy, extend beyond those women who are themselves hired. This will influence all of our thinking about pregnancy. Once we put a price tag on pregnancy, we change, and ultimately devalue, the meaning of the relationship. Once we allow some people to hire and thus inevitably control some women's pregnancies, we move closer to controlling all women's pregnancies.

The time to stop such nightmare visions is now. We stop it by not acknowledging the underlying principle of surrogate contracts, by not accepting the very concept of "surrogacy" for motherhood. A surrogate is a substitute. In some human relations, we can accept no substitutes. Any pregnant woman is the mother of the child she bears. Her gestational relationship establishes her motherhood. We will not accept the idea that we can look at a woman, heavy with child, and say the child is not hers. The fetus is part of the woman's body, *regardless of the source of the egg and sperm*. Biological motherhood is not a service, not a commodity, but a relationship. Motherhood can remain obvious. If a woman is carrying a baby, then it is her baby and she is its mother. Of course, it is true that a mother, any mother, can abdicate her motherhood, can give away a baby—but it is *hers* to give. And if we were to allow the selling of babies, then it is *hers* to sell.

And what can we do with fatherhood? How can we protect the relationship between a father and his child? What will make a man a father? One possibility is to stay with the model that we had: A father can continue to take his fatherhood from his relationship with the mother of the child. In a married couple, the father can continue to be, as he has been up to now, the husband of the mother.

This is not a perfect solution to the troubling question of fatherhood. It gives, in some ways, too much power to women over men's reproduction. And it gives, in other ways, too much power to men over women's reproduction. But this is not a new problem. We are not struggling here with questions of science and new technology. Here we are struggling with age-old questions of relationships, of family, of how we are bound together. We have not found perfect ways of dealing with these issues in all of history. But we have, in this society, been clear in rejecting the use of money in these relationships. We have said that in our society husbands and wives, mothers and fathers, and babies are not up for sale. Nothing in the new reproductive technology need change that.

But what of those infertile couples who do so desperately want babies and see surrogacy as their only option? My heart too goes out to them. Infertility is indeed a tragedy for many of those who experience it. But infertility is just as great a tragedy for those without the $25,000 or more to spend on surrogacy arrangements as it is for those with money. We as a society need to find solutions to infertility, but they must be solutions that are available to everyone and not just to the very rich.

The most obvious and most satisfactory solution would be prevention. Infertile couples have shown us how very desperate they are. We must recognize the tragedy this can be, and make preventing infertility a state and national priority. We need to fund more research on the causes of infertility and on the treatment of infertility.

Perhaps we need also to reconsider our adoption system. The nonmarket approach to adoption has some fine things to recommend it. We need to see if that system, both nationally and internationally, cannot be strengthened, made more equitable for all concerned.

In one sense, the use of "surrogates" has grown directly out of the failures of our adoption system. We have in adoption these days some of the disadvantages of the marketing of babies, with few of the advantages. Adoption has moved out of the public and into the private sector, with attorney-brokers handling more and more adoptions. Small wonder, with so many more couples approaching them for babies than there were babies available, that the brokers were encouraged to think of ways of producing more babies to meet the needs.

Surrogacy contracts developed as a way around laws against baby-selling—with the genetic tie between the man and the child, the brokers could claim that the child was the father's, and that the mother was being paid not for her baby but for her services. Surrogacy is an attempt to solve the problem of a baby shortage for infertile would-be adopters. The advantage that surrogacy offers is that it encourages women to enter into pregnancies they would not otherwise have had, and so produces more babies for adoption. The straight-out selling of babies, allowing mothers to put their babies on the open market, would do the same thing, without the unique dangers of surrogacy. Those dangers are, to sum up:

1. The encouragement of a "breeder" mentality in the production of human beings, using a combination of genetic materials and human services for the greatest profit, with the specific dangers of creating baby farming of white embryos in the bodies of third-world women and American women of color.
2. The development of "production standards" for pregnancy, which grow out of thinking of pregnancy not as a relationship between a woman and her fetus but as a service she provides for others. Such standards may ultimately lead to the control of all women in all pregnancies.

3. The reinforcement of genetic and eugenic values over the value of relationships, with the reidentification of motherhood as the hosting of the seed, and the woman herself as a vessel for someone else's child.

Those engaged in surrogacy brokering tell us that if we do not bring surrogacy into the open market, it, like adoption, will continue to exist in gray or black market forms. And they are probably right. Preventing the open sale of babies has not prevented couples from having to spend much money on getting babies, nor prevented brokers from making money out of matching babies to adopters.

I disagree with the brokers not over acknowledging the problem but over choosing the solutions. There are grave costs to any form of open market in baby-selling. If we wish to legalize baby-selling, let us acknowledge what we are doing and offer the appropriate protections to the parties involved. If we choose to allow a woman to sell her baby, so be it. But let us recognize that it is indeed *her* baby to sell, *her* baby that she is selling. And if we do not wish to permit baby-selling, then there is nothing in the new reproductive technology that forces us to do so. We do not have to give the support of the state to a view of babies as purchasable commodities or motherhood as a salable service.

In sum, the legislation that I feel we need must recognize that *the gestational mother is the mother*. Any pregnant woman is the mother of the child she bears, regardless of the source of the egg or the sperm. The rights and the responsibilities of motherhood are the same for all gestational mothers, regardless of the source of the egg and the sperm.

Therefore, *purchasing a baby from its mother, regardless of the source of the egg and the sperm, is purchasing a baby*. Until or unless we legalize baby-selling, the law cannot acknowledge paid surrogacy arrangements. Surrogacy is not to be used as a way around the laws against the sale of babies: It is itself a variation of baby-selling.

Further, *accepting a baby as a gift from its mother, regardless of the source of the egg and the sperm, is a form of adoption*. The laws that govern the rights and the responsibilities of all parties to an adoption must apply to so-called surrogate arrangements as well.

Chapter 19

The Terror of Surrogate Motherhood
Fantasies, Realities, and Viable Legislation

ISADORE SCHMUKLER AND BETSY P. AIGEN

Why does surrogate motherhood create so much antagonism and anger? Why should there be such outrage against women who are willing to help an infertile couple create a family of their own, especially if these women enjoy childbearing, already have children of their own, and can significantly increase their self-esteem in the process? And what is so evil about paying someone for this?

It is becoming increasingly clear that surrogate motherhood arouses panic and fear because it is seen as challenging cherished cultural values, such as the sanctity of motherhood and the family, and is being forbidden on that basis. We feel that this is an effort to legislate morality, equivalent to past efforts against drinking or abortion, most likely promoting similar results. Certain conservative and religious groups are attempting again to define for all of us what we should believe as right and wrong, what we can and cannot do. The legislature should question whether they have the right to eliminate people's freedom because others have a different idea about what is moral or correct.

In addition, the couples, the surrogates, and the intermediary agencies are accused of many evils, such as exploitation, ruthlessness, and encouraging mothers to desert their children. This is most often done in complete ignorance of the actual motives and feelings of the participants. Ignorance allows glib labels such as "reproductive prostitution" and "baby-selling" to be hurled at the surrogacy process with impunity. It is quite amazing to us when, for example, we hear charges that the surrogate is exploited, that those making these charges never provide evidence by asking the surrogates. Of course not! The surrogates would tell them that they are *not* being exploited. Who wants to hear *that*? All the critics seem to *know* that surrogacy exploits women. They know it *a priori*, without the chore of having to find out. If surrogate motherhood has the *potential* for exploitation, that's good enough for them.

Let's take a closer look at the corruption of morals that surrogacy is accused of. Protection of these morals has been labeled "public policy," and the recent New Jersey Supreme Court decision regarding the Baby M case outlines two basic aspects of such

---

ISADORE SCHMUKLER AND BETSY P. AIGEN • Surrogate Mother Program of New York, New York, New York 10024.

policy: (a) "that children be brought up by their natural parents, the surrogacy contract guaranteeing the separation of the child from its natural mother," and (b) "that adoption not be influenced by the payment of money, the surrogacy contract being based on such payment" (New Jersey Supreme Court, 1987, p. 2). Surrogate motherhood is seen by the court as violating each of these two aspects of public policy.

These policies appear to us primarily as cultural values that have been accorded legal status. It is our position that these values are a product of pervasive irrational fears. Experiences such as surrogacy, which are seen as undermining these values, are forbidden. Critical examination of such values is becoming increasingly important because the legitimacy of surrogacy is being determined by them. Additionally, they fuel very moralistic, self-righteous positions because they represent cherished cultural ideals whose correctness is seen as self-evident.

Abandonment Fears

> The surrogacy contract guarantees permanent separation of the child from one of its natural parents. Our policy, however, has long been that to the extent possible, children should remain with and be brought up by both of their natural parents. That was the first stated purpose of the previous adoption act. . . . "It is necessary and desirable (a) to protect the child from unnecessary separation from his natural parents." (New Jersey Supreme Court, 1987; p. 42)

Harold Cassidy, Mary Beth Whitehead's lawyer, has said:

> The single most important issue that ought to emerge from the Baby M case is the need for society to preserve and protect the ties between mothers and children. . . . Society must not sanction a public policy that would encourage mothers to "abandon" their children. (*New Jersey Record*, 1988, p. 14)

It becomes clear that surrogacy is seen as encouraging the evil of maternal abandonment. Surrogacy is portrayed as a form of stealing children, of forcing ordinary mothers to hand over their beloved children to "baby snatchers." Even in the absence of the payment of a fee to the surrogate, there is a clear moralistic underpinning to the arguments against surrogacy, which is rarely stated overtly: That choosing to have a baby for someone else is reprehensible because it represents a rejection of the infant by its biological mother. Society sees the cherished ideal of mother love and the mother–infant bond being threatened, and surrogacy is the corrupting agent.

Well, isn't all that true? By viewing the surrogate as just another woman carrying a child that she wants to get rid of by giving it to a couple for adoption, the courts and the press have perpetrated and perpetuated such an image.

Situations like surrogacy inevitably stimulate deep anxiety and discomfort on a massive level because they evoke one of our primal fears as human beings: Being rejected and thrown away by our mothers. We identify with the infant and perceive him as being orphaned by his mother, whom we see as "using" him. This is the way surrogate mothers have most often been portrayed both in the press and by critics. This unconscious fantasy of rejection is fueled by the negative feelings we all have about our mothers and by fears of not having been totally "wanted."

It is, of course, true that, biologically, the surrogate is the "real" mother. But this ignores the circumstances and motivation for her pregnancy, as if these were irrelevant details. However, these are precisely the central points about being a surrogate mother. The court and others fervently deny the possibility of a woman's wanting to bear a child for someone else, a child that she therefore does not consider primarily as "hers." If a woman sees herself as a stand-in or double for another woman for whom she is bearing the child, and feels from the beginning of conception that this child belongs to the other woman and her husband, the biological father, rather than to herself, what type of abandonment is this? It is because the woman has chosen to biologically substitute for an infertile woman less fortunate than herself that she defines the experience for herself as an act of "giving" rather than "giving away" and rejecting a child.

This is the real emotional state and attitude of the surrogate, and it has been totally denied by and distorted by the New Jersey Supreme Court. For instance, "She [the child] is the offspring of someone who gave birth to her only to obtain money" (New Jersey Supreme Court, 1987, p. 51), "It [surrogacy] takes the child from the mother regardless of her wishes and her maternal fitness, and it does all of this, it accomplishes all of its goals, through the use of money" (p. 53). How does surrogate motherhood take a child from the mother "regardless of her wishes or maternal fitness"? The court is on a one-way track: It keeps trying to see the surrogate mother as wanting this child for herself. What does the surrogate mother's "maternal fitness" have to do with anything? It can have relevance only in a process that is seen as forcibly separating a child from its mother against her wishes. The court cannot absorb or deal with a situation where this is not the case, and it keeps addressing and judging the entire surrogate experience as if it were.

In a similar way, the surrender of parental rights, from the *surrogate's* experience, merely makes legal what has been her primary belief from the beginning: that the child is for the couple, not for herself. Unfortunately, because of the emotional power of the "bad mother" fantasy that surrogacy evokes, critics do not wish to know the *reality* of how surrogates themselves feel. Under the guise of protecting surrogates' rights, such critics really wish to proclaim the obligations of biological motherhood, regardless of what women actually want to do or how they feel. They refuse, for example, to allow a surrogate mother to surrender her parental rights, claiming that they are fundamental legal rights that cannot be relinquished by contract. This is tantamount to changing a right to be a mother into an obligation to be one. It is as if these people were saying, "The law says you have to be a good mother and raise this baby, and the baby is yours, whether you think so or not." Critics use the idea of a right as a method of coercing the surrogate mother to fulfill what they think is her obligation to her child. This makes a travesty of the concept of rights; it curtails freedom of choice instead of expanding it.

It is one thing to have a public policy that protects the rights of biological parents to raise children whom they are attached to and want, or that defends the child from "unnecessary separation from his natural parents." But to use such a policy to forbid experiences to which it was never meant to apply is a travesty. The court is implying that the biological mother is morally obligated to raise the child, purely by virtue of the biological relationship, and that experiences like surrogacy are inherently wrong, exactly because they create situations in which this biological mother doesn't want to raise this baby. Well, why is *that*? *Is* it better for a woman not to help others to have a baby, just to avoid such a situation? Is *that* what is meant by the public policy of the adoption law that the court refers to? Or is it the private view of the judges or others that is being held up as "public policy," as common law and value? Is this the widely held value that the court says it is? Where are the polls or referendums to show it?

Fears of Being Used as an Object

The second major aspect of public policy that the courts feel is violated by surrogacy is "that adoption not be influenced by the payment of money." Because of the need to deny the crucial differences between the surrogate pregnancy and the typical unwanted pregnancy, in which a woman wants to surrender her child, the courts have pushed surrogacy into adoption law, which forbids payment to the mother. The original intent of this law was to prevent poor women from being pressured to give up their babies, making their decision "involuntary."

It is clear, however, that the introduction of money into such situations involves other values.

> There are, in a civilized society, some things that money cannot buy. . . The long term effects of surrogacy contracts are not known, but feared—the impact on the child who learns her life was bought, that she is the offspring of someone who gave birth to her only to obtain money; the impact on the natural mother as the full weight of her isolation is felt along with the full reality of the sale of her body and child. (New Jersey Supreme Court, 1987, pp. 50–51)

The real evil of money emerges: Its power to corrupt and seduce human beings to treat each other as commodities, as objects to be bought and sold, coldly and without feeling; a mother sells herself and her baby as objects.

The examples the New Jersey Supreme Court lists as "things that money cannot buy" in a "civilized society" are the following:

> Employers can no longer buy labor at the lowest price they can bargain for, even though that labor is "voluntary" . . . or buy women's labor for less money than paid to men for the same job . . . or purchase agreement of children to perform oppressive labor . . . or purchase the agreement of workers to subject themselves to unhealthful working conditions. . . . There are, in short, values that society deems more important than granting to wealth whatever it can buy, be it labor, love, or life. Whether this principle recommends prohibition of surrogacy, which presumably sometimes results in great satisfaction to all parties, is not for us to say. (New Jersey Supreme Court, 1987, p. 51)

Thus, although the court admits that "the great satisfaction to all of the parties"—which has actually occurred in almost all surrogate outcomes—would put surrogacy in a different category, it goes on to ignore this consideration and suggests that surrogacy is another example of human oppression and exploitation. It seems to us that the mind of the court is menaced by any thought of buying human services. This is quite understandable in that the court, like all of us, lives in a "civilized society" where money buys "human labor" and an endless variety of human services every day.

Money allows human beings to indulge their impulses to be served or serviced by others, without any sympathy or feeling for those being "used." Actually, one need only review the examples offered by the court of what "money cannot buy" to realize that all of these abuses were perpetuated for centuries against victims such as workers, children, and women. One need only think of the long use of slavery to understand the powerful wish to use others, and it is no wonder that there are laws against "baby-selling." These abuses are all fueled by human impulses, impulses that are common and only recently banned by the introduction of "civilized laws." It is our understanding that the introduction of money in surrogacy provokes repressed guilt over wishes to use others as objects. As Freud said, the repressed impulse always pushes for return, and society is hypervigilant against any situation that gives even the appearance of exploitation or devaluation.

Because surrogacy has the *potential* for abuse, the court assumes that such abuses are constantly occurring in practice. "The negative consequences of baby-selling are potentially present in the surrogacy context, especially the potential for placing and adopting a child without regard to the interest of the child or the natural mother" (New Jersey Supreme Court, 1987, p. 27). The comparison is to babies being sold into slavery, to be exploited: "In surrogacy, the highest bidders will presumably become the adoptive parents regardless of suitability, so long as payment of money is permitted" (New Jersey Supreme Court, 1987, p. 48). The implication of a slave auction, complete with "bidders," is clear. The actual reality of helping very adequate couples to have children is completely lost sight of.

The court wishes to exorcise what it considers to be "bad" motives. "Nowhere does this Court find any legal prohibition against surrogacy when the surrogate mother volunteers, without any payment, to act as a surrogate and is given the right to change her mind and to assert her parental rights" (New Jersey Supreme Court, 1987, p. 94). This seems to mean that surrogacy is okay if one's motives are "pure," untainted by financial gain, and shows the crucial role that moralistic judgments of character have played in the court's decision. If money is eliminated, the surrogate no longer is mercenary or heartless, the couple is no longer exploitative, the infant is no longer an object or a commodity being either sold to or stolen by the couple. The evil is exorcised, and the results are now benign.

Once surrogacy is judged to be in the category of evil human impulses and activities, stereotyped images of the motives and characters of the participants are made.

> The child . . . is the offspring of someone who gave birth to her only to obtain money; the impact on the natural mother as the full weight of her isolation is felt along with the full reality of the sale of her body and child; the impact on the natural father and adoptive mother, once they realize the consequences of their conduct. (New Jersey Supreme Court, 1987, p. 51)

Thus, all parties are seen as morally corrupt, sinners who should be hanging their heads in shame. In this type of primitive caricature, the characterizations are black and white, in this case all "bad"; there is no allowance for complexity, for other "good" motives being attributed to anyone involved. Roles are attributed to the participants that do great violence to the facts. The court cannot see that surrogates most often are not poor, are not "forced" into anything, are not deprived or degraded, and that, on the contrary, they feel enhanced and emotionally gratified. The couples are not unfit, "unsuitable," corrupt, or exploitative. The surrogates do not want to keep these children, not because they are heartless deserters but because they consider these children to belong to others.

The Psychology of Feminist Criticism of Surrogate Motherhood

Some feminists attack surrogacy as degrading and dehumanizing in reducing women to being "biological objects" and "breeders." They claim that surrogacy exploits women by seducing them with money to engage in "a form of prostitution."

The terms used to describe the role of the surrogate mother are identical with those used originally to attack the subjugation of women by men. Feminists react to surrogacy as a male conspiracy to "use" women. The fee paid to the surrogate mother, who offers her biological identity as a childbearer, has somehow been confused with a man's payment to a woman for the sexual use of her body. These feminists react to surrogate arrangements as if the husband in the infertile couple is "cheating" on his wife and paying for the reproductive "favors" of another women.

To cast surrogate motherhood in sexual terms is a gross distortion of reality. It neglects the infertile wife's vital and often dominant role in choosing surrogacy as a solution to her own infertility, as well as the advantages she feels in being able to "have" her husband's child through a surrogate. On the other side, the surrogate is often more identified with the plight of the woman than the man, and sees herself as wanting to be a surrogate primarily for the wife of the couple.

Surrogacy provides a role for women that causes discomfort among people who have difficulty accepting women's biological identity. Feminists have a long history of ambivalence toward women's being defined as childbearers, and they have an equally long history of rebellion against such a definition of themselves. It has been difficult for many women to perceive being a "breeder" in a positive way, and the term itself betrays contempt and devaluation of the childbearing role.

It is threatening for women to proclaim that childbearing—the use of their biology and physiology—is a source of such great personal value that they fulfill themselves. The issue of personal fulfillment is never addressed by feminist critics; its omission reduces surrogates to reproductive objects. The actual lived experience of the surrogate mothers is never referred to.

Many feminists, although espousing the principle of women's rights to control their bodies and to "reproductive freedom," wish to deny such rights to women in specific instances, when they do not like the choices other women are making. In other words, women should be able to have abortions, under the principle of freedom of choice and control of their own bodies, but should not bear a child for someone else.

At a moral level, it is amazing to us to see feminists fervently proclaim a woman's right to abort and thus destroy a potential life, yet deny a woman the right to create a life that wouldn't otherwise exist, and a life that is desperately wanted by another woman. It is unclear why women helping other women is exploitative, or why women who love being pregnant and pride themselves on their capacity to give birth are not acceptable. Many feminists seem to have "bought into" traditional cultural definitions and ideas about motherhood in an unquestioning way. It is certainly no accident that on the issue of surrogacy, feminists are in bed with churchmen, two groups that have rarely desired each other in the past.

Legislating Surrogacy—What Works and What Doesn't

Surrogate parenting has been practiced in the United States for over 37 years.[1] Twelve years ago the first surrogate contract was arranged. *The New York Times* (1987) estimated 2000 births. The American Organization of Surrogate Parenting Practitioners is able to document approximately 1000 births. It is difficult to establish a specific number for two reasons: New babies are born each month, and many arrangements are done privately, not through agencies, and are not recorded as surrogate births.

---

[1] Vicky and Eric Solo, born in Chicago, February 1954 and February 1958, by the same surrogate.

Of all the births that have taken place, only six birth mothers have not relinquished the babies.[2] The Baby M trial gave surrogacy national attention, albeit in an extremely negative perspective.

Without knowledge, understanding, or facts about the process, many states have rushed into legislation with a knee-jerk reaction to the Baby M trial. Bills originating in Florida, Indiana, Kentucky, Louisiana, Michigan, and Nebraska have tried to discourage surrogacy by declaring contracts invalid or banning fee payment. Michigan's legislation is currently being challenged, while Arkansas and Nevada have passed pro-surrogacy legislation.

In the states that have attempted to end surrogacy, the surrogate agencies report that the practice is still flourishing, but without legislation to protect it. In the next few years, other states will be dealing with forming legislation. We would like to critique the negative legislation in a constructive manner while making specific suggestions for regulation of surrogacy.

There are strong, paid professional antisurrogacy lobbies—i.e., the National Coalition Against Surrogacy, the National Committee for Adoption, in addition to the Catholic Church—that are attempting, entirely on the basis of prejudice and ignorance of surrogacy, to influence legislators to draft bills. The pro-surrogacy point of view is infrequently heard, while the antisurrogacy position is sensationalized and is favored by the press in its so-called objective reporting. Moreover, both couples and surrogate birth mothers understandably prefer anonymity and seldom speak out.

Two examples of bills that have been influenced by this lobby that have currently been introduced are California's Assembly Bill 3200, and New York's bill introduced into the Assembly and the Senate as A.10851-A and S.9134, respectively. I am vehemently opposed to any bill that (1) makes contracts void and unenforceable, (2) prohibits payment to surrogates, (3) bans agencies from being involved with surrogacy, and (4) makes surrogacy a criminal offense with criminal penalties (fine and/or jail) for those involved. This type of bill, in reality, attempts to end surrogate parenting as an option for childless couples who wish to build their families. It would be poor public policy to allow private surrogacy without the benefit of an experienced agency's being responsible for prescreening, couple/surrogate matching, counseling, and guidance, and without contracts to protect all parties involved. It would be poor public policy not to allow any compensation to the surrogate beyond the most basic pregnancy expenses. This would most certainly reduce the quality of the interested and available women and would leave all parties unprotected.

Surrogate parenting is not a new way to build families. In many cultures and at other times in our history, surrogacy has been seen as a positive solution to a societal problem. Several children now in their 30s, such as Eric and Vicky Solo (see footnote 1), have come forward to say how grateful and proud they are of their parents' courage, a courage that gave them existence and life that they would not otherwise have had.

Antisurrogacy legislation assumes that surrogate mothers, infertile couples, and all the children involved will be emotionally damaged by such arrangements to build families. There is absolutely no research to show that this is the case. On the contrary, published accounts show that in over 99% of the surrogate births that have

---

[2]Survey compiled by American Organization of Surrogate Parenting Practitioners, Indianapolis, Indiana.

occurred, all of the participants were satisfied with the results. Contrary to distorted and biased opinion, less than 1% of all surrogates to date have regretted their decision (see footnote 2). Furthermore, the authors of this type of bill have clearly not studied, or chosen to recognize, any of the current studies examining motivations of surrogate mothers, which have found surrogates to be capable, informed, stable, and competent women who are able to make conscientious and careful decisions regarding surrogate parenting. Nor have they bothered to read any of the six postpartum studies available. Surrogates overwhelmingly report emotional satisfaction and self-growth owing to their participation (Einwohner, in progress; Forst, 1988; Hanafin & Reading, 1989; Hardwick, 1989; Schwartz, 1989; Ulrich-Resnick, 1989).

These results are different in many respects from those gathered about the traditional adoption population, to which people have liked to *force* a comparison.[3] Assumptions about, and laws pertaining to, surrogate parenting cannot be drawn from analogies to adoption, which is in reality very different from surrogacy.

Several provisions of this type of bill create potentially disastrous consequences for future participants:

1. All those considering participating in a surrogate mother pregnancy are prohibited from availing themselves of knowledgeable professionals, such as mental health experts or surrogate agencies. Peer group support provided by the agency is extremely important for both couple and surrogate. In addition, the psychological counseling and guidance of a program can help participants solve their problems in a dignified and humanitarian manner.

2. Surrogacy is seen as *legal*, but professionals helping those parties to perform this "legal" act are seen as felons and liable to criminal penalties (i.e., fine and/or jail terms).

3. All surrogate contracts are void and unenforceable. Couples are allowed to engage in surrogacy but *only by themselves*, without any support or aid. Each arrangement would have to be worked out in isolation, as if it were the first. All the hard-won experience of 2000 preceding births would be unavailable to them. Inevitably, mistakes that could have been avoided will be made, frequently with damaging results. Allowing a woman to become a surrogate mother only so long as she does not enter into any type of agreement as to the responsibilities of the parents or the future of the child is clearly an act of political irresponsibility and neglect. It seems malevolent in its intent and would certainly be malevolent in its consequences.

4. Prohibiting payment to the surrogate will lead to the most feared outcome regarding surrogacy. Fewer women will volunteer, and these will not necessarily be the best qualified; yet they will be chosen, without the appropriate medical and psychological safeguards, because couples with no choice will feel even more desperate than they already do. Wealthier couples who can afford going out of state will be favored, and surrogacy will ironically become an arrangement for the rich. *The worst result will be in the coercion and pressure by childless couples on their friends and family members to "volunteer" to be a surrogate for them.* This will inevitably lead to disastrous outcomes, including custody battles, broken families, and emotional trauma for all parties. Such outcomes have been avoided until now because of fee payment, and because of the overseeing of most arrangements by responsible agencies and experienced professionals.

---

[3]Andrews, Lori B., Esq., Balboni, Michael, Esq., and Podell, Richard J., Esq.; Testimony before Assembly Standing Committee on Judiciary Assembly and Task Force on Women's Issues; December 6, 1988.

5. The result of all this is to leave all participants in surrogate arrangements in an extremely vulnerable position. Surrogate parenting is a complicated emotional, legal, interpersonal agreement that needs experienced professional supervision and support to prevent the occurrence of potential problems. Psychological screening of surrogates and couples, counseling on typical emotional reactions that can arise for the couple and the surrogate, and matching of specific couples with specific surrogates for the best "fit" all provide safeguards against poor outcomes. Outlawing such safeguards by making felons of the professionals who provide them cannot possibly improve the situation for individuals engaging in surrogacy.

6. Legislation that does not distinguish between surrogacy using a surrogate's egg and *in vitro* fertilization using the infertile couple's embryo is primitive. The denial of such differences points to the philistine level of understanding behind bills of this kind.

7. At a legal level, this type of bill unnecessarily interferes with the right to procreate, which encompasses the right to conceive, bear, and rear children, and the right to contract. The bill further violates the right of couples and surrogates to be aided by professionals. If tested, such a bill would be found unconstitutional.[4]

For all of these reasons, individuals should consider the reality of surrogacy in light of the existing facts, and not be swayed by hysterical and confounded fears and prejudices. This type of bill would eliminate an important option now available to infertile couples. Instead of limiting or eliminating surrogacy, it will merely drive the entire practice underground. Infertile couples will still reach out to surrogacy, but in secret, and without professional help or accountability. A bill that neglects regulation and hides from its responsibilities will certainly result in future tragedies.

What we need is bold, thoughtful, creative legislation that will provide standards and guidelines pertaining to the rights of voluntary surrogates, infertile couples, and the babies born by these arrangements.

After 2 years of work, the American Bar Association Family Law Section has written a Model Surrogacy Act, including specific recommendations for the regulation of surrogacy.[5] The American Organization of Surrogate Parenting Practitioners is also working to set standards for professional surrogate services, including screening, counseling, and legal protection for both couples and surrogates. The group unanimously agreed to support the American Bar Association's Family Law Section Model Surrogacy Act. We have proposed several standards to the organization that are already included in the surrogate mother program that we run, and a number of which are included in the American Bar Association Act. For example:

1. The birth mother does not sign away her parental rights before the delivery.
2. The birth mother has the opportunity to change her mind after the birth of the child. This would put the onus on the surrogate mother agencies to do more extensive screening. It would also serve the best interest of the child, who would be settled in a permanent home and not be "treated like a Ping-Pong ball," in the very rare instances of dispute.

[4]*Family Law Quarterly*, Surrogate Parenthood and Adoption Statutes: Can a Square Peg Fit into a Round Hole? (Chicago, Illinois: Volume XXII, Number 2, Summer 1988), p. 199.
[5]*Family Law Quarterly*, Draft of American Bar Association Model Surrogacy Act (Chicago, Illinois: Volume XXII, Number 2, Summer 1988), p. 123.

3. The birth mother's bodily integrity must be respected, and she must have control of all medical decisions, such as choice of doctor, hospital, medication, and method of birthing, and, specifically, that no contract can dictate whether she should abort or not.
4. The surrogate should be paid for her services a fee to be calculated by the month. Therefore, if she has a miscarriage in her fourth month or her seventh month, she is paid until that time. If she delivers a deformed child or if the baby is delivered stillborn, she should be paid the full $10,000 because she went through the full 9 months of pregnancy. This dispels the "baby-selling" argument; there may be no baby.
5. A surrogate must be represented by her own independent attorney.[6]

In contrast to the image of surrogate agencies carelessly accepting surrogates without regard for their welfare, it takes 3 to 6 months to be accepted into our program. We accept only one-third of the women who apply, and only after they pass three rigorous screening interviews. They are provided with reading material for and against surrogacy, and they have the option of speaking with other surrogates. We also meet with their husbands and families. The surrogates receive psychological counseling throughout the pregnancy, and they may continue counseling for up to a year after birth, not only for themselves but for their families, if necessary.

Fears of exploitation are often voiced by opponents of surrogacy when they link it with adoption. There are incomparable differences in profiles and life circumstances between a woman caught in a crisis situation with an unwanted pregnancy, who feels forced to give up her baby for adoption, and a surrogate who enters into a cooperative birthing arrangement voluntarily. The surrogate has legal, psychological, and medical counseling, and deliberates an average of 2 years before entering the agreement.

Women placing their children for adoption frequently (1) are in their teens, (2) have not had any other children, (3) are not married, (4) do not have a supportive home environment, and (5) are in poor financial circumstances and cannot support the child. In contrast, surrogate mothers (1) are older, with an average age of 26 to 27 years, (2) have birthed before and have children of their own, (3) are married or have a supportive home, (4) have an average income of $25,000, and (5) have a stable home environment (Aigen & Schmukler, 1987).

It is ironic, if not actually bizarre, that some people can favor a woman's having the right to abort and kill a potential life yet oppose that same woman's having the right to choose to create a life that would not otherwise exist, and one that is so desperately wanted by another woman. Women are doing this to allow other women to become mothers.

Surrogacy's worst opponents can point to only a handful of failures. Out of over 1000 documented births over the past 12 years in the United States, only 6 women have not relinquished the babies, and only about 12 others have had regrets. This is a 99% success rate.[7] Contrary to popular opinion, birth mothers generally report profound gratification, a feeling of heroism, and a long-standing sense of achievement. To date there have been six postpartum studies of surrogate mothers. All of

---

[6]Provisions included in the Surrogate Parenting Agreement of the Surrogate Mother Program of New York, 1989.

[7]Survey compiled by American Organization of Surrogate Parenting Practitioners, Indianapolis, Indiana, Spring 1988.

them have found these women to have been emotionally gratified and without regrets. Every woman who has birthed in our program has asked to birth a second time.

Notions of family and motherhood are changing. Surrogacy is needed, and it works. People will continue to seek out this last chance to build a family, and surrogate parenting should not be forced underground. Much unnecessary misery will be created by short-sighted, narrow-minded legislation. It is possible to deal responsibly with the medical, moral, emotional, and legal issues so that the rights of all parties are protected. There is no inherent conflict between the participants. Typically, the surrogate experience is joyful and gratifying for everyone involved.

AUTHORS' NOTES

The following are recommendations for anyone, and particularly legislators, interested in an objective investigation of surrogacy. The purpose is to gain a diversified perspective of the issues before forming an opinion or presenting a bill for legislation.

1. A body of scientific data now exists of studies with surrogate birth mothers. This includes motivational, socioeconomic, and six follow-up studies of women after they have birthed. This objective material is vital for anyone interested in a true investigation of the issue. (See References and Additional Reading.)

2. Legislators should speak directly with at least a dozen surrogates as well as with couples that have gone through the process. Surrogates can be contacted through their two national organizations: Surrogates by Choice, located in Dearborn, Michigan, and the National Association of Surrogate Mothers, in Los Angeles, California.

3. The American Organization of Surrogate Parenting Practitioners in Indianapolis, Indiana, should be contacted, and three or four member agencies should be interviewed. This will offer a full and different perspective of the realities and complexities involved in these arrangements. In this regard, the 50-page Surrogate Parenting Contract of the Surrogate Mother Program of New York can clarify how many sensitive issues can be adjudicated in a humanitarian way.

4. The *Family Law Quarterly*, Volume XXII, Number 2, Summer 1988, should be read in its entirety (see footnotes 4 and 5). It is completely devoted to legal issues involving surrogacy and includes a draft of the American Bar Associations' Model Surrogacy Act as drafted and approved by the Family Law section. In addition, Lori B. Andrews, project director of medical law at the American Bar Foundation, has been studying and writing extensively on surrogacy. She is a highly respected legal expert in the field, and no consideration of surrogacy would be complete without including her work. She testified at four of the five hearings of the New York State Assembly and Senate[8] (see also Andrews, 1981, 1984, 1987, 1989).

[8]New York State Joint Public Hearing of Assembly Standing Committee on Judiciary and Assembly Task Force on Women's Issues (New York: December 6, 1988); New York State Joint Public Hearing of New York State Assembly and New York State Judiciary Committee. Hearing on surrogate parenthood and new reproductive technologies (New York: October 16, 1986); New York State Senate Child Care Committee. Public hearing on surrogate parenting (White Plains, New York: April 10, 1988); New York State Senate Child Care Committee. Public hearing on surrogate parenting (Albany: May 7, 1988); New York State Senate Judiciary Committee, Senator John R. Dunne, Chairman. Surrogate parenting in New York: A proposal for legislative reform (Albany: January 1987).

5. New York State Senator John R. Dunne, chairman of the Judiciary Committee, and Senator Mary Goodhue, chairman of the Child Care Committee, have spent over a year investigating surrogacy. They held three public hearings that included testimony from national experts with diverse opinions. They compiled a brief titled "Surrogate Parenting in New York: A Proposal for Legislative Reform" and outlined a bill, S.1429. While we do not agree completely with the bill, it is a notable effort at dealing with the complex issues of regulating surrogacy. Because of its national scope, it can be used by any state as a model for drafting surrogacy legislation.

6. The complete testimony of the five legislative hearings listed in footnote 8 can be obtained by contacting the respective legislative offices. While New York and California[9] hearings are cited, the witnesses included experts from across the country. A wealth of information, for and against surrogacy, is included in this testimony.

7. The Congress of the United States Office of Technological Assessment published a report on infertility in May 1988 (U.S. Congress, 1988). While the section on surrogacy was already out of date with respect to agencies and number of births when printed, the report contains a great deal of information. Additionally, a survey of the surrogate mother agencies was conducted by Amy Zuckerman-Overvold and is published in her book, *Surrogate Parenting* (1987).

THE FUTURE

Surrogate motherhood, since its inception, has had the legitimate goal of allowing new families to be created. The primary reaction, however, has been terror, as if the process were a deliberate effort to undermine society's most cherished ideals, to encourage mothers to abandon their children, to steal children from their mothers and sell them into slavery. The culture has felt assaulted and has reacted in a typically paranoid way, attributing to the participants malevolent motives that correspond to these perceived "evil" goals. Thus, the couples are seen as mercenary, the intermediaries as ruthless "baby brokers," and the surrogates as both deluded and heartless.

We have tried to show that frightening human impulses and painful early experiences are "stirred up" by the idea of surrogate arrangements, to the point where these impulses and experiences are "seen" in surrogacy, rather than the more benevolent reality. As legislatures begin to grapple with the legitimacy of surrogacy, it is crucial that they do not mistake their fantasies for reality, or biased subjective views for the facts. Is this a case of selling babies as commodities or slaves, or does it have more to do with enabling couples to become families by enabling parenthood? Is this a case of an underprivileged, deprived woman being forced to abandon her child, or does it bear more resemblance to a middle-class, average mother, trying to further the goals of her children and family by being paid for using her procreative capacity, a capacity she values and gains great satisfaction in using, particularly to allow others to enjoy what she has enjoyed: Children?

Regulation of potential abuses is a legitimate concern that should be addressed. But the possibility of *potential* abuses, of *potential* difficulties that may arise, should not lead to the mistaken belief that abuses are inevitable or in any way typical. Sur-

---

[9]California Assembly Judiciary Committee. Public hearing on surrogacy (Sacramento: April 8, 1988).

rogate motherhood is based not on a conflict of interest but on mutuality of interests among the participants. Out of over 900 surrogate births (750 registered; 150–200 estimated additionally, undocumented; see Overvold, 1987), only 7 have encountered difficulties, a very small fraction. Is it possible that this is because surrogacy has been a "successful" experience for almost all who have participated?

References

Aigen, B. P., & Schmukler, I. (1987). Motivations of surrogate mothers: Parenthood and self-actualization. Unpublished.
Andrews, L. B. (1981). Removing the stigma of surrogate motherhood. *Family Advocate, 4,* 20.
Andrews, L. B. (1984). *New conceptions.* New York: St. Martin's Press.
Andrews, L. B. (1987). The aftermath of Baby M: Proposed state laws on surrogate motherhood. *Hastings Center Report, October/November.*
Andrews, L. (1989). *Between strangers.* New York: Harper & Row.
Einwohner, J. L. (n.d.). Additional study in progress, unpublished.
Family Law Quarterly (Summer 1988). Volume XXII, Number 2.
Forst, K. (1988). *Grief experiences: Social support networks of surrogate mothers.* Masters dissertation, Colorado State University.
Hanafin, H., & Reading, A. (1989). *Assessing the anxiety level and attitudes towards pregnancy in surrogates.* Los Angeles: Cedars-Sinai, Department of Psychological Studies.
Hardwick, S. (1989). Doctoral dissertation in process. Hofstra University.
New Jersey Record. (1988). Surrogate motherhood. January 14, p. 14.
New Jersey Supreme Court. (1987, September term). In the case of Baby M.
The New York Times. (1987). Surrogacy.
Overvold, A. Z. (1987). *Surrogate parenting.* New York: Pharos.
Schwartz, S. (1989). *Study on infertile women choosing adoption vs. surrogacy.* Doctoral dissertation, Cambridge School.
Ulrich-Resnick, R. (1989). *Surrogate mothers: Relationship between early attachment and the relinquishment of a child.* Doctoral dissertation, Fielding Institute.
U. S. Congress, Office of the Technology Assessment (1988, May). *Infertility: Medical and social choices* (OTA-BA-358). Washington, DC: U. S. Government Printing Office.

Additional Reading

Aigen, B. P. (1986). In the matter of Baby M. (Amicus curiae brief on behalf of Dr. Betsy P. Aigen, Psy.D., submitted by Annette Tobia, Esq.). Trenton, NJ: Supreme Court of New Jersey, Docket No. 27,050, Civil Action.
Aigen, B. P. (1988–1989). All benefit from cooperative birthing arrangements (Decree). New York: American Adoption Congress, Volume 7, Number 1.
American Bar Association (1989). National Conference of Commissioners on Uniform State Laws, Docket 113B.
American Organization of Surrogate Parenting Practitioners, Indianapolis, IN.
Dunne, J. R., and Goodhue, M. (1988). *Surrogate parenting in New York: A proposal for legislative reform* (S.1429).
Einwohner, J. L. (1987, August). *Psychological characteristics of surrogate mothers.* Paper presented at the annual convention of the American Psychological Association, New York.
Franks, D. D. (1981). *Psychiatric evaluation of women in a surrogate mother program* (Vol. 138, pp. 1378–1379). New York: Academic Press.

Hanafin, H. (1984). *Surrogate mother: Exploratory study*. Doctoral dissertation, California School of Professional Psychology, Los Angeles.

Hanafin, H. L. (1984, August). Paper presented at a meeting of the American Psychological Association.

Hollos, M. (1987, August 31). Paper presented at the annual meeting of the Association.

Parker, P. J. (1987). Motivation of surrogate mothers: Initial findings. *American Journal of Psychology, 140,* 117–118.

Parker, P. J. (n.d.) Additional study, unpublished.

Taub, N. & Cohen, S. (1989). *Reproductive laws for the 1990s*. Clifton, NJ: Humana Press.

Chapter 20
Lesbian Parenting
A Personal Odyssey

APRIL MARTIN

The 1980s have witnessed the emergence of a completely new family constellation. While there have probably always been lesbian families, until the past decade these were mainly the result of a heterosexual union that later dissolved. What is new in the past decade, by contrast, is the planned lesbian family. There has been a veritable baby boom among lesbians who know that they want to adopt or bear, and raise, children.

There are reasons for the current baby boom. It could not have happened in any previous era. The intact, heterosexual, two-parent family with gender-defined roles is no longer the uniform model of family life in our society. High divorce rates, along with a loosening of sex roles, have resulted in a wide variety of acceptable family constellations. A child in a single-parent family, a child in a reconstituted stepfamily, a child split between two different households is no longer stigmatized. The phrase "from a broken home" has become anachronistic. In addition, many unmarried heterosexual women, emboldened by changing mores, have chosen to become single mothers. The old stigma of illegitimacy has largely dissolved. At the same time, the civil rights movement has embraced sexual minorities, and gays and lesbians have been able to cast off much of the stigma of being "sick" or "sinful." With a new positive sense of identity, many lesbians have been able to reconsider old assumptions that their "deviant" life-styles must leave them childless. They have begun to feel that they have as much to offer a child as anyone else.

My lover, Susan, and I have been together for 10 years. Before that I was involved with men. I'd wanted children from as far back as I could remember, always assuming it would be in the context of a conventional heterosexual marriage. At times when I was between relationships, I had contemplated the possibility that if the right man never came along, I might choose to have a child alone. Then much to my surprise, the right woman came along when I was 29.

Susan's involvements had been primarily, though not exclusively, with men. She had been quite involved in helping to raise her sister's children but had never given

---

APRIL MARTIN • Private practice, 429 West 24th Street, New York, New York 10011.

much thought to the idea of having her own. Early in our relationship, however, we realized that we wanted to make a family.

From the beginning, Susan and I conceived of our relationship as a marriage. We knew we wanted the kind of closeness that results from making a home together, pooling our financial resources, sharing decision making, and looking forward to our middle and later years together.

It is not, for us, a matter of seeing the heterosexual model of marriage as a standard, or an ideal to be approximated. In fact, one of the appealing things about the gay and lesbian community is that there is an acceptance of diversity. There is more tolerance in the gay and lesbian world, generally, than one finds in heterosexual society for different ways of having a relationship. Gays and lesbians can make commitments with a variety of living arrangements, financial agreements, and understandings about emotional and sexual fidelity. In the straight world, many equivalent relationships would be pressured by inquiries of "Aren't you two ever going to get married?"

Lesbians with children also have more options in the lesbian world for how to arrange their lives. These include living communally, living as a single parent while sharing parenting with other women friends, and dozens of other possible arrangements. Many lesbians, though, like Susan and me, choose to set up a two-parent nuclear family. Susan and I have done it this way because it works for us personally. It appeals to our basic preference for monogamy. It fits well with our fantasies of what we want for ourselves and our children. And perhaps it also reflects a certain lack of creativity on our part or a certain conservatism in our natures. At any rate, our choices are our own.

There are some differences, however, between a lesbian or gay marriage and a heterosexual marriage. Internally, of course, is the fact that gender doesn't preassign any division of labor. We are free to negotiate the chores and duties of living on the basis of our abilities and preferences. The assignment of tasks has a fluidity to it that responds to our changing needs at any given time.

The major differences, however, between a lesbian or gay marriage and a heterosexual marriage are in the way society regards us. We are denied the benefits of legal sanctions, joint taxes, inheritance laws. Then our lack of a legalized union is used as justification for denying us the benefits of recognition by employers, insurance companies, landlords, and hospital visitation policies. Our lifelong commitments are not taken seriously, often even by our own friends and families. It often takes a lot of patient educating to get family and friends to see that a gay or lesbian marriage deserves and requires the same respect as any other marriage.

Though it was not all smooth sailing for us, we were fairly fortunate in having our marriage respected by our families, neighbors, and friends. Our situation was helped by our living in an urban area with a large gay and lesbian population. We were always able to be open and direct about being a couple. It was in this context, then, that we decided to have children.

At the time we didn't know anyone who had ever done it before. We set about researching the options for the next 3 years, feeling very much like pioneers facing uncharted territory. There were women on the West Coast who had done it, we heard, but none that we knew of in our area. We found a couple of pamphlets and articles that talked about lesbians' having children and about the mechanics of insemination. We spoke to doctors, therapists, friends, and family. Endless hours were spent discussing with each other the ramifications of bringing children into our lives.

The changes that becoming a parent effects on one's life are so many and so enormous that they can never be fully anticipated. Next to these changes, the specific issues that set lesbian parenting apart from heterosexual parenting are very small indeed. By far the bigger questions are whether or not one wants the work of childrearing, the presence of new little people in one's household, the changes in one's life plans, and the dramatic shift in focus that the role of parenting brings. Compared with that, the questions about whether or not to parent as a *lesbian*, while they need to be addressed and answered, are not as difficult.

We knew we wanted two children. Each of us has one sibling, and it seemed familiar to be a family of four. Also, it seemed especially important to us that if our offspring were going to grow up in an unusual type of family, each should have the companionship of a sibling so as not to feel isolated.

For various reasons, Susan and I each chose to be a biological mother. One factor in this decision was that we were not at ease with the thought of only one of us having the biological ties to both children. We didn't want either of us ever to feel as if she was not the "real" mother. With each of us having one biological and one nonbiological child, we felt that the equality and equivalency of our roles as mothers would be more manifest, both to us and to the outside world. Beyond this, of course, were also some deeper, more personal desires in each of us to conceive and give birth to a baby.

We decided to bear our two children at the same time. I'm not entirely sure why, in retrospect, except that we were eager to get on with our family. We felt we had the time and resources to care for two infants together and would enjoy seeing their parallel development. Perhaps we also were unconsciously hoping that their closeness in age might compensate for any distance they might feel because of not being biologically related to each other. It was very important to us that our children experience themselves as siblings, and that the world they encounter regard them as such, and not as unrelated children raised in the same household. Toward that end, we decided to give them the same last name—a hyphenated combination of my last name and Susan's. For us it was pretty much the same as expecting twins.

Old attitudes die hard, and a comother may have difficulty getting people to understand that she is a full parent. Society easily grasps that a heterosexual adoptive parent is a parent, even though he or she may not have been present from the child's beginnings. But a comother often has to struggle for her status, despite having shared all the joys, toils, and expenses from planning and conception through delivery and sleepless nights. This can be exacerbated by the child's early bonding with the biological mother. Starting at a few months of age and continuing until perhaps age 2 or 3, the child will generally show a preference for one parent. In a heterosexual marriage we say, of course, that the child wants its mommy. When there are two mommies, we may say that the child wants its *real* mommy. This may feel like quite a slap in the face to the nonbiological mother. The lesbian comother, lacking the social role recognition that helps fathers through times of rejection, may feel the stress of this period more keenly. We have seen this happen in lesbian families we know where there is only one child. Despite our having a biological child each, we have experienced some of this also. It has been important for us to take actions that keep affirming our positions as full and equal parents of *both* children. This has meant going together to the pediatrician, to parents' night at nursery school, and similar situations. It has also meant correcting friends and relatives when they talk to one child about "Mommy" and refer only to the biological mother.

We considered our options for getting pregnant. It was immediately apparent to us that we did not want to have to introduce a sexual relationship with a man into our lives. Getting pregnant can require months of trying, and we anticipated that the strain on us of having one or the other of us regularly sleeping with someone else could be pretty unpleasant. There was no question that, for us, alternative insemination with donated sperm was the way to go. Then followed the questions about how to locate a donor. A possibility that we rejected immediately was to ask someone we knew. While many lesbians do it this way, we felt we could not consider it.

There are no right answers as to how this should be done. Lesbians who choose a known donor sometimes do it because they are also choosing a man who will play a fathering role in the child's life to some extent. Some lesbians want a donor to agree *not* to have any involvement with the child, yet still prefer to have the donor be someone they know personally. There are several reasons for this. For one thing, knowing the donor gives them vastly more information about him than can be had through most anonymous donor arrangements. For another thing, some women feel that the child and/or society will manage more easily if there is someone's name on the "father" line of the birth certificate. A third reason for using a known donor is that it affords the child the option, later in life, of making contact with him should the child desire it. I know of two situations in which a woman chose her lover's brother as a donor, as a way of having the child be a true genetic blend of both women. In other situations, known donors have ranged from dear friends to passing acquaintances to men who have responded to an ad in the newspaper. They have been men who lived in the neighborhood or men who lived thousands of miles away.

It was our choice, though, to use unknown donors. It is probably the more conservative route to go, choosing safety over the possible advantages of having the donors be known to us. We felt very frightened about the things that could go wrong if we used known donors. What would stop a donor who professed to want no contact with the child from changing his mind once that child became a reality? We would have no legal protection, really, against a donor's being awarded visitation rights or joint custody or even outright custody. The courts are not favorable to lesbian mothers and are often, these days, favorable to fathers who want parental responsibilities. The thought of having someone invade the sanctity of our family, disrupt our children's lives, and cause unimaginable anguish for all of us was horrifying. We have known of many a heterosexual woman who truly loved the man she chose and married, yet who ended up in ugly painful battles with him over the children once the marriage fell apart. It just seemed to us to be too risky to gamble on a known donor's being someone who would respect our wishes and our status as the sole parents. As someone I know put it, it would be confusing biology with sociology—that is, assuming someone's suitability as a donor of genetic material qualified him as suitable for membership in our family.

Next to the fears of what could go wrong using a known donor, the advantages seemed to us to pale. It does make sense that if everything goes well with a known donor (i.e., he really does honor an agreement to have no involvement with the child, or else he does live up to a commitment to be involved in a way that is harmonious with everyone), the child might benefit from having his or her father be a tangible reality, but we just couldn't take the chance.

We then thought about how to locate an anonymous donor. The options seemed to be to go through a medical setting or a sperm bank, or to have a friend serve as a go-between, giving her the responsibility for making a selection based on our wishes, and trusting her to keep everyone's identities secret. We had a friend who offered, and we spent many evenings discussing it, but again there seemed to be too many problems. The chances of the donor's finding out who we are were much greater if he were known to someone who knows us. Also, at the time we thought of looking for a gay man to be the donor, feeling this would make him less likely to claim custody rights later on should our identities be divulged. Although this was before AIDS had become widespread in the gay male community, we were still concerned about the high rate of sexually transmitted diseases among gay men. We opted instead for a medical setting.

There are sperm banks that assist women who want inseminations. The Oakland Sperm Bank in California was established as a feminist resource. There are facilities on the East Coast as well, but at the time we couldn't locate them. I had some reason to suspect I might have fertility problems, so we decided that our best course was to find a fertility specialist who was willing to do donor inseminations on single women. We decided that I would try to get pregnant first, and as soon as it worked, Susan would try. I began calling ads in the Yellow Pages.

Some places I called said immediately that they wouldn't consider inseminating a single woman. One place said they would consider it if I would subject myself to a battery of psychological evaluations to determine if I was fit to be a mother. I didn't think they had any more ability than I had to judge my merits as a potential mother, and I disliked the idea that unmarried women are singled out for this particular humiliation. While many men are wonderful fathers, I resented the notion that the mere presence of a man in the home was the criterion for assumption that the child would be adequately cared for. Another place I called responded warmly and positively, and without judgment or reservation, so I set up an appointment.

The donors were part of a donor pool, an organized fertility service to which a physician could subscribe. The service screened potential donors from among the physicians at a major local hospital, then provided sperm to the fertility specialist according to the required specifications. I was asked to choose race, height (short, medium, or tall), and complexion (fair, medium, dark). I was also given the option to choose religious background, and to write in any other requirements. We didn't care about religion but did write in a few preferences for other characteristics. I don't think they were actually considered, though, because I know that the sperm specimens they ordered for me were coded only as ABA, meaning Caucasian, medium height, fair complexion. Having no more control than that was frightening. We simply had to trust that people we didn't know, and whom even our physician didn't know, were in fact being conscientious about their medical histories and good health.

The only thing I was asked to sign was a paper stating that it was entirely my choice to become pregnant as an unmarried woman, and that I would not hold the physician responsible for any consequences for my decision. Though we did not tell the doctor at first that we were lesbians, he did come to know eventually and did not seem to have any particular feelings about it one way or another. We will always be grateful to him for his respectful manner and his help.

The mechanics of donor insemination are incredibly simple. The donor masturbates and ejaculates into a clean specimen jar. In my case, the specimen was then usually sent by taxi to the fertility clinic where I would be waiting. An assistant would check the specimen under the microscope to make sure the sperm count and motility looked good. The semen is then drawn into a syringe, which is inserted through a speculum into the vagina. The sperm are deposited right near the opening of the uterus. A plastic-covered sponge is put in the vagina to retain the semen, and the patient is asked to lie quietly for a little while. I had been placed on a fertility drug because of some ovulatory dysfunction. With the drug, I could gauge fairly precisely when ovulation would occur. Two or three inseminations would be scheduled on the days around ovulation. I got pregnant in the second month of trying.

There is nothing medically complicated about the process. Women who don't have the money to do it through a physician (it can be *very* expensive) or who just don't want to deal with a medical setting can do it at home with a turkey baster.

Susan started trying right away. She also got pregnant in her second month of trying. So, the beginning of 1981 found us expecting one baby in August and another at the end of September.

My family was delighted for us. These were to be the first grandchildren. We had begun about a year earlier to discuss with them our plans to have a family. They had had time to adjust to the idea, and to see how very excited and happy we were about it. Though they expressed some initial apprehensiveness, by the time we actually got pregnant they were enthusiastic supporters. Our friends cheered us on and gave us a double baby shower. I'm sure many of our neighbors didn't know what to make of us. We waddled down the street together, sometimes arm in arm. The salesperson at the maternity boutique was a bit baffled that we chose some items such that both of us could wear them, and the bill for the shopping spree was charged to our mutual address.

We chose an obstetrician who, though heterosexual herself, was extremely supportive. Exhausted from having recently given birth to her own second baby, she thought the idea of having two mommies in the family was wonderful. We went to our obstetric appointments together and listened to the heartbeats of our children-to-be. We also went to films on childbirth at the hospital, and to Lamaze classes.

There were four other couples in the Lamaze class, all of them heterosexual. We would practice first with me breathing and Susan coaching, then switching places so Susan could practice getting through contractions while I held the stopwatch. We were a bit shy at first with the other couples, but eventually we warmed to each other and felt pretty well accepted.

There is a gay pride button around that reads, "How dare you presume I'm heterosexual!" There were times during my pregnancy when I wished I had a maternity blouse with that inscription. Being a lesbian hasn't always been part of my identity, but it clearly has come to be an important part of it over the years. I often hear heterosexuals say they don't think it's anyone's business if someone is gay, and that gay people should just keep private issues to themselves. But it's not as if heterosexuality is a private issue. It is displayed everywhere—billboards, television, shop windows, the street. And there is the presumption, always, that unless one actively declares oneself to be different, one is part of the majority. It is not a relief to me to be seen as heterosexual. I have worked hard to understand and embrace the feelings I have for women. I've also worked hard to understand society's fluctuations of tolerance and intolerance for differences, for minorities, for women, for sexuality. It is both the burden and the contribution that minorities make to be the gadflies of society's conscience. We help to protect society from the disease and stagnation of a narrowly focused, homogeneous self-righteousness. The presence of diversity helps keep us all a little more humble and a little more alive. I have a certain gratitude for being in that position, and a sense of community with other minorities because of it. It was at times especially difficult, then, to walk down the street pregnant and know that other gays and lesbians were merely dismissing me as one of the mainstream.

Michael George was born by cesarean section after 12 hours of labor on August 13. He was the most wonderful sight we'd ever seen. Susan was with me throughout the labor and in the operating room during the surgery, for which I was awake. (They had trouble finding a surgical gown that would fit over her 8-months-pregnant belly.) She saw him first and held him right away. Then they took him away to be cleaned up and examined while I lay in the recovery room and Susan called our families. While we were planning his future, a doctor came in and gave us the devastating news that Michael was born with a condition called achondroplasia—a form of dwarfism.

A male achondroplastic dwarf can expect to reach an adult height of 4'3" or so, with a relatively normal-size torso and proportionally shorter arms and legs. Other than his size and proportions, though, Michael was not impaired in any way—his intelligence was fine and his expected life-span was normal. In the midst of incredible pain and incredible joy—alternating often within the same minute—we began to learn about dwarfism.

Achondroplasia occurs 90% of the time as a spontaneous mutation of a single gene. No one knows why the gene mutates or how to predict it. It has no known relationship to the genetic family histories of either parent. It just happens. Once the gene has mutated, however, it becomes a dominant gene—meaning that the offspring of someone with the gene for achondroplasia will definitely be dwarfs if they inherit the gene, which they have a 50% chance of doing if only one parent is a dwarf. I called the fertility doctor, who managed to trace the donor. The donor was unquestionably normal. We had to accept that we were just participants in one of nature's vagaries.

My father set to work right away with plans to build Michael a set of extra-small furniture and riding toys. Everyone in the family admired how wonderful he was. Susan's immediate and unreserved rapture with Michael gave comfort to my sagging spirit. As thrilled as I was to have him, I was also afraid for him, and felt as if I'd failed in some way to give him everything he deserved. Never having even met a dwarf, I had no idea what kind of life he could expect. Would he feel like an outcast? Would he have lovers, get married, have children? Would he be able to achieve things in his life? Through our network of friends and family we learned of the Johns Hopkins work on dwarfism, and of an organization called Little People of America. We met a wonderful woman and her family, including her dwarf daughter, Anna. Anna played the piano for us, rode her bicycle, and seemed to be absorbed in the usual assortment of birthday parties, friends, and school activities typical of any 7-year-old. Her life was so hearteningly ordinary that I began to feel a real hopefulness. We learned of dwarfs who were in many of the major professions, and dwarfs with good marriages. It was clear that all Michael would need to have a rich and satisfying life was to feel good about who he was.

People so often ask whether we think our being lesbians will have *negative* effects on our children. We came to realize that our lesbianism gave us some particular *advantages* in understanding Michael. Being gay in a predominantly heterosexual world had forced us to grow—to go through a process of learning how to value ourselves independent of society's judgments. It was immensely helpful to understand that Michael would be going through the same process—i.e., learning to accept and value his differentness, and finding the strength that comes from adopting a broader world view. That there would be some painful moments for him no longer seemed so terrible. We could help him use those moments to grow instead of retreat. I don't think

I could have ever come to that without the experience of coming to terms with my lesbianism. And I certainly couldn't have done it without the loving support of Susan and so many others. With excitement, we pursued the networking process that would make us a part of the Little People's community, much as we had pursued connections to the lesbian and gay community years earlier.

Seven weeks after Michael's birth, Emily Carol arrived after a nice, normal, 6-hour labor and delivery. While I was helping Susan through the delivery, Michael was in the hospital lobby with a friend so I could run down and nurse him as necessary. Emily looked absolutely perfect, but I was so frightened for her that I didn't dare to get excited until we got the word from the pediatrician. The word was that she couldn't be healthier. Barely 24 hours later we bundled her home and began a life with two babies.

We had felt so proud of ourselves for learning how to handle Michael—we'd been parents for 7 weeks already and we figured we were pros by now. We hadn't counted on how different two babies can be. The things that soothed Michael were intolerable to Emily, and the things we eventually discovered would work for her would have set him howling. To add to the household chaos, I had to go back to work the week after Emily was born, having already taken 2 months away from my practice. Susan did a heroic job of caring for both babies while I was seeing patients. She breathed an audible sigh of relief every time I came in on a break from work.

My office is in the same building as our apartment. I arranged my work schedule so that I could nurse Michael at reasonable intervals between patients. Sometimes he'd get hungry before I arrived and Susan would nurse him until I got there. It was a help, at least for a few weeks, that she was able to nurse. After a while, though, he wouldn't accept her milk. Even when Susan's breast milk was put in a bottle, he became able to distinguish it from mine and rejected it.

Emily refused to nurse. We tried everything we could think of, and got suggestions from every resource we could find. Nothing worked. The nursing situation made Emily absolutely frantic despite our most gentle, soothing efforts. We were told to give her no bottle feedings, even if she didn't eat for a few days. She didn't eat for a few days. I tried. Susan tried. Emily would nurse for about 30 seconds and then start to cry. We decided not to let this become a battle of wills, and Emily became a very contented bottle-fed baby.

As Michael and I continued to have the special contact of a nursing relationship, Susan and I noticed some difficult feelings engendered in both of us. For one thing, the sheer amount of time nursing took left me proportionately less time for Emily. I felt left out of some of the early contact with her. Susan similarly felt left out of some of the contact with Michael. She felt especially awful at times when nothing she could do would comfort him, yet my arrival (with milk) would soothe him instantly. One solution we found was to let Susan have exclusive contact with Michael at bathtime. (Michael loved bathing; Emily hated it.) Meanwhile, I took whatever opportunities I could find to spend time with Emily. Despite feeling that we were basically handling things very well, we were never completely free of feelings of deprivation, guilt, and inadequacy about the inequities of our relationships with the two babies. These feelings were probably magnified by our physical exhaustion, but they were certainly offset by the deep pleasure of it all. Life was intense.

Two days after Christmas—Michael and Emily were 4-1/2 months and 3 months old, respectively—we were in the car on our way to visit my mother and stepfather. The babies fell asleep in their car seats as usual. Emily woke up as soon as we got there. Michael continued sleeping. So as not to wake him, we brought the whole car seat, with him sleeping in it, into the house and set it down. We went through about 5 minutes of exchanging greetings, removing coats. When I checked on Michael a few minutes later, he had stopped breathing. He was limp in my arms. We tried mouth-to-mouth resuscitation during the few seconds it took to get in the car and rush to the hospital. At the hospital they revived his heartbeat but said he was probably too brain-damaged to survive. Susan and I spent the night with him in the hospital. He died the next morning. His death was termed a SIDS (sudden infant death syndrome).

Anyone who has ever lost a child will know what we felt and lived through. Those who haven't are better off never knowing what that pain is like. I can't imagine that life on earth holds anything worse. It was the strength of our love for each other, and the love and support of our friends and families, that helped us survive.

We were luckier than people who lose their only child. We didn't also lose our roles as parents. But that brighter side to our misfortune is something we can appreciate only in retrospect. In the months of anguish that follow losing a child, there is no way to feel lucky about anything. It only hurt when people would say, "At least you still have Emily." Of course we were overjoyed to have Emily, but it didn't lessen the pain of losing Michael.

Wanting Emily not to be deprived or hurt by our grieving, we made special efforts to give her attention that was cheerful, playful, and loving. I found I could manage it only for a little while until thoughts of Michael would make me need time alone to cry. Then Susan would take over with Emily until she needed time for her own grieving, by which time I would have recovered.

We decided to have another baby. I wanted very much to become pregnant again, and we both wanted a family with two children. I started trying to get pregnant again about 2 months after Michael died.

Sometimes, perhaps, our bodies know what we can't admit to ourselves consciously—that it was not time yet to have another baby. I was under phenomenal stress—mourning, parenting, working—and the result was a stretch of infertility that lasted for 2 years. Driven by grief and longing, I went to the fertility clinic many times every month, going through what seemed like an endless series of procedures, fertility drugs, insemination, consultations, and sonograms. I became obsessed and quite depressed. I didn't know anyone who could really understand what I felt, and I was putting tremendous strain on Susan. In desperation, I joined Resolve, an organization providing support to infertile couples. I attended a support group for women—seven heterosexually married women and me. It isn't easy being the only lesbian in a group of strangers with whom one is supposed to talk intimately. I did it with my heart pounding, and if I hadn't been so desperate I would never have gone. But I did get tremendous help and support there. In a couple of months I was able to face the possibility that I might never be able to conceive again. I was able to separate my need to *bear* a child from my desire to *have* another child. Susan and I agreed that we would give it 3 more months, by which time our financial resources would be pretty well used up. If I didn't conceive by then, she would get pregnant and have another child for us.

As it happened, I got pregnant that very month. Our son, Jesse Eugene, was born in August 1984—arriving after 22 hours of labor and a cesarean section—looking wonderfully healthy and beautiful. During all that time—from Michael's death to Jesse's birth—Susan got the short end of the stick. The loss of Michael was every bit as hard for her as it was for me. He was every bit as much her son as mine, and her heart could not have been more broken. But people are slow to grasp the concept of a lesbian family. Even some of our close friends, both gay and straight, would somehow perceive the situation as if Michael were *my* child and Emily were Susan's. They would offer me sympathy and condolences about losing Michael, and tell Susan that she should take good care of me. She stood there at times feeling as if her grief was invisible. We made an effort, whenever it seemed appropriate, to let people know that Susan's loss was equal to mine. Some of them were able to recognize the assumptions they'd been making and repair their approaches to us, for which we were very grateful. Still, though, Susan got passed over.

There were other reasons why Susan did not get as much support as she needed. One is that she seemed to buy into the idea that she had to be strong to support me through this, so she took on that role herself. And in my neediness during that painful time I took advantage of her willingness to be my rock. In short, we both gave *me* the opportunity to grieve loudly and openly for many, many months. She gave me comfort unfailingly, whenever I was in pain, and that gave me the strength to work, and to live, and to care for Emily. She was patient and loving through my insufferable crankiness during the infertility. The pregnancy with Jesse had some frightening (but ultimately insignificant) complications, and together we held our breath until he was born. At that point, when I became able to truly feel hopeful again, all Susan's unacknowledged pain caught up with her.

Jesse's presence was painful at times to Susan because it brought back so many memories of Michael. It was frightening to begin to love him because we feared he might never wake up from his next nap. He was born in August, like Michael, so he went through each little developmental advance at the same time of year Michael did. We stayed awake at night listening to him breathe. Christmas found us both frightened, exhausted. Susan was irritable a lot. I tried to be understanding but also felt overwhelmed. We fought, we cried, and we muddled through.

Things got easier with the new year. Jesse not only survived past the critical age for most SIDS deaths, he grew to such strapping abundance that we all relaxed. Emily, who had undoubtedly felt the strain on the family and had become a rather cautious child, began to blossom. She became willing to get on with her somewhat delayed toilet training, and this coincided with her becoming much more willing to take risks in general. Though she has always been a very special, joyful, uniquely imaginative child, she now became freer to be difficult and obstinate at times—signs to us that she was feeling the confidence to become more independent.

As of now, Emily is 6 years old and Jesse is 3. She is wise, subtle, private, with a dry sense of humor and a wonderful rapport with other children. He is cheerful, precocious, devilish, incredibly sweet and open. I couldn't feel more blessed.

People often ask us what we plan to tell the children about our family structure, and who the donors were. (It feels more accurate to use the term *donor* than the word *father*, which has implications of a relationship that doesn't exist in this situation.) We plan, of course, to tell them the truth—and have in fact already begun the process. I call it a process because I don't think it is a static piece of information that gets imparted to the children once and then belongs to them. At different ages the questions about their origins will have different meanings, based on their cognitive and emotional levels of development. Both children already know that we are a family of two mommies. They see that most other families have a mommy and a daddy, though they also have seen many other lesbian families and know that our family structure is not unique in the world. The children hear a lot of talk in our house about gay and lesbian issues. They have been on the Gay Pride Day march with us every year. Emily understands that being gay and being heterosexual are different ways of loving, but that there are more heterosexuals than gays. She also has been told that some heterosexuals have a hard time understanding why we're different and even think we're wrong, and that we march to help them see that our way of loving is a good way.

The children know that we wanted a family and planned to have them. They know that Emily grew in Susan's belly, and Jesse in mine. Recently, a discussion came up concerning the biology of reproduction. Until then, Emily wasn't aware that a man is necessary for conception. Sparked by her interest in a TV program that discussed the mating behavior of animals, I explained about one seed coming from the male and one from the female. I went on to explain that if the two parents are a mommy and a daddy, the mommy gets the seed from the daddy to combine with her own. Because we had no daddies in our family, though, we had gone to the doctor to get some male seeds. That explanation clearly sufficed for the moment. It has not yet occurred to her to ask where the doctor gets the seeds. We'll give her a while to come up with that question on her own, while opening up the topic of reproduction from time to time to encourage her curiosity.

As they evidence readiness to hear, the children will know that some generous and caring men are willing to donate sperm to women who want to have babies. We will tell them what little we know about the donors, and encourage them to express their feelings about it. We are prepared, I hope, to be able to listen with interest and compassion, and without guilt or defensiveness, to anything they might feel about not having a father or not knowing who the donor is.

I can't predict what my children will feel about growing up in a lesbian family. It is possible that it may not be a problem at all for them. My own parents had made some courageous choices in their lives—marrying out of their religions, for one. I was aware, growing up, that my family was different. While there were some isolated moments of wanting to be like everyone else, I admired my parents' independence. I remember feeling proud of being both Jewish and Catholic, and of having a mother who was a scientist. It is my fond hope that my children will have similar feelings about their family, though that will depend on many factors over which I have no control. For one, it will depend on who Emily and Jesse turn out to be. If either of them cares very deeply about wanting to just like everyone else, then it may be harder for them. In general, we feel we can most be of help to them by just being willing to listen to their feelings about it. After all, most of us end up with some things about the "givens" of our lives that we wish were different. If we are angry or sad about our circumstances, we deserve to have those feelings heard with sympathy. Ultimately, we make peace with the aspects of our lives that we cannot change by weighing the negative feelings alongside the gratitude and love for the good things in our lives. Jesse and Emily are as wanted and loved as they could be, and we expect that will count for a lot.

Most children who are told or come to realize that their mother is a lesbian are children of separation and divorce. They have usually had and lost a father, or maybe had and lost a mother, if she doesn't get custody. They have to cope with the real loss of one parent, as well as the confusion and loss around so many assumptions they had made about who their parents are. They have to deal with feeling they were lied to for so long. They may feel the lesbian mother's own shame and guilt or the father's anger about it and conclude that lesbianism really *is* something bad. They have probably grown up in a household in which gayness wasn't talked about in any constructive way, and so they have no tools with which to understand why people are gay, why it isn't talked about, why some people think it's bad. These kids are left alone to deal with difficult feelings and, indeed, have a right to be angry and upset about the situation. Yet even under circumstances like these, many of these kids manage to come to a loving understanding of both parents and the situation. The ones who don't at first may, in time. Some children never do get over the hurt.

The planned lesbian family, though, is in a completely different situation. Having one's parents be different becomes the *only* issue. It need not be muddied up by separation, loss, fights, court battles, lies, shame, secrecy. And I am personally inclined to think that differentness, by itself, presents not a hardship but an opportunity for growth.

So far, to my knowledge, Emily has been invited to every birthday party in her social circle. Her friends come and play at our house. The other first-grade parents are friendly and chatty with us. If there are any parents who have disparaging things to say about us, we are unaware of it. Any such comments have been beyond our earshot, which is all we can ask. Neither the children nor we have ever been treated less than respectfully. On one occasion I called the parents of a school chum of Emily's about PTA business. The phone was answered by Emily's friend, and we exchanged a few words. As she passed the receiver to her mother, I heard her say, "It's Emily's mom. Well, it's one of them—she's got two." It was said about as casually as if she'd said I lived down the block. The children who troop in and out of our house with increasing frequency seem to have little difficulty grasping that we are "the parents." Jesse, in nursery school for the first time, is starting to get his share of invitations to play dates and birthday parties. We have made a point of going to school, meeting with the teachers, and offering to help in any way with their understanding of us as a family. We have asked that when they discuss families in school, they make an effort to include the two-mommy family constellation.

When we were first looking into nursery schools I made an appointment for one afternoon with the director of a nearby school. Susan unexpectedly freed her schedule and wanted to come along. I called the director, and not wanting to make lengthy explanations on the phone, just informed her that "my spouse is coming with me to our appointment." There is always a certain amount of anxiety for us in these situations. The director, for her part, accepted us with warmth and interest when we arrived.

Having children has required of us that we "come out" as lesbians over and over again, to people with whom we would ordinarily never get personal. Susan regularly stops in at the bakery with Jesse. The young woman there always gives Jesse a cookie. One day I happened to go in with Jesse. The saleswoman, making conversation with Jesse, asked him, "Where's your mommy?" He pointed to me. Then she asked me who the other woman is who always comes in with him. I was publicly on the spot—in this as in countless other situations—knowing my children were drawing conclusions from whatever they heard me answer. I followed my rule of "When in doubt, tell it like it is." I explained that he has two mommies. She looked puzzled. She is from a different culture, and English is not her first language. I didn't think the word *lesbian* would mean much to her, so I just explained again that we are a different kind of family—two women together who have children. She thought about it some more, then smiled broadly and said, "Oh!" and offered Jesse his cookie.

At home the kids refer to Susan and me as Mommy Bear and Mommy Seal, respectively. Bear and Seal were pet names Susan and I had for each other before we had children. Because I was the seal, when I was pregnant we joked that I was carrying a baby bear (that is, Susan's baby), while Susan carried the baby seal. Thus, in our playful family mythology, we refer to the kids as Emily Seal and Jesse Bear—names that they love. With our close friends who know us, the children will say, "Mom Bear baked that pie" or "Mom Seal is at a meeting," or Emily will refer to Susan and Jesse as in "the Bears went to the store." They seem clearly to understand, however, that to the outside world we need more formal designations. Whenever it is necessary to refer to one of us in a way that distinguishes between us—that is, where just plain "Mommy" isn't enough—we have taught them to call us Mommy Susan and Mommy April.

Sometimes people ask whether we feel that Jesse needs male role models. Yes, of course, he does. For that matter, so does Emily. Men are half the people in the world, and we want both our children to feel at ease with them. I don't honestly know whether Jesse has more need than Emily to have a man around with whom to identify. It is certainly true that in the normal course of development, some boys identify most with their mothers and some girls identify with and emulate their fathers primarily, without there being any concomitant identity problems. And children have been growing up in families without men for centuries. There have always been families where the men have gone off to war or migrated to find work or were never involved to start with. The children were then raised by a mother and her mother, or a mother and her sisters, or other such arrangements. They surely identify to greater or lesser degrees with the caregiving women in their lives. In addition, they pick and choose role models from among the men outside the family (as well as from other women outside the family). Jesse and Emily have exposure to a number of men. They have an involved grandfather, and about 8 or 10 men who are part of our circle of friends. I am satisfied that all of the men we are close to are admirable and good people. If my children want to identify with any of them I would be delighted. Meanwhile, Susan and I hope we are providing pretty good models in ourselves of how to be a person.

We have no particular concerns or wishes regarding our children's eventual sexual/affectional preferences. Not that it would matter if we did. Ultimately, if people grow up in a nurturing environment, they will be whoever they will be. The only result that can be achieved by trying to control someone's sexual orientation is the creation of a tormented psyche, divided against itself. It seems fairly safe to say that Jesse and Emily will not likely suffer from such torment. They will, of course, be subject to all of the gross and subtle pressures society applies to suppress and devalue homoerotic love, while heterosexuality is proclaimed the only legitimate path. At home, however, they will grow up feeling our respect for human variety. We are aware that sexual preference may be decided early, or it may shift at later points in life. We hope to encourage our children to look in their own hearts for what they feel, and to treat those feelings, whatever they are, with respect. Ultimately, we care very much about the quality of love they find in their lives, and not a whit about the gender of the loved one.

Suggested Reading

Anonymous, S., & Anonymous, M. (1979). *Woman controlled conception*. Berkeley: Womanshare Books.

Hanscombe, G. E., & Forster, J. (1981). *Rocking the cradle; Lesbian mothers: A challenge in family living*. Boston: Alyson.

Martin, A. (1982). Some issues in the treatment of gay and lesbian patients. *Psychotherapy: Theory, Research, and Practice, 19(3)*, 341–348.

Pies, C. (1985). *Considering parenthood, a workbook for lesbians*. San Francisco: Spinsters/Aunt Lute.

Pollack, S., & Vaughn, J. (1987). *Politics of the heart, a lesbian parenting anthology*. Ithaca, NY: Firebrand Books.

Rich, A. (1976). *Of woman born, motherhood as an experience and institution*. New York: Norton.

Santa Cruz Woman's Health Collective (1979). *Lesbian health matters*! Santa Cruz, CA: Santa Cruz Woman's Health Center, 250 Locust Street, Santa Cruz, CA 95060.

Saphira, M. (1984). *Amazon mothers*. Ponsonby, Auckland: Papers, Inc., P. O. Box 47-398.

Vida, G. (1978). *Our right to love—A lesbian resource book*, Englewood Cliffs, NJ: Prentice-Hall.

Chapter 21

Bearing the Unbearable
The Psychological Impact of AIDS

STEPHEN B. GOLDMAN

Acquired immune deficiency syndrome. AIDS. The most horrible affliction—on an individual or epidemiological level—anyone ever imagined. The kind of nightmare one always dreads and then reassures oneself is just the guilt-ridden concoction of an overbearing superego. Anxiety-driven obsessions, like the fairy tales that children need to deal with in order to gain a sense of mastery over the dreaded and unknown. And now it turns out that the worst of them is true.

And gets worse every day. Not only in the numbers of victims (more than 74,000 cases reported in the United States as of September, 1988), which is terrifying in itself, but also in the constantly multiplying forms the disease can assume. The initially discovered "opportunistic infections" were cruel enough: pneumocystis carinii pneumonia (PCP), a recalcitrant and enervating infection caused by ubiquitous organisms that a healthy immune system is able to keep at bay, and Kaposi's sarcoma (KS), a skin cancer that begins as small, unobtrusive lesions on the skin's surface and can then rapidly spread into a horrifying series of disfiguring purple growths, sometimes all over the face and body and sometimes internally where it can damage organ systems. But new horrors develop regularly. Many AIDS patients develop neurological diseases, including meningitis, encephalitis, and brain tumors (usually lymphomas), with neuropsychiatric impairments ranging from mild memory deficits to outright dementia.

Direct dealings with this illness produce a basically altered set of emotional expectations. At a distance, most people are able to rely upon denial: "This is awful, but it can't/won't happen to me or those close to me." There is usually some degree of comfortable detachment unless a ruthless reality destroys it. This process is very painful and disorienting, and, particularly for those of us in the helping professions, it affects our professional as well as personal lives.

In preparing this chapter, I initially considered my own experiences with AIDS patients and HIV-positive individuals. (Someone who is seropositive on the HIV antibody test has been exposed to the virus and is probably infected to some extent.

STEPHEN B. GOLDMAN • Psychology Externship Program, New Hope Guild Centers, Brooklyn, New York.

Estimates of how many among such individuals will develop symptoms and actually be diagnosed with AIDS vary yearly; it ranges from 50% to as high as 90%, depending upon the population studied.) In addition, I read whatever papers, both professional and journalistic, were available. Finally, I conducted interviews, individually and in groups, with AIDS patients, their lovers, friends, and families, and with health care professionals (mainly in mental health) who work with this population.

The Patients

My own experience with AIDS has been predominantly with gay men, and a similar emphasis occurs in most of the writings on the subject. I attempted to balance this presentation by interviewing professionals who work with women and children with AIDS and with intravenous drug abusers, but the bias still exists. This is probably due to the fact that gay men are the largest group affected. They were also the earliest group affected in this country (heterosexuals predominate among infected Africans), so that they were the first to form self-help organizations and community care networks. For example, among those I interviewed were many volunteers and professionals affiliated with the Gay Men's Health Crisis (GMHC) in New York City. I appreciate their indispensable cooperation.

Owing to the common use of defense mechanisms such as denial, no one is really equipped to deal with a diagnosis of AIDS, no matter how much one has been anticipating it. According to Richard Wein, former Director of Group Services at GMHC, the typical reaction to actually receiving a diagnosis is denial or detachment. The patient may suddenly achieve "instant mental health" and have no problems to talk about. Generally, if recently diagnosed patients are interested in any kind of counseling during this early stage, it has to be short-term and time-limited. Mr. Wein recommends that therapists and health workers not challenge that initial reaction; the patient needs time to ready himself for a new reality. When that time comes, one hears frequent phrases like "everything's changed; nothing will ever be the same again." At that point, their perspective is greatly altered and most patients are terrified of separation and loss. Some of these people act out their fears counterphobically, such as by taking distance from their friends and family in order to protect themselves and others from the pain of loss. Others are more aware of their true feelings; in therapy groups, for example, they may become very upset about the illness of other group members, a change in the composition of the group, or even a brief interruption in meetings. Mr. Wein suggests that AIDS patients in groups should not have enforced vacations; that is, if possible, groups should maintain continuity, even if some group members or the leader are not able to participate, so that individual patients can maintain a sense of connection and do not feel abandoned.

Another common theme among gay men with AIDS is the double dilemma they must face if their family is unaware of their homosexuality. In the situation where someone with AIDS has kept his gayness a secret from his family, he may realize that he needs their help after being diagnosed; or he may simply desire more closeness or reconciliation with the family while he is still functional, but be stymied out of fear of hurting them or of incurring their rejection because of his sexual orientation. For many people, acknowledging that one is a person with AIDS (PWA) is tantamount to stating that you are gay, and that may be an issue that the individual and his family have avoided for years. Most PWAs belong to minority groups in some sense (gays, drug abusers, infants, hemophiliacs), and this complicates the interpersonal aspects of dealing with their illness.

On the other hand, there are many cases where a gay PWA's family was quite aware of his sexual orientation, even though it was never spoken of. A psychologist with AIDS states that the hardest moment since getting diagnosed was "telling my mother." Sometimes, sharing the knowledge that he has AIDS allows the family and the patient to be more open with each other and to become closer than before.

In March 1986, I attended a professional workshop on psychological issues concerning AIDS. The instructor was Lewis Katoff, a psychologist who is currently the director of client services at GMHC. Dr. Katoff described Kübler-Ross's (1969) "stages of death and dying," including denial, anger, resignation, and, eventually, acceptance. He commented at that workshop that he had always had trouble comprehending the stage labeled "acceptance"; he could not imagine anyone—particularly a young person—actually becoming comfortable with his or her own death. Just a year later, in March 1987, I was organizing a panel on the psychological aspects of AIDS for the New York State Psychological Association. When I invited Dr. Katoff to be a panel member, he informed me that he had been diagnosed with AIDS 6 months before, following a case of PCP. He was willing to be a panelist if he could describe his own experiences as a PWA as well as a mental health professional.

At that panel, Dr. Katoff's comments were wise, funny, and profoundly moving. He discussed the inner conflicts that a PWA must face concerning medical treatment. It is important to believe in the method of treatment if it is to work for you. This psychological truth is lost on many medical doctors, who tend, at the least, to be unresponsive to the emotional states of patients. Dr. Katoff stated that he always defines his physicians as "consultants"; that is, it is up to him to make the important decisions about treatment after getting opinions from doctors. After all, he is the one who will either survive or suffer serious consequences from the choices that are made. For example, in the hospital when he had the pneumonia that led to his diagnosis of AIDS, he "refused to be a patient." He wore regular clothes instead of a hospital gown (except during surgery) and took charge of as many situations concerning his treatment as possible. This active attitude toward one's health promotes healing, whereas passive resignation sends many PWAs on a downward spiral into despair and physical deterioration.

Initially, Dr. Katoff believed that 2 years was the maximum time he could expect to live. Now, since he has maintained relatively good health for more than 2 years, he tends to see AIDS less as a fatal condition and more as a chronic illness. Paradoxically, he has learned to appreciate life more fully since he was diagnosed. Viewing New York City's Central Park in the spring, he wondered, "Are these the last cherry blossoms I will ever see, the last autumn colors, the last view of Central Park in the snow?" In concluding the panel discussion, I suggested that Dr. Katoff had discovered the real final stage in the process of dying—and of living: courage.

It has been estimated that approximately 2 million Americans have been exposed to the AIDS virus (Buckingham, 1987); as noted earlier, we do not yet know what percentage of them will eventually develop AIDS. However, many clinicians and researchers have noted that a positive HIV antibody test result, even without any symptoms, can provoke a serious psychological crisis in many people. It is for this reason that "taking the test" must be considered a very important decision, and that is also why all ethical testing sites provide pre- and post-test counseling (anonymously, if desired). For some individuals in the high-risk groups, even a negative antibody test result may not be sufficient to quell their anxieties, particularly if they are prone to hypochondriacal or psychosomatic reactions. Several gay male patients developed minor, but tenacious, symptoms, such as upper respiratory discomfort (clogged ears, sinus problems) or gastrointestinal problems, which appeared to have no discernible organic basis. Even after discovering they were antibody-negative, some of these patients continued to obsess about the possibility that they suffered from an AIDS-related disorder and to experience a great deal of anxiety. Buckingham and others warn clinicians to assess the suicidal potential of the "worried well" patient, as well as the potential for acting out feelings in dangerous or self-destructive ways. For example, after finding that they are antibody-positive, some people may engage in unsafe sex as a means of expressing hostility or hopelessness in the face of uncertainty about their future health. Self-help groups, as well as professionally led group discussions, are often helpful in this area; one recently formed group in the New York City metropolitan area is called The Body Positive.

Saul was a 40-year-old man who had been in psychoanalytic therapy with me for about 6 years and had terminated following our mutual agreement that he had made substantial progress in being able to recognize and express his feelings and that his relationships had become much richer. He understood that he could return for more sessions if he felt it was necessary, and 2 years later he did. The precipitating crisis was his discovery of two tiny purple lesions on his left calf (they resembled tattoos of miniature tornadoes). Biopsies indicated that they were KS lesions and he suddenly found himself to be an AIDS patient. Or, at least, a person with AIDS. Because Saul did not feel sick: He was not tired, although he had long grueling days as a schoolteacher. He exercised regularly, enjoyed dancing on weekends, had a good appetite (too good, he said, always concerned about his weight), and looked perfectly healthy. (Shortly after resuming psychotherapy, he discovered that he also had thrush, or oral candidiasis, a frequent indicator of a compromised immune system.)

Saul began to realize that he was relating to his friends problematically and wanted help in understanding their reactions. He recognized that, as much as he wanted to be taken care of, he felt mortified by his physical and emotional helplessness; he was pushing people away with his hostile demands and subsequent withdrawal. The old patterns of his interpersonal life were reasserting themselves owing to his depressed and regressed emotional state. He felt that he was receiving good medical care and had gotten some useful counseling at a volunteer agency that deals with AIDS patients. But he wanted "to be treated like a person and not a patient." Therapy had helped him in the past to feel more like a person—in fact, to simply "feel" more—and so he had returned to see me.

Obviously, there were strong transference and countertransference elements in this former patient's desire, during this traumatic time, to reestablish a relationship with the psychotherapist he had worked with for many years. And these were helpful to both of us in creating a supportive fabric within which to explore Saul's experiences with people and his relationship to life and death. (I will discuss the therapist's reactions in a later section.) But there was a difference in the basic assumptions that lay beneath our discussions. We both understood that Saul needed to get the most out of his life now, instead of forgoing gratification in the present for fulfillment in the future.

For example, Saul had planned to take a long trip to Hawaii during his summer vacation. With the recent knowledge of his diagnosis, he was tempted to cancel this long-anticipated trip. He had intended to purchase an expensive camera, an atypical gesture of generosity to himself. Now, he said, he should forgo that pleasure and get a cheap camera instead; after all, with an AIDS diagnosis he could not expect to get much use from it. Instead of remaining neutral, as in the earlier therapy, or exploring the childhood roots of his parsimony, I urged him to action instead. Clearly, he should buy the best camera he could find and get the most fulfillment and pleasure out of every hour he spends with it. Now, every hour counts more than before. (As Dr. Katoff stated: "Live three years in three days.") Saul recognized my genuine concern for him (in the psychoanalytic sense, I became a "new object" for him); he accepted the suggestion, went on the trip, and had a great time. He continued to function well for about 2 years after this; eventually he declined and departed this "vale of tears."

Several of the psychotherapists I interviewed had observed an interesting phenomenon. Individuals who are HIV-positive, but who have not developed AIDS, tend to be more acutely anxious than those actually diagnosed with AIDS. They are often described psychiatrically as having anxiety or panic disorders or adjustment disorders with anxiety features, whereas PWAs are more typically diagnosed with depression or adjustment disorder with depressive features. That is why so many clinicians who do counseling before and after the HIV antibody test urge therapists not to challenge the use of denial in HIV-positive patients too aggressively. (This position would have to be modified, of course, if the patient were acting out his feelings in a dangerous or self-destructive manner as noted previously.) The uncertain situation that many thousands currently find themselves in—namely, a positive antibody test but no symptoms or only minor ones—is very difficult to live with. They may want to live normally and to plan for the future, which would be salutary behavior for the immune system (which seems to thrive on positive feelings and to shrink in the face of negative emotions), but often they are too paralyzed with fear or hypochondriacal preoccupations to focus on their current activities.

With the recent expansion of medical treatment to handle many of the opportunistic infections effectively, or even prophylactically (e.g., regular use of antibiotics to prevent (PCP), PWAs are beginning to see their diagnosis as something other than a death sentence. Instead, they define it as a lifelong job of maintenance, similar to other chronic conditions, such as diabetes. They are also beginning to feel somewhat less stigmatized and to feel freer to discuss their condition, both medical and psychological, with friends and families, as well as in self-help groups.

On the other hand, as the illness progresses and some PWAs find their bodies "wasting away" for lack of nourishment and numerous infections, the issue of life versus death comes to the fore. It has been mercifully rare in history that so many young and functional people have had to face the issues around death and dying that older people gradually deal with. For the aged, the end of life has been anticipated and may even be welcomed among the infirm and lonely. And society has always participated in dealing with the end of lives in ways the culture deems appropriate. For PWAs there are few paradigms upon which they can lean. It has been problematic for them even to discuss the issue with loved ones, since it is a frightening unknown to everyone.

For gay men, the issue is further complicated by whether or not their families are aware and accepting (or not) of their sexual orientation. In those situations where the family does not know about the PWA's life, or where they are actively hostile toward it, many surprising and cruel events may occur. For example, when two men have lived together for many years and perhaps purchased property together, they tend to bequeath their possessions to each other, as in most spousal arrangements. However, the family of a deceased PWA may contest his will, even against his expressed wishes, and, until recently, many courts would uphold the family and treat the "life partner" of the deceased as a nonperson. Similarly, where a PWA expresses the desire that no extraordinary measures should be taken to keep him alive if he reaches that horrible point where he can no longer make his wishes known (e.g., becoming demented or comatose and kept alive by a respirator), physicians or hospital administrators may decline to follow his instructions out of "moral" or, more typically, legalistic concerns. These situations are gradually changing. Attorneys have developed legally airtight wills that can pass court challenges successfully; similarly, devices such as "living wills" allow individuals to determine the limits of medical treatment when they have reached the point where they are no longer truly alive.

When a PWA is in psychotherapy and begins to face his own demise, and possibly even expresses a desire to hasten it, the therapist is put in a rare position of ambiguous trust. Caught between the patient's hope and despair, the therapist may well be stymied and feel personally bereft. Even after conscientiously exploring a patient's suicidal musings to determine how much they represent a transference test for the therapist (e.g., "Can you really save me as my mother would have, or will you be helpless and ineffectual as my father was?"), a painful and inexorable reality may remain. Eventually, for the declining AIDS patient, a confrontation with death will occur, and it will not be amenable to psychodynamic interpretation.

Robert is a 40-year-old attorney who had been in psychoanalytic therapy with me for 3 years when he was diagnosed with AIDS. He had originally sought help because of a persistent depression (unresolvable grief reaction) following his lover's death by suicide. He rapidly developed a strong attachment to me and became distraught if he was ever late or missed a session, which occurred only once when he was "stuck in the subway." Although his depression was greatly ameliorated, some of his grief and longing to join his dead lover remained.

He stayed quite healthy for 2 years following his AIDS diagnosis, but then began to decline. Diarrhea, fevers, and rapid weight loss quickly transformed him from a vibrant, active man in a prime phase of his life into a helpless and emaciated invalid, unable even to control his own bodily functions. Shortly after being diagnosed, Robert began to talk about suicidal wishes and the magical hope that he would be reconciled with his lover and with his mother, who had died when he was in his later teens. Initially, I tended not to take these wishes too seriously and to interpret them in the light of Robert's "lifelong love affair with the grim reaper." Eventually, as I gained more knowledge about AIDS and as Robert became sicker, I encouraged him to talk candidly about his death wishes, with me and with close friends and in his therapy group, so that he would not feel so alone in his secret relationship with death. He did not need to protect me or those he was close to from the facts of his life and death.

Robert then had a dream that his mother was holding him in her arms. She was telling him that his cat had to be "put to sleep." He disagreed, but was paralyzed to express anything. She put the cat in a box with a clear cover, like a "casket," and injected something into the box to put it to sleep. The dream represents the struggle between the part of this man that wants to live but feels paralyzed about doing so, and the aspect of himself (the cat) that longs for solace and equates that with death and a mystical symbiosis with mother. The meaning of the dream was clear to the patient. I exhorted him to recognize what represents life and what stands for death in his current situation and to make active, conscious decisions about them. For example, Robert had never "come out" about his homosexuality to his father and his siblings, who were still alive, for fear of upsetting them or of being rejected. He realized that this situation symbolically represented death; he was not fully alive and not genuinely himself in relation to his family. The false self had eventually come to feel hollow and exhausted and had become a drain on the real person hidden beneath it. Robert decided to be himself and to risk rejection for the sake of a more authentic life. He informed his father and his siblings of his condition and the facts of his life and, fortunately, encountered acceptance and support from them. Again, a more neutral or passive attitude on my part would have been inappropriate and certainly unhelpful.

Another corollary of the chronic disease model that is displacing that of an acute illness is the increasing appearance of neurological disorders. Recent evidence suggests that HIV may directly infect brain cells, resulting in some forms of chronic degenerative diseases of the central nervous system (Perry & Jacobsen, 1986). The three commonest forms of AIDS-related cerebral pathology are meningitis, primary neoplasms (especially lymphomas), and encephalitis. Discussing the neuropsychiatric manifestations of AIDS, Perry and Jacobsen found that the common functional diagnoses of chronic depression or acute psychosis may mask organically determined problems. Early symptoms of neurological disease typically include visual motor difficulties, loss of memory, and cognitive deficits. These can be differentiated by neuropsychological tests, although they might be missed during interviews or mistaken as indications of depression. Similarly, the authors found that neuropsychiatric symptoms of "AIDS-spectrum disorders" that appear as some form of acute psychosis can easily be misdiagnosed as schizophrenia or an acute paranoid disorder. In these cases, the predominating symptoms include grandiosity, suspicion, delusions and hallucinations, agitation, confusion, and changes in affect.

Since the life expectancy of current PWAs is increasing along with improving medical management of corollary infections, clinicians should consider a patient's friends, family, and community resources in planning ongoing care. Supportive psychotherapy, even with patients who have cognitive deficits, may help them to deal with limit setting, reality testing, and their sense of overall alienation. Perry and Jacobsen (1986) urge that psychotherapists be especially aware of countertransference problems when working with patients "who represent minority groups that traditionally have been the objects of irrational attitudes" (p. 141). That is to say, don't add injury to insult by adopting a judgmental or moralistic attitude when dealing with patients who have already had their self-esteem harmed by social attitudes.

Families, Friends, and Lovers

If AIDS places an unbearable and truly monstrous burden on the individual, we must acknowledge that this illness also takes a devastating emotional and material toll from those who are close to a PWA. John Martin and his colleagues, Mary Clare Lennon and Laura Lee Dean, at Columbia University's School of Public Health, have completed a series of exceptionally sensitive, relevant, and skillfully conducted studies of AIDS-related bereavement. They conclude that "a secondary epidemic of bereavement is also growing" (Martin, 1987, p. 47), which will overburden medical and mental health care providers.

For families, as noted earlier, the issue is complicated if they are unaware of a PWA's sexuality or, less often, drug use. Early in the epidemic, it was evident that this country's widespread denigration of, and prejudice toward gay people, intravenous drug users, and black people was generalized to all people with AIDS. (Many of the earliest stricken were Haitian in origin, and the epidemic has ravaged several African countries, predominantly among heterosexuals.) Owing to this generalized fear (of contagion) and loathing (of those who are different), even PWAs who did not belong to one of these groups were ostracized. The television news documented numerous examples of young children and hemophiliacs who were shunned and ill-treated by neighbors and even public officials (e.g., children kept out of schools, despite the improbability of transmission of the virus).

Families of PWAs are therefore vulnerable to a kind of double whammy. Unless they are already aware, and accepting, of their family member's life-style, they must first deal with their shock at discovering that their child or sibling or even, sometimes, spouse has been leading a secret life. At the same time, they are confronted with an even more painful fact about their relative's life: his illness and probable demise.

Probably the hardest thing a parent ever has to bear is the death of a child. This is a truism that has lately been uttered too often, with deep anguish and grief. Each of the 40,000 human beings who have thus far died of AIDS had a set of parents—many of them living and grieving—as well as brothers, sisters, other relatives, and, sometimes, spouses and children. Many of the men also had primary relationships with other men: lovers or "life partners." These family members of lovers or friends became caretakers of the PWA during the last, and probably worst, part of his illness.

The caretakers are often inundated with overwhelming and conflicting feelings. They may be devoting huge amounts of time, energy, and, sometimes, material resources to this process of caretaking. In most circumstances, when people make that kind of investment they expect a positive result—some kind of "successful outcome." In the current AIDS situation, if the disease runs its usual course, the outcome is the patient's demise and the termination of his relationship with his caretakers. If they define success as cure or as keeping the patient alive indefinitely, they are devastated when he dies; they may feel that all their efforts were in vain. Besides the sense of deep loss, they may also feel like failures: They were unable to save the PWA, and his demise may be experienced as a blow to their self-esteem. This complicates the grieving process, which is already unusual and difficult for the survivors of this particular illness. On the other hand, many caretakers discover within themselves a degree of selflessness they had not previously recognized. The human connectedness they provide by remaining close to a PWA—even though the patient may be demanding, difficult, overactive, and even unable to manage basic bodily functions—resonates back to them as a heightened sense of oneness with humankind. This can serve as a crucial buffer against both the loss and the narcissistic injury of failing to keep the patient alive.

The complications of AIDS-related bereavement were detailed by Lennon and Martin (1987) in a series of studies focusing primarily on AIDS-related bereavement among gay men. They concluded that the mourning process is particularly difficult for young gay men to resolve because of several factors that distinguish this group from others who have suffered many losses. First of all, they note the prematurity of both the deceased and the survivors; in most cases, they are in the prime of their lives, so that the death seems out of sync with the normal rhythm of the human life cycle. This is further complicated by the uncertain outcome of each opportunistic infection during a long illness. And, unlike most bereavement circumstances, many gay men face a frequent, sequential series of losses, so that the normal process of grieving is repeatedly interrupted and the total amount of mourning becomes overwhelming.

The "debilitating, at times disfiguring, and universally stigmatizing characteristics" (Lennon & Martin, 1987) of a long AIDS illness increases the trauma for those who cared for the patient. This is especially true when the surviving caretakers are gay men, who may be suffering enormous anxiety about their own health. Within some communities, the devastation is so immense that the survivors face "major disruptions in their social network." In 1985, Dean and Martin (1987) interviewed 745 gay males. They found that the average individual knew 4 people who either had AIDS or had already died from AIDS; this average individual had experienced 2.5 actual losses and anticipated another 1.3 losses at the time of the interview.

Martin and his associates developed a grief scale with which to study the gay male survivors of AIDS. The primary items constitute the "obsessional review" group, which includes a strong yearning to have the deceased back, a need to cry for him, and a preoccupation with thoughts about him. A secondary group of items on the scale comprises symptoms of detachment and denial. Using the grief scale, Lennon and Martin found that the loss of a lover, as opposed to a close friend, resulted in only marginally higher grief scores, as did the frequency of contact with the deceased individual. Grief reactions were significantly stronger among men who functioned as caretakers during their lover's illness. (These results seem to parallel bereavement studies of heterosexual spouses.) Those caretakers who felt they had inadequate support systems (such as people to talk with about their emotions) during their lover's illness had stronger grief reactions than those who felt they had sufficient emotional support. In addition, those men who themselves had symptoms of AIDS-related illness were likely to have more intense grief reactions.

These findings underscore the value of counseling and psychotherapy, as well as self-help groups, for caretakers during a long AIDS illness. Many mental health agencies are beginning to recognize this and are following the lead of gay community groups, such as GMHC, which has special therapy groups for parents and for "care partners" of PWAs.

Born of a cruel necessity, communal ways of sharing the burden of unbearable losses are emerging. Perhaps the most impressive occurred on Sunday, October 11, 1987, in the city of Washington, D.C., during the Gay Rights March on Washington. A gigantic "quilt," consisting of 2000 panels (and which would, by 1988, consist of over 8000 panels)—each one to commemorate a person lost to AIDS—was unfurled on a lawn the size of two football fields next to the Capitol. Canvas walkways crisscrossed the quilt; by making a contribution to The Names Project, which had organized this massive communal mourning, one could get a directory showing the location of all the people commemorated there. Friends, lovers, and family members of deceased PWAs searched for the names of those they had lost. Sometime, they encountered an unexpected shock: someone they had not realized was lost to AIDS. Old and young, thousands of parents and lovers and sisters and friends embraced each other, tears streaming down their cheeks. It was the kind of mass grieving one encounters only during times of war or plague.

Health Care Workers (Especially Psychotherapists)

The AIDS epidemic poses many unusual dilemmas for health care professionals. Despite the constant barrage of information in professional journals and in the general media, physicians' knowledgeability about AIDS varies more than in any other medical condition. The level of expertise covers the gamut from those who see PWAs daily and keep up with research on a regular basis to physicians and other professionals who are not only astonishingly ignorant about many basic facts but also anxiety-ridden and prejudiced against anyone infected with the virus.

The *New York Times* (June 9, 1987) reported on a study of physicians in New York City and San Francisco about the stress effects of treating AIDS patients. Responses to questionnaires show that many doctors have obsessive thoughts and nightmares about becoming infected with the virus, as well as experiencing a good deal of manifest anxiety. Ninety-one percent of respondents experienced "at least mild anxiety," while 40% thought about the risk of developing AIDS at least weekly. Some of the reasons offered for these findings include the expectation of medical students and young doctors that everything is curable using modern medical technologies. As they become stymied by this disease, they feel impotent and frustrated. Also, the younger doctors are often in the same age range as their AIDS patients; this makes them face the issue of their own mortality at an earlier point in their lives. Of particular interest is the finding that female physicians report less stress about treating AIDS patients than do the male doctors. The male doctors try to avoid entering patients' rooms far more often than do the females. Authors speculate that these results might be related to male physicians' uneasiness about male homosexuality, or they may simply indicate that women are more comfortable in the caretaking role in which physicians are often placed since there is no "cure" for AIDS. (As noted earlier, there are many treatments for the various infections to which the PWA is susceptible, but the underlying immune deficiency remains.)

Most young physicians and other health care professionals are used to curing their patients; except for those who specialize in areas where frequent fatalities occur, such as oncology and gerontology, many doctors rarely deal with seriously ill or moribund patients. How much truer this is of psychotherapists, who set long-term goals and describe themselves as dealing with "problems in living." For many of us, accepting and acknowledging that our patients with AIDS probably have a grossly circumscribed life-span is a soul-wrenching experience. As noted earlier, those therapists who typically encourage their patients to endure current frustrations for the sake of future growth must, of necessity and of humanity, take a more active, "here-and-now" emphasis.

Michelina Santorelli interviewed 60 psychotherapists who work with PWAs at least some of the time. She explored "the need for professional training, the role of the psychotherapist, and psychotherapists' dilemmas and personal reactions to working with persons with AIDS." Interestingly, 38% of respondents did not actively choose to work with PWAs, but found themselves doing so when one or more of their clients developed the illness during the course of psychotherapy.

Although 60% of the group studied indicated that "good clinical skills" constituted the most essential factor in working with PWAs, just as with anyone, 76% noted that psychotherapy was different with such patients. Most respondents emphasized the importance of keeping up with medical developments and counseling patients about "safer sex" medical practices. They tend to set more goals and to deal with concrete present issues much more actively with these patients; 95% believed that psychotherapeutic treatment with PWAs is effective.

Dr. Santorelli concluded that therapists who deal with PWAs on a regular basis are overwhelmed; there is a severe burnout problem among these practitioners. She recommended limiting the number of AIDS patients per therapist and emphasized the importance of consultations and support. (Psychologists are less likely than social workers to make use of a support network.)

In a talk to the Group Services Department of GMHC, Lorraine Smithberg focused on the need to "care for the caretakers." The stress of dealing with life-and-death issues and powerful affects in patients who are often regressed can take a serious toll on psychotherapists. Too much "selflessness" can be dangerous; the tension that builds up in the therapist can be expressed as psychosomatic conditions, which may mirror some of the patient's symptoms, or be discharged through self-destructive activities. Dr. Smithberg reiterated the need for therapists to have good sources of support, such as their own therapy, supervision, and, particularly, groups of other therapists who work with PWAs, where they can express their own fear and rage and be heard and understood.

In this time of plague, psychotherapists may find themselves in strange situations, performing unusual functions. As we now live in cruel and unexpected circumstances, so must we find new and flexible responses if we are to cope. When, after many years of therapy, my patient Saul (discussed earlier) died from AIDS, I attended his funeral. Many of the people present were familiar to me, some because they had been in one of my therapy groups along with Saul, and some because he had spoken of them in his sessions. The format was informal because Saul's wish was to be cremated and not to have a religious funeral service. Instead, his closest friends, who had nurtured and supported him during his illness, brought photograph albums showing Saul throughout his life, from infancy to death.

In addition, they had decided to invite those who had gathered to share their feelings and recollections of Saul. People were initially hesitant and confused. There was no rabbi, in this case, or any kind of traditional religious leader to perform the usual rites and to confer the usual blessings and reassurances to the group. Even when the "minister" does not know the deceased and merely voices platitudes, the bereaved may experience a degree of consolation, if only from the awareness that the "leader" is conducting the proper ceremony. In this case, no one was formally assigned that function, and, in retrospect, it seems both ironic and inevitable, since the "priest-father" role derives from the individual-as-a-child's relationship to his own "idealized" father, and Saul's own father was absent or unavailable to him throughout his childhood. He had painfully come to acknowledge this disappointment during the course of his therapy and to relinquish residual fantasies of his father's changing; Saul's father died about 5 years before he did. Of course, Saul insisted that no rabbi be present; if the hurt child in him finally accepted the reality of no fathering, he must not have wanted his spirit to be falsely consoled by the paternalism of traditional religion, which he abhorred.

I decided to express my feelings about Saul, partly to get the process under way and partly to share my own grief in a communal way. I talked about how much Saul had grown over the years and how strongly he had responded to his friends' caring; and about how sad he felt that he couldn't express his love and gratitude in the regressed state into which had had fallen in his final months. I also revealed some of the specific things he would have wanted to say to those closest to him, a sharing of knowledge that a psychotherapist is almost never justified in doing during the usual practice of our profession; these are not usual times. Almost all who were present stood up and spoke of their relationship with Saul and told of incidents both sad and funny. Tears and laughter were shared among us. It seemed that, in these strange times, the need for a "priest-father" had been transferred to the psychotherapist, even after a patient's death, as it often is nowadays during life.

REFERENCES

Buckingham, S. L. (1987). The HIV antibody test: Psychosocial issues. *Social Casework: The Journal of Contemporary Social Work, 68*(4), 132–141.
Dean, L. L., & Martin, J. L. (1987, August 25). *Social losses, bereavement and grief reactions: Issues in data collection, assessment and definitions.* Paper presented at the 95th Annual Convention of the American Psychological Association, New York.
Kübler-Ross, E. (1969). *On death and dying.* New York: Macmillan.
Lennon, M. C. & Martin, J. L. (1987, August 25). *Factors affecting grief reactions to AIDS-related bereavement.* Paper presented at the 95th Annual Convention of the American Psychological Association, New York.
Martin, J. L. (1987). *AIDS-related bereavement among gay men: Sexual behavior risk factors and psychological consequences.* Unpublished manuscript.
Perry, S. & Jacobsen, P. (1986). Neuropsychiatric manifestations of AIDS-spectrum disorders. *Hospital and Community Psychiatry, 37,* 135–141.
Santorelli, M. (1988). *The psychotherapeutic treatment of persons with AIDS: Mental health professionals' perspectives.* Unpublished dissertation.
Smithberg, L. (1988, January 29). *Utilizing group dynamics to help the healers.* Presentation at Gay Men's Health Crisis, New York.

Chapter 22
Toward a Sense of Immortality
Case Studies of Voluntarily Childless Couples

SUSAN BRAM

During the decade of the 1970s we witnessed a revolution in sex roles and family patterns in the United States and western Europe. Whereas, in previous eras, the locus of social change had been the church or factory, during the 1970s it was closer to home—indeed, within the very heart of the family itself. So many changes took place in such a short period of time, in fact, that it is difficult to list them all. Of primary importance was the increasing participation of women in education and work outside the home (Hoffman, 1977). Of equal and related significance was the transformation in attitudes and behavior in the area of reproduction. For example, there was a tendency in the 1970s for women to begin childbearing at a later age than in the 1960s (United States Bureau of the Census, 1981). Fewer children were born per family and birth rates reached their lowest points during that decade (National Center for Health Statistics, 1981). The children that were born were spaced more closely together, so that women would ultimately spend a smaller portion of their lives as childbearers or childrearers. Consistent with these trends there was an unprecedented increase in the rate of voluntary childlessness—the proportion of women of childbearing age who remained childless out of choice, rather than because of infertility (United States Bureau of the Census, 1981). Large-scale surveys and census data for that period suggested to some researchers that the proportion of women choosing to remain childless would be as high as 30% by the year 2000 (Westoff, 1978).

As the 1980s draw to a close, we can see that this decade has been quite different from the preceding one. There has been at least a partial return to many of the structures and values of the traditional family that were predominant in the 1950s. Although they began most conspicuously among conservative groups that overtly deplored the changes of the 1970s, it is now clear that these changes have begun to permeate society at large. For example, at the same time that we have an unprecedented number of women and mothers working outside the home (U.S. Bureau of the Census, 1986),

In order to protect the confidentiality of the individuals described here, all major identifying markers and names have been changed.

SUSAN BRAM • New York State Psychiatric Institute, Columbia Presbyterian Medical Center, New York, New York 10032.

there is a greater emphasis on the importance of women being mothers, even "super moms" (Ehrensaft, 1987). Although economic necessity and cultural values prevent a total return to the early post-World War II era (i.e., two incomes are now usually needed to support a family), there are similarities between the 1950s and the 1980s in the extent to which childbearing and childrearing are again a focus of major attention, especially for women. While men are now urged to participate in childrearing more actively than in the past (Cath, Gurwitt, & Ross, 1982), the continued demands of the workplace and the fact that the man's income is still usually higher than the woman's have limited the extent to which men are actually involved in childrearing. As a result of such social factors, women are again faced with the decision of when and how to have a child (e.g., to be a single parent, to share parenting, to utilize the new reproductive technologies, to adopt), rather than whether or not to have a child. In effect, we have entered the period of a new "parenthood imperative."

There are many ramifications of the revived emphasis on childbearing. Despite vast developments in reproductive technology, women actually may feel less free to control childbearing than in the past. The educated middle-class woman (and adolescent) has gotten the message from the media that she should be able to do everything—work, marry, create a family, and care for her children, with nominal amounts of help from men or institutions such as day-care centers. Strong, pronatalist pressures are ubiquitous—on television, in the press, in stores, in political campaigns—leaving those who are not able to have children (because of infertility, age, or economic situation) feeling left out in the cold. Clearly, the choice to remain voluntarily childless has lost some of its "cachet." Thus, couples who made the decision to forgo parenthood in the 1970s must now create their own social supports. Because working parents are exceedingly busy, their lives are increasingly divergent from the lives of nonparents. As a result, a new feeling of divisiveness has arisen, particularly among women of childbearing age. The emphasis on a plurality of choices for women and men, so freeing in the 1970s (Dixon, 1970), has been replaced by a narrower set of options that are not truly available to everyone.

It is particularly timely, then, that we look at the lives of the voluntarily childless—individuals who chose to resist the traditional pronatalist norms of the early 1970s and have maintained their "deviant" lifestyle through to the present. We shall see how they survived the vicissitudes of social trends and attitudes toward reproduction while creating lives based on goals other than parenthood. One of our aims here is to counter social stereotypes and prejudices about childlessness. For example, there is a common assumption that the childless couple chooses to *avoid* parenthood because of a dislike of children, psychological immaturity, or personal inadequacy. Our data reveal, however, that the childless couple usually decides to forego childbearing in order to pursue other goals that are equally important to them but happen to be exclusive of parenting (Bram, 1974, 1978, 1984). We shall have an opportunity to consider how the voluntarily childless lives can be understood as meaningful and purposeful to the individuals and to society. In addition, we shall consider how, despite some commonalities, the voluntarily childless are a diversified and individualistic group, rather than a homogeneous one. Yet, the needs and concerns they address in their lives are significant to us all in this era.

In this chapter I will describe the lives of four voluntarily childless couples who were interviewed several times over a 7- to 10-year period, from the early 1970s to the 1980s as part of a larger study of childless couples and parents (Bram, 1985).

During that time their ages ranged from the mid-20s to mid-30s, and they were married an average of 5 to 15 years. I thus had the opportunity to get to know them during a critical period in their lives—the transition from young to middle adulthood—and during an important societal transition—from the 1970s to the 1980s. For many of the couples, the first interview in the study represented their chance to "come out" as voluntarily childless; during the 7 to 10 intervening years, they became much less reticent and, in some cases, were publicly involved in organizations and groups devoted to childlessness (such as NON, the National Organization for Non-Parents). Following a description of the four couples, I will discuss ways in which their lives can be understood as an attempt to find a new path toward a sense of immortality.

Nature Lovers: Mr. and Ms. A

Mr. and Ms. A were zealous and active nature lovers. When they were first interviewed in the early 1970s, Mr. A was 34, Ms. A was 37, and they had been married 6 years. They were living in a bright and airy apartment decorated with desert plants and photos of the mountains, creating an image that was reminiscent of the West Coast, where they had first lived during the early years of their marriage. Born in the rural Southwest, Mr. A worked full time as an engineer, as had his father, and was employed by a government agency that focused on ecological issues. Ms. A had trained in public health and worked as a dental hygienist, but she was about to leave her job to see what it would be like to stay home full time.

The primary reason the As gave for not wanting to have children was the limitation it would place on the spontaneity of their life together. Both of them felt it was important that they be able to drop everything at a moment's notice and go out into the wilderness—to backpack, canoe, or camp—activities Ms. A had introduced to her husband when they were first dating. Ms. A felt that children would tie them down to a house, a plot of land, and set of responsibilities that were too constraining for their relationship. In addition, they were both concerned about the financial problems that children could create and the burden that would then fall upon the husband. When discussing this issue, they referred to their memories of families that had struggled through the Depression era and the tension that their own parents had undergone. Of the two spouses, only Ms. A expressed the fear that she would prove to be inadequate to the tasks of parenting, especially the physical stresses of pregnancy, childbirth, and early parenthood. She acknowledged that Mr. A, in contrast, would probably have no difficulty with parenthood and that he would be a good father. In summing up, she stated, "I prefer to live in the present. [It seems that] people with children have to think more about the future." Mr. A concurred, admitting that he did not have a very positive view of the future. He would not want to expose a growing child to the crowding, pollution, crime, and political tensions that he envisioned in the world at large during the upcoming decades.

In describing their marriage, Mr. and Ms. A both stressed the extent to which they shared interests and activities, as well as trust and loyalty. Mr. A felt that they did everything together, and he thanked his wife for his enduring love of the out-of-doors as well as the healthy life-style they had developed together. She also felt this was one of their strengths as a couple, but at the same time she wished for a bit more freedom in her own life, acknowledging that the responsibilities of being a wife had made her feel like less of a "free spirit" than she would have preferred. She cherished the image of her "life as a vagabond—traveling in foreign countries" with no obligations whatsoever. Overall, however, both Mr. and Ms. A were very happy with their current lives and their marriage, and when describing the future (the next 5 years and the next 25 years), they both talked about continuing to live just as they currently were, except that they wanted to move back to the western part of the country.

Indeed, 7 years later, the As were living on the West Coast again and had bought a home that came closer to their dream house than had the midwestern apartment in which they had previously lived. After nearly 15 years of marriage, they had developed a very stable life-style together with, at least superficially, a traditional division of labor. Mr. A was the sole breadwinner and had been for many years. Ms. A stayed home full time and carried out most of the household tasks, in addition to pursuing her interests in botany, weaving, and art. They were still both committed to, and happy with, their decision to remain childless, but Mr. A was especially relieved that he had not brought a child into the world. He spoke of the difficulties he would have had raising an adolescent in the contemporary culture—with drugs, crime, and sexual tensions—and doubted his own ability to set a good example for a teenager.

In regard to their own lives, Mr. and Ms. A appeared to be as contented as any other couple interviewed, still making full use of their time together to enjoy common interests. Their marital complaints had been reduced to relatively trivial domestic issues—bill paying and housecleaning—and these were not the source of any great tension between them. Again, their wish for the future was to continue just as they were, living "healthy, active lives."

A Religious Couple: Mr. and Ms. B

Mr. and Ms. B described their life as based upon a profound and articulate fundamentalist religious faith that they both had acquired as adults. When they were first interviewed they had been married about 6 years and were 30 years old. Mr. B was working full time as an automotive engineer and Ms. B was a high school science teacher. They had both come from working-class families in the rural midwest and continued to live a relatively modest life-style, in a trailer court outside a midwestern city. They lived frugally so as to save their money for travel and entertainment. Their personal warmth was particularly striking to the interviewers—they were the only individuals in the study who invited the researchers to join them in a home-cooked meal.

Mr. and Ms. B stated that they had entered marriage with mixed feelings about having children. In contrast to the stereotypical childless couple, it was the husband rather than the wife who had been more committed to a childless life-style at first. Within a few years of marriage, however, they had both come to the conclusion that Mr. B should have a vasectomy. They explained that their primary reason for not wanting children had to do with their particular view of the world and the future. They were convinced that the next decade would bring worldwide destruction marked by famine, overcrowding, and large-scale human suffering. Thus, it would not have made sense to have a family or to risk bringing a child into the world. On a more personal level, they also feared that having children would disrupt the special closeness they felt as a couple, as well as the financial freedom and spontaneity they had established in their lives.

In describing their marriage, both Mr. and Ms. B were extremely positive and stated emphatically that there were no qualities they wished to change in the other. For example, Ms. B. said, "We enjoy being together as much as we can—just sitting home, watching TV, and reading, and we hate to leave each other, even for a few hours." She felt her marriage had given her a partnership and companionship, as well as sexual satisfaction, and that she had developed a "brighter, happier outlook on her personal life" because of her husband. Mr. B was even more idyllic in his description. He said, "It's a storybook marriage, a dream come true, ideal and perfect in every way." He also stated that his life had improved since his marriage—he had more friends and a better income, and his wife had been a "good Christian influence" on him.

It is clear that for the Bs, the church had become their special family. When they described the most satisfying things in life, they both listed religion and church after marriage, and it was obvious that their fundamentalist faith was central to their view of the future.

When asked what they wanted to be doing in the next 5 and 25 years, Ms. B said, "We won't be here in 25 years. I don't think that man will take care of all his problems or use his weapons carefully enough." Mr. B was even more explicit. His view of the future was that it would come to a catastrophic end when world war broke out between the United States and China, to be survived only by the followers of Christ. His own plan for the future was to be "influencing people toward Christ"—a task he expected would take up nearly all his time.

By 1980 several important changes had occurred in the lives of Mr. and Ms. B. Large-scale layoffs in industry had left Mr. B without a job and Ms. B had become their sole support. As a result, they had moved further west to be closer to Ms. B's family of origin. Despite their difficulties (or, perhaps, because of them), their commitment to each other was still very strong and they had no regrets about remaining childless. In fact, Ms. B found that she was increasingly glad of their decision not to have children. Moreover, their "doomsday view" had been radically transformed, so that they both felt substantially more optimistic about the future. As Ms. B said, "I'm less concerned about the world situation now, so I find I'm more supportive of my friends who have children. I feel closer to God and am more confident that He will take care of us. I'm very optimistic now."

Although their sense of urgency about the future had greatly diminished, they still planned to dedicate the rest of their lives to the work of Christ and were actively engaged in evangelical activities at the time of the follow-up interview.

A Dual Career Couple: Mr. and Ms. C

At the time of the first interview, Ms. C was a 28-year-old full-time law student who had been married 6½ years and was living in a university town with her husband, a full-time student in architecture. She was an energetic woman who spoke enthusiastically about her life goals and her decision to remain childless. Her strong commitment to voluntary childlessness was indicated by her decision to pursue a tubal ligation, despite the fact that the medical procedure was rarely available to childless women at that time. She explained that she had known as early as age 12 that she did not want to follow in the footsteps of her mother, who had been a full-time parent and homemaker. Instead, she preferred to focus on her studies, her career, and her political activities in the community.

When Mr. and Ms. C met in college, Ms. C felt that he was the first person to understand and support her professional and political goals. He, in turn, felt she was sympathetic to his creative interests. Although he had given much less thought to the childbearing decision, she persuaded him to choose to remain childless by explaining that he would have to stay home with the children, since she intended to work outside the home full time. Thus, the choice of childlessness was made before marriage and it grew stronger as their marital relationship developed. Both partners emphasized the extent to which having children would disrupt their lives, their work, and their relationship with each other. Ms. C also mentioned that she felt inadequate to the task of raising children and was unenthusiastic about the experiences of pregnancy and childbirth. Mr. C felt that, although in general he might be a good parent, he would much prefer children who were old enough to be independent—adolescents and young adults.

Mr. and Ms. C had a very close and egalitarian marriage. They had carefully worked out a life-style that would allow the equal participation of each spouse in housekeeping, shopping, and decision making, by sacrificing some of their parents' middle class standards of cleanliness and order. They enjoyed each other's company and spent so much time together that each spoke of beginning to need some time for privacy. They also wanted more time to carry out their political and community interests. For example, Ms. C was involved in several organizations that focused on feminist causes in the local area, and Mr. C was working with others to develop ways to contribute to political causes through the application of their creative skills.

Seven years later, at the time of the follow-up interview, Ms. C was permanently childless, having received the tubal ligation, and both spouses were still committed to a childless life-style with a focus on work and community. Ms. C had achieved prominence as a representative for a national women's organization and was still living with her husband, although they were contemplating a trial separation so that Mr. C could accept a job in another city. They were clearly still attached to each other, but stated that their interests had begun to diverge during recent years, causing them to feel somewhat dissatisfied with their marriage. Ms. C had taken up meditation and felt it had changed her view of the world to the point that she was "mellower" and less active than before. Mr. C had become more successful in his work and felt that he was putting more effort into the marriage than his wife. They both were looking forward to the time apart as an opportunity to sort out their views of the future, although individually they spoke of wishing to pursue the same goals as in the present—achievement, creativity, and world change.

Adventurers: Mr. and Ms. D

Mr. and Ms. D were about 30, came from an upper-middle-class suburb and a small midwestern town, respectively, and were married 4 years at the time of the first interview. They each had a wide diversity of interests and personal goals, which could best be summed up by one word: *eclectic*. Ms. D was an editor and described herself as a "professional dilettante." One of the aspects of her job that pleased her the most was the opportunity to meet a diverse group of individuals, such as writers and editors, who would come to her for professional advice. Mr. D had an administrative position at a large university and, when first interviewed, was in transition to a second career as an urban planner. Among the numerous reasons they gave for not wanting to have children was the restriction it would place on their freedom and personal dreams. As Ms. D said, "Children would have a negative effect on the freedom of expansion between us." They also both mentioned the loss of money and time, as well as the increased responsibility that comes with parenthood.

When Mr. and Ms. D described their marriage, they emphasized the dialectic between freedom and stability, activity and stagnation. Ms. D, for example, liked the companionship of the marriage, as well as the travels and adventures she shared with her husband. However, she also felt that she did not have enough excitement in her life and she desired more stimulation and a change from her everyday routine, "more of a challenge." She stated that marriage caused her to "give up her footloose ways" and to channel her energy into a career. Mr. D stressed the personal growth he experienced in his marriage as a positive factor, but he wished for more certainty in his life. At the same time, he stated he felt too restricted in his life since being married. Thus, both spouses stressed "activity" in describing the current sources of satisfaction in their married life, but wished for more stability as well.

When the Ds looked toward the future they expressed their desire to transcend the mundane in their everyday life. Ms. D wanted to travel more, to see every country in the world, and finally to settle down in Asia. Mr. D had perhaps the most ambitious dream of any of the individuals we interviewed: he wanted to become an astronaut and travel to the moon!

Seven years later, Mr. and Ms. D had separated and were in the process of getting a divorce. Mr. D's life had not changed very much, however. He remained in the same home in which they had previously lived together, was working full time as an urban planner, and, with the occasional companionship of new women in his life, was still pursuing many of his original interests and hobbies. In contrast, Ms. D had changed her life in a major way. She had moved to another city, was living with another man, and had entered a new career in business. Moreover, she was reconsidering her wish to remain childless. She was beginning to think that the desire to forgo children had stemmed from her relationship with Mr. D and that her new relationship with a man was one in which being a parent would be feasible and satisfying. Her enthusiasm for world travel and high adventure was beginning to diminish, and she was beginning to focus on activities closer to home, such as artwork and handicrafts, which she pursued in her free time.

Summary and Conclusion

I have described four voluntarily childless couples during a significant time period of their lives and in society, when both personal and cultural values have been in flux. As mentioned above, I found that the voluntarily childless couples here (and in our larger study) could best be described as individuals who are searching for personal meaning in their lives, rather than as reacting against childbearing or parenthood, as many had previously assumed. Moreover, in their quest for purpose, they have developed idiosyncratic life-styles that do not fall easily into any one stereotype of childlessness. As I have shown in this chapter, each couple appears to have a major theme that serves to guide and organize them, at least in this stage of their lives. Mr. and Ms. A are oriented toward nature and their love for the out-of-doors. Mr. and Ms. B share a strong religious faith that binds them and focuses their lives. Mr. and Ms. C are primarily work-oriented. Mr. and Ms. D are each adventurers, whose emphasis in life has been on experience.

It is worth noting, however, that despite their unique life-styles, all four couples share some features with the entire group of voluntarily childless couples studied and described elsewhere (Bram, 1974, 1978, 1985). They all have a tendency to emphasize self-actualization in their lives, to stress some form of achievement or creativity, to work toward egalitarianism in their marriages, and to have some sex-role innovation in their life-styles. Moreover, they share a desire for a transcendent purpose, a "sense of immortality" that is often expressed through childbearing among couples who become parents.

In trying to understand the underlying motivations of the voluntarily childless couples, I found the work of R. J. Lifton (1967) to be most useful. His in-depth research on survivors of historical periods marked by crisis and upheaval led him to a theoretical model of human behavior based on the "compelling universal urge to maintain an inner sense of continuity over time and space," and "sense of immortality" that is most often provided by collective and cultural institutions. Lifton points out that during a time of rapid change, social institutions are often not sufficiently organized to provide an experience of continuity, so that individuals must determine or create a mode of transcendence for themselves. He describes five such modes: (1) the "natural mode," being survived by nature itself, living on in natural elements, (2) the "theological mode," the religious idea of a spiritual conquest of death, or a belief in the afterlife, (3) the "work mode," living on through one's job, accomplishments, or creative work, (4) the "experiential mode," a transcendence of the issues of time and death through the pleasure associated with experience itself, and (5) the "biological mode," living on through one's offspring.

Clearly, having children is the most common way to attempt to acquire a sense of immortality. If people do not have children, however, they are faced with a dilemma. As one voluntarily childless woman said, "If you decide not to have children, you miss one of the major stepping-stones and rites of passage in adult life. You look ahead of you, and instead of seeing, as many people do, pregnancy, childbirth, parenthood, and all the stages of rearing children, you see an empty path heading straight toward death." Whereas some couples we interviewed spoke of planning to dedicate buildings in their names or donate books to libraries, others felt that their lives themselves could give them a sense of continuity and a way to cope with their own finiteness.

Indeed, it is of great interest to me that in my work with voluntarily childless couples nearly all the themes that emerged fit into Lifton's model for attaining a sense of immortality. To be completely true to our data, however, I would add one additional category that may be specific to the decades of the 1970s and 1980s—the "communal mode." Although I chose not to represent that theme in this chapter, it is clear that many of the couples in my original study had organized their lives around their ties to community on a broad scale and on a local level. Some had decided to live communally and others planned to do so in the future. Some were working on a community level (as were Mr. and Ms. B and C), and some found that their ties with friends and neighbors were central to their sense of purpose in life.

The voluntarily childless can thus be understood as responding to universal and contemporary issues of self, gender, marriage, and family, as well as of community and society. Although it may be tempting to dismiss the voluntarily childless, or to label them as "social deviants," in fact, as we have seen, they share with all of us the need to cope with current social changes and with cultural discontinuities. An examination of their lives reveals that they are struggling with universal concerns as well as existential issues. At a time when gender, class, and social boundaries are in flux and choices seem to be diminishing, it can be edifying to discover that there are still some viable options available to men and women, and that there are multiple routes to a "sense of immortality."

References

Bram, S. (1974). *To have or have not: A social psychological study of voluntarily childless couples, parents-to-be, and parents.* Unpublished doctoral dissertation, University of Michigan.

Bram, S. (1978). Through the looking glass: Voluntary childlessness as a mirror of contemporary changes in the meaning of parenthood. In W. B. Miller, L. F. Newman (Eds.), *The first child and family formation* (pp. 368–391), Chapel Hill, North Carolina: Carolina Population Center.

Bram, S. (1984). Voluntarily childless women: Traditional or nontraditional? *Sex Roles: A Journal of Research, 10,* (3/4), 195–206.

Bram, S. (1985). Childlessness revisited: A longitudinal study of voluntarily childless couples, delayed parents, and parents. *Lifestyles: A Journal of Changing Patterns, 8*(1), 46–66.

Cath, S. H., A. R. Gurwitt, & J. M. Ross (Eds.). (1982). *Father and child: Developmental and clinical perspectives.* Boston: Little, Brown.

Dixon, R. (1970). Hallelujah the pill? *Trans-Action,* November-December, 44–49, 92.

Ehrensaft, D. (1987). *Parenting together.* New York: Free Press.

Hoffman, L. W. (1977). Changes in family roles, socialization, and sex differences. *American Psychologist, 32,* 644–657.

Lifton, R. J. (1967). *Boundaries: Psychological man in revolution.* New York: Vintage.

National Center for Health Statistics (1981). *Monthly Vital Statistics Report,* September 17.

Petchesky, R. (1984). *Abortion and woman's choice: The State, sexuality, and reproductive freedom.* Boston: Northeastern University.

United States Bureau of the Census (1981). Current Population Reports, Series P-20, No. 363, *Population profile of the United States.*

United States Bureau of the Census (1986). Current Population Reports, Series P-20, No. 406, *Fertility of American women.*

Westoff, C. (1978). Some speculations on the future of marriage and fertility. *Family Planning Perspectives, 10,* 79–82.

Chapter 23
21st Century
Changing Concepts of Masculinity and Femininity

ALICE EICHHOLZ

There has been a riptide lashing at the coastline of our understandings about gender identity in the last 20 years. Our former heroes, those guides to definition of self, are dying, both figuratively and literally. New heroes haven't yet replaced them, leaving few models for guiding us to what it means to be a woman or a man these days.

Why now? The answer usually run the gamut—economic necessity, civil and women's rights, antiwar movement, social protest. All were important aspects of our cultural change, for sure. But why did all these challenges crop up in the 1960s and 1970s and not before or later? A different answer to why our concepts of masculinity and femininity are being challenged might be found in an exploration of what we now know about those concepts from an interdisciplinary perspective focusing on biology, psychology, and sociology viewed in historical context. Reviewed here is the work of three contributors to this important discussion.

First, Alice Rossi's (1977, 1985) work in biosocial perspectives of gender can be viewed in a historical perspective once realizing how little we humans knew of our own biology, physiology, and anatomy before the 20th century, or still understand on a mass basis today. Then, Lillian Rubin's (1983) work describes the psychosocial development of boys and girls and what patterns exist simply because of the way we respond to childhood and structure childrearing. Finally, Mark Gerzon's (1982) work evaluates the public and private archetypes of masculinity, with some intriguing suggestions for altering them given the challenge men's roles face. Once we have a clearer understanding of the forces facing gender identity, we may be able to deepen our understanding of why the forces exist today and what that means for the future.

Over the last several months, in discussions with large groups of adults about the material presented here, we have started by posing the question "What do you remember about being a boy or girl before you were 2?" Not surprising, rarely does anyone have a strong memory from this early time. Yet the most powerful determinants of gender have been set in place before age 2. Biology and culture have already had their say and leave their remnants in our unconscious. When the question is posed again with the age changed to 5 years, more memories come into play. It is the develop-

---

ALICE EICHHOLZ • Vermont College of Norwich University, Montpelier, Vermont 05602.

ment of a sense of self and language acquisition that allows us to attach words to feelings and events between the ages of 2 and 5, which make it easier to have conscious recall of them. Even for many people, it is difficult to recall much before age 5 except when encouraged in psychotherapy.

At each stage of development in these early years, former "memories" take a backseat, making room for the concentrated effort needed for the task at hand—first, motor skills, and then, language acquisition, and, finally, what has been called the "second birth"—that of one's sense of self. While some of these continue to develop long past the formative years, childhood is a critical phase of our beginnings. We never "forget" the early experiences and feelings associated with them. They remain aspects of our sense of self unconsciously called upon when present-day situations, events, traumas remind us of the hidden past. What exists in our conscious awareness depends totally on experience. But first we have to clarify what "experience" means. Traditionally, experience was defined in the social sciences as "nurture." What you did to someone—the experience you provided for them was thought to determine outcome. Nature or biology was not considered experience in the same way. But nature is as much a part of experience as nurture. Just our increased understanding of life *in utero* has extended the definition and understanding of the word *experience*.

For purposes here, experience will be considered the composite and interaction involving biological propensities, environmental milieu, and the defensive structures set up between conscious and unconscious processes during psychological development. Environment milieu includes not only the culture into which we are born but the particular family constellation and its relationship to, and impact on, the broader culture. This milieu has an impact on development of self and the ability to move back and forth between conscious and unconscious experience.

Biological influences are critical at particular times in development, psychological influences at certain times, and cultural influences at other times. It is the interweaving of these facets of our experience that makes us the people we are. It is not a cause-and-effect relationship but a dialectical kind of involvement among these three spheres of our lives. Consequently, the research that looks at how these components affect our development is not always easy to conduct and is by necessity very complex.

Biological propensities of experience have their critical say first. What has happened to our knowledge and understanding about biological components in the 20th century has had a profound effect on our understanding of what it means to be a woman or a man. It begins with the sperm containing a particular set of chromosomes reaching the ovum that is to be fertilized. Whether the fetus will be boy or girl is determined by sperm carrying an XX chromosome for females or an XY chromosome for males. On rare occasions there is an extra chromosome attached.

Determinants for both primary and secondary sex characteristics and a road map for hormones are laid out by the chromosomes. The earliest view of endocrinology, as outlined by Rossi (1977) and the one commonly taught through most of the 20th century in high school biology, was that it was a closed system with hormones traveling only between the pituitary, adrenal glands, and gonads, functioning independent of the environment, including the other physiological systems. There was not thought to be any connection between the flow of hormones and the nervous system. But since the 1950s three facts have been discovered. First, the hypothalamus and therefore the cortex and nervous system are indeed related. When the level of testosterone increases massively in male fetuses *in utero* at 12 weeks and begins the differentiation of males from females, those hormones circulate throughout the nervous system when the brain is at a critical point of development and not just through the endocrine system. Second, blood flows *from* the hypothalamus *to* the pituitary. Third, the nervous system receives electrical signals from the brain and is subject to "behavioral" influence and moderating influence of the gonadal hormones. This means that not only do hormones influence the nervous system, but social stimuli *may* impinge on hormonal secretion through the nervous system.

Rossi (1977) is also struck by the discrepancy between the demands of a complex, technological society today and the inherited physiology from the past and how our knowledge has stockaded our perceptions of sex differences. Humans are still only genetically equipped with their primate heritage, which was adaptive for the last 40,000 years. The female hip bone structure, for example, has not changed, while nutrition has increased the likelihood that children are larger than in the past when coming through the birth canal. While the general impression by many is that androgens are the "aggressive" hormones, Rossi describes them more as "activity" hormones.

A graphic example of how previously held understanding of biology influences our definitions of masculinity and femininity is in the relationship between male and female contributions in conception. What we know now is that it is a complicated interactive process between hormones and neural impulses with both male and female playing critically active roles. Previously it had been assumed that the flagellum of the sperm was responsible for the journey to the ovum. With new information from biology, we now know that while sperm are generally active, the *direction* to their activity is the result of transportation created by the impact of sexual stimulation on the female neural impulses to the hypothalamus. This activates the posterior pituitary and releases oxytocin in the woman to produce uterine contractions with the potential to guide the sperm on its way—a much more interactive and interdependent sense of necessity for both male and female in conception than previously held.

Without accounting for biological contributions to the nature of "experience," a skewed understanding of masculinity and femininity is likely to occur. What all this means for our understanding of masculinity and femininity is that biological contributions shape what is learned about sexual roles—what we come to accept as our gender identity and behavior. Any changes in those roles need to account for the difference with which men and women easily learn certain sexual behaviors, particularly, as Rossi (1977) continues, in parenting.

Throughout most of the 20th century, the controversy between "nature" proponents and "nurture" proponents of experience has been quite hostile. By the 1960s and 1970s with an intensity in demands for equality and increased knowledge, newer approaches to this dichotomy have made it possible to see both nature and nurture as important parts of experience. Why did the demands become heightened then? Why not 20 years earlier or later? We need more information before we can answer this question.

It was a time when many people were insisting on being valued in different ways than the culture had previously allowed. The question is raised: Can something be both different and equal at the same time? The cultural push has been that if you wanted to be considered equal, you had to be the same. But if, instead of the mathematical model, equal means of *same value*, then it is easier to look at the behavioral differences between men and women, valuing potentials in a different light.

Among the behavioral differences research attributes to men and women (Farrell, 1986; Gilligan, 1982; Hite, 1987; Rossi, 1977; Rubin, 1983) are the following: (1)

Women have role-embracing behavior; men have role-distancing behavior. (2) Women have discomfort with impersonal situations; men have discomfort in intimate situations. (3) Women have greater empathy, affiliation, and nonverbal ability; men have greater large motor skill mastery, autonomy, and cognitive achievement. (4) Women tend to approach a crying infant; men tend to ignore or withdraw in response to infant crying. (5) Women tend to learn contextually and narratively; men tend to learn in formal, linear, abstract ways. (6) Women seek love first; men seek work first.

All of these behaviors have potential value, depending on the situation. To understand how it happens that these differences exist and how it might be possible for both men and women to have all these behaviors in their repertoire of human reactions, not only biological propensities, an understanding of the psychosocial context in which the behaviors arise needs to be considered. Socialization may account for many of the differences, but as Rossi (1985) points out, behavioral differences continue to exist in families of solo moms, solo dads, and communal or alternative family forms.

While sociologists and psychologists work readily across disciplines in their research because their procedures are similar, rarely are biological variables included in social research. Biologists more often tend to account for environmental differences. As Rossi (1985) summarizes:

> Organisms are not passive objects acted upon by internal genetic forces, as some sociobiologists claim, nor are they passive objects acted upon by external environmental forces, as some social scientists claim. Genes, organisms, and environment interpenetrate and mutually determine each other. To discuss biological predispositions is to attempt a specification of biological processes, in the same way sociologists try to specify social process. Awareness of *both* social and biological processes adds a synergistic increment to knowledge, knowledge that can then be used to provide the means for modification and change; they do not imply that we are locked into an unchangeable body or social system. Ignorance of biological processes may doom efforts at social change to failure because we misidentify what the targets for change should be and, hence, what our means should be to attain the change we desire. (p. 179)

How do these differences in gender behavior evolve not only from biology but through psychological development as well? The psychological job of establishing "self" includes concretizing both gender identity and ego boundaries, often talked about these days as the two central things to the process of separation/individuation. Even this concept of "self" is looked at differently in the 20th century than from our historical past. Changes in both length of life and health have pressed the concept of development of self through longer and longer stages of human growth than simply childhood. What we understand and value about childhood has different meaning than in the past. What was begun by Freud in the 19th century in the discussion of id, ego, and superego, or more appropriately translated (Bettelheim, 1984) as the it, the I, and the over-I, has been carried further by a group of object relations theorists: Winnicott, Mahler, Bowlby, and Klein among them. Object relations theory helps account for why our concepts of masculinity and femininity are being challenged so universally today.

One of the more lucid descriptions of this process of development of self for both boys and girls has been written by Lillian Rubin (1983). While both our biology and social heritage create the aura under which a child develops, how they are each interpreted can make a difference in the course of development. That special kind of attachment in bonding between mother and child, for example, a highly discussed and debated aspect of development today, is not an innate part of our past. There is persuasive evidence that mother–infant bonding is a recent aspect of human relations (deMause, 1974; Shorter, 1975; Stone, 1977) and not at all a given in our collective past when children not were extensively abused, abandoned, intruded upon, or treated with considerable ambivalence. The process of establishing the emotional bond between mother and child is new in history and bonding between fathers and children even much more recent. Yet in our culture today, the fact is that

> a woman, if not the mother, is almost always the primary caregiver of infancy. *And, no fact of our early life has greater consequences for how girls and boys develop into women and men, [and] therefore for how we relate to each other in our adult years.* [emphasis in original] For when social fact is combined with the biological reality of our infantile dependency, the stage is set for developmental consequences of which we have only recently become aware—consequences that are intimately related to the difficulties we encounter. (Rubin, 1983, p. 43)

In the first stage of life the human infant needs to become attached to another human being in order to have basic needs fulfilled. Unlike the rest of the animal kingdom where infants are able to move to a source of food, for example, the human infant has to have it provided for an extended period of time.

> From the beginning, life is a process of forming attachments, internalizing representations from the external world, and making identifications with significant people from that world. Since it is mother [or woman] who is the primary caregiver—who feeds us, shelters us, comforts us, holds us in her arms to allay our fears—it is she with whom we make our first attachment . . . within which we do not yet know self from other. For each of us, then, whether a girl or boy, it is a woman who is in this primary position in our inner life—a woman who is the object of our most profound attachment, a woman who becomes our first loved other. (Rubin, 1983, pp. 49–50)

When infancy passes and the child first crawls and then stands and walks, a new stage of development takes place, one in which the child learns to separate self from other. This movement away, while exciting and adventuresome, is also filled with tension and anxiety. We still need that human attachment. It is

> the period when the issues of separation and unity come clamorously to the fore—when the child lives in ambivalent oscillation between the desire first for one, then the other. . . . But there is no perfect parenting, no possibility of meeting and assuaging every anxiety a small child's experiences . . . . Separation and unity—the excitement and fear, the triumph and anxiety they generate—will remain continuing themes in adult life. How these needs were dealt with when we were small children makes a difference, of course . . . . And long after the conflict between our need for separation and our desire for unity has left center stage, these issues will live inside us to influence the next act. (Rubin, 1983, pp. 51–52)

How boys and girls fare in separation and unity's central themes of gender identity and ego boundaries is profoundly affected by the fact that for most of us, that process involved a woman as the first and primary "other," in this new era of emotional bonding. Rubin suggests that what evolves is many of the behavioral differences cited above, but which may, if our arrangements for childrearing were altered, afford more access to a broader range of human potentials that do not have to be gender-bound.

For a boy, establishing a gender identity is a profound upheaval in his internal world since it means he must renounce his connection to this first person outside of himself and seek a deeper attachment with a man who up until that time has been a distant and often absent, shadowy figure. This process builds a set of defenses that act as a rigid barrier against his previous emotional connection to a woman. Rubin suggests that giving up this early connection may explain a part of the aggressiveness in men, particularly directed against women. If we take Rossi's perspective into consideration, we might say that the aggressiveness that we observe to be "natural" in men may be one of the possible results of the intense psychic energy against attachment interacting with the need for activity associated with hormonal levels. Perhaps if other means of directing activity were available, aggressiveness would not be quite so "natural," or if gender identity in boys was possible in positive attachments to men earlier along *with* women, the renunciation would not be so radical.

For a girl there are different obstacles in the separation/individuation process influenced by our childrearing arrangements. While the girl has an easier time with the positive gender identification, the process of defining herself as a separate, autonomous person is harder. While there is little need to build defenses against attachment, making boundaries less rigid, the boundaries that are developed will be more permeable, making it harder to see where she ends and another person begins. This makes her internal life more complex but means less skill in negotiating the outside world on a one-to-one basis since the internalization of father takes place much later, after gender identity has been formed.

> For, when a boy internalizes father and banishes mother, he is left with only one significant other who is actively experienced in his inner psychic life, only one with whom he must negotiate. For a girl, there are two. It may not seem like much, but the difference in psychic structure, therefore in personality development, is enormous. For it means that a woman's inner relational negotiations become triangular while a man's remain dyadic. (Rubin, 1983, p. 59)

Men tend to be unifocused and women multifocused in all kinds of life circumstances and decisions. Through the process of observing dialogue and interviewing numerous couples, Rubin is left with the haunting refrain back to the problems of separation and unity. Women voice problems with separation, want connection. Men push for separateness, feel overwhelmed or intruded upon. But it doesn't have to be that way. To correct the imbalance that is created by the childrearing structures requires only that, from birth, children have two parents to nurture them.

> Each child would have two objects of attachment and two figures with whom they would make that early and crucial identification. For boys, therefore, the connection to a male self would be more direct, defined positively by primary identification with a male figure rather than negatively by the renunciation of the female . . . . For girls, a primary attachment to and identification with both parents would mean that separation would be less fraught with conflict and confusion in childhood, and the development of a well-bounded and autonomous sense of self less problematic in adulthood. For both women and men, boundaries would be firm where necessary to maintain separation and permeable where unity was the desired result. For both, self and gender would be less rigidly and stereotypically defined and experienced—the artificial distinctions we now hold between masculine and feminine swept away by early childhood experiences that would permit the internalization of the best of both in all of us. (Rubin, 1983, p. 204)

Well, maybe. At least that is the challenge in this last decade of the 20th century. But even that task of helping women and men see that both are capable of nurturing infants *seems* to go against the grain of what we have internalized about gender roles from our cultural past and may be influenced by our biological propensities. Without taking both into consideration, arranging family constellations and child care situations that promote the importance of both male and female roles in the nurturing of infants before selfhood won't be easy.

Men may need, for example, more training in listening to infants cry and knowing confidently how to respond since their hormonal cues may not make this easy. A far more complicated problem is the reality that over 50% of women with children under 1 year of age are back in the work force, meaning that people other than the parents, usually women, are interacting for long periods of time while children go through their "second birth" of developing a sense of self. This seems to revert back to an earlier form of childrearing when parents abandoned, either emotionally or physically, children to others outside the family. Different dialogues with others, it is true, are important for children to have, as is food on the table. But in the process what we have learned about the positive growth and development of children seems to take a backseat, despite the best of intentions of parents and the culture.

The continual controversy about government's role in child care will, no doubt, take us well into the 21st century, with the constant question "Who cares for the children?" hotly debated and emotionally connected not only to our own childrearing experience but to our feelings about gender roles, as well. Few families are in the financial position of the couple on the television show "Day by Day." Here the father quit his job on the stock market to open a day care center in their home with his wife in order to raise their daughter together. Even fewer white families, let alone black families, are in the position to have both parents full-time professionals (even one an obstetrician) with the luck of the draw of being home most of the time to extensively interact with their children. And yet these are the models for shared childrearing that most Americans see.

The mass media is filled with examples of men "taking care of" children, on their own as well, usually in situations that are humorous and less likely to be similar to real-life daily routines and events. How many nurturing men are involved in the child care centers that spring up to care for the children of two-career families or single-parent households when work becomes a necessity?

Rubin's wonderful optimism of the early 1980s may fast be become an unrealistic possibility, except in a small percentage of households. How many men who do share the caring of their infants think about themselves as full-time fathers with full-time careers instead of half-time fathers with their "life's work" being outside their parenthood? How many women think about themselves as full-time mothers "helping out" with the family finances instead of fulfillment from the work and motherhood?

Let's see if we can extend the cultural context in which these challenges and new understandings exist. Culture is an adaptive mechanism for the way individuals and small and large groups of people decide to coexist together. It does not exist outside of the collective unconscious of individuals. It both deeply affects and is affected by the development of all the "selves" that make it up. Consequently, it is profoundly affected by how the culture arranges the primary care of small children developing their sense of self.

If we described the culture now as being in a transition between reasonably stable (albeit usually oppressive) definitions of gender to more fluid definitions where behavioral skills are more than likely shared, what kind of heroes or models present themselves? Mark Gerzon (1982) helps to illuminate the spot we currently exist in by looking at the choice of heroes in both private and public life for manhood.

He uses the concept of archetype or modal personality defined as personally powerful unconscious images that are useful to large numbers of people who share common life or unconscious experiences. One such common experience in this culture is patriarchy. Another one might be similar patterns of childrearing, though Gerzon does not address this specifically.

The two public archetypes he presents are the Frontiersman, the one who alone conquers the earth and tames the forests, and the Soldier, the protector who abuses his body in order to defend. Both are strong images of masculinity in boys growing up in our culture. Gerzon describes the balance between these two public heroes of Frontiersman and Soldier as peace-loving champions of freedom ready to kill to prove it. The frontier now is often translated into space as the final frontier. But no actual frontier is even necessary to make the image work for boys. It is an unconscious ideal with the potential to be translated a variety of ways.

Interestingly enough, given Rubin's and Rossi's discussion, to maintain these two models as heroes requires denial of dependency and powerful defensive boundaries or character armor, just the stuff generated from the dynamics of the psychosocial constellation of childrearing of boys during development as we have known it with women as sole caregivers.

Three models or heroes in the private sphere are described by Gerzon as the Breadwinner, the Expert, and the Lord. Again, it is fascinating how the nature of these heroes personify Rubin's and Rossi's discussion of differences in men's and women's gender behavior. To the Breadwinner, work comes first before other considerations and that, by necessity, makes him unifocused. The Expert, as Gerzon describes him, is a role-distancing person who relies on cognitive achievement to distance himself from others. The Lord, also a role-distancing hero, is one who avoids his own inner life in exchange for nurturing others' inner struggles. No better graphic example of the Lord exists than the "fallen heroes" of television ministries who avoided confronting their own inner moral conflicts.

Taking on the role of one or more of these heroes excuses one from particular kinds of vulnerability and responsibility, while at the same time appearing not to. What comparable heroes exist for women in the culture today? Though Gerzon does not address this question, a quick look at culture as translated by the media would suggest that there is one unifying heroine for women—the Superwoman who is independent, a supermom, whose body is perfect as well--the ultimate of independence, sexuality, and nurturance all neatly packaged and marketed. Even the discussion of "the Goddess" in New Age thinking, despite the best of intentions, plays into this phenomenon, making it seem as if vulnerability and responsibility for life circumstances can be overlooked by some special gifts or understandings. In many ways, it seems as if women, in their thrust for equal value, are still falling into the same trap of equality meaning no difference instead of valuing differences and building on them.

What Gerzon doesn't talk about, or Rubin for that matter, is what happens to aggressiveness in little girls in the dynamics where they are raised by women. Gerzon's heroes for men are as much a part of little girls' imagery of what masculinity means as it is boys'. Girls and women, in some respects, ask boys and men to do their "dirty work" of aggression for them. Another option in the dynamics of patriarchy is for girls to repress their own aggression and internalize it as low self-esteem, including ways of "accepting" physical and sexual abuse. One might even suggest that patriarchy could not exist without the physical and sexual abuse of girls to keep the dynamic intact.

Gerzon has some intriguing suggestions for choices of heroes that would change this equation and make it more possible to value our differences in gender behavior through providing a broader range of choices for each sex to use, depending on the needs for the situation. For each of the public and private heroes he has a comparable hero that incorporates some of the traditionally more feminine behaviors and skills, without making men the same as women. For the Frontiersman, the less defended hero who is capable of interdependence is the Healer, with a commitment to healing the wounds in the earth made by Frontiersman. The choice instead of Soldier is the Mediator, able to hear contrary points of view and understand the "enemy" because he understands himself from within rather than projecting it onto others. Rather than work coming first for the Breadwinner, the choice is Companion, who has the opportunity to share in work, love, and family. In the workplace and education, rather than the Expert, the choice is that of Colleague, one who values all contributions and skills, realizing everyone's expertise in their own experience. Finally, rather than the Lord representing that distanced role of responding to hurt and pain, whether spiritual, psychic, or physical, the Nurturer understands the closeness and humanity necessary in healing, including his own.

It is not hard to see that these choices for new heroes incorporate many of the gender behaviors previously associated as the domain of women. But Gerzon's descriptions are clearly gender-inclusive, not exclusive. How these choices are to become real options is the challenge. The fact the heroes are changing is unmistakable.

We come back to the question Why now? What is making the former concepts of masculinity and femininity change? What has made the challenge come in this last third of the 20th century? If we look at what the heroes of masculinity have been and why they failed, we may find an answer that goes beyond the explanation of economic necessity, women's and civil rights, and antiwar movement responses and helps to explain why those forces finally became undeniable as well. All of these pushes have existed in the culture for a long time, but something has made them take hold with a tenacity now.

What if Gerzon's archetypical "heroes," the Frontiersman and the Soldier, failed in their purpose of providing road maps for definitions of masculinity by failing to protect and provide the basic security that both men and women had accepted as the prerogative of masculinity? World War II taught us many lessons about our civilization, perhaps the most powerful of which is that both our "protectors" and our enemies could not only kill to preserve peace but *annihilate* scores of people within the course of *minutes*. Within a few minutes "Little Boy" was delivered from the belly of the Enola Gay—named for the pilot's mother, an ordinary woman. It was an annihilation we saw in photographs and moving pictures, bringing it closer to home and making it very hard to deny its reality. It was an annihilation created by what masculinity meant. Symbolically, as well as literally, fathers died. As Naomi Goldenberg (1979) has poignantly observed, when fathers die, we turn inward.

Today we can talk about the trauma we faced when we saw leaders and schoolchildren blown away on television news, or a space shuttle with ordinary people, some even our neighbors, explode miles above the earth. But in 1945 we were just beginning to learn how an entire culture can experience trauma within minutes.

Sometimes it takes awhile to react to the impact of trauma or to understand its implications. By the late 1950s the reminders of the trauma of war came billowing back to us. The Supreme Court ordered desegregation in southern schools, while the nation saw, this time in their homes on television, police dogs and fire hoses trying to quell the support for desegregation. Rosa Parks sat down in the front of a bus and Betty Freidan challenged the feminine mystique. The Russians launched into a new frontier—outer space. We were again slowly edging our way into unknown territory in Asia. All were nagging reminders of how useless the role of protector, as it had been championed, had been and was. Women had learned in the war that their labors were equal to men's, even if the impetus was original to "help out," temporarily.

The ideals the culture held out about manhood were no longer useful. In many ways, manhood continues to be the more aggressively challenged concept. What if women, unconsciously and collectively, being reminded by the new threats to security like those they experienced mostly unconsciously, secretly, as young women and children in the 1940s, said, "These heroes don't do what I thought they would. They don't protect me or my children. They can't. There must be an alternative." A crisis developed in our confidence about heroes, those leaders in whom we invested exterior expressions of development of self. Those who felt little access to those definitions of public heroes began to see the fallacy in the private ones as well, becoming the most outspoken critics, trying to exercise their collectivity into definitions of new heroes for both men and women.

The crushing blow for the men who were still invested in the concepts of Frontiersman and Soldier was defeat in Southeast Asia. Those who thought they were acting on the respected and admired definitions of masculinity found their heroes challenged beyond comprehension. It forced them to confront the inadequacy in the concepts of the private heroes as well. In numerous ways, it is symbolically important that the National Vietnam War Memorial was designed by a woman, is in the earth, as opposed to rising above it, is black instead of the usual white, and includes the names of those killed or missing. It personalized our pain instead of championing our heroes. It was the systematic reading of their names that was the focus of nearly every demonstration for peace, an attempt to remember the individuals and not think about them as numbers or unsung "heroes." We can read their names and acknowledge their personal meaning to each of us, whether we knew them or not.

In large numbers, in small consciousness-raising groups, women pressed for alternatives to the former definitions of masculinity and femininity. But any definitions that do not account for our biological propensities and the basic needs of human infants for constancy in attachment and emotional support in separation will fall short of making it possible for both men and women to become healers, companions, mediators, colleagues, and nurturers together.

As we approach the 21st century, the challenge is to create a culture that makes these alternatives possible instead of sanctifying the already composted notions of masculinity and femininity.

References

Bettelheim, B. (1984). *Freud and man's soul*. New York: Random House.
deMause, L. (Ed.). (1974). *History of childhood*. New York: Psychohistory Press.

Farrell, W. (1986). *Why men are the way they are.* New York: McGraw-Hill.
Gerzon, M. (1982). *A choice of heroes: The changing face of American manhood.* Boston: Houghton Mifflin.
Gilligan, C. (1982). *In a different voice.* Cambridge, MA: Harvard University Press.
Goldenberg, N. (1979). *Changing of the gods.* Boston: Beacon.
Hite, S. (1987). *Women and love.* New York: Knopf.
Rossi, A. (1977). A biosocial perspective in parenting. *Daedelus, 106,* 1–31.
Rossi, A. (1985). *Gender and the life course.* Hawthorne, NY: Aldine.
Rubin, L. (1983). *Intimate strangers: Men and women together.* New York: Harper & Row.
Shorter, E. (1975). *Making of the modern family.* New York: Basic Books.
Stone, L. (1977). *The family, sex and marriage in England, 1500–1800.* New York: Harper & Row.

Overview
Reflections

JOAN OFFERMAN-ZUCKERBERG

In this collection, academic psychologists, psychoanalysts, psychohistorians, sociologists, and an attorney have joined forces to comment on the intricate interplay of gender dynamics today. On every level, from the unconscious reservoir of tradition to the preconscious world of automatic, habitual reactions, to the realm of commitment and conscious lip service to change, we are being challenged. On every level of society—religious, moralistic, legalistic, ethical—we are being asked to redefine our notions of masculinity and femininity. We are being asked to demystify parenthood and treat it with techno-logic instead of psycho-logic (a far more emotive and irrational form of reacting). We are being asked to tolerate and endorse new personal freedoms, homosexual parenting, equalitarian couples. Our bodies no longer define and/or limit our creative-generative potential. In every way, we are crossing boundaries and blazing new trials.

In entering an androgynous zone (i.e., a rich blend of masculinity and femininity), we create a new frontier—one marked by new choices and new anxieties. We are creating the possibilities of forging a new human race, one not imprisoned by restrictive and culturally imposed gender roles. Gender is a biological given, but it needn't shackle or constrain.

We live in a nuclear age and we live in a world of AIDS, threatened from within and without. Yes, personal freedom and man's technological brilliance can, of course, be abused, leading to annihilation. The hope is that personal freedom and scientific knowledge can be harnessed for the good.

As scientists we are committed to keeping a balanced perspective in the face of highly emotional and controversial issues. Legislation will come and go; babies will always be wanted under- or overground; men will be men, and women, women; much will be the same 100 years from now; much will be different. Our humanity will be tested.

I believe, though, that it is the spirit and conviction of this book to have faith, to step forward (not without an occasional look back), and finally, with eyes open, to dare.

JOAN OFFERMAN-ZUCKERBERG • Psychoanalytic Society of the Postdoctoral Program for Study and Research in Psychology, New York, New York; Brooklyn Institute for Psychotherapy, Brooklyn, New York 11215; National Institute for the Psychotherapies, New York, New York 10019; Yeshiva University, New York, New York 10033.

Index

Abortion
　of female fetus, 179, 180
　for gender selection, 179, 180, 184
　postviability, 221
　previability, 221
　spontaneous
　　artificial insemination-related, 154
　　in vitro fertilization-related, 167
　women's right to, 221, 222, 240
Achondroplasia, 255–256
Acquired immune deficiency syndrome (AIDS)
　artificial insemination and, 113, 152–153, 253
　bereavement related to, 269–271
　incidence, 263
　neurological effects, 263, 269
　opportunistic infections of, 263, 267, 270–271
　psychological effects, 263–274
　　on family, 265, 267–271
　　on friends, 269–271
　　on health care workers, 272–274
　　on lovers, 269–271
　　on patients, 264–269
Adam and Eve, 198
Adaptation, androgyny as, 31
Adoptee
　as birthmother, 148
　in cooperative adoption, 139–143, 145–147, 148
　psychological infertility, 148
　response to adoption, 136–137
　agency-type, 134
　annual number of, 138
　artificial insemination versus, 115
　attachment behavior and, 136, 137
　birthmothers' reactions, 137
　children available for, 123–134
　closed, 134, 140
　cooperative, 133, 138–148
　　advantage, 141–145
　　definition, 134–135
　　parenting issues, 145–146
　　problems, 147–148
　　society's response, 147
　fertilization, 134; *see also* Surrogate motherhood
　independent, 134
　mother's responsibility regarding, 221–222
　open, 134
　as parenting, 137–138
　relative, 134
　sealed-records, 135–136, 140
　surrogate motherhood versus, 124
Adoption broker, 232
Adoption law, surrogate motherhood and, 236, 237, 238–239
Agency, gender stereotypes and 47, 51, 54, 58, 62–63
　in egalitarian marriage, 53, 61–62
　socialization for, 12
　in traditional marriage, 49, 50, 52, 58
Aggression
　anabolic steroid-related, 1565
　as female trait, 292–293
　female-directed, 290
　as male trait, 24, 29, 156, 290
　sex ratio and, 184
Alcohol, as male infertility cause, 112
Altruism
　of sperm doctors, 100, 102
　of surrogate mothers, 129–130
American Adoption Congress, 136

American Bar Association, 243-244, 245
American Bar Foundation Society, 152
American Organization of Surrogate Parenting Practitioners, 240, 243, 245
Ammons Quick Test, 124, 125
Amniocentesis, 173-178, 198
Andrews, Lori B., 245
Androgens, 155, 287
Androgyny
  definition, 62
  physical attractiveness and, 63
  Plato on, 17-18
  psychological, 30-32
  sex role stereotypes versus, 31-32, 62
Antiabortion movement, 197
Antibody
  to human immune deficiency virus, 152
    test for, 152-153, 265-166, 267
  to ova, 180
Anticancer drugs, as male infertility cause, 112
Anxiety
  artificial insemination-related, 113
  castration, 28, 194
  genital, 192, 199
  infertility-related, 94, 95, 96
  separation, 28
Archetype
  of hero, 292-294
  sociocultural, 30, 31, 93-110
Artificial insemination (AI)
  gender selection and, 180, 181
  uterine, 166
Artificial insemination, by donor (AID), 93-110, 151-161
  adoption versus, 115
  AIDS and, 113, 152-153, 253
  animal analogues, 155
  attitudes towards
    of public, 96-98, 107
    religious affiliation and, 98
    of sperm donors, 99-102, 103, 114-115
  children conceived by, 105-106
    hyperkinesis of, 105
    intelligence quotient, 105-106, 107
    knowledge of birth origin, 117-118
    knowledge of sperm donor's identity, 97-98, 100, 119
    number of, 93, 112
  donor
    anonymity, 97-98, 101-102, 113, 114-115, 118, 159
    attitudes of, 99-102, 103, 114-115

  characteristics, 99-100, 102-103, 114
    health screening, 105, 114
    homosexual, 115, 253
    legal liability, 114
    mother's fantasies about, 117
    motivations, 100-101
    rejection, 115
    selection, 151-152, 159, 253
  effects on marriage, 106-107, 116
  failure, 113
  first, 111, 166
  genetic linkage factor, 97, 104
  hormonal aspects, 155-156
  incest and, 114
  legal aspects, 124
  lesbians' use of, 97, 98, 101, 104 111, 158, 160, 252-253
    sperm donors attitudes towards, 102, 103
  medical aspects, 151-153, 253-254
  motivations for, 115-116
  parents
    characteristics, 116
    psychosocial assessment, 117
  psychological factors, 113, 115, 116, 153-160, 167
  secrecy regarding, 98-99, 117-118, 227-228
  sense of immortality and, 116
  sex-role stereotypes and, 160
  single women's use of, 103-105, 111
    characteristics, 103-104
    public attitudes towards, 97, 98, 101
    sperm donor's attitudes towards, 102, 103
  success rate, 94, 113
  techniques, 112-113
Artificial insemination, homologous, 93-94
  public attitudes towards, 96-97
Arts, female body imagery in, 192
Assertiveness, as male trait, 24, 25
Atallah, Lillian, 118-119
Attachment behavior, 289
  adoption and, 136, 137
  definition, 136
  shared parenting and, 73, 74, 76
Autonomy
  in egalitarian marriage, 61
  intimacy relationships, 15
  as male trait, 29
  in mother-son relationships, 28
Azoospermia, 112, 116

INDEX

Baby M, 5, 126, 128, 218, 223, 241; see also Stern, Elizabeth; Stern, William; Whitehead-Gould, Mary Beth
  mass media coverage of, 206–208
  New Jersey Court decision regarding, 235–236, 237, 238, 239
  women's reactions to, 205–215
    "good mother" image, 211–212
    self-identification, 210–211
    women's rights movement and, 209
Baby selling
  laws against, 238
  surrogate motherhood as, 229, 230, 232, 233, 239
Beauvoir, Simone de, 191
Behavioral differences, male-female, 298–288; see also Gender development; Gender stereotype traits
Bem Sex-Role Inventory, 48
Bender Gestalt Test, 106
Bereavement, AIDS-related, 269–271
Bible, male infertility mentioned in, 112
Biology
  femininity and, 191, 193
  sexual differentiation and, 286–287
  sexual inequality and, 191, 1933
  social constructionist perspective, 193
Biopsy, endometrial, 166
Birthfamily, 133–134
Birthfather, in cooperative adoption, 147
Birthmother
  adoptee as, 148
  in cooperative adoption, 139, 140–142, 143–145, 147, 148
  response to adoption, 137
Birth order
  gender selection and, 180, 181, 182–183, 185–186
  psychological effects, 186
  psychological effects, 185–186
Birthparent, see also Birthfather; Birthmother; Surrogate mother
  in cooperative adoption, 139–141, 142
Birth rate, 275
Bisexuality, 18
Blood donor, 100, 102, 103
Body ego, female, 192, 192, 194–196
Body Positive, The, 266
Bonding
  in father–child relationship, 73–74, 288–289
  maternal–fetal, 219–220
  in mother–child relationship, 73, 74, 117, 288–289

Boundary situation, 67
Boys
  gender development: see Gender development, male
  preference for
    amniocentesis and, 177
    gender selection and, 179, 180, 181, 182, 183
    women's rights movement and, 180, 181
  separation–individuation, 27–28, 29, 194, 290
Breast feeding, 76
Brown, Louise, 166

Caretakers, of AIDS patients, 270, 271
Castration anxiety/complex, 19, 28, 194
Catecholamines, 155
Center for Disease Control, 152
Cesarean section, 183–184
Chastity belt, 183–184
Childbearing, see also Motherhood; Pregnancy
  men's involvement, 276
  women's right to choose, 123
    feminist perspective, 217–225
Childbirth
  "cloacal" theory of, 36
  existential perspective, 67, 68
  natural, 192, 199
  by older women, 186, 275
  women's fear of, 67
Child care center, 591
Childlessness, see also Infertility
  voluntary, 70
    case examples, 276–283
    incidence, 275
    motivation for, 282–283
    incidence, 275
    motivation for, 282–2833
    sense of immortality and, 282–283
Childbearing
  father's involvement, 23–24, 72, 291
  shared parenting in, 72–77, 290
Children
  artificial insemination-conceived, 105–106
    hyperkinesis, 105
    intelligence quotient, 105–106, 107
    knowledge of birth origin, 117–118
    knowledge of sperm donor's identity, 97–98, 100, 119
    number of, 93, 112
  available for adoption, 123–124

childbirth theory of, 36
death of, 67–68, 257–258
gender development by: *see* Gender development
handicapped, 126
in vitro fertilization-conceived, 98, 166
"wrong gender," 183
Chromosomal abnormalities, 186
Civilization, Freud on, 4–5
Clitoridectomy, 183–184
Cloacal theory, of childbirth, 36
Clomiphene citrate, 96
"Coming out"
by homosexuals with AIDS, 264–165, 169
by lesbians, 260
Commonwealth, 278
Communication
male–female patterns, 20
in shared parenting families, 76
Communion, gender stereotypes and, 47, 54, 62–63
inegalitarian marriage, 52–53, 61–62
in traditional marriage, 49, 50, 52, 58
Competition
as male trait, 29
sexual, 24, 25, 184
Conception: *see* Fertilization
Control, as male trait, 29
Countertransference
with AIDS patients, 266, 269
in infertility case, 85, 86–87, 88, 90–91
Courtship rituals, 56
Couvade, 36
Creativity, male, 198
Cultural factors
in gender development, 291–294
in gender selection, 179
Custody, surrogate motherhood and, 219–220, 223, 224; *see also* Baby M

Death
awareness of, 67
of children, 67–68, 257–258
Decision-making
as boundary situation, 67
in egalitarian marriage, 61
regarding parenthood, 67, 68–69, 71
in shared parenting, 73
Dementia, AIDS-related, 263
Dependency needs, 29, 69
Depression
infertility-related, 94, 11, 164
testosterone-related, 155

Desegregation, 294
Dickinson, Robert L., 111
Disability, pregnancy-related, 217–218
Disease, sexually-transmitted, 105, 194; *see also* Acquired immune deficiency syndrome (AIDS)
Disengagement, 75
Disidentification, 12–13, 15, 28
Dominance, 29, 155, 156
Donor
of ova, 222
of sperm
anonymity, 97–98, 101–102, 113, 114–115, 118, 159
attitudes of, 99–102, 103, 114–115
characteristics, 99–100, 102–103, 114
health screening, 105, 114
homosexual, 115, 253
legal liability, 114
mother's fantasies about, 117
motivations, 100–101
rejection, 115
selection, 151–152, 159, 253
Down's syndrome, 186
Drugs, as male infertility cause, 112
Dunne, John R., 246
Dwarfism, 255–256

Ecriture feminine, 192
Educational factors, in gender selection, 181
Egg: *see* Ova
Ego, 288
Ego boundary, 288, 289, 290
Ejaculation, premature, 93
Embryo, *see also* Fetus
preimplantation, 230
Embryo transfer, 134, 221, 222, 230–233, 243
Emotionality, male–female comparison, 20
Employment
of mothers, 275–286, 291
of pregnant women, 217–218
of single women, 70
Endocrinology, 286–287
Endorphins, 155
Enola Gay, 293
Environmental factors, in infertility, 155, 156
Essentialism, biological, 191–102
Ethnic factors, in gender selection, 180, 181
Existential perspective, on parenthood, 67–68
Experience, 286–298
Eysenck Personality Inventory, 114

Faith, 10

INDEX

Family
　adoptive
　　in cooperative adoption, 138, 139, 142
　　definition, 133
　of AIDS patients, 265, 267–271
　lesbian, 249
　non-traditional, 249
　single-parent, 291; *see also* Women, single
　social change and, 275–276
　two-career, 291
Family size
　decreased, 275
　gender selection and, 180–181, 183
Fantasy
　gestation-related, 14
　reunion-related, 10, 11
Father
　childbearing involvement, 23–24, 72, 291
　infants' attachment to, 36–37
　role, 36, 37
　　changing, 23–24
　transference by, 69
　types, 36, 37, 41–42
Father–child relationship, 24
　bonding in, 73–74, 288–289
　mother–child relationship comparison, 74–76
Fatherhood
　psychological reactions to, 69
　　psychoanalytical preparation for, 35–46
　social, 228, 229
　surrogate motherhood and, 229, 231–232
Father–son relationship
　castration anxiety and, 28
　gender development and, 28
　in New Guinea, 13
　Oedipus complex and, 36, 37, 76
Fellatio, 13
Femininity, *see also* Gender development, female
　biological concepts of, 287
　changing concepts of, 285–291, 292–293, 294
　distortions, 14
　female biology and, 191, 193
　receptive nature of, 14
　sexual tensions and, 9–16
Feminist perspective
　on gender selection, 180, 181
　on motherhood, 70, 191
　on parenthood, 223–224
　on reproductive choice, 217–225
　on surrogate motherhood, 218–220,

Feminist perspective
　on surrogate motherhood (*cont.*)
　　239–240
Fertility, sociocultural value of, 111
Fertilization
　gender selection and, 179–180
　hormonal/neural factors in, 287
　in vitro, 97, 98, 166
　　case study, 83–92
　children of, 98, 116
　failure rate, 228
　first, 85
　psychological aspects, 167–169
　sperm donor's attitudes, 102
　success rate, 228
　technique, 166–167
Fetus
　antiabortion movement's portrayal of, 197
　bonding with mother, 136, 219–220
　mother's rights regarding, 197–198
　sex determination, 177–178
　sexual differentiation, 286–287
　sonogram, 173–174, 175, 177–178, 198, 200
Footbinding, 183–184
Frankenstein (Shelley), 5
Freud, Sigmund, 18, 36, 198, 288
　on civilization, 4–5
　gender development theory, 18–19, 190
　on God, 4–5
　ignorance of female psychology, 190
　on love, 11
　on repressed impulses, 238
Friedan, Betty, 294
Friends, of AIDS patients, 269–271

Gamete intrafallopian tubal transfer, 166
Gay Men's Health Crisis (GMHC), 264, 265, 271, 273
Gay Rights March, 271
Gender development, 190, 191
　cultural factors, 291–294
　early memories of, 285–286
　female, 27–28
　　biological essentialism and, 191–192
　　body ego and, 194–196
　　mother–daughter relationship and, 14, 27–28
　　psychoanalysis of, 190, 194–196
　　psychosexual stages, 196
　Freud's theory of, 18–19, 190
　male, 12–13, 27
　　disidentification and, 12–13, 15, 28
　　female-directed aggression and, 290
　　interpersonal consequences, 28–30
　　intrapsychic consequences, 28–30

optimal, 199
mother–child bonding and, 289
Gender identity, 62–63
  development of: *see* Gender development
Gender selection, 179–187
  birth order and, 180, 181, 182–183, 185
  cultural factors, 179
  educational factors, 179
  educational factors, 181
  ethnic factors, 180, 181
  political factors, 180, 181
  reasons for, 182
  religious factors, 180, 181
  sex ratio effects, 180–181, 182, 183, 184
  socioeconomic effects, 183–186
  technique, 179–180, 181
Gender stereotype traits, 19–22, 47–65
  in egalitarian marriages, 52–53, 60–63
  leader–follower roles, 29, 48–53, 54, 55, 57–58, 61
  maintenance of relationships, 54–54
  physical attractiveness and, 55, 56, 63
  principles in, 50–54
  Relationship Balance Model, 50–52
  in traditional marriages, 52, 53, 57–60
Genetic screening, 222
Gestation, *see also* Pregnancy
  as motherhood determinant, 218–221
Girl
  aggressiveness of, 292–293
  gender development: *see* Gender development, female
  gender selection and, 179, 182
  physical abuse of, 293
  separation–individuation, 27–28, 194, 290
  sexual abuse of, 293
God, Freud on, 4–5
Gonorrhea, 112
Goodhue, Mary B., 127, 246
Group Personality Projective Test, 94
Guilt
  infertility-related, 94, 95, 228
  surrogate motherhood-related, 238–239

Handmaid's Tale, The (Atwood), 197
Health care workers, AIDS patients' interactions, 272–274
Hero, 292–294
Heroine, 292
Herpes, 112
Hoffman, Dustin, 33
Homosexual(s)

with AIDS
  "coming out" by, 264–265, 269
  psychological reactions, 264–265, 267–269
  AIDS-related bereavement, 270–271
  AIDS-related fear, 266
  as sperm donor, 115, 253
Homosexuality, 12, 184
Hormonal factors
  artificial insemination and, 155–156
  in fetal sexual differentiation, 296–298
  in sperm production, 155, 156
Hospital, pregnant women's rights in, 197
Housework, father's participation in, 23–24
Hubbard, Ruth, 224
Human immune deficiency virus (HIV)
  antibody response, 152; *see also*
    Human immune deficiency virus (HIV) antibody test
  exposure incidence, 265
  sperm contaminated with, 113, 152–153, 253
Human immune deficiency virus (HIV) antibody test, 152–153, 265–266, 267
Human immune deficiency virus (HIV)-positive individuals, 263, 264, 265, 267
Hunter, John, 111
Husband–wife relationship, 24; *see also* Marriage
Hypospadias, 93
Hypothalamus, 286, 287
Hysterectomy, 183–184
Hysterosalpingography, 166
Hysteroscopy, 166

Id, 288
IDANT Laboratories, 151, 152, 155, 157, 159
Illegitimacy, 136, 249
Illinois Test of Psycholinguistic Abilities (ITPA), 106
Immortality, sense of, 282–283
Impotence, 93, 99, 116
Incest, 114
Incompatibility, social, 62
India, intimacy relationships, 15
Infant, attachment behavior of, 136, 137, 289
Infertility
  of both partners
    incidence, 93
    surrogacy and, 229
  environmental factors, 155, 156
  incidence, 93, 153
  psychogenic, 3, 95–96

psychological effect, 94–95
Infertility, female, 153
  acceptance of, 196
  of adoptees, 148
  definition, 93
  incidence, 93
  psychoanalytic case study, 81–92
    countertransference, 85, 86–87, 88, 90–91
    transference, 81, 87–88, 90–91
  psychogenic, 148
  psychological effects, 163–171
    linear stages of, 165
  stress-related, 113
Infertility, male
  acceptance of, 118
  assessment, 153–154
  biblical mention of, 112
  causes, 112
  diagnosis, 166
  incidence, 93, 112
  psychogenic, 164
  psychological effects, 112
  treatment, 166
    psychological interventions, 154–155
Inheritance, matrilinear, 179
Initiation rite, male, 13
Intelligence quotient
  of artificial insemination-conceived children, 105–106, 107
  of surrogate mothers, 125
Intersubjectivity, 196
Intimacy relationships
  cross-cultural comparison, 15, 15
  femininity and, 14
  male anxieties regarding, 11, 12–13, 29–30, 31
  male gender development and, 12–13
  in primitive cultures, 13
  wish for reunion in, 10–12

Katoff, Lewis, 265, 267
Keane, Noel, 123

Language acquisition, 286
Laparoscopy, 84
Leadership, as gender stereotype trait, 9, 48–53, 54, 55
  in egalitarian marriage, 52–53, 61
  in traditional marriage, 52, 53, 57–58, 60
Lesbians
  artificial insemination use by, 104, 111, 158, 160, 252–254
  "coming out" by, 260
  parenting by, 249–262
Lethal Secrets (Baran and Pannon), 119
Libido, hormonal factors, 155
Little People of America, 255, 256
Living will, of AIDS patients, 268
Locus of control, of women, 197
Loss, sense of, infertility-related, 95, 164, 168
Love, wish for oneness and, 11–12
Lovers, of AIDS patients, 269–289
Luteinized unruptured follicle syndrome, 96

Maclean's, 207
Mademoiselle, 207
Male–female differences, 287–288
  gender stereotype traits, 48–66
    in egalitarian marriage, 52–53, 60–63
    leader–follower roles, 29, 48–53, 54, 55, 57–58, 61
    maintenance of relationships and, 54–57
    principles in, 50–52
    Relationship Balance Model, 50–52
    in traditional marriage, 52, 53, 57–60
  socialization and, 193
Marijuana, as male infertility cause, 112
Marine Corps, 13
Marlow–Crowne Social Desirability Scale, 168
Marriage
  artificial insemination's effects on, 106–107, 116
  gender stereotype traits in, 48–66
    in egalitarian marriage, 52–53, 60–63
    leader–follower roles, 29, 48–53, 54, 55, 57–58, 61
    principles in, 50–52
    Relationship Balance Model, 50–52
    in traditional marriage, 52, 53, 57–60
  lesbian, 249–262
Masculinity, *see also* Gender development, male
  archetypical heroes and, 292–294
  biological concepts, of 287
  changing concepts of, 285–292, 293, 294
Masochism, 11, 14, 15
Mass media
  Baby M coverage by, 206–208
  motherhood portrayal by, 276
  shared parenting portrayal by, 291
Mastectomy, 183–184
Men, *see also* Boys; Father
  dominant, 184
  psychological integration, 17–34

internal conflicts, 24–27
interpersonal consequences, 28–30
intrapsychic consequences, 28–30
psychological androgyny and, 30–32
wish for reunion, 11–12
Menstruation, 192, 193
Minnesota Multiphasic Personality Inventory (MMPI), 85, 124, 125
Miscarriage: *see* Abortion, spontaneous
Model Surrogacy Act, 243–244, 245
Molestation, 184
Mother
 changing role, 23–24
 definition, 218, 219, 220
 genetic, 218
 gestational, 218, 219; *see also* Birthmother
 rights regarding fetus, 197–198
 as "supermom," 276, 292
 single, 249; *see also* Women, single
 surrogate: *see* Surrogate mother
 working, 291
  number of, 275–276
Mother–child relationship
 bonding in, 73, 74, 288–289
  artificial insemination and, 117
  fetal, 136
 father–child relationship comparison, 74–76
 genetic ties in, 221, 222
Mother–daughter relationship
 gender development and, 14, 27–28
 separation–individuation and, 194
Motherhood
 decision-making regarding, 276
 feminist perspective, 70, 191
 gestation as determinant, 218–221
 mass media portrayal of, 276
 reparative aspects, 196
 surrogate: *see* Surrogate motherhood
Mother–son relationship
 disidentification in, 12–13, 15, 28
 in New Guinea, 13
 separation–individuation in, 27–28, 29, 290
Ms., 207
Mumps, as male infertility cause, 112

Narcissistic injury, 164, 168, 169, 189, 194
National Association of Surrogate Mothers, 245
National Organization for Non-Parents, 277
National Review, 207
National Vietnam War Memorial, 294
Nature–nurture, 21–22, 287

Nervous system, fertilization and, 286–287
Neurological effects, of AIDS, 263, 269
New Guinea, masculinity concept in, 13
Newsweek, 207
Nurture, *see also* Nature–nurture
 experience as, 286

Oakland Sperm Bank, 253
Object loss, 194–195
Object relations theory, 288
Occupations, female-dominated, 184
Oceanic feeling, 10, 11
Oedipus complex, 37, 76
 negative, 36
Oligospermia, 112
Oral deprivation, 194
Organ donor, 100, 102
Organ selling, 229
Ova
 antibodies, 180
 donation, 230
 experimentation with, 98
Ova bank, 222
Ovulation
 stress-related suppression, 113
 timing, 179, 181
Oxytocin, 287

Parent(s)
 adoptive, 137, 141; *see also* Family, adoptive
  in cooperative adoption, 140, 144–146
 of AIDS patients, 265, 268–269, 270
 as gender role model, 22
Parenthood, 67–78
 changing social context of, 70–78
 decision-making regarding of, 67, 68–69, 71
 dependency needs and, 69
 determination of, 218, 223
 existential aspects, 67–68
 feminist perspective, 223–224
 responsibility of, 68
 role model for, 71
 traditional, 72
Parenting
 by adoptive couples, 137–138, 145–146
 by lesbians, 249–262
 sex role and, 37
 shared, 72–77, 290
Parks, Rosa, 294
Patriarchy, 292, 293
Penis envy, 19, 194–195

Perganol, 166
Personality traits, *see also* Gender stereotype traits
  of surrogate mothers, 124–132, 231, 242, 244
Person with AIDS (PWA), *see also* Acquired immune deficiency syndrome (AIDS)
  psychological reactions of, 264–265, 267–260
Pesticides, as male infertility cause, 112
Phallic monism, 190
Physical abuse, of girls, 293
Physical attractiveness
  androgyny and, 63
  gender stereotypes and, 55, 56, 63
Physician
  AIDS patients and, 272
  artificial insemination involvement, 115, 117
  reproductive technology involvement, 98
Planned Parenthood, 183
Plato, 17–18
Pneumonia, *Pneumocystis carinii*, 263, 265, 267
Political factors, in gender selection, 180, 181
Polyandry, 184
Pope John Paul II, 6
Pornography, 12, 184
Power, 9, 15, 61
Preembryo, 230
Pregnancy, *see also* Motherhood
  as disability, 217–218
  father's involvement, 37
  glorification of, 2219, 220–221
Prolactin, 155
Protection of others, as male trait, 29
Psychoanalysis
  of father-to-be, 35–46
  of female gender development, 190, 194–196
  infertility case study, 81–92
    countertransference, 85, 86–87, 88, 90–91
    transference, 81, 87–88, 90–91
Psychological effects
  of AIDS, 263–274
    on family, 265, 267–271
    on friends, 269–271
    on health care workers, 272–274
    on lovers, 269–271
    on patients, 264–269
  of infertility, 94–95, 163–171
    in females, 163–171

in males, 112
Psychological factors
  in artificial insemination, 113, 115, 116, 153–160, 167
  in birth order, 185–186
  in *in vitro* fertilization, 167–169
Psychological integration, 17–34
  female, 26–27
  male, 17–34
    internal conflicts, 24–27
    interpersonal consequences, 28–30
    intrapsychic consequences, 28–30
    psychological androgyny and, 30–32
Psychological screening, of surrogate mothers, 124–132
Psychology, female, 22
  Freud's ignorance of, 190
Psychopathology, male–female comparison, 20–21
Psychotherapy
  for AIDS patients' families, 271
  counterference in, 85, 86–87, 88, 90–91, 266, 269
  for infertile women, 96
  for sterile males, 154–155
  transference in, 69, 81, 87–88, 90–91, 268
Purdah, 184

Quiet Man, The (film), 32–33

Rape, 184
Relationship Balance Model, 50–52
Religion, sex ratio and, 184
Religious factors
  in artificial insemination, 155
  in gender selection, 180, 181
Reproductive choice, 123
  feminist perspective, 217–225
Reproductive technology, *see also* Artificial insemination; Embryo transfer; Fertilization, *in vitro*; Gamete intrafallopian tubal transfer
  government involvement, 98
  negative aspects, 196–201
  physicians' regulation of, 98
  positive aspects, 200
  social change and, 223
  surrogate motherhood and, 230–231
  women's sense of self and, 189–201
    antibiology position, 193
    body ego and, 192, 194–196
    essentialist position, 191–192
    feminist position, 191, 193

social constructionist position, 193
RESOLVE, 257
Reunion, universal wish for, 10–12
RH incompatibility, 112
Roe v *Wade*, 123
Role model
  gender, 292–294
  for parenthood, 71
Role sharing, in parenthood, 72–77, 290
Rorschach Inkblot Test, 124–125
Rothman, Barbara Katz, 219, 224

Sadism, 11
Sambia, 13
Santorelli, Michelina, 272, 273
Sarcoma, Kaposi's, 263, 266
Second Sex, The (de Beauvoir), 191
Self, sense of, 286
  development of, 288–289; *see also* Gender development
  reproductive technology and, 189–201
    antibiology position, 193
    body ego and, 192, 194–196
    essentialist position, 191–192
    feminist position, 191, 193
    social constructionist position, 193
Self-actualization, 2, 15
Self-esteem, 194, 195
Self-help groups, for AIDS patients caretakers, 271
Self-object merger, 10, 11
Self-unification, 18
Semen: *see* Sperm
Separation–individuation, 195, 288
  by boys, 27–28, 29, 194, 290
  by girls, 27–28, 194, 290
  shared parenting and, 74–75
Serotonin, 155
Sex characteristics, 286
Sex ratio, gender selection effects, 180–181, 182, 1983, 184
Sex role
  biological concepts of, 287
  changing, 22–24
  parenting and, 37
  stereotypes, *see also* Gender stereotype traits
    androgyny versus, 31–32, 62
    artificial insemination and, 160
    birth order and, 185–186
    social incompatibility and, 62
    in traditional marriage, 61
Sexual abuse, of girls, 293

Sexual differentiation, fetal, 286–287
Sexual inequality, female biology and, 191, 193
Sexual intercourse
  as birth analogy, 9–10
  experiential levels, 9–10
  ovulation timing and, 179, 181
Sexual object, women as, 191, 192
Shared fate theory, 138
Shared parenting, 72–77, 290
Siblings, in lesbian families, 251
Sims, Marion, 111
Smithberg, Lorraine, 273
Social change
  family and, 275–276
  parenthood and, 70–78
  reproductive technology and, 223
Social constructionism, 193
Socialization, 193
  for agency, 12
  femininity distortions and, 14
  male–female differences and, 288
  shared parenting and, 75
Solo, Eric, 241
Solo, Vicky, 241
Sonogram, fetal, 173–174, 175, 177–178, 198, 200
Sperm
  cryopreserved, 151–152; *see also* Artificial insemination, by donor
    AIDS-contaminated, 113, 152–153, 253
    fresh sperm versus, 113
  of husband, 94
  sperm quality, 105–106
  defective, 112
  in fertilization, 287
  in gender selection, 179–180
Sperm bank, 94, 112, 253
Sperm count, 112
Sperm donor: *see* Donor, of sperm
Sperm–mucus incompatibility, 200
Sperm production, 155, 156
Stepchildren, 147
Stereotypes
  gender, 19–22, 47–66
    in egalitarian marriages, 52–53, 60–63
    leader–follower roles, 29, 48–53, 54, 55, 57–58, 61
    maintenance of relationships and, 54–57
    physical attractiveness and, 55, 56, 63
    Relationship Balance Model, 50–52
    in traditional marriages, 52, 53, 57–60
  sex-role

androgyny versus, 31–32, 62
artificial insemination and, 160
birth order and, 185–186
social incompatibility and, 62
surrogate motherhood-related, 239
Stern, Elizabeth, 206, 207, 209, 212–213, 214
Stern, William, 207, 209, 212, 213
Steroid, adrenal, 155
Stress
  as infertility cause, 95–96
  ovulation effects, 113
  sperm production effects, 155
Sudden infant death syndrome, 257, 258
Superego, 288
"Super mom," 276, 292
Surrogate mother
  altruism of, 129–130
  case examples, 126–131
  characteristics, 124–132, 231, 242, 244
  educational background, 125
  intelligence quotient, 1255
  legal rights, 243–244
  parental rights, 219–220
  postpartum studies, 244–245
  prior pregnancies, 125
  screening, 243
    psychological, 124–132
Surrogate motherhood
  as adoption, 233, 236, 238–239
  adoption versus, 124
  baby selling as, 239
  births resulting from, 240
  brokers, 230–231, 233
  cooperative adoption and, 136
  custody conflicts regarding, 219–220, 223, 224, 240–241, 244
  with embryo transfer, 230–233, 243
  feminist perspective, 218–220, 239–240
  financial aspects, 126, 130–131, 238–239
    guaranteed payment, 244
    payment prohibition, 242
  future developments regarding, 246–247
  genetic linkage factor, 230–233
  history, 123, 240
  as legal contract, 208–209, 231, 232, 236, 240
  legalization, 229
  legislation regarding, 219, 240–246
  public attitudes towards, 235
  recommendations regarding, 245–246
  reproductive technology and, 124, 230–231
  social policy and, 227–233, 235–239

abandonment fears and, 236–237
adoption law and, 236, 237, 238–239
technique, 124
Surrogate Parenting (Zuckerman-Overvold), 246
Surrogates by Choice, 245

Taylor Anxiety Scale, 168
Testosterone, 155–156
  fetal, 286–287
Test-tube baby, 85; *see also* Fertilization, *in vitro*
Time, 207
Tobacco, as male infertility cause, 112
Tootsie, 33
Toxic poisons, as male infertility cause, 112
Transference
  by AIDS patients, 268
  by father, 69
  in infertility case, 81, 87–88, 90–91
Transformation, 10
Transsexualism, 12

Ultrasonographic visualization, of fetus: *see* Sonogram, fetal
Uterine insemination, 166

Vietnam War, 294
Volunteers, women as, 184

WABC, 208
War, trauma of, 293–294
Wayne, John, 32–33
Wechsler Intelligence Scale for Children-Revised (WISC-R), 106
Wein, Richard, 264
Whitehead-Gould, Mary Beth, 206, 207, 208–212, 214, 218, 236
Womb envy, 198
Women
  gender selection implications for, 183–186
  "inner space" of, 192, 198–199
  locus of control, 197
  older
    childbirth by, 186, 275
    desire for motherhood, 1–2
  psychological integration, 26–27
  sense of self
    antibiology position, 193
    body ego and, 194–196
    development, 286; *see also* Gender development, female
    essentialist position, 191–192

feminist position on, 191
reproductive technology and, 189–202
social constructionist position, 193
as sexual objects, 191, 192
single
artificial insemination use by, 97, 98, 101, 102, 103–105, 111, 124, 158
as mothers, 249
in work force, 70

Women's rights movement, *see also* Feminist perspective
Baby M case and, 209
gender selection and, 180, 181

XX chromosome, 286
XY chromosome, 286

Yalom, Irvin, 67